Mind, Brain and the Quantum

To the memory of
Hans Motz
(1909–1987)

Mind, Brain and the Quantum
The Compound 'I'

Michael Lockwood

Basil Blackwell

Copyright © Michael Lockwood 1989

First published 1989

Basil Blackwell Ltd
108 Cowley Road, Oxford, OX4 1JF, UK

Basil Blackwell, Inc.
3 Cambridge Center
Cambridge, Massachusetts 02142, USA

British Library Cataloguing in Publication Data

Lockwood, Michael
Mind, brain and the quantum.
1. Mind. – philosophical perspectives
I. Title
128'2
ISBN 0–631–16183–X

Library of Congress Cataloging in Publication Data

Lockwood, Michael.
Mind, brain, and the quantum.
Bibliography: p.
Includes index
1. Mind and body.   2. Quantum theory.
I. Title.
BF161.I57 1989   128'.2   88–35124
ISBN 0–631–16183–X

Typeset in 10 on 12pt Sabon
by Hope Services
Printed in Great Britain by
Billings & Son Ltd, Worcester

We are that in which the earth comes to appreciate itself.

(Ancient Chinese aphorism)

Contents

Preface

This book is the outcome of over two decades of thinking about the mind–body problem and the interpretation of quantum mechanics, both of which have fascinated me since my schooldays. If I have hitherto written little on these issues, and have published even less, this has been due largely to my inability, until comparatively recently, to arrive at any settled view of either of them.

The reader may be puzzled that I should be writing a book which encompasses both of these subjects, since they are not usually thought to have much connection with each other. But it seems to me clear that they do; and in two distinct ways. First, in reflecting on the relation of consciousness to the *matter* of the brain, philosophers have been apt to take matter for granted, assuming that it is mind rather than matter that is philosophically problematic. This has much to do with the fact that they tend to think of matter along essentially Newtonian lines. The Newtonian conception of matter is incorrect, however, and it is high time that philosophers began properly to take on board the conception that has replaced it. Quantum mechanics just is the theory of matter, as currently conceived. So it is with the matter of Schrödinger, Heisenberg and Dirac that mind has to be brought to terms, not the reassuringly solid stuff of Galileo, Descartes or Newton. This matter, the matter of quantum mechanics, is deeply problematic, and philosophically ill-understood.

Most philosophers who have tackled the mind–body problem have, as I say, tended to regard matter as having a conceptual solidity to match its supposed literal solidity; they have regarded it as a constant, so to speak, in the metaphysical equation. So the mind–body problem itself has, by most contemporary philosophers, been seen as calling for mind to be accommodated to the material world – all the 'give' being on the side of mind. Some wonderfully Procrustean devices have been invoked to that end: so-called *eliminative materialism* and *behaviourism* (which I discuss briefly in chapters 2 and 3) being extreme examples. This prejudice in favour of the material seems to me devoid of any sound scientific foundation. Quantum mechanics has robbed matter of its conceptual quite as much as its literal solidity. Mind and matter are alike in being profoundly mysterious, philosophically speaking. And what the mind–body problem calls for, almost certainly, is a *mutual* accommodation: one which involves conceptual adjustment on both sides of the mind–body divide.

There is a further consideration which links the two subjects of this book. As I now see it, we cannot hope to make sense of quantum mechanics until we succeed in making headway with the so-called *measurement problem*: the problem of understanding what, in quantum-mechanical terms, happens when we observe a physical system. Popular understanding of the theory would have it that, according to quantum mechanics, observation invariably involves a physical interference with the system being observed; and that is why the observer comes to play an active role in the theory. But this, as I explain in chapter 11, is a gross misconception (albeit one that many physicists, who really ought to know better, have had a hand in perpetuating). The apparent 'entanglement', within quantum mechanics, of observer with observed, is a far subtler and far more mysterious affair than the popular account would suggest. It cannot in general be understood in terms of any (ordinary) physical effect that the activities of the observer may have on the objects of observation. What the quantum-mechanical measurement problem is really alerting us to, I shall argue, is a deep problem as to how *consciousness* (specifically, the consciousness of the observer) fits into, or maps on to, the physical world. And that, of course, is the question that lies at the heart of the traditional philosophical mind–body problem.

It is this traditional problem that is the subject of the first ten chapters of the book, though rather more attention is paid to the neuropsychological dimension of the problem than is customary in philosophical discussions. Much of this part of the book will be familiar territory to philosophers; less so, however, to scientists and other educated lay people. And since the book is aimed at a fairly general readership, I have written it in a way that presupposes no previous acquaintance with philosophy (or, for that matter, neuroscience). Similarly, the discussion of quantum mechanics presupposes no prior knowledge of physics. In both parts of the book, the discussion of matters that will be largely familiar, to philosophers and physicists respectively, is intended to prepare the ground for my own preferred views of the relation between mind and body and what I believe to be the correct way to understand quantum mechanics. The conclusions for which I argue involve radical departures, both from common sense and from philosophical orthodoxy, albeit that I am building on the ideas of others. I make no apology, however, for the radical character of these conclusions. If there is one thing I am sure of, it is that a correct conception of these matters is bound in one way or another to involve a drastic revision of our customary way of looking at the world, fully comparable to the Copernican or Einsteinian revolutions. Thus the real objection to the positions defended here (as one of the pioneers of quantum mechanics is alleged to have said of a colleague's theories) is, in all probability, not so much that they are crazy, but that they are not crazy enough.

I have taken pains, wherever possible, to use plain English in place of technical jargon, and to explain the technical terms of which I do make use. Likewise, I have tried to avoid formulae, whether it be the symbolic logic beloved of many philosophers, or the calculus and linear algebra that make relativity and quantum mechanics seem so forbidding to the uninitiated. It is the language of geometry, principally, that I have employed to get across the fundamentals of quantum theory, relying heavily on the analogies between Hilbert space and ordinary three-dimensional Euclidean space. But this is not, for all that, a 'popular' book, if by that is meant one that sacrifices accuracy and logical rigour for the sake of providing an easy read. Rather, I have tried to be clear, without disguising the difficulties or riding roughshod over the subtleties of the issues. There is not, I believe, any 'royal road' to quantum mechanics, and probably not to philosophy either. Parts of the book are thus, inevitably, hard going. But then the issues *are* hard, even to get to grips with, let alone to resolve satisfactorily. My hope is that I have nowhere made them any harder than they have to be.

This book bears the influence of so many friends and colleagues that it would be impossible to name them all. But I owe a special debt of gratitude to Raziel Abelson, Freddie Ayer, Harvey Brown, David Deutsch, John Durant, John Foster, Grant Gillett, Dick Hare, Rom Harré, John Lucas, Howard Robinson, Fred Sommers, Kathy Wilkes, Bob Weingard, my dear friend Hans Motz, and the members of the Rewley House Philosophical Society, for their encouragement over the years, and for much valuable and stimulating discussion. Harvey Brown, David Deutsch, Ian Marshall and Hans Motz helped me greatly, both by the stimulus of their own ideas (some of which are discussed in the text) and by reading and commenting on large parts of the manuscript. I am indebted also to three anonymous referees, to Peter Smith, who produced a marvellously detailed critique of the first draft of chapter 8, and to John Foster and Richard Swinburne, for their comments on an earlier version of chapter 10. No author can have been better served by his copy-editor than was I by Stephen Ball. As a trained philosopher with a background in science, he was able to give invaluable advice on content as well as form. (He is also responsible for a couple of the jokes!) The comments and criticisms accumulated from these various sources have resulted in numerous corrections and improvements. Finally, thanks are due to Angie Sandham for her generous help with the index and diagrams.

It is a very great sadness to me that Hans Motz did not live to see the book completed.

Michael Lockwood
Oxford University Department for External Studies

Acknowledgements

The authors and publishers are grateful to the following for permission of reproduce figures previously published elsewhere: Cambridge University Press for figure 4.4 (from Colin Blakemore, *Mechanics of the Mind*. Cambridge: Cambridge University Press, 1977, 80); Encyclopaedia Britannica Inc. for figure 7.4 (from *The New Encyclopaedia Brittanica*, *Micropaedia*, vol. VII. Chicago: Encyclopaedia Brittanica, Inc., 1984, 103); Macmillan Magazines Limited for figure 4.6 (reprinted by permission from Ramachandran, 1987, in *Nature*, vol. 328, 645. Copyright © 1987 Macmillan Magazines Ltd); Oxford University Press for figure 7.5 (from Churchland, 1986, in *Mind*, vol. xcv, No. 379, 301).

1

The Riddle of Consciousness

Regarded from the standpoint of physical science, the most puzzling thing about consciousness (or awareness or sentience: I use these terms as synonyms) is the fact that it exists at all. There is on the face of it absolutely nothing in the laws of physics and chemistry, as currently understood, that is capable of accounting for the extraordinary capacity of that lump of matter that we call the brain – once likened by Alan Turing to 'a lump of cold porridge' – to sustain an 'inner life'. This is not to deny, of course, that some progress has been made in explaining how the brain encodes and processes the information that arrives from the sense organs, and how it controls behaviour. What remains mysterious is why this complex *physico-chemical* activity should be associated with any subjective states at all: why, in Timothy Sprigge's memorable phrase, there should be a 'what it is like to *be*' you or me (Sprigge, 1971, pp. 167–8; see also Nagel, 1979b).

One must avoid the mistake of thinking that this is simply a matter of scientists not yet knowing enough about how the brain functions, in physico-chemical terms. For it seems clear that more knowledge of the same general kind that neuroscience currently offers could not – in principle could not – shed any further light on the fundamental problem that consciousness raises. Suppose, as is probably impossible in practice, that we had a perfect understanding of the functioning of the brain, in physico-chemical and/or information-processing terms. It would seemingly remain a complete enigma why certain of the *brain's* operations should be associated with *conscious* thought, desire, sensation, passion, perception and purpose – in contrast to the operations of, say, an electronic computer, at least as currently constructed and programmed.

Not everyone would agree with these sentiments. One frequently encounters, both amongst lay people and amongst scientists, what might be termed a 'no-nonsense' materialism, according to which so-called conscious states and processes are just physico-chemical states and processes in the brain. (I say 'so-called', because these same people will sometimes deny that words such as 'consciousness', 'sentience' and the like – at least as used by philosophers – have any clear meaning.) Nor is this brand of materialism by any means unknown in the philosophical literature. One of its clearest exponents is Thomas Hobbes (1588–1679) who, in his *Elements of Philosophy* (Ch. XXV, Sec. 2) writes 'Sense . . ., in the sentient, can be nothing else but motion in some of the internal parts of the sentient'.

Perhaps I should make it clear that 'no-nonsense' materialism, as I understand it, is characterized not so much by what it asserts, namely the identity of conscious states and processes with certain physiological states and processes, but by an accompanying failure to appreciate that there is anything philosophically problematic about such an identification. I am not saying that the identification is necessarily mistaken. But it is clear that there are some exceedingly formidable philosophical obstacles that will have somehow to be overcome if such an identification is to be made to work. Hobbes, for one, seems blithely unaware of these obstacles, or of the philosophical problems that the identification leaves unresolved.

Like the ancient atomists Leucippus, Democritus and Epicurus, Hobbes conceives the world as consisting exclusively of *bodies*, that is material objects, situated in space and possessed only of the sort of properties that would feature in the science of mechanics: properties the philosopher John Locke (1632–1704) was later to call *primary qualities*. 'Motion, magnitude and figure' (i.e. shape) are the only fundamental ones that Hobbes mentions. Roughness and smoothness are, as he points out, obviously definable in terms of 'figure' (*Elements of Philosophy*, Ch. XXV, Sec. 10). And, less obviously, hardness, he thinks, can be defined in terms of motion; a body may be said to be hard, says Hobbes, to the extent that it is impossible for any (undetached) part of it to move without the whole doing so (Ch. VIII, Sec. 2). (The current technical term for what Hobbes calls 'hardness' is 'rigidity'.) But material things ostensibly have a host of properties, Locke's so-called *secondary* qualities, that are not obviously reducible to motion, size, shape and the like: colour, for example, or taste. These, says Hobbes, 'cannot be accidents [properties] of the object' (Ch. XXV, Sec. 10). When we look at a ripe tomato, the redness that we experience does not, according to Hobbes, really belong to the tomato itself: 'light and colour, and heat and sound are . . . but phantasms in the sentients [sentient beings]' (Ch. XXV, Sec. 3). Such a 'phantasm' lies at the end of a chain of events initiated by the object, whereby motion is conveyed from one material object to another:

For whensoever the action of the object reacheth the body of the sentient, that action is by some nerve propagated to the brain.

(Sec. 4)

[I]n all motion which proceeds by perpetual propagation, the first part being moved moves the second, the second the third, and so on to the last . . . And in what point of time the first or foremost part proceeded to the place of the second, which is thrust on, in the same point of time the last save one proceeded into the place of the last yielding part; which by reaction, in the same instant, if the reaction be strong enough, makes a phantasm; and a phantasm being made, perception is made together with it.

(Sec. 3)

Considered as a piece of speculative physiology, this is unobjectionable (though we should no longer consider mechanics adequate to the task of accounting for the physiological processes involved in perception). But the philosophical problem of accommodating, say, our perception of colour within a material universe conceived as essentially devoid of colour remains stubbornly with us. All that Hobbes has succeeded in doing, in philosophical terms, is to shift the problem from the external world into the brain. Very well; so the tomato itself is not intrinsically possessed of any such fundamental property as colour. It merely possesses, in virtue of the magnitude, shape and motion of its parts, the power, when suitably illuminated, to set in train a sequence of events, the upshot of which is the generation of a 'phantasm' of redness in the brain of a normal, and appropriately situated, human observer. But what, *in material terms, is* a phantasm of redness? Hobbes tells us, in his *Human Nature* (Ch. II), that 'colour is but an *apparition* unto us of that *motion*, agitation, or alteration, which the *object* worketh in the *brain*'. That, however, invites the further question: what, in material terms, is an 'apparition'? How is a motion or agitation in the brain supposed to appear to us as colour, given that we ourselves are not supposed to consist in anything over and above our bodies? How is that *appearance* of colour to be accommodated within a conception of the *brain* as devoid of any properties beyond those of motion, size, shape and so on? How, indeed, is it to be accommodated within our *contemporary* conception of the brain? How could any set of purely physico-chemical states capture the qualitative richness with which our senses present us, even granted that it is a mistake to read this qualitative richness into the external world?

The key point here is this. A certain explanatory strategy has been invoked to square the apparent qualitative motley of the external physical world with a radically more austere conception of its fundamental underlying character. Contrary to appearances, the objects that we observe do not, in fact, possess anything but primary qualities; but different distributions of these primary qualities, especially in regard to the microscopic parts of objects, give them the power to evoke in the consciousness of the observer qualitatively very different effects. In Boyle's celebrated analogy, they are like keys which differ only in their size and shape, but have the power to open an enormous variety of different doors: in this case doors of perception. The difficulty then, for the would-be thoroughgoing materialist, is that there is no way of reapplying this strategy at the level of the conscious effects themselves. The qualitative motley has been effectively swept under the carpet of the mind. But there it remains, and there is no obvious way in which it can be expelled from the universe altogether.

Hobbes, in a sense, gives the game away, when he refers to colour as an 'apparition of motion'; what he finds himself *wanting* to say is that a certain motion or 'agitation' in the brain of a sentient observer triggers a certain sort of appearance or sensory impression in the observer's mind. This is fine for a mind–body dualist such as René Descartes (1596–1650). But it is a way of talking that is simply not available to a materialist like Hobbes; when we reach the end of the line that links the perceived object to the relevant part of the brain, what we must have is not a motion that in turn *causes* an appearance or impression of colour, but one that precisely *is* the impression or appearance.

The point of view adopted by Hobbes is a very ancient one – almost as ancient as philosophy itself. Certainly it was adopted by the atomists of the fifth century BC. It is intriguing, therefore, to find a fragment from the writings of Democritus in which he appears to acknowledge the difficulty just raised. The intellect (*dianoia*) is engaged in an argument with the senses (*aistheseis*) about what is 'real':

The intellect: Ostensibly there is colour, ostensibly sweetness, ostensibly bitterness, actually only atoms and the void.

The senses: Poor intellect, do you hope to defeat us while you borrow from our evidence?

(Diels and Kranz, 1951, B 125)

(The Greek word here translated 'ostensibly' is *nomoi*, which really means, in this context, 'according to the standard or conventional way of regarding things'. The passage is preserved in Galen's *On Medical Experience*, and is quoted approvingly by Erwin Schrödinger, one of the principal progenitors of modern quantum mechanics, in a chapter of his book *Mind and Matter* entitled 'The Mystery of the Sensual Qualities'

(Schrödinger, 1967, p. 177; the translation is his). Schrödinger himself, incidentally, is an example of a scientist who was acutely aware of the philosophical difficulties that beset materialism.)

The point Democritus would appear to be making – against himself, moreover – is that there is something presumptively self-torpedoing about a theory that is founded upon a set of phenomena, in this case our ordinary perceptions, to which it then ends up denying reality. For if there are no secondary qualities, even within the human body, then it seems to follow, absurdly, that there are no *perceptions* of secondary qualities.

That is a rather sloppy way of putting it, because of course it all depends on what one means by perceptions of secondary qualities. Some philosophers, of whom Hobbes is one and David Hume possibly another, adopt an *error theory* of colour (see Mackie, 1980, pp. 51–2, 58–9, 136). That is to say, they hold that our pre-reflective, or at any rate pre-philosophical, conception of the material world is actually mistaken, in so far as it holds that physical objects really are coloured. According to the error theory, our tendency to believe that objects are coloured is a consequence of an illegitimate projection on to the external world of things that are going on exclusively in our own minds. I am, as it happens, by no means persuaded that this error theory is correct. It is a question of whether our ordinary use of colour words really is logically committed to a false conception of what goes on, when we look at ripe tomatoes and the like, or is largely neutral as between different scientific accounts of the matter. But suppose, for the sake of argument, that our ordinary use of colour concepts, in application to the external world, is indeed logically committed to an incorrect view of what actually occurs in perception, and that the correct view is more or less what Democritus, Hobbes and others in this tradition say it is. Then in one sense it will not, of course, be literally true that there are such things as perceptions of colour, if by that are meant perceptions of coloured material things. Clearly, there is nothing self-undermining about a theory which is required, in the end, to *redescribe* the data on which it is based; so that we say not that we perceive coloured objects, but that we perceive objects which thereby induce in us certain sorts of sensory impression. But, and this is the crucial point, it would still be true to say that there were perceptions of colour in a different sense. I have in mind the sense in which a person may quite properly be said to see, say, a red patch when, with her eyes closed, pressure is applied to her eyeball, or when some region of the visual cortex of her brain is electrically stimulated, just as much as when she is viewing a ripe tomato. Perceptions of colour in this sense, the criterion for whose occurrence lies purely in the subjective character of a person's experience, have not been and, one would think, *could not* be shown not to exist. Consequently, it is a condition of adequacy of any comprehensive theory of reality that it can accommodate such occurrences; and on the face of it – as Democritus himself apparently realized – it is very difficult to see how a Democritean theory according to which there is simply nothing, ultimately, but variously shaped atoms clashing in the void is, even in principle, capable of accommodating them.

I have deliberately represented this problem in a way that is (a) somewhat repetitious and (b) not philosophically very rigorous. My aim in these pages has been to provide the reader with a feel for the challenge that the senses set the would-be materialist. A more careful statement of the difficulty, and possible ways of dealing with it, will come later. It will be useful to have a label for the specific problem we have just been discussing: henceforth I shall refer to it as the *problem of phenomenal qualities*. By 'phenomenal qualities' I mean, for example, the red that is, so to speak, *in me* when I look at that tomato – what, for a Hobbesian brand of materialist, might be dubbed 'the red in the head'. There is a host of questions that can be raised about the status of phenomenal qualities. Are they qualities or properties *of* anything? And if so what? Are these qualities, or the things whose qualities or properties they are, spatially located? How do we come to know phenomenal qualities, and is it possible for us to be mistaken about their intrinsic character? I wish, for the moment, to leave all these questions open, though they will be addressed later in the book. Thus far I have been speaking only of perceptual phenomenal qualities, such as colours and tastes. But I would also wish to include under this head the (qualities involved in the) subjective impressions associated with all feeling and sensation, such as itches, feelings of giddiness, drowsiness, light-headedness and nausea, and the phenomenal core that remains when one has mentally subtracted from an emotion those aspects that consist in our having certain conscious thoughts and desires. (Some philosophers use the term *qualia* for what I am calling phenomenal qualities; but I have a particular reason which I shall explain later, having to do with the history of that term, for wishing to avoid it.)

The problem of phenomenal qualities is only one of many that mind raises for materialism. There are three others that I shall be discussing in this book, the first of which is that of the unity of consciousness. Descartes observed that there is a natural unity to the conscious mind that distinguishes it from anything material – or, as he puts it, *extended*, that is to say, which occupies space. It is a largely arbitrary and conventional matter how, for the purposes of thinking about the material world, we slice it up into different objects. No doubt certain parcels of matter tend naturally to cohere or to possess a certain functional unity;

but cohesion and functional unity are only matters of degree. The unity of consciousness, by contrast, seems to be absolute and not a matter of convention – a natural given that is prior to all conceptualization. As Descartes himself puts it, in his *Meditations*:

> I must begin by observing the great difference between mind and body . . . When I consider the mind – that is, myself, in so far as I am merely a conscious being – I can distinguish no parts within myself; I understand myself to be a single and complete thing. . . Nor can the faculties of will, feeling, understanding and so on be called its parts; for it is one and the same mind that wills, feels, and understands. On the other hand, I cannot think of any corporeal or extended object without being readily able to divide it in thought . . .
>
> (Sixth Meditation)

This problem of the unity of consciousness is the subject of chapter 6, where I shall examine Nagel's claim, grounded in some findings of modern neuropsychology, that this Cartesian all-or-nothing unity is an illusion (Nagel, 1979a).

Another problem, which is also highly relevant to perception, is that of *meaning* or, relatedly, what philosophers sometimes call *intentionality*; intentionality really means object-directedness, in the sense in which a perception can present itself as a perception *of* a tomato, and a thought be *about* Paris (or, respectively, pink rats and Eldorado; the 'objects' in question, sometimes known as intentional objects, need not actually exist). Intentionality is really just one aspect of meaningfulness; it is to mind what reference is to language. But it is deeply puzzling how mental goings-on can be meaningful, how, in particular, they can be of or about anything – all the more so if these mental goings-on are to be identified with neurophysiological goings-on. Of course, we are in one sense perfectly familiar with material objects and events having meaning and referring to certain specific things. Consider the ink marks on a page, or the pressure waves in air when people converse, or the operations of an electronic computer programmed to perform a specific task. These things, however, have meaning only because people have invested them with meaning; and what makes this possible is that the operations of their own minds or brains are already meaningful. But how, then, do *they* come to have meaning?

There is an instructive parallel here between the strategies that have historically been employed in relation to the secondary qualities and those employed in relation to meaning, especially linguistic meaning. Indeed, both owe their modern expression to the seventeenth-century scientific Enlightenment. In the one case it is denied that physical objects are *intrinsically* coloured, say. In the other, it is denied that words, in their various physical embodiments, are *intrinsically* meaningful. Intrinsic colour and intrinsic meaning are, as it were, chased back into what is held to be their only proper habitat, the mind. And anything outside the mind is allowed to have colour, or meaning, only in a derivative sense, by standing in a suitable (perhaps merely dispositional) relation to *mental* goings-on.

This whole Cartesian picture – for it is in Descartes that one finds it most clearly – is as problematic as it is seductive. It can seem to lead inevitably to mind–body dualism; and it results in mind being distanced from the external world, in a way that makes it difficult to see how the latter can ever be an object of genuine knowledge. Little wonder, then, that much post-war twentieth-century philosophy has been aimed at showing that the Cartesian picture is somehow radically mistaken. I shall have something to say later, in chapters 9 and 16, about one of the boldest and most intriguing attempts to wean us away from the Cartesian picture, that found in some recent writings of John McDowell (1986). But let me say straight away that I myself – unfashionably perhaps – am of the opinion that the Cartesian picture is essentially correct, as far as it goes, and that we need to build on the philosophical edifice forged in the seventeenth century, instead of attempting to demolish it altogether.

Bear in mind, though, that what I mean here by the Cartesian picture is not explicitly committed, as Descartes himself was, to mind–body dualism; rather it is a view that Galileo, Descartes, Hobbes, Boyle, Locke and Hume all shared. Also bear in mind that what we are talking about here is a philosophical picture. The scientific picture that emerged in the seventeenth century has, I believe, been effectively shattered by Einstein, Bohr, Heisenberg, Schrödinger and Dirac. And philosophy needs, however belatedly, to come to terms with this scientific revolution.

This brings me to the final problem that I wish to highlight in this chapter, the *problem of our perception of time*. From the point of view of consciousness, time is perceived in terms of a moving present steadily advancing into the future, or, equivalently, a constant dynamic metamorphosis of future into present, present into past (see figure 1.1). Common sense generalizes this to the world as a whole, a conception that Isaac Newton was able to incorporate in his mechanics. Though, to be sure, there was nothing in his differential equations that necessitated the time parameter's being interpreted in this way, by the same token there was nothing to prevent its being so interpreted. From this Newtonian point of view, then, there is nothing surprising or problematic in the fact that we perceive time (or better, perhaps, perceive temporally) in the way we do, on the assumption that our states of mind just are states of the brain. For they are simply participants in an overall, objective, universal march of time, and are accordingly experienced as such.

But modern physics, specifically Einstein's theory of relativity, has rendered obsolete this whole way of looking at time. Time has become a fourth dimension; and an individual persisting object, such as a human body, is to be conceived as a four-dimensional 'worm', laid out in space-time, each three-dimensional time-slice of which corresponds to the object as it is at a particular moment in its history. (The set of space-time points occupied by this 'worm' – if one ignores the fact that it has spatial thickness as well as temporal length – is known as the object's *world-line*.) In this conception there is no universal march or flow of time. There cannot be, because there is no universal present; and consequently there is no universal past or future. There is nothing in *special* relativity to prevent one, *locally*, from defining a 'now' on the basis of one's current experience, and then defining the 'present' as the three-dimensional so-called *simultaneity plane* that encompasses everything happening anywhere in the universe that is simultaneous with that local 'now'. But the latter definition will be wholly dependent on one's current state of motion. What this means is that, relative to such a definition, the very slightest change in motion will result in spatially removed events swinging forward from the 'past' into the 'future' and conversely – in the case of distant stars and galaxies by perhaps thousands or millions of years – as this instantaneously defined simultaneity plane tips back and forth on the pivot of one's momentary local 'now' (see figure 1.2). Moreover, in *general* relativity, which takes account of gravitation and involves curved space-time, there is not even a uniquely defined simultaneity plane relative to the observer's state of motion. What one chooses to regard as 'now', at some distant region, will also depend on a largely arbitrary choice of coordinate system.

This makes trouble, incidentally, for a conception of time that many philosophers from Aristotle to the present day have wished to defend, according to which the future is *open*, partially undefined, in contrast to the past, which is fixed, closed, a *fait accompli*. The motivation for such a view lies mainly in a desire to defend free will, to enable us to regard the future (in words I once saw in the *Reader's Digest*) as 'not there waiting for us, but something we make as we go along'. In the context of relativity (as is pointed out by Hilary Putnam, 1979), such a view appears not so much false as meaningless. As we have seen, different observers, and the same observer at different times, slice the space-time continuum at different angles (or the space-time analogues of angles), corresponding to their different instantaneous states of motion. Which, then, of all these instantaneous time slices through the continuum, an infinity of which will intersect any given space-time point, is to be regarded as *the* present

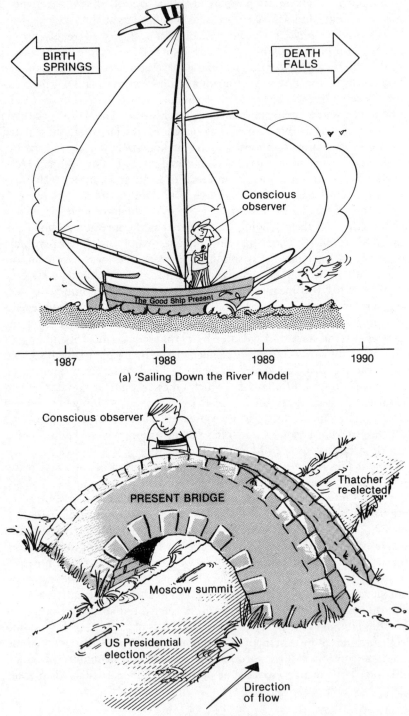

(a) 'Sailing Down the River' Model

(b) 'Poohsticks' Model

Figure 1.1 (opposite)   *Two models of temporal flow (as of June 1988).*
In (a) the River of Time carries us forward, and specific times and events are to be thought of as stationary and arrayed along the bank(s) of the river. In (b) we remain stationary on Present Bridge, while the River of Time carries events (like sticks floating on the surface) towards us from the future, then under the bridge and away into the past. (The reference is to the stick-racing game played by Pooh, Piglet and Roo in A. A. Milne's The House at Pooh Corner.) The models are essentially equivalent, since all that is really implied by the flow of time is a relative motion of the present, with respect to times and events, such that the interval separating the present from future events is constantly narrowing, whilst that separating the present from past events is constantly widening.

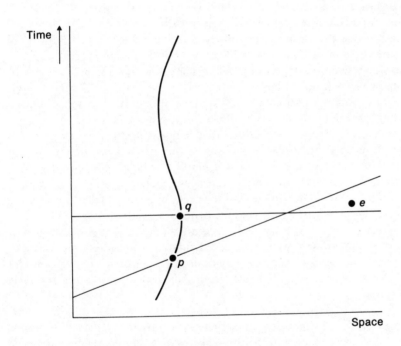

Figure 1.2 *The wavy line represents someone's world-line.*
The straight lines represent the instantaneous 'presents' or simultaneity planes corresponding to the two different points (i.e. events) p and q on this world-line. Any event below the line is past relative to such a 'present'; any event above the line is future. Note that the distant event e is past relative to the earlier 'present' associated with the point p, but future relative to the later 'present' associated with the point q. (The simultaneity plane corresponding to a given point on a world-line is conventionally represented by a line having the same angle to the space axis as a tangent to the world-line, at that point, has to the time axis.)

that divides the fixed from the open? Not only does relativity not tell us; it is wholly contrary to the spirit of the theory (a marring of the symmetry that renders it a thing of such beauty) that there should actually be any such *preferred* frame of reference, relative to whose simultaneity planes, things are *really and absolutely* past, present or future.

Actually, there was always something a bit fishy about the 'flow' conception of time; so that it is perhaps arguable that relativity has, philosophically speaking, had the effect mainly of rubbing our noses in a difficulty that should have been evident all along, given sufficient philosophical acuity. The commonest way of posing this difficulty that arises quite independently of relativity is to ask the question 'How fast does time flow?' To which the only possible answer is 'One hour per hour' – one that seems comic in its tautologousness, rather than being informative in the way that a measure of any genuine process ought to be. One way of diagnosing what has gone wrong here might be somewhat as follows. First, there is, of course, such a thing as *change*. There's nothing particularly mysterious about it: for something to change is simply for it to have different attributes at different times. Thus understood, change is something that happens *in* time, not *to* time. But somehow, perhaps because changes in things (changes, indeed, in our states of consciousness) are the sole *manifestation* of time, we have got it into our heads that time itself is a process of change, with its own inner dynamic – a dynamic process, so to speak, in its own right – rather than merely the arena in which genuine processes occur.

None of this, however, really gets to the heart of the question why there is something problematic about time in relation to consciousness, or why this is *especially* problematic in the light of relativity. Consider the following piece of dialogue, from Paul Davies's *God and the New Physics*:

Physicist: . . . I don't deny that there is an ordered sequence of events, with a definite before–after or past–future relation between them. I am simply denying the existence of *the* past, *the* present and *the* future. There clearly is not *a* present, for you and I have both experienced many 'presents' in our life. Some events lie in the past or future of other events, but the events themselves are simply *there*, they don't *happen* one by one . . .

Sceptic: Surely my consciousness moves forward from today to tomorrow?

Physicist: No! Your mind *is* conscious both today and tomorrow. Nothing *moves* forward, backward or sideways . . . The physicist views spacetime as laid out like a map, with time extending along one side. Events are marked as points on the map . . . It's all *there* . . .

Sceptic: You still haven't explained to me why I *feel* the flow of time.

Physicist: I'm not a neurologist. It has probably got something to do with short-term memory processes.

Sceptic: You're claiming it's all in the mind – an illusion?

Physicist: You would be unwise to appeal to your feelings to attribute physical qualities to the external world. Haven't you ever felt dizzy?

Sceptic: Of course.

Physicist: So, I maintain that the whirling of time is like the whirling of space – a sort of temporal dizziness – which is given a false impression of reality by our confused language, with its tense structure and meaningless phrases about the past, present and future.

(Davies 1984, pp. 129, 131–2)

This is a splendid piece of popular science writing (and, by the way, make no mistake about it: the position of 'Physicist' here is unquestionably that of Davies himself). Moreover, I have not the least doubt that Davies is right in suggesting that the appearance of temporal flow has 'something to do with short-term memory processes'. But, philosophically speaking, Physicist's words somehow fail to satisfy – though I'm bound to admit that the whole problem has about it an elusive, now-you-see-it-now-you-don't quality, which makes it difficult to be sure that one's residual unease marks a genuine unresolved philosophical difficulty. On the face of it, however, what we have here is yet another instance of the strategy that we have encountered twice before in this chapter, in regard to the secondary qualities and intentionality, and have twice found wanting. Temporal flow has no place within the physicist's world-view, so we must consign it to the mind. And having done so, the assumption seems to be, we don't have to worry about it any more. But then what is going on in the mind? And what is the place of that within the physicist's world-view? The analogy with dizziness, ingenious though it is, nevertheless seems on reflection to be singularly unhelpful. The illusion involved in dizziness, in which things seem to be whirling around us, is, as Physicist says, an illusion about the *external* world. And, to that extent, it raises no special philosophical problem; for physiologically explicable reasons dizziness causes the brain to receive a set of signals similar to those it would be receiving were things really whirling around us, and which accordingly induce a set of sensations that we are naturally predisposed to interpret as indicating a rotation of our surroundings – though the interpretation is, of course, one that the intellect rejects out of hand. But temporal flow, by contrast, if it is an illusion at all, is not an illusion about the *external* world, particularly. Rather it relates to the very nature of experience; at the most fundamental level, it has to do with the intrinsic character of our own stream of consciousness. Temporal flow seems to be of the very essence of consciousness and, as such, as inescapable a feature of our being as is consciousness itself.

In any case, this issue, like all the others, is one to which we shall return in due course. After this whistle-stop tour, we must now go back over the ground with rather more philosophical circumspection and also with closer attention to the question what is true as a matter of scientific fact. Or what *might* be true: in matters that lie beyond the frontiers of present day scientific knowledge, I shall consider myself free to indulge in armchair speculation!

2

Physicalism and Materialism: A Tale of Two 'isms'

In Carl Sagan's novel *Contact* there is a scene in which Dr Arroway, the agnostic scientist-heroine, has a meeting with a politically influential television evangelist, Palmer Joss, who has opposed her plan to build (to specifications supplied by an alien intelligence) a mysterious machine of unknown purpose. At one point the conversation takes a philosophical turn:

> 'I give you my word, Dr. Arroway, I'll carefully ponder what you've said this evening. You've raised some questions I should have answers for. But in the same spirit, let me ask you a few questions. Okay?'
>
> She nodded, and he continued. 'Think of what consciousness feels like, what it feels like this moment. Does that *feel* like billions of tiny atoms wiggling in place? And beyond the biological mechanism, where in science can a child learn what love is?. . .
>
> (Sagan, 1985, p. 255)

Now what are we to make of this, as an argument? Actually, there are two arguments here. As regards the first of these – 'Does that *feel* like etc.' – I am tempted to echo a famous remark attributed to Wittgenstein. Upon meeting a friend in the corridor, Wittgenstein is alleged to have said: 'Tell me, why do people always say it was *natural* for men to assume that the sun went round the earth rather than that the earth was rotating?' The friend responded, 'Well, obviously, because it just *looks* as if the sun is going round the earth.' To which Wittgenstein replied, 'Well, what would it have looked like if it had looked as if the earth was rotating?' (The story is told by Elizabeth Anscombe (1959, p. 151) and also, in the version I have quoted, in Tom Stoppard's play *Jumpers* (Stoppard, 1972, p. 75). In a similar spirit, Dr Arroway should perhaps have asked Palmer Joss: 'What would consciousness have felt like if it had *felt* like billions of tiny atoms wiggling in place?'

One may be tempted to argue as follows. 'We are in no position to have any philosophically well-grounded expectation as to what we ought, specifically, to be experiencing if there were nothing more to consciousness than "billions of tiny atoms wiggling in place". For, after all, the assumption that *that* is all that is going on gives us no grounds, a priori, for expecting that we should be having any experiences at all.'

But this argument seems to me mistaken. Palmer Joss does, I think, have a valid point (which is not to deny that the Wittgensteinian riposte has some force also). While it remains totally mysterious why anything going on in the brain should be associated with conscious experiences at all, if materialism is true we should nevertheless expect some kind of 'fit' between the phenomenal character of our experiences and the physical character of the goings-on in our brain which are constitutive of our having these experiences. *What* kind of fit, however, it is difficult to say, in advance of a more specific indication as to the sort of materialism one has in mind.

One thing that is needed in this context is a general way of thinking about the manner in which any particular state, be it a state of consciousness, characterized by the presence of some particular phenomenal quality, or a physical state, say the instantaneous state of a pendulum bob, forms part of a system of possible states. The requisite notion, highly relevant to the general question of fit as between conscious states and states of the brain (and also to the understanding of quantum mechanics), is that of a so-called *state space*, which will be the subject of chapter 7. Palmer Joss's first question also raises something that is known in the philosophical literature as the *grain problem*: how can a mass of highly-structured individual operations, whether at the level of atoms or of brain cells, constitute the physical realization of something as smooth and uniform as a patch of homogeneous (phenomenal) colour or a phenomenally flawless and sustained musical note? Again, this is perhaps more of a problem for some forms of materialism than for others. It is certainly a problem for the position I wish ultimately to defend in this book and will accordingly have to be confronted in due course.

(Incidentally, I say 'brain' in this context, and will continue to do so. But I do not wish, at this stage, wholly to prejudge the question whether experiences should be regarded as confined to the brain, or even to the body. Perhaps we should not think of them as being anywhere, even if materialism is true. But these are questions that will be addressed in a later chapter.)

Now what about Palmer Joss's second point: 'where in science can a child learn what love is?' Well, psychology is a science, so why not from psychology if she's a bright child? I suppose there are two things to be said here. First, what is presumably meant by 'science' is so-called 'hard science': here, physics, chemistry and physiology. And secondly, the real point of the question, presumably, is that to know what love is one has to know *what it is like* to love someone; and that is something that one cannot simply get out a science textbook, unaided by any relevant *experience*. Now love (whether of the romantic or, say, parent–child variety) is far too complex, ill-understood and psychologically elusive a phenomenon for the purposes of the present discussion, and too steeped in intentionality. In philosophy, as in science, it is usually better to start with the relatively simple. So I shall concentrate instead on phenomenal colour (though colour too is a great deal more complex than most people imagine).

What is really at stake here is the question whether there is anything that in principle is going to be *left out* of any description, however comprehensive in its own terms, which is couched purely in the language of physics. (I haven't forgotten chemistry and physiology, to which I shall shortly return.) This is very vague as it stands, so I must try to make it more precise. In the first place, the concepts and modes of description employed by physicists are constantly being amended and augmented. Hence, the 'language of physics' must be interpreted generously, so as to include anything that might come to be added to the basic vocabulary of physics, in consequence of theoretical physicists going on doing essentially the same sort of things that they do at present. (Certain kinds of very radical conceptual shift, such as would involve the introduction of mentalistic terms into the basic level of description – rather as Aristotle contended that the planets were moved by love – must obviously be excluded, if the 'language of physics' is not to become all-encompassing simply by definition.)

Secondly, it needs to be spelled out just what it is for something not to be left out of a given description. What we are really talking about here is *reducibility* (or reductionism). But the term is ambiguous and can mean one of (at least) two things. Consider, for example, the question whether physiology is in principle reducible to physics. I would argue that in one sense it probably is and in another sense pretty clearly is not. The sense in which it is presumably not reducible to physics is as follows. Given a statement couched in the language of physiology, one could not, even in principle, translate it into a logically equivalent (though obviously vastly more complicated) statement couched purely in the language of physics. We might say, then, that physiology is not *strongly* reducible to physics. This is as much as to say that physiology employs its own autonomous set of concepts and modes of explanation. And I imagine this is true of chemistry as well: I should think that chemistry is not strongly reducible to physics (or, at any rate, not as it stands), and that physiology is not strongly reducible even to physics and chemistry combined.

On the other hand, there is another – to my mind philosophically more interesting – sense, in which contemporary physiology probably is reducible to physics (and *a fortiori* to a combination of physics and chemistry). Suppose one were given (a) a sufficiently detailed account of what was going on in, say, the brain, couched purely in terms of the concepts (or language) of physics, (b) a sufficient grasp of the relevant physiological concepts (or vocabulary) and (c) sufficient ratiocinative power (which in practice would probably be way beyond the capacity of any actual human being). Then one would, I imagine, be in a position to deduce what was going on in the brain in physiological terms: to know whether or not any given statement about it, couched in the language of physiology, was true. Physiology could then be said to be *weakly* reducible to physics. This, as I say, seems to be the more interesting notion, since a failure of strong reducibility may be attributable to the nature of our conceptual scheme or language, rather than to the nature of the reality to which the concepts or language correspond.

(The situation, here, parallels a stock philosophical example. Statements about nations, it is often said – rightly, in my view – cannot be translated into logically equivalent statements that make reference only to the doings and interactions of individuals and spatial regions. In my terms, then, nation talk is not strongly reducible to talk about persons, strips of terrain and the like. But suppose someone possesses the concept of a nation, and is told, in language that makes no reference to nations, sufficiently many facts about what various people are doing and in what places. Then they will surely, in principle, be in a position to tell what is going on in nation terms. Nation talk is thus weakly reducible to person/ place talk.)

Our original question was whether anything is, of necessity, left out of descriptions of the world that are couched purely in the language of physics – whether, that is to say, such descriptions are inherently liable, in virtue of the existence of states of awareness, to involve omissions that no further elaboration, in purely physical terms, could repair. This question may now be recast as the question whether *psychology*, in its old-fashioned sense of the study of the mind, where mind includes states of awareness, is even weakly reducible to physics. (Purely behaviouristic psychology presumably *is* weakly reducible to physics, wherein, I dare say, lay its principal appeal.) The thesis that in the domain we're concerned with, there are only physical facts is what I shall henceforth refer to as *physicalism*. And I suggest (though this is not intended as a definition) that we should regard physicalism as being true just in case psychology is, in my sense, weakly reducible to physics.

One thing that I should perhaps make clear is that, given this definition of weak reducibility, one way in which statements which ostensibly refer to, say, phenomenal qualities could turn out to be reducible to physiology, and hence to physics, would be if such statements were all of them false – if there somehow turned not to be any such thing as the experiencing of phenomenal qualities! This is because reducibility here turns on the question whether, given a correct account of what is going on couched in the language of physics or physiology, together with the relevant psychological concepts and sufficient ratiocinative power, one could deduce what is *actually* happening at the level of the awareness of phenomenal qualities. If nothing is really going on in these terms – if it is simply some sort of illusion that it is – then the condition for reducibility is satisfied trivially. That nothing *is* going on in these terms is not quite as ridiculous a suggestion as it sounds (though it is one that I myself find it very difficult to take seriously). The suggestion would be that our ordinary mode of describing our so-called 'inner lives' – what philosophers nowadays refer to as *folk psychology* – presupposes a false theory of what is really going on. On this view, it would strictly speaking be invariably false to say such things as 'I am feeling nauseous'. It would be false in the same sort of way and for the same sort of reasons that it would be false to say 'The rain god is angry', on hearing a clap of thunder. What would be needed in both cases is the replacement of such language by something scientifically acceptable – and in the first case, that would mean replacing the statement by some appropriate neuro-physiological analogue. The view according to which all psychological descriptions that resist being weakly reduced to the language of physics, chemistry and physiology are to be regarded as, strictly speaking, false, goes by the name of *eliminative materialism* (Rorty, 1971; Stich, 1983). My own reaction to the growth of eliminative materialism amongst would-be physicalists is that it is symptomatic of extreme philosophical desperation. Since I am also inclined to think that physicalism is an untenable position, I would judge that they have good reason to be desperate.

It is essential, however, to make a distinction here between different types of psychological concepts. Concepts like those of belief and desire, I shall be arguing in chapter 10, are indeed, to a degree, *theory-laden*; it is true that their content derives, in part, from a common-sense theory about how the mind functions. So it may just be possible to argue that, to the extent that this theory might turn out to be false in the light of a proper scientific understanding of the brain, beliefs and desires might turn out, strictly speaking, not to exist. But the question then is whether all psychological concepts are theory-laden in this sense. It seems to me that they are not, and that there is a realm of 'raw feels' and brute sensation, where the corresponding psychological concepts are purely descriptive and classificatory, importing no element of theory whatsoever. Anyone who agrees with me about this will regard as downright absurd the idea of 'eliminating' such things as sensations and phenomenal qualities. This ostensible absurdity is nicely captured in the following anonymous limerick:

> There was a faith-healer of Deal
> Who said 'Although pain isn't real,
> If I sit on a pin
> And it punctures my skin,
> I dislike what I *fancy* I feel.'

Physicalism, as I have defined it, implies, but is not implied by, *materialism*. Materialism is the theory that everything that exists is material. I shall not attempt to define precisely what I mean by 'material'; but, roughly speaking, those things are material that occupy or take place in space, and whose existence is ultimately constituted by the properties and relations, actions and interactions of particles and fields, or whatever basic entities physics treats of. For our purposes, a materialist is someone who denies that mental states, processes and events exist *over and above* bodily states, processes and events (or the material environment, if one thinks that mentality somehow spills over into some of that with which the body interacts).

Why, then, does materialism not imply physicalism? Because there may be more to matter than can be captured in the language of physics, more than any description couched purely in the language of physics is capable of conveying.

Compare two possible philosophical positions. First, there is that held by Descartes, who thought that the (conscious) mind was a distinct, immaterial *substance* (in the philosopher's sense of a persisting entity), lacking a spatial location but nevertheless causally interacting with matter. This position is neither physicalist nor materialist. Now consider a different sort of position, according to which mind does not exist over and above the brain: states of awareness *are* brain states, and are located in space (to the extent, anyway, that the states of any material object may be said to be). But those brain states that are identical with states of awareness have, besides their physical or physiological properties, certain additional mental properties. Thus the patch of phenomenal red or (better perhaps) the state of one's being aware of such a patch, is just a state of one's brain; but its having the subjective character it does (as an experience of red, for example, as opposed to yellow) is a property of that state additional to its physical or physiological properties. What I have in mind is a view which postulates a dualism of attributes, where Descartes postulated a dualism of basic types of thing. Such a view is an example of one that is materialist without being physicalist. It is not a particularly attractive view nor is it the only way one could be a materialist without being a physicalist; I cite it simply to illustrate what seems to me to be a crucial distinction. There is, however, another, more interesting way in which a theory could be materialist without being physicalist. But its explanation calls for the introduction of a new concept.

The concept in question, which has figured large in much recent philosophical discussion, is that of the *supervenience* of the psychological on the physical. Start with some collection M of true psychological statements, and consider it in relation to the set P of all conceivably relevant physical statements, including but not necessarily restricted to statements about the brain. Let all these statements be ones that record the state of affairs that obtains at some particular time *t*. Then imagine that an alternative state of affairs had obtained at *t*, in which some of the statements in the set M were false (in which one did not, after all, want to watch that programme on the television, or in which one felt elation instead of depression). The doctrine of the supervenience of the psychological on the physical then tells us that, as a matter of necessity, some of the statements in the set P would have to be false as well. Briefly, for every difference at the mental state level, there must be some corresponding difference of physical state, on which difference the difference of mental state in some sense depends. Clearly, there are going to be different versions of the supervenience doctrine, according to the kind of dependence or necessity that is held to obtain here. But philosophers who invoke the notion usually have in mind something stronger than mere *lawlike* dependence, such as might obtain if there were certain laws of nature according to which, as a matter of brute contingent fact, the occurrence of every distinct kind of mental state was accompanied by a corresponding distinct kind of physical state.

What is it, then, that they have in mind? Well, consider the following two statements: (a) 'Iron is a metal', (b) 'Iron is composed of atoms with atomic number 26'. Is there any way in which either of these statements *could have been* false? Surely not. The first is, as one would ordinarily say, true by definition. It is part of our *concept* of iron that it is a kind of metal. (Or, perhaps, part of our concept of a metal that iron is a metal.) Let us say, then, that (a) is a *conceptual truth*: its truth is guaranteed by the logic of the relevant concepts. However (b) is different. Its truth is not guaranteed by our concepts of iron or of atomic number. Not, at any rate, if we are talking about the ordinary person's concept of iron, as opposed to the scientist's, or about the concept of iron that a scientist would have had a hundred years ago. Nevertheless, (b) – assuming that it is in fact true, and that scientists are not mistaken about the atomic number of iron – could not have been false. Even God could not have brought it about that *iron* had a different atomic number from that which it in fact has. For anything that had had a different atomic number, however much it had resembled iron, just wouldn't have been iron.

Why is this? Well, it is because it was always part of our concept of iron that to be iron was to have a particular sort of underlying nature, the nature in question being whatever it is that provides the deep explanation for iron's characteristic attributes under normal conditions: its density, appearance, tendency to rust, behaviour when heated to different temperatures or when heated and then suddenly cooled, and so forth. And we now know that it is the number of protons in the nucleus of iron atoms that provides the deep explanation for all of these things. So our prior concept of iron, in conjunction with what we now know, jointly render this a necessary truth about iron. The American philosopher Saul Kripke, who has done most to clarify these matters, has suggested the term *metaphysical necessity* for the sort of necessity that (b) has (see Kripke, 1980). But this makes it sound far more mysterious than it really is; certainly, there is nothing particularly metaphysical about it. The necessity that attaches to (a) and (b) could equally be regarded as a kind of shadow cast on the world by our concepts. It is just that in (a) our concepts by themselves determine where the shadow will fall, whereas in (b) the direction of the shadow, so to speak, is determined by how things are independently of our concepts. In what follows, 'necessary' or 'necessarily', without further qualification, will connote the kind of necessity possessed by (b); I shall speak of 'conceptual truth' or 'conceptual necessity' whenever I have in mind the kind of necessity exemplified by (a). (By a conceptual truth I mean what many philosophers would call an *analytic* proposition.)

While we're engaged in making distinctions, there is another that will come in handy: the distinction between *type* and *token* states or occurrences. Suppose you and I both have a headache. (Or suppose I had a headache last Thursday, and then another one today.) There is then a sense in which we are in the same state, but another sense in which, of course, we are not; how can *I* have *your* headache? (And how can I have the very same headache on two distinct occasions?) This may be expressed by saying that our respective states (or the states I was in last Thursday and today) are different *tokens* of the same *type*. (The distinction has been imported into philosophy from theoretical linguistics, where it proved convenient to make such a distinction in relation to linguistic expressions: the senses in which you and I can and cannot be said to utter the same word, phrase or sentence.)

To return, then, to supervenience, there are two sorts of necessity that people who invoke this notion normally have in mind. Sometimes it is some kind of conceptual necessity, according to which it is ultimately logically incoherent that the mental should ever float free of the physical in the way that a failure of supervenience would imply. More usually, however, it is the kind of necessity that attaches to (b), such as would make the flow of electricity in a wire supervenient upon a migration of charged particles (albeit that electrons in a wire move in the opposite direction to this notional 'flow'!). Though it required empirical investigation to establish this relationship, it is nevertheless necessary, in the sense that there could not have been a genuine electric current in the absence of such a motion of charged particles, any more than there could have been genuine iron which was not composed of atoms of atomic number 26.

A convenient way of putting this is to say that there is no *possible world* in which there exist electric currents without a migration of charged particles, or iron that is not composed of atoms of atomic number 26 (or, one might add, in which I derived from a different sperm and egg from those from which I originated in the actual world: anyone, however similar to me, who had had a different parentage in this biological sense just wouldn't have been *me*). There is, by definition, a distinct possible world for every distinct way things might have been – meaning by 'things' absolutely everything, the entire universe. (Suppose one had an all-powerful deity, constrained only by the laws of logic. Then there is a possible world for every distinct way such a deity could have arranged matters, either by suitable intervention, guiding the course of history, or by the way He set up the universe in the first place, framing laws of nature and so forth.) In this sense, there are no doubt possible worlds in which something other than the motion of charged particles gives rise to superficially similar effects in superficially similar circumstances – making bulbs light up, causing sensations and physiological effects similar to those we associate with electric shock, and so forth. But this something else just wouldn't count as the flow of electricity. Anyway, when I speak of supervenience in what follows, it is to be understood in terms of this latter kind of necessity.

One could consistently hold that the truth of statements couched in the language of psychology was, in this sense, supervenient upon that of statements couched in the language of physics – in contrast to someone who held that brain states, say, possessed mental properties simply in addition to their physical ones – without, once again, holding that psychology was either strongly or weakly *reducible* to physics. Such a view would be a version of materialism, because it would be logically committed to denying that mental states existed over and above states of the material world; but it would not be physicalist, in my sense. Given, as I hope to show, that physicalism is untenable, an otherwise unobjectionable theory of this general form would have much to recommend it.

3

Functionalism

The great white hope of physicalists and materialists, in recent years, has been a doctrine called *functionalism* (Putnam, 1971; Dennett, 1978; Loar, 1982; Smith and Jones, 1986). It is a theory born of the computer age and taken up with enthusiasm by many researchers within the field of artificial intelligence. The virtues of, and motivation behind, functionalism can perhaps best be appreciated if one considers the inadequacies of that earlier theory that went by the name of *behaviourism*. As a methodological approach in psychology, behaviourism involved treating human and other organisms as essentially *black boxes*. What behaviourist psychologists said, in effect, was: 'Ignore what goes on inside an animal, human or otherwise. That's a job for the physiologists. Regard an animal simply as something which receives certain inputs from the environment, that is to say *stimuli*, and emits certain outputs, that is to say behavioural *responses*. Our job, as psychologists, is to work out a set of laws that relate responses and stimuli, thus enabling us to predict, at least statistically, what responses will emerge, over a period of time, if the animal is subjected to this, that or the other stimulus regime.' The corresponding philosophical doctrine was that mentalistic vocabulary is really just a shorthand way of talking about physical stimuli, behaviour and the relation between them. Thus, the 'cognitive content' or 'cash value' of saying of a motorist that he is in a bad mood might be held to consist in such facts as that, if someone were to cut in front of him, he would immediately tense up, punch the horn, make rude gestures out of the window, or something similar. Of course, he might not do any of these things. But then that would presumably be because he was exercising great self-control; and that in turn would be given some suitable behaviouristic construal. In any case, it might still be true that he was strongly disposed to act thus; and maybe there would be suitable behavioural criteria for saying this. The theory is not really worth spending time over. What I think most gives the game away is the 'something similar' in the above example. For we are entitled to ask what it is that makes certain stimuli or certain responses relevantly similar, in this context. It would seem that one cannot really give an answer, except against the background of a theory as to what is going on inside. Relative to such a theory, stimuli are similar if they affect the internal mechanism in a relevantly similar way; and responses are similar if they are the sorts of responses that are liable to be induced by relevantly similar internal states. And what does '*relevantly* similar' mean here? Something like: similar, relative to the system's overall functioning.

Philosophical behaviourism is an absurd theory, a straw man. Practically the only philosophers who ever held it, at any rate in the crude form just outlined, were certain *logical positivists*: philosophers, that is, who were wedded to a theory of meaning according to which knowing the meaning of a proposition is a matter of knowing its method of verification. For it is, to be sure, mainly on the basis of our observation of people's behaviour and the physical stimuli to which they are being subjected that we verify or falsify propositions about their mental states. But even these logical positivists tended to baulk at applying the theory to propositions in which mental states are ascribed to *oneself*. As Ogden and Richards pointed out, in *The Meaning of Meaning* (1949, p. 23), this would place the behaviourist 'under the logical necessity of affecting general anaesthesia'!

But it is still worth asking: where precisely has behaviourism gone wrong, considered simply as an attempt to defend physicalism? Something it might be profitable to ask a philosophical or a methodological behaviourist (if one could still be found) is: what's so special about the skin? That is to say, why all this emphasis on *overt* behaviour and *external* stimuli? Why isn't what goes on *inside* the organism of equal significance? As far as philosophical behaviourism goes, the answer is pretty obvious: it is intended to be a theory about what propositions involving psychological vocabulary actually *mean*. And it is difficult to see how what is going on in the brain, for example, or indeed anything that most ordinary users of the language don't know about, can enter into the meaning of such statements. When it is put that way, it becomes evident that philosophical behaviourists have set their sights much higher than they are required to, if their underlying motivation is to defend physicalism. They are looking for a way of construing psychology that would render it strongly reducible to physics; whereas this is simply not necessary. It is enough so to construe propositions involving mentalistic vocabulary that they are weakly reducible to physics or physiology: to construe them in such a way that their truth or falsity could in principle be deduced from the physical facts by anyone possessing the relevant concepts.

From the standpoint of this lesser, though still wholly adequate, physicalist ambition, the emphasis on overt behaviour and external stimuli is indeed quite arbitrary. We need to consider what goes on inside, *how* it is that such-and-such inputs lead to such-and-such outputs. As far as the content of ordinary everyday psychological concepts goes (or the meaning of our mentalistic vocabulary), it is of course perfectly true that they cannot embody any esoteric knowledge, of the kind thrown up by neurophysiology. But there is a way in which the 'what is going on inside' could enter into our concepts without importing any physiology. This is if the 'inner' states and events are treated at a level of *abstractness* that renders our psychological concepts neutral with respect to the question what, precisely, a given mental state might amount to in physico-chemical or physiological terms.

Such abstract descriptions of processes are a commonplace in the age of the computer. Most of us are familiar with flow charts, decision trees, block-diagram models and the like – and, indeed, with computer programs. What all of these things have in common is that they delineate the structure of a process, whilst leaving it largely unspecified just how this structure is (or is to be) physically realized. (Computer programs, for example, clearly admit of a potential infinity of physically different realizations.) This then, is the key idea underlying functionalism. The suggestion is that what it is about a given token mental state or occurrence that makes it a state or occurrence of a particular type – a desire for food, say, or a belief that it is going to rain, or a surge of joy, or a pang of anxiety – is its occupying a particular niche within a complex causal network of possible states which mediates, as a whole, the causal relationship between sensory (and other) inputs and behavioural (and other) outputs. Any state that is appropriately causally related to other actual and possible states, that are in their turn causally related to one another in the right sort of way, so as to constitute a network of the appropriate kind, will, as a matter of conceptual necessity, be a desire for food, say, as opposed to a desire for a holiday in the Seychelles or a feeling of resentment against one's boss.

States that are related to each other as are, say, all desires, or all beliefs, or all intentions, or all visual perceptions will presumably be in some sense states of a single system within the brain. So the functionalist approach suggests, though it does not necessitate, a block-diagram conception of the mind, somewhat reminiscent of the old 'faculty' psychology. It will be natural to break the mind down, conceptually, into subsystems which receive certain inputs, either from the external world or from other subsystems, which operate upon them in certain ways, and which then deliver corresponding outputs either to the external world or to other subsystems. It must be emphasized, however, that these subsystems, represented by blocks, need not correspond to physically distinct components within the brain; rather they may represent different modes of functioning of what is, in physical terms, the same component or set of components.

Now each such subsystem could be broken down, in its turn, in block-diagram fashion. But – and I take it that this is a central tenet of functionalism – there will come a point, as this functional dissection proceeds, at which it becomes permissible to deal with what is going on inside such a block in the way behaviourists treated the internal workings of humans and other animals. At a certain, sufficiently detailed level of analysis, these *subsystems* may themselves be treated as black boxes, in the sense that, as regards what is going on in psychological terms, it may matter *what* they do, what the causal relationship is between input and output; but now *how* they do it, not how that relationship is mediated.

In order to indicate, very roughly, what such a functional breakdown might look like, at any rate at the first, crudest level of analysis, I offer the reader a functional map of the human mind (figure 3.1). I need hardly say that it is not to be taken very seriously; it is meant to be illustrative, rather than a carefully thought-out piece of functional analysis in its own right. Arrows represent routes along which causal influences pass, without specifying what form the causal influences take. But given the nature of the blocks that the arrows link, it should be fairly obvious what sort of thing I have in mind. For example, the arrow from Senses to Beliefs is meant to indicate such causal transitions as hearing a hooting sound and immediately forming the belief that the taxi one ordered has arrived. Likewise, the arrow from Practical Reason to Intentions is intended to indicate coming to a conclusion as to what it is best to do, and then forming a corresponding intention to do it. The fact, by the way, that arrows pass from Desires to Intentions, and from Desires to Actions, without passing through Practical Reason, is intended to show how so-called *weakness of will* is possible. A judgement about what it is best to do, generated by Practical Reason, normally generates a strong desire to do it. But such a desire may well be in conflict with some even stronger desire to act contrary to this considered judgement, thus causing one to act in a way that one knows full well to be irrational. New Year's resolutions are an excellent example of good intentions that usually lose out in a battle with base desire allied to habit – thereby, incidentally, generally causing one to abandon one's resolution. (Weakness of will in general need not, however, be a matter of giving in to *base* desires. Bernard Williams recently drew my attention to a nice example from Iris Murdoch's *The Bell* (1959), pp. 16–17.) A well-brought up young woman persuades herself that she has every right, being in a state of physical and emotional exhaustion, not to give up her seat in the London

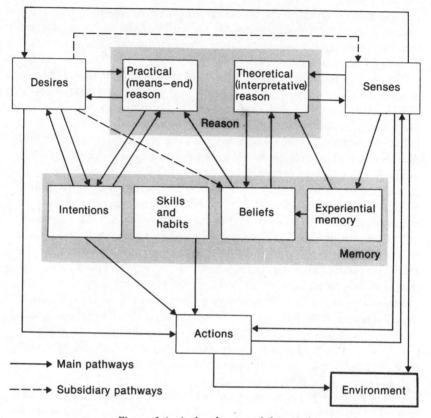

Figure 3.1 *A sketch map of the mind.*

Underground to an old lady, and that it would be far better if she remained seated. But, needless to say, upbringing triumphs and she gives up her seat regardless.)

The more one reflects on the matter, the more one is tempted to join each box to every other, with arrows going in both directions; but this is a temptation which I have resisted. What I have been talking about, up to now, is what might be called *strong* philosophical functionalism. (Block, 1978, p. 268, calls this '*a priori*' functionalism or 'Functionalism' with a capital letter.) Such a view holds that our *concept* of a particular mental state type is that of a state whose tokens have such-and-such a causal–functional role *vis-à-vis* tokens of other mental state types (the nature of which is to be similarly defined), and ultimately, *vis-à-vis* sensory input and behavioural output. That a state of this type is thus-and-so causally–functionally related to states of other types is held to be a conceptual truth; something that was not so related could not, as a matter of logic, be *that* type of mental state. The idea is that somebody knowing this conceptual truth who then discovers that, as a matter of empirical scientific fact, the token states which fulfil that role in the human brain do so in virtue of belonging to a particular neural state type, is thereby enabled to *deduce* that anyone in that neural state is experiencing pain, say. This is largely the point of strong functionalism, philosophically speaking. It allows for physicalism, in my sense of weak reducibility, to be true.

This brings me back to figure 3.1. I have put in continuous arrows only where there is a causal relationship so central to our common-sense conception of how the mind works that, from the standpoint of strong functionalism, it could plausibly be held to be an ingredient in our concept of the state in question. Dotted arrows represent causal relations which undoubtedly exist but do not seem to fit into this category. The one joining Desires to Senses is meant to indicate a phenomenon, experimentally well-established but probably unknown to most people, according to which one's desires can make a direct difference to how things look (sound, taste, etc.). I gather, for example, that the colour of a cherry will often be judged more vivid by someone who is very hungry (on the assumption that she likes cherries) than an exactly matching colour sample. The arrow joining Desires to Beliefs is intended to indicate the phenomenon whereby a desire to believe something can result in one's actually believing it. This is an entirely familiar phenomenon, but would not, for a different reason, plausibly be held to be an ingredient in our *concepts* of belief or desire; and that is that such causation would strike most of us as an example of *aberrant* mental functioning. This relates to what is sometimes referred to as the *normativity of the mental*; our mental concepts seem to some extent to pivot on a conception of how a conscious agent *ought ideally* to function. (Normativity of the mental might be thought also to exclude the lines of causation, on my diagram, that render weakness of will possible. But the point here, I think, is that weakness of will, as an ever-present possibility, is a consequence of the existence of causal pathways that are a necessary prerequisite of normal, desirable mental functioning. Were desires capable of issuing in action only via Practical Reason, there would be no room for spontaneity, and it would often be impossible to make suitably *rapid* responses to situations not catered for by appropriate pre-existent intentions.)

Strong functionalism says that, for every psychologically distinct type of mental state M, there is a distinct corresponding functional role R; and it is a conceptual truth that a state is of type M if and only if it fulfils the role R. This is, indeed, a very strong claim. But there are two weaker forms of functionalism that have been embraced by philosophers.

Moderate functionalism says only that it is a conceptual truth that, for every psychologically distinct type of mental state M, there is *some* distinct functional role R, such that a mental state is of type M if and only if it fulfils the role R. Which functional role corresponds to which type of mental state has, in general, to be determined by empirical investigation. Moderate functionalists hold it to be a conceptual truth that the identity of a mental state, both as a mental state at all, and as the kind of mental state that it is, is given by its functional role. But they would deny that the nature of the functional role that defines it as the type of state that it is can be read off from our concept of the state.

Finally, *weak functionalism* (of which one could, if one wished, define several subspecies) does not make any *conceptual* claims at all. It holds merely that, as a matter of empirical fact, every psychologically distinct type of mental state M is associated with a corresponding distinct functional role R, and that its playing the role R is what its being a mental state of type M actually consists in. The weak functionalist advances this equation between type of mental state (and type *as* mental state), and functional role, not in any sense as a conceptual truth, but as a scientific or metaphysical *theory*, according to which it is *in fact* the causal–functional role of a mental state that makes it a mental state at all, and the type of mental state that it is, and which gives it the subjective character that it has. (Moderate and weak functionalism are both subspecies of what Block, 1978, p. 268, calls *empirical* functionalism or *Psychofunctionalism*.)

It seems to me to follow from all three versions of functionalism that any given type mental state (pain, say) would necessarily have the particular causal–functional role it does; anything that had had a relevantly different causal–functional role just wouldn't have been pain. Only in the case of strong functionalism, however, will this be true as matter of *conceptual* necessity.

It is vital to understand that, from a functionalist standpoint, be it strong, moderate or weak, we have no guarantee that your pains and mine will, in physical respects, be all that similar: what it is that plays the causal–functional role of pain in my brain, might, in physiological terms, be something very different from what plays that role in yours. Given that we belong to the same species, this is a highly improbable supposition. But what if we were talking, not about something unlearned, such as (physical) pain, but a belief that a given political party will lose the next election? Or what if one of us were an extraterrestrial? Functionalists usually cite it as an advantage of their theory that we wouldn't need to be convinced that a Martian was *biologically* all that similar to ourselves in order to be justified, on the basis of behaviour, in concluding that he/she/it very probably possessed desires, beliefs and the like, engaged in genuine thinking, and was capable of enjoyment and suffering. Their assumption seems to be that similar causal relations between sensory input and behavioural output will generally constitute good presumptive evidence for a similarity of internal functional organization. But the assumption must be treated with considerable caution. If two unrelated organisms exhibit similar appropriate behaviour, in situations such as would have occurred fairly frequently in their evolutionary history, that constitutes only very weak evidence for a similarity of underlying functional organization. If in addition they exhibit similar appropriate behaviour, in a range of situations such as would have occurred rarely if at all in their evolutionary history, that is stronger evidence. What, however, would be especially telling is if they exhibit similar *in*appropriate behaviour, whether in certain naturally occurring or certain highly contrived situations. The point here is that the occurrence of *adaptive* behaviour, in naturally occurring situations at least, can always be accounted for simply on the basis of its having been evolutionarily selected for. But *mal*adaptive behaviour patterns must be thought of as an accidental by-product of the particular mechanisms arrived at for generating adaptive behaviour. Similar maladaptive behaviour, in similar circumstances, is thus good evidence for a similarity of mechanism – that is, underlying functional organization. By the same token, a similarity of behaviour on the part of two chess-playing computer programs, with respect to a variety of highly fantastical states of the board (such as one sometimes encounters in chess problems), would be better evidence for a similarity in the logic of the programs than would their making similar moves in the course of normal play – for which, presumably, they've primarily been designed. And better evidence still that they had a similar logic would be if they turned out to have similar 'bugs'.

Thus far, I have been talking about functionalism as a philosophical theory. As with behaviourism, however, there is a methodological version too. Methodological functionalism sees the task of psychology as that of giving a functional explanation of mental processes. There is not necessarily any assumption, here, that the functional role of a mental state is what makes it a mental state, or the type of mental state that it is; the approach is essentially neutral as between different *philosophical* positions on the nature of mind. This methodological functionalism has a name. It is called *cognitive science*, and comprises both cognitive psychology and research into artificial intelligence (AI), in so far as the latter is concerned with getting computers to perform or to simulate (a crucial distinction to which some workers in this field seem amazingly insensitive) cognitive tasks in what is, functionally speaking, a similar manner to that in which we ourselves perform them.

There are, in the literature, three stock arguments against philosophical functionalism. Each argument has its devotees and its critics; and one thing that helps perpetuate the controversy is unclarity about precisely which form of functionalism the arguments are supposed to be arguments against. For what it's worth, all three arguments seem to me to be pretty powerful against strong and moderate functionalism, but ineffective against weak functionalism.

First, we have the *Chinese mind* argument (Block, 1978, pp. 279–81). Let us assume that functionalism is true and that the functional roles constitutive of mental states are, in our own case, fulfilled by brain states. (This does not follow from functionalism alone. It does not follow simply from the truth of functionalism that they are physical states at all; even if functionalism is true, the requisite causal–functional roles might, in us, be played by states of some immaterial substance, as envisaged by Descartes. Perhaps, as Descartes himself thought, there is some inherent limitation on what causal–functional roles *could* be played by the states of any material thing, so that nothing material could ever possess mentality. But no functionalist actually believes that.) Now the population of China is already very large. Suppose, the argument runs, it were to increase until it were equal to the number of neurons in the average human brain. Then we could in principle make it function like the human brain, with each Chinese citizen being instructed to play the role of a single neuron, receiving and passing on (via telephone, say) messages from other Chinese citizens, in a manner exactly parallel to that of actual neurons. (I shall ignore the practical difficulties created by the fact that each individual neuron may be acting in a way that is simultaneously responsive to incoming signals from as many as ten thousand others; perhaps that wouldn't matter if the pace of the process were kept sufficiently slow, as would be consistent with its still being a functional analogue of actual brain processes.) We could even arrange matters so that the Chinese population was, as a whole, controlling the behaviour of a robot, capable of motions similar to our own and possessing sensors that paralleled our own sense organs. If functionalism is true, it would then seem to follow that one would thereby have succeeded in creating something that possessed a mind in its own right, over and above all the individual minds of all the individual Chinese people.

Well, it doesn't *quite* follow, even with the extra assumptions we have already made. We should have to assume that the functional organization of the brain that would be relevant to mentality is such as would entitle one to ignore the internal functional organization of individual neurons, and also of the processes that occur in the synapses across which the neurons communicate with each other. But that also seems reasonable from a functionalist perspective. Indeed, it seems overwhelmingly reasonable from the standpoint of strong functionalism, which would have us believe that the requisite causal–functional roles can in principle be read off from our ordinary psychological concepts; for these must presumably be highly macroscopic with respect to the functioning of individual brain cells.

One must be clear what the intended force of this argument is. I suppose there are some people for whom it would seem quite obvious that this would *not* be a way of creating a collective Chinese mind: the very idea, someone might think, is absurd. If that were the point, however, the functionalist could quite reasonably reply that what we had here was not so much an argument as a brute appeal to intuition that, in effect, simply begged the question at issue. 'How do you *know* that this wouldn't be a way of creating a Chinese mind?', the functionalist could retort. No, the most that the argument could be claimed to establish is that it is, at any rate, an *open question* whether a collective Chinese mind would emerge from the envisaged exercise. But that more modest claim, if it can be sustained, is actually quite sufficient to dish strong functionalism. It shouldn't *be* an open question if strong functionalism is true, given that strong functionalism holds that, for any given mental state type, it is a conceptual truth that being a mental state of that type means possessing a particular type of causal–functional role. On the contrary, given very plausible factual assumptions, it should then follow logically that a collective Chinese mind would have been brought into being. The fact that it doesn't in the least strike us that way is surely strong presumptive evidence that strong functionalism is incorrect, in so far as it purports to be giving an account of the *content* of our ordinary psychological concepts.

By the same token, the fact that the existence of a collective mind, here, would seem to be an open question places a decided question mark over moderate functionalism too. The only difference is that, for moderate functionalism, the precise nature of the causal–functional role relevant to the determination of any particular type mental state is left open, as far as our concepts go; though it is still a conceptual truth that there is *some* causal–functional specification, such that anything that answered to it would, of necessity, be a mental state of that type. Given that fact, the moderate functionalist could always say that the reason why it strikes us as an open question whether a collective mind would emerge in such a case is that, from the description of the enterprise, it is not really possible to tell whether the *relevant* causal–functional features – relevant, indeed, to making something a mental state at all – would actually have been successfully reproduced. For example, it may, after all, matter that the internal functional organization of the neurons has been neglected.

Weak functionalists, clearly, have least reason to be discomfited by the

Chinese mind argument. They can cheerfully admit that most people would consider it an open question whether – or even, highly improbable that – the imagined exercise would generate a collective Chinese mind. 'All that shows', they would say, 'is that most ordinary people do not share our theory. But that has no tendency to show that the theory is incorrect. For that one would need contrary evidence. No scientist, after all, would regard the fact that most ordinary people find the effects predicted by Einstein's theory of relativity intuitively difficult to credit as having any bearing on the question whether the theory is actually true.'

One thing that should perhaps be pointed out, regarding the Chinese mind argument, is that it exploits an intuition that I think most of us have, but which seems rather difficult rationally to justify. This is an extreme intuitive reluctance to believe that mentality could be generated by a mechanism the fundamental components of which were physically quite large, so that the machinery involved was, so to speak, open to casual inspection. People are far more willing to believe that consciousness could emerge from microchips. I take it that this prejudice in favour of the microscopic – for prejudice is what it seems to be – is what governs our response to John Searle's observation (1984, pp. 28–9): that if functional organization were all that mattered, there would be no bar in principle to generating consciousness by way of a contraption made out of empty beer cans and powered by windmills! But this same intuition is exploited by such philosophers of the Enlightenment as Leibniz and Locke. Locke (in his *Essay Concerning Human Understanding* IV.x.10) notes the prejudice in favour of the microscopic quite explicitly, and tries to extend downwards, so to speak, our corresponding reluctance to ascribe to matter in the large the power to generate mentality:

> Divide matter into as minute parts as you will, which we are apt to imagine a sort of spiritualizing or making a thinking thing of it; vary the figure and motion of it as much as you please; a globe, cube, prism, cylinder, &c., whose diameters are but 1,000,000th part of a gry [one gry = 100th of an inch], will operate no otherwise upon other bodies of proportionable bulk than those of an inch or foot diameter; and you may as rationally expect to produce sense, thought, and knowledge, by putting together in a certain figure and motion gross particles of matter, as by those that are the very minutest that do anywhere exist. They knock, impel, and resist one another just as the greater do, and that is all they can do.

Then there is Leibniz's famous image of the mill (in his *Monadology*, sec. 17):

It must be confessed . . . that Perception, and that which depends upon it, are inexplicable by mechanical causes, that is to say, by figures and motions. Supposing that there were a machine whose structure produced thought, sensation, and perception, we could conceive of it as increased in size with the same proportions until one was able to enter into its interior, as he would into a mill. Now on going into it he would find only pieces working upon one another, but never would he find anything to explain Perception.

To this I suppose one could retort by asking Leibniz how he expected to know if he *had* found something that explained Perception. Except that that is supposed to be *his* point: one wouldn't know and hence nothing one encountered *could* explain Perception. I'm not sure who comes out ahead in such an exchange. But in any event, functionalists would doubtless reply that, assuming their theory to be correct, one *would* know what to look for, at least in principle. It would be like walking into a vastly magnified computer, such that one could watch the electrons streaming by, and trying to work out what program it was running. Not, one supposes, an impossible task for a being of sufficient ratiocinative power. Only the proverbial problem of not seeing the wood for the trees. (Or the bytes for the bits.)

I spoke of a prejudice in favour of the microscopic. Nevertheless, Locke's splendid remark that we are 'apt to regard' a division of matter 'into its minutest parts . . . as a kind of spiritualizing . . . of it', assumes a somewhat new significance in the light of quantum mechanics. Matter in the small turns out to be not in the least like a scaled-down version of the proverbial billiard balls. Indeed, solid matter as conceived by common sense and Newtonian mechanics (to the extent that it is not simply an illusion) has turned out to be an essentially large-scale phenomenon, rather as is heat with respect to molecular motion. It makes no sense to describe individual atoms or elementary particles as 'solid' or 'fluid', any more than it makes sense to ascribe to them a temperature.

The ultimate 'spiritualization' of matter was, of course, that carried out in the early eighteenth century by George Berkeley (1685–1753), Bishop of Cloyne, according to whom matter was, roughly speaking, in the mind. Berkeley's theory (which we shall be examining in chapter 10) elicited a celebrated response from Doctor Johnson who, according to Boswell, kicked a stone, saying 'I refute it *thus*' (*Life of Johnson*, 6 August 1763). This story prompted a modern poet (whose name I have unfortunately been unable to discover) to write, presumably with quantum mechanics in mind:

Kick the rock Sam Johnson,
Break your bones,
But cloudy, cloudy is the stuff of stones.

The prejudice in favour of the microscopic might, in a sense, be vindicated if it could be convincingly argued that consciousness was somehow an inherently quantum-mechanical phenomenon. This is a fairly old idea (with little, formerly, to back it up beyond some half-formulated notion that since quantum mechanics is mysterious and so is consciousness, these two mysteries may perhaps be related). It is, however, one that takes on a new appeal in the light of some very recent work suggesting that there are quantum-mechanical phenomena the exploitation of which within the brain could, in a sense, give mind causal–functional powers that are in principle denied to mechanical computation devices constructed along classical lines.

But we are rapidly getting ahead of ourselves. We shall return to an examination of quantum mechanics, and its possible implications for the mind–body problem, in later chapters. Our immediate task is to examine the other two standard arguments against functionalism that I alluded to earlier, which generally go by the name of the *absent qualia* (Block, 1978, p. 281) and *inverted qualia* arguments. As I explained earlier, 'qualia' is essentially another name for what I have been calling 'phenomenal qualities'.

I want to approach the absent qualia argument in a somewhat roundabout way, via the concept of so-called kinaesthetic sensations. Kinaesthetic sensations, I was taught years ago when I studied psychology, are a class of *sui generis* sensations (that is, distinct from those of touch, sound, sight, taste, smell and so on) which are traceable to the stimulation of sensory receptors in the muscles; they are what enable one to know how one's limbs and so on are moving, and, if they are at rest, in what attitude they lie. They stand, so one was always told, to the states and doings of the muscles as do, say, auditory sensations to the vibrations in the ear.

Richard Swinburne, however, has largely persuaded me of something that, when he first put it to me, I found somewhat startling. Briefly, *there are no such things as kinaesthetic sensations*. It is perfectly true, as a matter of physiology, that there is a special class of sensory receptors which send signals to the brain that enable us to register the relative position and movement of our limbs. And it is also true that we have a host of sensations that are in some sense caused by the motion and configuration of our bodily parts. But these have nothing to do with the receptors just mentioned. Broadly speaking, these perfectly genuine sensations are traceable to the stimulation of touch and pain receptors, and are registered as feelings of pressure or milder forms of sensations more intense versions of which might be described as aches. It is not, or at any rate not primarily, on the basis of these that we are able to monitor the doings of our muscles and limbs. Rather we *just know* where our limbs are and how they are moving: we know it directly, without the mediation of any sensations, kinaesthetic or otherwise. The same claim (as someone pointed out to me) is made by Anscombe (1963, pp. 13–15).

Now I am not one hundred per cent convinced that Anscombe and Swinburne are right about this, though clearly, they might be. The suggestion is perfectly coherent. And the main point is: it seems to make precious little difference, as regards the way we function, whether they are right or wrong. Let X be some specific psychological state, as it occurs in us, which incorporates or consists in the experience of a particular phenomenal quality, for example a continuous tone of some specific (perceived) pitch and intensity. Then, as matter of logic, there could surely exist another sort of being, functionally equivalent to us at the level relevant to psychology, in whom the causal–functional role that, in us, is played by X, was played instead by a state Y that was not associated with any phenomenal qualities at all. And if so, it follows that there is more to what makes a psychological state the state that it is than is encapsulated in its causal–functional role. Hence functionalism would be inadequate, as a theory about psychological states in general.

The same point is sometimes made by appealing to a curious phenomenon known as *blind-sight* (Weiskrantz et al., 1974). A patient had been suffering from flashing lights in an oval area of his visual field, which were followed by headaches and vomiting. This distressing and somewhat disabling condition, which proved to be due to a malformation of the blood vessels in part of the visual cortex of the brain, failed to respond either to migraine drugs or to the severing of some of the nerves associated with the sympathetic nervous system. So it was finally decided to excise the brain tissue that included the malformation. The result was that the patient reported that he was unable any longer to see anything within the larger part of his right visual field. Experiments were then carried out that involved presenting the patient with different shapes, for example a letter 'O' and 'X' or lines at different angles, in such a way that they only projected on to that part of the retina that corresponded to the 'blind' area; and the patient was asked to guess what the shape was or whether the lines were horizontal or diagonal. Similarly, spots of light were presented to this same area, and the patient was asked to point in the corresponding direction. To the amazement of the patient himself, who insisted that he could see nothing in that part of his visual field, his 'guesses' turned out to be remarkably accurate, provided the stimuli were above a certain size. On being pressed, he would say only, apropos of the experiment that required him to discriminate between an 'O' and an 'X', that he had a 'feeling' of smoothness or jaggedness. He appeared, in short, to be able to derive visual information without consciously apprehending the phenomenal qualities with which visual perception is normally associated. Other such patients have been studied since (Weiskrantz, 1986).

The trouble, however, about appealing to such empirical phenomena is that, as things are, it clearly does make a very significant causal–functional difference whether certain phenomenal qualities are present or absent. It causes people to behave differently, not least in respect of their linguistic behaviour. Indeed, kinaesthesis and blind-sight both call for a significant amendment to the diagram that I presented earlier. In figure 3.1 there is just a single box labelled 'Senses'. What is clearly needed is for this to be replaced by a pair of boxes, 'Sensory Receptors' and 'Sensations', with an arrow leading from each directly to Beliefs, and a third arrow leading from Sensory Receptors to Sensations. The distinction between blind-sight and ordinary sight may then be represented, in terms of the amended diagram, as follows. In ordinary sight, the causal influence passes from Sensory Receptors to Beliefs via Sensations; in blind-sight, by contrast, it passes from Sensory Receptors to Beliefs without passing through Sensations – a pattern of causation which, if Anscombe and Swinburne are right, is the norm for kinaesthesis.

Of course, proponents of the absent qualia argument will protest that this misses the point. No doubt in *us* the presence or absence of phenomenal qualities does make a difference, if only for the boring reason that it is a difference that we are capable of detecting. The important philosophical moral to be drawn from blind-sight, kinaesthesis and the like is that the apprehension of phenomenal qualities isn't necessary, if information from our sensory receptors is to enable beings to form beliefs about the world and behave appropriately. And from this it follows, with high probability, that beings could exist – call them human analogues – who apprehended no phenomenal qualities at all, but whose overall functional organization was the same as ours. Where we experience phenomenal qualities, something would happen to them that played precisely the same causal–functional role in their overall functioning that the apprehension of phenomenal qualities plays in ours. Were we to communicate with them, they would tend to assume, understandably but erroneously, that what we meant by a feeling of pain or the look of a tomato was whatever nonphenomenal goings-on occupy, for them, the very same causal-functional niche that these phenomenal qualities occupy in us.

'But what', someone might ask, 'about the very distinction, which for us seems so significant, between states and processes that are, and those that are not, associated with phenomenal qualities? How could that be functionally mirrored in a being that experienced no phenomenal qualities at all?' The answer must be that it is mirrored in some difference *within* the nonphenomenal. Someone might object that no difference within the nonphenomenal could seem to any conscious being to be as significant as the difference between the phenomenal and nonphenomenal. But I take it that a being's judgements of *relative* significance are what really count, in functional terms. And I see no reason why some difference within the nonphenomenal should not, for a being who was incapable of experiencing any phenomenal qualities, rank as highly in *order* of significance as the difference between the phenomenal and nonphenomenal does for us.

(A mathematical analogy suggests itself at this point. But since what I am about to say will be largely opaque to those innocent of set theory, I suggest that nonmathematicians skip this paragraph. The analogy I have in mind is that of nonstandard models of, say, Zermelo–Fraenkel set theory. Now it is well known that any theory formulated, as is Zermelo–Fraenkel set theory, in first-order predicate logic, admits of a denumerable model: one that involves only denumerably infinite sets. Yet it follows from the Zermelo–Fraenkel axioms that there exist nondenumerably infinite sets. So how can a theory which says that there are nondenumerable sets have a model in which there are none? This is the *Skolem–Löwenheim paradox*. The answer is very simple. In a nondenumerable model of the system, a predicate which, as standardly intepreted, would say of any set to which it was applied that it was nondenumerably infinite, comes to say something else instead. The very distinction between denumerable and nondenumerable infinities is mapped on to another, structurally analogous distinction that can be applied *within* the realm of the denumerable sets. For nondenumerable–denumerable read phenomenal–nonphenomenal, and for a human being and the corresponding human analogue read, respectively, a standard and a denumerable model of axiomatic set theory. For the axiomatic system itself read the abstractly conceived functional system of which the human being and the human analogue constitute different concrete realizations.)

The *inverted qualia* argument (Shoemaker, 1975, 1982; Block, 1978, pp. 304–5) is similar to the absent qualia argument. Instead of imagining a being, functionally similar to ourselves, who lacked some or all of the phenomenal qualities we experience, we are asked instead to imagine a being in which the same phenomenal qualities occupied different causal–functional niches. Most frequently encountered in the literature is the *inverted spectrum*. In its commonest version, we are asked to imagine a being who, under conditions in which we would experience a given phenomenal colour, would instead experience the so-called *complementary* colour: green instead of red (and conversely), blue instead of yellow, and so on. (Two colours are said to be complementary if light of those colours would combine to produce white light.) This is somewhat unsatisfactory as an example since it neglects one important dimension of our colour judgements. What I have in mind is our propensity to judge red and yellow as 'warm' colours, in contrast to blue and green, which are judged to be 'cool'. Specification of a precise shade of colour requires three parameters: those most commonly chosen are *hue, saturation* (the amount of colour present) and *luminance* (lightness–darkness). Hues are what are represented along the spectrum. If we ignore saturation and luminance, the different hues, the spectral colours, may be arranged in a circle, rather like the points of the compass. Think of red as north, blue as west, green as south and yellow as east. Take another such circle, place it above the first, and then flip it over along the line that runs from blue-green (south-west) to orange (north-east) (see figure 3.2). This has the effect of systematically redistributing the hues, all except for blue-green and orange which stay put, in a way that preserves our judgements of warmth and coolness: red changes places with yellow, blue with green and violet-indigo with yellow-green (both of which are neutral on the warmth–coolness scale). This reflected colour circle seems to me to serve the purposes of the thought-experiment rather better than the standard inverted spectrum, which is produced by rotating the colour circle through 180 degrees.

(It still, however, suffers from the fault, also found in the comple-mentarity-based inversion, of mapping the original hues on to ones of unequal luminance; yellow, for example is of greater luminance than red.

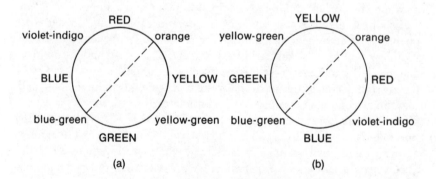

Figure 3.2 *The reflected colour circle.*
This is a variant of the standard inverted spectrum, designed to preserve warmth–coolness.
Normal colour vision is represented by (a), while (b) represents the vision of someone who sees phenomenal yellow when we see phenomenal red, and so on. One gets from (a) to (b) by reflecting (a) along the axis indicated by the broken line.

I see no simple way in which this could be fixed without disturbing the perceived *purity* of the colours. Thus, reducing the luminance of yellow has the unfortunate effect of shifting it in the direction of brown. Whether the functionalist could derive any particular comfort from this difficulty is quite another matter.)

Larry Hardin, incidentally, maintains (1984) that this neglected warmth–coolness dimension of phenomenal colour has a known physiological correlate. I shall briefly elaborate in the next chapter, when we make a brief excursion into neurophysiology.

The claim then is that a being could exist, functionally identical to ourselves at the level relevant to mentality, but whose experiences of phenomenal colour were mirror images of our own. And does this not show, once again, that a theory that would equate psychological state types with causal–functional state types is incapable of capturing the phenomenal aspects of consciousness?

As with the Chinese mind argument, the absent and inverted qualia arguments seem to me to be pretty powerful against strong and moderate functionalism. There is nothing contradictory, logically absurd or conceptually incoherent in the *idea* of a being, functionally equivalent to ourselves at the requisite level, but who experiences different phenomenal qualities from us, or none at all. This is so even if, with the moderate functionalist, one thinks that the requisite level is impossible to know a priori (that is, by reflecting on what is logically implied by the relevant concepts). But how much force does the argument have against weak functionalism? How heavily, if at all, do these arguments weigh against the claim that, as a matter not of conceptual necessity but of scientific fact, there is some causal–functional role such that anything that has that role, however the role is physically realized, must be an apprehension of, say, phenomenal red? On the face of it very little. For we should not normally suppose that our capacity to imagine something had any particular tendency to show that it was scientifically possible (as witness fairy stories and the bulk of so-called 'science' fiction).

But weak functionalism seems to me untenable for other reasons. I remarked earlier that, on each of our three versions of functionalism, the equation of mental state types with causal–functional types would be necessarily true if it were true at all: if the equation holds in the actual world, then there is not even a possible world in which it fails to hold. The same can be said of all identity claims. It follows (the point is implicit in Kripke, 1980, and is made explicitly by Hirsch, 1986) that someone who understands a true proposition of the form '*X* is identical with *Y*' or '*X*s are identical with *Y*s', can fail to be in a position to deduce its truth, only if having a conception of *X* (and/or having a conception of *Y*) is subjectively indistinguishable from having a conception of *W*, where W is distinct from X (or from Y). As it stands, this may strike the reader as a somewhat obscure remark. But an example should make it clear what is meant.

Consider the dispute in the eighteenth century between those who believed heat to consist in the motion of molecules and those who wished to equate it with the presence of caloric fluid. Clearly it is not (or was not then) a conceptual truth that the heat of an object consists in the motion of its molecules, since no amount of reflection simply on what is meant by this proposition could possibly have enabled anyone to deduce its truth and, correspondingly, the falsity of the caloric theory. Now there isn't even a possible world in which heat *is* the presence of caloric fluid. But there are possible worlds in which some rarefied substance, with the properties ascribed to caloric fluid, is responsible for giving rise to the sort of casually observable phenomena by which, in the actual world, heat is characteristically identified: expansion, glowing, sensations of warmth, and so forth. Assuming that the inhabitants of such a world use the same word 'heat' for whatever underlies these phenomena, the right thing to say is not that, in their world, heat *is* the presence of caloric fluid, but rather that their word 'heat' refers not to heat (which is necessarily molecular motion), but to something else instead, which consists (likewise necessarily) in the presence of a certain fluid. Yet, for all that, the conception they associate with their word 'heat' may be subjectively indistinguishable from that which we associate with our word 'heat' (or at any rate did, before the kinetic theory gained the ascendancy). And it is precisely this that prevented the dispute between proponents of the kinetic and caloric theories from being decided on purely conceptual, a priori grounds. In advance of further empirical investigation, people had no way of knowing which kind of possible world (if either) they were living in; they couldn't tell for sure whether the actual world was one in which 'heat' referred to (what is in fact) molecular motion or one in which it referred to (what is in fact) the presence of a rarefied fluid.

Suppose now that a functionalist theory of the mind had been worked out in some detail, so that pain, for example, was alleged to be identical, not merely with some causal–functional state or other, but with the specific causal–functional state S. According to both moderate and weak functionalism, one can understand this proposition (assuming it to be true) without thereby being in a position to deduce its truth: empirical investigation is required in order to establish it as true. And from this it follows that either (i) there are possible worlds in which people have a conception, subjectively indistinguishable from our conception of pain, which is nevertheless not a conception of *pain*, but of something else; or (ii) there are possible worlds in which people have a conception, subjectively indistinguishable from our conception of S, that is nevertheless not a conception of *S*, but of something distinct from *S*. Yet it is exceedingly difficult to see how either of these things could be. Indeed (i) seems downright absurd. To have a conception of pain, to know what pain is, it suffices to know what pain feels like. And by definition, surely, anything that feels like pain, in the relevant respects, just is pain, however it may be caused. For pain precisely is a feeling of a certain sort.

The problem with (i) lies in the ostensible immediacy of our concept of pain. But matters seem only marginally less clear cut in regard to (ii), where the difficulty lies rather in the relative *abstractness* of our conception of a specific causal–functional role, compounded as the notion essentially is of the concepts of state and cause. The concept of a specific causal–functional state is the concept of a state that is thus-and-so situated within a system of causally interrelated states, and is indifferent to the question how this system is concretely realized. What one refers to by the concept doesn't depend, therefore, on what, specifically, the world is like, or how one stands in relation to it (unless one thinks, implausibly, that the references of 'state' and 'cause' so depend). Compare the concept of long division, by which I mean the algorithm (abstractly regarded) that we all learned at school for dividing multi-digit numbers: take the smallest initial segment of the dividend (the number to be divided) that is at least as large as the divisor, divide the divisor into it, store the resulting quotient, append the next digit of the dividend to the remainder, divide the divisor into it, append the new quotient to the stored number, and so on. (This description isn't meant to be mathematically rigorous.) Alternative (ii) seems to me unimaginable in much the same way, and for much the same reasons, that it is impossible to conceive of a possible world in which people had a concept subjectively indistinguishable from our concept of long division, but which referred to a procedure different from that which we understand by the term. And if neither (i) nor (ii) can be sustained, then it follows that moderate and weak functionalism are both false.

Such intuitive appeal as attaches to functionalism in any of its forms derives mainly, it seems to me, from concentration on such things as beliefs and desires, which in general have no necessary association with phenomenal qualities and which can exist, moreover, and affect our behaviour accordingly, at such such times as we are not even aware of them. There really does seem to be a substantial causal–functional ingredient in our conception of desires and beliefs in relation to behaviour. Imagine a man standing on a high diving board over a swimming pool containing just three inches of water. (The example comes from a talk given by Richard Braithwaite on the BBC Third Programme in 1965.) On the assumption that the man wanted to go for a swim, we should naturally take his action in diving from the board as indicating that he believed that the pool was full. Conversely, on the assumption that he believed that the water in the pool was only three inches deep, we should naturally infer from his action in jumping from the board that he wanted to injure himself, perhaps to commit suicide. This is assuming a normal set of background beliefs; it would clearly make a difference if we knew that he believed he could fly, or was immortal. Beliefs, actions and desires form a kind of interlocking triad, such that a sufficient knowledge of any two enables us to infer the third. (At least, it does given a whole range of other assumptions that we normally take for granted, for example about a person's capacity to act on his or her desires.)

It is plausible, in the light of considerations of this sort, to conclude that it is at least a necessary condition of something's being a belief or a desire, of a particular sort, that it has a certain kind of causal–functional role with respect to a person's psychological-cum-behavioural functioning as a whole. It would be baffling if one was told that a being had genuine beliefs and desires, in the same sense that we do, but that they stood in a totally different causal–functional relation both to each other and to that being's actions (and even 'tryings'), from our own. Where, then, has the functionalist gone wrong? In three ways, it seems to me. First, in supposing that all psychological states are like beliefs and desires, in this respect. Secondly, in supposing that the causal–functional role is *all* there is to having a particular belief or desire. And thirdly, in supposing that it is *behavioural* inputs and *external, physical* stimuli to which the causal–functional roles of states such as beliefs and desires are ultimately answerable, albeit via the network of states to which they belong; this seems to me the bad inheritance from behaviourism. I suggest, on the contrary (and this is a point to which I shall return), that they are primarily answerable to *conscious* states and processes. It is their functional role in relation to these that qualifies them as *mental* states, even at such times as we are unaware of them.

Only thus can I make sense of what might otherwise strike one as a rather curious pair of intuitions, but ones that I suspect most people would share. I can accept the existence of unconscious beliefs and desires; indeed, most of our beliefs and desires are ones that we are aware of only intermittently. Yet I cannot make intuitive sense of there existing a being who possessed genuine beliefs and desires, but who, or which, lacked the capacity for consciousness altogether.

For all that there may be a functionalist element in many of our psychological concepts, functionalism as a global theory of mentality must thus be abandoned. It founders principally, as we have seen, on the rock of phenomenal content. Illumination on this and other problematic features of mind must now, it seems, be sought in a different direction.

4

Neuroscience

One way of distinguishing between different versions of physicalism or materialism is to ask: what is it, in physical or material terms, that is registered in consciousness? On what do conscious states supervene? Functionalism says it is the causal–functional role. What, then, should one say if one rejects functionalism? The obvious thing to say is that it is something about the physiological nitty-gritty of the relevant brain states or processes. The functionalist, one might complain, has mistakenly and arbitrarily emphasized causal–functional role to the exclusion of the specifics of its concrete physical realization.

But what exactly is known about these specifics? At this point a modest infusion of neuroscience might be helpful (though one mustn't expect too much of it, in philosophical terms). The brain, as everyone knows, contains a prodigious number of nerve cells or *neurons*. The normal complement is not very precisely known: estimates vary from 10,000 to 100,000 million. (There is also a vast number of cells of other kinds, especially *glial cells*, whose functions are not very well understood but which appear to include those of providing the neurons with nourishment and structural support.) A typical neuron has a *central body*, containing the cell nucleus, a long fibre or *axon*, and a shorter, tree-like structure, the branches of which are called *dendrites* (see figure 4.1). Across the cell wall of a neuron (which is a semi-permeable membrane made of fatty acids or *lipids*) there is a steep voltage gradient, which in the cell's *resting* state runs from a positive charge on the outside to a negative charge on the inside. Periodically, however, a wave of depolarization, known as the *action potential* or *spike*, in which the voltage gradient is locally and temporally reversed, will pass along the axon from the central body. This, which is called *firing*, takes place by way of a local exchange of potassium and sodium ions across the axon wall. When a neuron fires, the arrival of the action potential at the tip of the axon causes certain

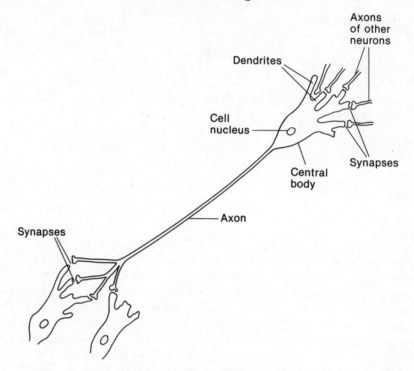

Figure 4.1 *Schematic neuron.* (Adapted from F. Crick and C. Asanuma, 1986.)

chemical *transmitter substances* to be emitted. These can affect neighbouring neurons, via their dendrites, in either of two ways. Every neuron
has a natural *base level* of spontaneous firing, and this natural *spiking
frequency* can be either increased or decreased in consequence of
transmitter substances being absorbed by the cell dendrites. The neuron
from whose axons the substances have been emitted is correspondingly
said to have an *excitatory* or *inhibitory* influence on the other cell. A
given neuron may be affected by as many as 10,000 other cells at a time;
whether its firing rate is increased or decreased will therefore depend on
whether the influences from all these other cells amount to a *net*
excitatory or inhibitory effect. The junction between a dendritic fibre and
a neighbouring axon, the small gap across which transmitter substances
diffuse, is known as a *synapse*; and it has been estimated by Gierer (1988,
p. 7) that the human cerebral cortex alone (of which more in a moment)
contains about 300,000 billion synaptic junctions, connected by something
of the order of 100,000 miles of nerve fibres. (If one were to add to these
the fibres in other parts of the brain, and place them end to end, they
would stretch halfway from here to the moon.)

It is tempting to compare this vast network of neurons with a very complicated system of electrical circuitry. In the nineteenth and early twentieth centuries, it was customary to compare it to a telephone exchange. Nowadays, the favoured model is the electronic computer. Doubtless there is much merit in this analogy, but there is a sense in which it is a bit one-sided. For it encourages us to think that the action potential is where the action is, so to speak; and that everything else is secondary. What happens in the synapses is regarded as important only in so far as it enables a message to be passed on from one neuron to the next: it is to the axons what the exchanges are to runners in a relay race.

Such a view, however, hardly squares with the current evidence. Recent research has begun to reveal, in the interstices of the neurons, a highly organized biochemical system of vast and bewildering subtlety and complexity, including hormones and the *neuropeptides* (so called because they belong to a class of chemicals first identified in the digestive tract). These include the mysterious *substance P* and also the *endorphins* and *enkephalins*, which, amongst other things, can affect mood and one's perceptions of pain and pleasure. Altogether, there appear to be thousands of different kinds of so-called transmitter substances, which now, however, turn out to affect the neurons in ways far more various and complex than mere excitation or inhibition. I say so-called, because that is already to label these substances in a way that encourages us to think of them as having, with respect to the neurons themselves, an essentially *subsidiary* function. But the biochemical system is highly structured, with particular substances being concentrated in particular centres and pathways, and appears to be able to encode information in its own right. These discoveries have led some workers to suggest that we should give up thinking of the brain as some vast electronic computer, and think of it instead as an enormous *gland*. No doubt this also is unduly one-sided, but perhaps no more so than the standard picture.

Whatever may be the truth of the matter, there is one crucial respect in which the brain is evidently quite unlike most present-day computers. For the latter operate in *serial* fashion, carrying out one operation at a time, whereas the brain clearly goes in for massive parallelism in its operations. Though this has been known for a long time, it is only within the last decade that the potential power of so-called *parallel distributed processing* has begun to be properly appreciated. This is a point to which we shall return in chapter 7.

Let me now say something about the architecture of the human brain (see figure 4.2). By far the largest parts are the two *cerebral hemispheres*. At the surface of these are several layers of *grey matter*, the *cerebral cortex*, comprising mainly the cell bodies of neurons whose axons project downwards, making up the so-called *white matter*. The cerebral cortex

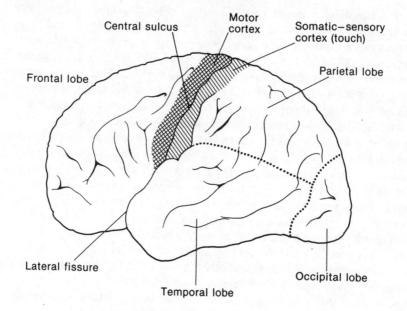

Figure 4.2 *The cerebral cortex.*

includes *motor* areas, which send signals to the muscles, *sensory projection* areas, which receive signals from the various sense organs, and the areas of so-called *association cortex*, which perform various cognitive tasks, often in association with particular sensory areas; these last also include the areas, mostly in the left hemisphere, that are concerned with the comprehension of language. The regions communicate with each other via neurons whose fibres run parallel to the surface of the hemispheres. Each hemisphere is traditionally divided into four *lobes*. At the back is the *occipital* lobe, which contains the visual projection and association areas. Immediately in front of the occipital cortex are the *parietal* lobe, at the top, and below it the *temporal* lobe, separated from the parietal lobe by the *lateral fissure*. The auditory projection areas are buried deep within this fissure. At the front of the brain is the *frontal* lobe, separated from the parietal lobe by another fissure known as the *central sulcus*. Bordering the central sulcus, immediately in front, is the *motor cortex*, concerned with activation and control of the muscles; and running parallel to the motor cortex, immediately behind the central sulcus, is the *somatic–sensory cortex*, the primary projection area for touch.

The frontal lobes appear to play a role in the integration of mental activity and the control of attention. More specifically, in human beings they seem to be involved with planning and also with social skills: injury to this area is commonly associated with irresponsible and socially obtuse behaviour. In other animals, frontal lesions have been found to impair performance on 'delayed choice' tasks, where animals are required to base their current responses not (or not merely) on the currently presented stimulus, but on, say, the stimulus last presented (or the last but one, or whatever). Specific high-level cognitive functions – roughly, thought and understanding – are generally ascribed to the temporal and parietal lobes, with the left hemisphere, especially certain regions on the temporal–parietal boundary, having the major responsibility for language; the corresponding areas in the right hemisphere appear mainly to be concerned with spatial and spatio-visual tasks. It should be said, however, that the standard parcelling out of functions between the frontal and temporal–parietal regions has been undermined somewhat by some very recent work, using the technique of *positron emission tomography*, or PET scanning; this allows one to see which areas of the brain are active when a subject is presented with various cognitive tasks. In an ingenious experiment, Petersen et al. (1988) appear to have established that the semantic processing of individually presented words takes place not in the left posterior temporal lobe, as had previously been thought, but in the left frontal lobe (specifically, the region known as area 47).

The two hemispheres are linked by a bundle of fibres known as the *corpus callosum* (of which more presently); and at the base of each hemisphere is a mass of grey matter known as the *corpus striatum*, which in human beings is again largely concerned with motor function. (In birds, the corpus striatum is far more highly developed than the cerebral cortex, and seems to fulfil many of the functions that, in us, are carried out cortically.)

Nestling beneath the hemispheres, at the back, is the *cerebellum*. It used to be thought that this was concerned merely with sensori-motor coordination and balance; but it is now becoming apparent that it has a wide range of integrative functions, roughly comparable to the activities of a super-efficient personal assistant working for a boss who is too busy to attend to details. People sometimes say things like: 'It is not *me* that knows how to play the piano, but my hands. The memory is in my hands, not in my head.' It is probably skills whose acquisition principally involves the modification, or 'retuning', of neural circuits within the cerebellum that elicit this feeling. What causes such skills to strike one as somehow 'distanced' from the self is presumably the fact that the requisite information-processing is largely being carried out subcortically, as indeed it would have to be given the rapidity with which activities such as typing or juggling can be performed. The most that the cortex can do,

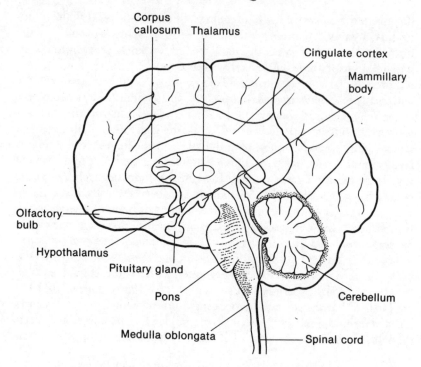

Figure 4.3 *Section through the middle of a human brain.*

here, is provide sensory information (from the cortical projection areas) and maintain a kind of global control.

At the base of the hemispheres, at the front, is the *limbic system*, which is concerned with reward and learning; that part of the limbic system that seems most centrally involved in the laying down of new long-term memories is the *hippocampus*. Damage to the hippocampus, if it is sufficiently severe, can leave people with nothing but short-term memory, living in a nightmare world where they are stranded, so to speak, on the island of the present, ostensibly unable to lay down new long-term memories. (One such person, the musician Clive Wearing, was the subject of a 1986 British television programme, 'Prisoner of Consciousness', in the Channel 4 *Equinox* series, in which he was interviewed by Jonathan Miller. The damage to Wearing's brain, which was caused by a brain infection, has left him with the skills and long-term memories he acquired before his illness, but apparently unable to retain new memories for more than about ten minutes. This means that he may find himself in a concert hall, able to play flawlessly, but not knowing where he is or how he got there.) I said that such people were *ostensibly* unable to lay down long-term memories, because it has recently emerged that they do possess a residual capacity to form long-term memories, which is the memory analogue of blind-sight. In one experiment, patients were shown a line-drawing in which many of the lines had been erased, and asked to work out what the picture represented; if they were unable to do this within a certain time, they were then shown the completed picture. When shown the same picture, days, weeks or months later, they had no conscious recollection of ever having seen it before, but were usually able to say immediately, or almost immediately, what it represented (Weiskrantz, 1986).

Also under the hemispheres, at the front, are the *olfactory tract* and *bulb*, through which signals from the receptors of taste and smell in the nose and mouth pass to the *olfactory cortex*. The olfactory cortex is, in evolutionary terms, the oldest part of the cortex and the part most highly developed in lower animals. (Incidentally, the close proximity of the olfactory system to the hippocampus, which is known to be involved with memory, may have something to do with the extraordinary power of tastes and smells to reawaken memories of the distant past; the classic instance, in literature, is the incident in the first volume of Proust's *Remembrance of Things Past* (1973, p. 61), where a flood of childhood reminiscence is precipitated by the taste of a madeleine cake.)

Immediately beneath the corpus callosum is the *diencephalon*, which includes the *thalamus, hypothalamus* and *amygdala*. The thalamus acts mainly as a relay station through which signals from the peripheral sense organs, with the sole exception of olfactory signals, are passed to the cortex. It may also, however, initiate various reflex responses, such as would cause a person to pull her hand away from a hot surface, accidentally touched, before any signals reached the cortex and triggered a conscious feeling of pain. The hypothalamus is concerned with the regulation of such things as appetite, respiration and body temperature; it is the major control centre of the *autonomic* nervous system, and helps to control hormonal output via the neighbouring *pituitary gland*. The amygdala is concerned with emotional responses, such as anger, and also with the sex drive. The *optic nerve* is joined to the diencephalon, from which it is, anatomically speaking, an offshoot; the retina itself is, in a sense, part of the brain, and engages in some very complex processing of information in its own right.

Beneath the diencephalon are, in turn, the *midbrain, pons* and *medulla oblongata*, which collectively make up the *brain stem*. This joins the diencephalon to the *spinal cord*. The pons acts as a relay station for signals passing between the cortex and the cerebellum, which is joined to the medulla oblongata by a pair of slim bundles of nerve fibres with the delightful name of the *inferior cerebellar peduncles*. In addition to various nuclei of grey matter, the brain stem contains a network of spider-like neurons that make up the *reticular formation*. This contains both ascending and descending pathways; amongst the ascending ones are those that comprise the *reticular activating system*.

The cortex as a whole seems unable to function at all unless it receives a constant stream of signals from the brain stem. And, according to the conventional wisdom, it is signals from the reticular activating system that are responsible for sustaining consciousness within the higher cortical (and possibly also diencephalic) regions. The reticular system is thought to control both the sleep–wakefulness cycle and also – partly under the influence of descending signals from the cortex itself (especially the frontal lobe) – one's focus of attention. Damage to the reticular activating system, or drug-induced suppression of its activities, are the usual causes of coma. And with brain-steam death, the medical profession now recognizes that the person is dead too, even though the body may still be alive, and may be kept alive for several weeks with intravenous feeding and the use of an artificial respirator.

This, as I say, is the conventional wisdom. But there are also some heterodox opinions in circulation which may merit a mention. On one view, the main reason why the brain stem is needed to sustain cortical activity is that communication between different areas of the cortex is somehow mediated by, or actually passes through, the brain stem. On this model, we are to think of the various minimal functional units of the cortex as like people sitting in separate offices in a large building, relying on the telephone to do any business with each other. And the brain stem is like the building's switchboard. This is an engaging idea; and it is certainly true that there are pathways that link different cortical areas via the brain stem. Nevertheless, the suggestion that it is the functioning of these pathways that sustains cortical activity generally, or at any rate that it is a necessary condition of consciousness, seems, in the light of the available evidence, pretty fanciful.

Another idea is that the reticular formation is not something that sustains conscious activities that take place elsewhere, but is itself the seat of consciousness, rather as Descartes (*Treatise on Man*) mistakenly believed the *pineal gland* to be. The claim is that this is where conscious processes actually take place, drawing information from the higher centres, and sending information to be processed there. That proposal again is more ingenious than plausible; my reasons for rejecting it will emerge shortly. But that said, the way in which the reticular activating system sustains consciousness remains deeply mysterious; and people should not allow themselves to be deterred from such speculation, through attaching to the conventional interpretation an authoritativeness which it cannot really claim.

I turn now to the neurophysiology of vision, our understanding of which has been transformed in the last few decades, mainly as a result of the work of the Nobel prize-winning physiologists David Hubel and Torsten Weisel. The starting point in neurophysiological terms is the stimulation, by incident photons of light, of the rods and cones at the back of the retina. In front of them there are layers of neurons (through which the light has to pass to get to the rods and cones! – the whole arrangement being the reverse of what one would expect) which perform the initial processing of these signals, before they are sent on to the brain.

At this point something occurs which is well worth mentioning, since it relates to what we were saying in the last chapter about our propensity to judge colours on a scale of warmth and coolness. There are three types of cone, with maximal sensitivities in the red, blue and green parts of the spectrum, respectively. The rods provide monochromatic information, being responsive only to *luminance* (lightness–darkness). Now (still within the retina) the cones feed into a pair of so-called *opponent* systems. Each is a system of neurons with a characteristic base level of firing. One of them increases its rate of firing in response to red, and decreases its rate of firing in response to green (though the maximal responses are to red and green of different wavelengths from those that maximally excite red- and green-sensitive cones). The other increases its rate of firing in response to yellow, and decreases it in response to blue (maximally, once again, in response to blue of a different frequency from that associated with blue-sensitive cones). In addition to these two chromatic systems, there is an achromatic opponent system that responds to lightness–darkness by increasing or decreasing its base firing rate. In contrast to the other two systems, whose base rate firings are associated with no contribution to phenomenal colour, the base output of the third system, in the presence of only base rate firings of the two chromatic systems, yields phenomenal dark grey. This is more or less the form in which information relating to hue, saturation and luminance is passed on to the brain.

The philosopher Larry Hardin suggests (1984) that this basic feature is preserved in whatever cortical goings-on immediately underlie our awareness of phenomenal colour. Red and yellow continue to imply heightened neural activity; green and blue continue to imply lowered activity. Suppose further, he says, that the cortical upshot of sensory inputs in some other modalities has a similar opponent character. In particular, make the not unreasonable supposition that this is true for our perceptions of literal warmth and coolness, which also correspond, respectively, to heightened and lowered cortical neural activity. Finally, assume that there is, somewhere within the cerebral hemispheres, what Hardin calls a *cross-modal polarity comparator*, which receives input from various different sensory projection areas and is capable of distinguishing between heightened and lowered activity therein. Then our characterization of colours as, respectively, warm or cool makes good sense. Nor is this just a metaphor. Or rather, it is a metaphor, but one with a sound, objective physiological basis. If Hardin is right, phenomenal red and yellow have something genuinely in common with phenomenal warm, as do phenomenal blue and green with phenomenal cool.

Hardin offers these considerations as a contribution to a systematic physicalistic *reduction* of phenomenal qualities to such physiological attributes as the relative spiking frequencies of groups of neurons. To what extent this is, in philosophical terms, a realistic ambition is a question to which I shall return. But there is a neurophysiological, or perhaps I should say neuropsychological, point too, which I shall be discussing at some length in chapter 7. Whatever opponent systems might turn out to underlie the phenomenal character of colour perception would have to be responsive to different features of the sensory input, or responsive to them in different ways, from those to which these relatively peripheral cells are responding; and this is because colour vision is not straightforwardly geared, as the responses of these cells are, to wavelength.

Sensory information is projected on to the cortex in the form of so-called *topographic maps*. For example, there is a point-by-point correspondence, in the area of the cortex which receives inputs from the touch receptors, between regions of the cortex and regions of the body surface. However, distance relations are not preserved. Regions of the skin that have a very high density of touch receptors, such as the hands, correspond to huge areas of the corresponding projection area, whereas those that have relatively few, such as the arms, legs and torso, correspond to areas small in relation to their actual size. This is sometimes graphically represented in the form of a grotesque picture of a human being in whom the proportions of the bodily parts correspond to the proportion of cortex devoted to their surface: huge head, mostly face, with an enormous tongue but narrow forehead, puny torso and limbs with large genitals (often omitted for reasons of misplaced delicacy or sexual neutrality), huge hands and enormous fingers. This figure, which is often shown stretched out along the relevant part of the cortex, goes by the name of the *somatic–sensory homunculus* (see figure 4.4). (The two sides of the body are represented, respectively, in the opposite hemispheres.)

The same principle applies to vision. The central part of the visual field corresponds to a disproportionately large region of the visual projection areas, in relation to the peripheral parts; and this is simply because there is a far higher concentration of rods and cones in the central part of the

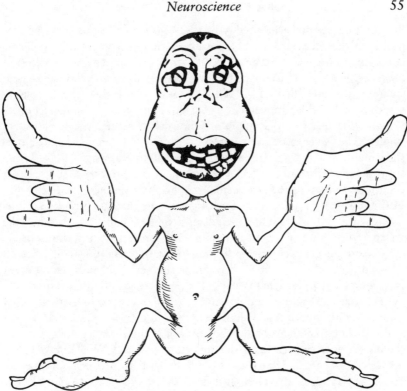

Figure 4.4 *The somatic–sensory homunculus.* (From Colin Blakemore, *Mechanics of the Mind.* Cambridge: Cambridge University Press, 1977, p. 80.)

retina (excluding the *blind spot*, marking the exit of the optic nerve, where there are none). But the *topological* relations between parts of the visual field are preserved: if one point on the retina lies between two others, so will the point to which it projects on the cortex, in relation to the points to which the others project; except that in all the visual projection areas so far studied the left and right halves of the visual field are represented separately, in the right and left hemispheres respectively. There is a crossing over of nerve fibres from the two eyes at the *optic chiasma.* Nerves originating in the right side of the retinas of both eyes project to the left side of the brain; those originating in the left side of the retinas of both eyes project to the right. And because the light rays cross at the pupil, the right and left sides of each retina correspond, respectively, to the left and right sides of the visual field.

Nerves from the retina enter the brain via two separate routes. One set projects to the *lateral geniculate nucleus* of the thalamus. From there fibres pass to the so-called *primary visual cortex* at the rear of the brain.

But another set projects directly to the *superior colliculus*, which is set much further forward in the cortex. A major role of the superior colliculus, which also receives inputs from the main visual projection areas, appears to be that of initiating certain sorts of reflex responses, such as the so-called *visual grasp reflex*: redirecting one's gaze in response to a sudden movement or flash of light at the periphery of one's visual field. The fact that there are these two distinct visual pathways suggests, however, a possible explanation for the phenomenon of blind-sight mentioned in the last chapter. Patients with blind-sight are suffering from a kind of lesion, called a *scotoma*, in the *primary* visual cortex, otherwise known as the *striate* cortex. This is the immediate destination of the fibres coming from the lateral geniculate nucleus. And it seems as though it is only such visual signals as are projected to, or through, the striate cortex, that give rise to the subjective impression of seeing, with all that this implies in terms of the apprehension of phenomenal qualities. (It does not follow that visual perception, in this sense, actually occurs *in*, or is supervenient upon what occurs in, the striate cortex itself. Hubel and Wiesel themselves deny the possibility of this, on the basis of a rather interesting argument that I shall examine later.)

Blind-sight may therefore be the result of visual signals passing into the higher cortical centres from the superior colliculus (Weiskrantz et al., 1974; Weiskrantz, 1986). If so, blind-sight is probably happening constantly in all of us. Though it is natural to think that our cognitive interpretation of the visual world is based entirely on the phenomenal quality of what is going on in the perceived visual field, this is unlikely to be true. Patterns of light entering the retina can often, probably, trigger recognition, even conscious recognition, without being required to pass through the stage of visual perception, as we normally understand it, at all. The superior colliculus belongs to what is, in evolutionary terms, an older visual system that plays an increasingly more dominant role as one goes down the phylogenetic scale. If one asks the question, 'What does the world look like to a fish?' the answer may be: 'It doesn't *look* like anything: fish find their way about by blind-sight.'

But to continue with the visual saga, the neurons that project along the optic nerve to the lateral geniculate nucleus mostly have spiking frequencies that are at their maximum when a circular spot of light, with a dark surround, impinges on the appropriate part of the retina; some respond maximally to a dark spot with a light surround. This is the form in which pattern information is relayed to the striate cortex, specifically to the neurons in what is known as *layer IV*, the lowest of four layers into which the striate cortex is divided. Up to and including this point, the signals from the two eyes are kept strictly segregated. At the higher layers of the striate cortex, to which the neurons in layer IV project, there is, however, a partial pooling of information from the two eyes. Moreover, the spot-by-spot pattern information is synthesized in such a way as to yield, instead, information about the presence and orientation of *edges* between dark and light areas, or of *bars* of light on dark or dark on light. There are cells known as *orientation cells*, which respond preferentially to bars or edges at a specific angle, projected on to the appropriate part of the retina. It was this remarkable discovery (deriving from their work on the visual system of the cat) that, above all, earned Hubel and Weisel their Nobel prize. Hubel and Weisel found that these *orientation* cells were arranged in long columns, running perpendicularly to the surface, such that the cells in a given column all responded maximally to a bar or edge with the same orientation. They also found, with lateral movement parallel to the surface, an alternating tendency for cells to respond maximally to bars projected on to the two different eyes. This showed that the striate cortex was divided into different *ocular-dominance* zones, as well as into different orientation zones, the vertical boundaries of the two zones being independent of each other.

The orientation cells turned out to fall into two categories. A *simple* cell responds maximally to a bar or edge, in a particular orientation, at a specific point in its *receptive field* – the receptive field being that portion of the retina from which the cell receives inputs. A *complex* cell, on the other hand, responds equally well to a bar or edge with the appropriate orientation, wherever, over a wide area of its receptive field, the bar or edge is located; this could be explained on the basis of its receiving input from several simple cells with overlapping receptive fields. Moreover, complex cells often respond preferentially to bars or edges that are *moving* in a direction perpendicular to their orientation; some show a preference for one direction of movement rather than the other (Hubel and Weisel, 1979).

The projection areas associated with the other senses are, at present, not nearly as well understood as the primary visual cortex: they still await their Hubel and Weisel. But the general principles that apply to the striate cortex appear to apply elsewhere; in the auditory cortex, for example, there appear to be ear-dominance columns similar to the ocular-dominance columns just mentioned. And, more to the point, the sensory projection areas, in general, seem to be concerned with stimulus *analysis* rather than simply with stimulus representation.

Beyond the striate cortex, within the visual system, there is a sequence of other *pre-striate* areas, which receive input directly or indirectly from the striate cortex (Zeki, 1974; Shipp and Zeki, 1985; Hubel and Livingstone, 1985). These are labelled V2 to V5 (V1 being the striate cortex). It is now thought that a major function of the striate cortex is to segregate information about colour, shape, depth and movement and

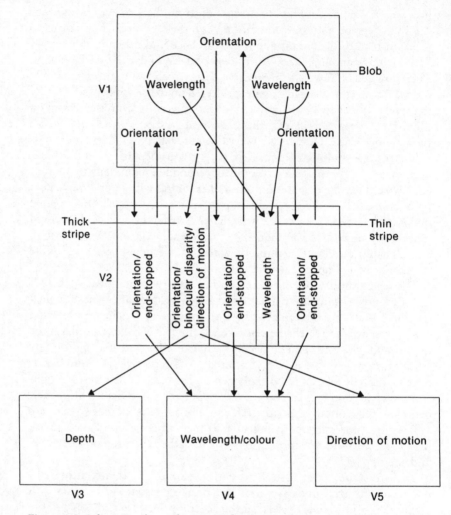

Figure 4.5 *Schematic chart of striate and pre-striate areas of the cortex, showing
neural connections.*
*Labelling of an area indicates the dominant and/or distinctive preferences of cells in that
area.*

distribute it to separate regions of the pre-striate cortex for further
processing. (Most of the relevant work has been done on monkeys.)
Dotted about within the striate cortex are clusters of cells, known as
blobs. Cells in these blobs show no orientation preference; but over half
of them show a preference for light of a particular wavelength. (This is
true of only a small number of the orientation cells.) Area V2 is shown

under appropriate staining to contain stripes that are alternately thin and thick. The thin stripes, which receive their input from the blobs of V1, contain cells two-thirds of which (in the macaque monkey) are wavelength-sensitive. Most of these are *double-opponent*: such a cell will have, say, a centre which responds positively to red and negatively to green, with a surround that gives the opposite responses. Many of them are what Hubel and Livingstone call *complex-unoriented*: they will respond to spots of the preferred size (and also, if wavelength-sensitive, colour boundary) over a wide area of their receptive fields.

The orientation cells of V1 feed into the interstripe areas of V2, which contain cells almost all of which show an orientation preference. But in addition, over half of these cells are what Hubel and Livingstone call *end-stopped*; they show a preference for an edge or bar of a particular length. Interestingly, as many fibres proceed back from the interstripe areas of V2 to the striate cortex as go the other way. Hubel and Livingstone (1985, p. 326) speculate that the information feeding back to the striate cortex from the end-stopped cells, in combination with that supplied by the ordinary orientation cells, may enable the striate cortex to compute curvature.

It is not clear from where exactly, in the striate cortex, the thick stripes of V2 receive their input. The cells there are not wavelength-sensitive, but are nearly all orientation-sensitive. These cells have two distinctive features. One is that most of them respond preferentially when similar stimuli are projected on to the two retinas in slightly different positions; they are responsive to what is called *binocular disparity*, which is an indicator of visual depth. Moreover, there is some evidence (Zeki, 1974) for an arrangement of these cells into columns corresponding to different depths, or degrees of disparity. The second thing that is distinctive about the cells in these thick stripes is that they show a high degree of preference for bars or edges moving in a particular direction.

Cells from the thick stripes of V2 project into area V5, which seems to be specialized for direction of motion, and also into area V3, which appears to be concerned with depth. Cells from the thin stripes and the interstripe areas of V2 project into area V4, which seems to be centrally concerned with colour; columns corresponding to different wavelength preferences have been reported by Zeki (1974). The cells in this area have some very interesting properties, which we shall be discussing in chapter 7. One general point is that, as one goes from the striate cortex (V1) to V2, and from V2 to V3–5, the receptive fields of the cells tend to get larger, sometimes, as in the movement cells of V5, by a very considerable factor; information from several cells with smaller receptive fields is clearly being pooled in some fashion.

What all this suggests is that information about movement, depth, shape and colour is processed in parallel. There is a division of labour within the visual system. And that supposition is amply confirmed by the psychological evidence (for example, Held and Shattuck, 1971; Ramachandran and Gregory, 1978; Levinson and Sekuler, 1980; Carney et al., 1987).

Now in one sense this is all very surprising and deeply puzzling. What our image of self somehow leads us to expect is the neural equivalent of an inner film screen. But what the physiologists tell us is actually there, inside our heads, is nothing much like that at all. The two halves of the field appear to be separately located, wildly distorted in terms of relative scale; and worse, different visual features are predominantly represented on different topographic maps. Surely, we say, there must be some super-projection area, where all the information is brought together in the form we know it. This is a point of view with which the physiologists themselves appear to have some sympathy. Mishkin and Appenzeller (1987, p. 64) have gone so far as to propose the inferior temporal cortex as the place where the neurons 'synthesize a complete representation of the object'.

That said, our intuitive expectations must be set against functional considerations. However visual information is processed in the brain, it must be done in such a way as to facilitate thought about, and appropriate action in respect of, whatever visual signals we receive from the environment. And how could an inner film show – albeit in 3D – do that for us? We'd still need systems that told us where edges were, and the like, if we were to be capable of the most elementary pattern-recognition. Indeed, the more one thinks about it, the more one comes to realize that an inner film show would, in functional terms, be a wholly pointless inner duplication of the retinal image.

Moreover, the very idea of an inner screen on which a visual image is cast can rapidly lead to philosophical incoherence. It encourages people to ask nonsensical questions, such as the old chestnut of how we succeed in seeing things the right way up, given that the retinal image is upside down; and this invites the conclusion that there must be some process in the brain which takes the image and turns it up the right way. The correct response, of course, is to point out that this is a pseudoquestion that can only be prompted by some illicit conception of an inner homunculus, who is viewing the said screen. What sometimes helps people caught in the grip of this supposed puzzle is to point out to them that if there is no such homunculus, the problem doesn't even arise; but on the other hand, if there is, the difficulty can be solved at a stroke by assuming that the homunculus is viewing the image standing on its head! Of course, the real problem with the homunculus idea is that it leads to what philosophers call an *infinite regress*. For we shall now need a theory about how the homunculus sees. (Is there another image inside *its* brain being viewed by yet another homunculus. . .?) In functional terms, it doesn't matter two pins whether the 'image' is upside down, back to front, lying on its side or broken up into tiny pieces and scattered liberally throughout the head, provided only that it, or its parts, are appropriately causally–functionally related to whatever brain processes underlie belief, desire, action and the like.

But functionality isn't everything. At least, it isn't unless you happen to be a convinced functionalist. And besides, there are good *functional* reasons for being dissatisfied with the account the physiologists offer us, *considered as an analysis of what lies behind actual conscious perception.* Here I can do no better than to quote Hubel and Weisel themselves:

> What is common to all regions [of the cortex] is the local nature of the wiring. The information carried into the cortex by a single fiber can in principle make itself felt through the entire thickness in about three or four synapses, whereas the lateral spread, produced by branching trees of axons and dendrites, is limited for all practical purposes to a few millimeters, a small proportion of the vast extent of the cortex.
>
> The implications of this are far-reaching. Whatever any given region of the cortex does, it does locally. At stages where there is any kind of detailed, systematic topographical mapping the analysis must be piecemeal. For example, in the somatic sensory cortex the messages concerning one finger can be combined and compared with an input from elsewhere on that same finger or with input from a neighboring finger, but they can hardly be combined with the influence from the trunk or from a foot. The same applies to the visual world. Given the detailed order of the input to the primary visual cortex, there is no likelihood that the region will do anything to correlate information coming in from both far above and far below the horizon, or from both the left and the right part of the visual scene. It follows that this cannot by any stretch of the imagination be the place where actual perception is enshrined. Whatever these cortical areas are doing, it must be some kind of local analysis of the sensory world. One can only assume that as the information is relayed from one cortical area to the next the map becomes progressively more blurred and the information carried more abstract. (Hubel and Weisel, 1979, pp. 132–3)

This thought-provoking passage raises a host of questions. First, why does there have to be such a thing as '*the* place where actual perception is enshrined'? The physiologists seem to be revealing a hierarchy of projection areas, containing cells which are sensitive to progressively more complex and abstract features of the visual scene. It is natural to suppose that there must be some hitherto undiscovered area in the brain, a super-projection area, where the information from all these different centres is 'synthesized' so as to yield 'actual perception'. But could it not be, instead, that perception, in its subjective aspects, represents a partial but simultaneous awareness of what is going on in all these centres? The natural reply is that this would leave unexplained how all these spatially separate neural goings-on somehow *fuse* into a single unified awareness. Indeed it would. But that problem would arise more or less whatever the physiological basis of vision turned out to be. It must be a mistake to suppose that any *special* problem is raised by the fact, for example, that colour and movement are processed in spatially separated areas – a problem, that is, given that what we see is, say, moving-patch-of-colour. After all, corresponding topographic points in the two maps are at any rate joined by neurons. Suppose one were to effect a fusion of the two areas, by gradually shortening the axons of these neurons, pulling the two systems together, until they were spatially superimposed, with neurons sensitive, respectively, to colour and movement in the same region of the visual field, sitting side by side in the brain. Would that do anything to alleviate the philosophical difficulty? Surely not. To the extent that it is a genuine problem at all, it would arise even if we had succeeded in finding that hypothetical super-projection area, in which all the information that the visual field seems to contain was found to be simultaneously encoded.

It is important, however, to be clear just what the problem is, in philosophical terms. What we are talking about here is not so much the problem of the unity of consciousness as a whole. Rather it is the perceived unity of items *within* consciousness: the unity of the visual field itself and, within the visual field, the unity of that moving red shape; what makes our perception something more than just the simultaneous perception of movement, redness and, say, squareness. No doubt it has something centrally to do with our ability to assign all these attributes to the same region of visual space. But how, then, does a perception of a single place arise out of a vast plurality of distinct topographic representations that, as a matter of fact, all correspond to the same pair of points on the retina? These are not problems to be shrugged aside. On the other hand, it is far from clear what, in *physiological* terms, would *count* as a solution to them. And to the extent that we don't know what *would* count, perhaps we cannot know either what *wouldn't*.

Some very interesting experimental results that are relevant to this question of the perceived unity of conscious visual perception have been reported by Ramachandran (1987). Ramachandran was interested in the question how it is possible for the brain to give us a perception of a moving object in which motion and colour are appropriately synchronized, given that colour and movement are processed in parallel. His experiment involved a well-known optical illusion, in which an arrangement of four black disks from which wedges have been removed creates the appearance of a square (see figure 4.6). A red square on a green background was displayed on a computer monitor, with the four disks on a moveable transparent overlay. Ramachandran found that movement of the four disks created the illusion that the red square was moving too, in the same direction. Moreover, the illusion was at its most pronounced when the luminance (lightness) of the red square and the green background were precisely the same. When the luminance contrast between the disks and the background was reduced, so was the illusion of movement of the red square. And when the luminance of the disks was made the same as that of the background, with only a colour contrast, several of the subjects spontaneously reported that they couldn't actually see the disks moving at all, even though they were.

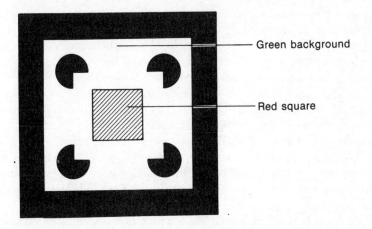

Figure 4.6 *Illusory square superimposed, by means of a transparent overlay, on a computer monitor display of a red square on a green background.* (From Ramachandran, 1987, p. 645.)

What Ramachandran has concluded from these results is that it is overwhelmingly (though of course not exclusively) movements in luminance boundaries, rather than in colour boundaries, that causes us to perceive movement in the visual scene. That, of course, is precisely what the foregoing account of the physiology would lead one to expect. Ramachandran postulates a mechanism he calls *capture*, according to which colours in the neighbourhood of the movement of luminance boundaries are picked up and attributed to the moving object. The moving configuration is, as Ramachandran puts it, 'impressionistically painted in' with the colours in the immediate vicinity, which are accordingly seen to move 'with' the object. He speculates that it may be in area V2 that this mechanism comes into play, with cells in the interstripe areas 'borrowing' colours from the immediately neighbouring thin stripes.

I find this notion of capture very intriguing. Something of this sort, it seems to me, must be involved quite generally in consciousness. But, in spite of Ramachandran's gestures in the direction of a physiological basis for the specific phenomenon he describes, capture remains, in neuro-physiological terms, an uncashed metaphor.

I want, however, to return to the distinction between unity *of* consciousness and unity *within* consciousness, since it seems to me a crucial distinction which has not received from philosophers the attention it deserves. And it bears centrally on the remarks Hubel and Weisel make about the local character of cortical analysis. There is a well-known psychological experiment in which the subject is made to look at flashes of light in different parts of the visual field and listen to sounds coming from different directions, and is asked to make judgements about the order in which they occur, when they are very closely spaced in time. It has been discovered that people are good at judging which of two sounds, or which of two flashes, came first; but they are, by comparison, rather bad at judging whether a flash came before or after a sound. Is it that we can't look and listen at the same time? That's what some psychologists seem to think – that all we can really do *consciously* is listen to the sound or look at the flash. The theory then is that whatever we choose not to attend to goes straight into short-term memory, without our being conscious of it at the precise time it occurs; and retrieving it after the event doesn't really help us to answer the question.

But I don't believe that explanation. I think the evidence from our own experience that we *can* simultaneously attend to auditory and visual presentations is overwhelming. The point seems to me to be rather that to be simultaneously or successively conscious of two things is not the same as being conscious of them *as* simultaneous or successive. Or, to put it another way, *phenomenal* awareness – what encompasses the subjective looks, sounds and feels within our stream of consciousness – is distinct from *cognitive* awareness: what we know or believe, what judgements we are capable of making, about or on the basis of phenomenal awareness. Suppose, for example, we are gazing at a group of black dots on a piece of paper. Remove one, and that may make a difference to how the group looks; but from this it doesn't follow that, either before or after, we could have said how many dots there were. Whatever is implied in the unity of consciousness, it emphatically does not imply an unrestricted ability to make global judgements about what is phenomenally presented to us in awareness.

There is a lot of evidence about the effect of lesions in various higher areas in the visual cortex to which the striate and pre-striate cortex project. Pohl (1973) discovered that the removal of tissue from the posterior parietal cortex, near the top of the brain, in monkeys, left them unable to perceive spatial relations whilst still able to tell distinctive objects apart. The ability to distinguish objects, on the other hand, seems to depend on an area in the inferior temporal cortex, where Gross has discovered cells that respond selectively to a complex shape wherever it is in the visual field (see Mishkin and Appenzeller, 1987, pp. 64, 68).

There is also an area of the pre-striate occipital cortex, damage to which, in humans, results in a bizarre condition known as *visual agnosia*; patients still insist that they can *see*, but are unable to engage in certain . kinds of pattern recognition. Luria (1973), who has studied a number of such patients, says of them that they suffer from an 'inability to combine individual impressions into complete patterns' and are 'compelled to *deduce* the meaning of the image . . . by drawing conclusions from individual details and by carrying out intensive work where a normal subject perceives the whole form immediately.' Like an 'archaeologist attempting to decode a text in an unfamiliar script', the patient 'understands the meaning of each sign although the meaning of the whole text remains unknown.' Here's a typical case:

This patient carefully examines the picture of a pair of spectacles shown to him. He is confused and does not know what the picture represents. He starts to guess. 'There is a circle . . . and another circle . . . and a stick . . . a cross-bar . . . why, it must be a bicycle.' He looks at the picture of a cock with feathers of different colours in his tail, but not immediately recognizing the object as a whole he declares: 'this is a fire, here are the flames'.

(Luria, 1973, p. 116)

Asked to draw an object, such patients do what some young children will do: they draw the parts, but seem unable to draw the object as an integrated whole. It should be emphasized that these patients show no general intellectual impairment, nor do they have any difficulty recognizing objects by touch.

Bálint, who studied such patients before the First World War, said of them that they suffered from 'a decrease in the range of visual perception', and seemed unable to see more than one object at a time; for example, they couldn't trace a line with a pencil, because if they looked at the pencil they lost the line, and vice versa. But on the other hand it could not be said of them that their visual field was constricted in any ordinary sense; for the problem was independent of the size of the object as projected on to the retina. What they appeared to be suffering from was indeed, in a sense, a constriction of the field, but one measured, as Bálint rather neatly put it, in *'units of meaning rather than in units of space'*. We appear to have here a kind of *semantic analogue* of tunnel vision.

It is very difficult to imagine what it would be like to be one of these patients. But the general message seems clear. We must distinguish between two senses in which visual judgements can be more than purely local. One is the sense in which we can make judgements which are based on what is going on in a relatively large part of the visual field. The perception of spatial relations, which Pohl's monkeys lacked, is clearly the central case of non-local analysis in that sense. But Luria's and Bálint's patients did not, apparently, lack that ability. What they were unable to do was form more than the most elementary visual *Gestalts*; they could engage only in visual analysis that was, so to speak, semantically local. It really does seem, from Luria's and Bálint's reports, that visual perceptions no longer comprise, for these patients, a unified visual field in the way ours do (although it's exceedingly difficult to imagine what that would be like). And this suggests a rather satisfying dovetailing of the phenomenal and the functional. The perceived unity of the visual field might be conceived as being of a piece with these two types of functional non-locality that I have tried to distinguish: our capacity to make judgements about spatial relations and our capacity to form visual Gestalts. From this point of view, one's difficulty in temporally ordering flashes with respect to sounds could be regarded as integrally bound up with the fact that there is no *audio-visual* field. The temptation is to invoke this fact in order to explain our inability to form audio-visual Gestalts at the purely phenomenal level. But it seems to me that this may get things back to front, and that we ought rather appeal to this inability to form audio-visual Gestalts by way of partial explanation of what this lack of a unitary field actually consists in.

Thus far, then, it seems quite possible, in spite of what Hubel and Weisel say, that the goings-on in the striate cortex constitute at least an element in that set of processes that are subjectively registered as seeing. After all, damage to those higher centres that are involved with the kind of spatially and semantically non-local analysis, of which the striate cortex is incapable, do not render subjects blind, but simply unable to perform the corresponding cognitive tasks. There is, however, another consideration that might seem to weigh against this suggestion. First, there is the fact that all of Hubel and Weisel's work was done with *anaesthetized* animals. Things that go on in the brain regardless of whether or not an animal is conscious cannot, by definition, one might say, be part of a conscious process, such as visual perception. Perhaps. Certainly, one's first temptation is to say something like that. But then no one has the least idea what the physiological basis of conscious perception is. There are several possibilities here. One is that there is a certain subset of brain neurons, whose firings, at significantly above or below base level, are constitutive of one's stream of consciousness. So that if (sufficiently many of) these fire, this will be registered in consciousness. From this point of view, the fact that the neurons in the striate cortex are fully functional in a state of complete unconsciousness indeed proves that they can play no *constitutive* role in *conscious* visual perception, though doubtless they play a causal role, sending off signals to other centres which *are* constitutively involved in actual seeing.

But there are other possibilities too. One is that the firings of a given cluster of neurons are not classifiable as conscious or unconscious *as such* at all. Rather, these firings can participate constitutively in a conscious state or process or not, simply depending on what signals are passing between this cluster and some other clusters; the awareness status of a given set of neuronal firings would then depend on the *relation* of these firings to other things going on in the brain. A final possibility is that there are centres in the brain, of which the striate cortex may be one, which are capable of functioning in either of two modes, a conscious or an unconscious mode; which mode they are operating in at any particular moment will be causally dependent on the signals they are receiving from the brain stem. For philosophical reasons that will emerge in chapter 10, this last is the theory that I myself am inclined to favour. But either of these two latter suggestions would be consistent with the events in the striate cortex being, on occasion, a constitutive part of genuine conscious perception, though of course lying anaesthetized on a laboratory bench is not such an occasion.

One fact that we have been neglecting in the foregoing discussion is that the striate cortex, in either of the two hemispheres, represents only half of the visual field; and what is more this also appears to be true for all the higher cortical projection areas for vision that have been studied so far. What corresponds, physiologically, to the phenomenal fact that we have a single visual field, and not two separate ones, representing the left and right sides of each retina? The answer would appear to be the corpus callosum, the bundle of fibres through which the two hemispheres communicate. But there are two ways in which the passage of visual information between the two hemispheres might generate a unitary field. It might do so by enabling visual information from the two hemispheres to be pooled in some single cortical area, presumably in one hemisphere or the other; and here, perhaps, is where genuine perception takes place. Or alternatively, the physiological basis of the perceived unity of the visual field may simply be the fact of their being connected, in the way they are, by fibres that cross the corpus callosum. That, the suggestion would be, is what makes the projection areas in the two hemispheres, spatially distinct though they are, add up to a system which is nevertheless *functionally* integrated. And after all, it is arguably, as we saw earlier, a kind of superstition to think that substantial spatial separation is in some special way incompatible with phenomenal unity.

Anyway, there are these two possibilities. And one might think that there was a fairly simple way of testing which was correct. Disable the fibres in the corpus callosum that link the two sets of visual projection areas, and ask patients what they see. If they say they can still see things in all parts of what they used to think of as their visual field, but that the field has now become divided, in a way that makes it difficult for them to answer questions that require them to compare, or otherwise relate, things in the two halves, that would vindicate the second hypothesis. If, on the other hand, they say the sorts of things that people would say if they were blind in one or other half of the visual field, that would support the first hypothesis; and depending on which half of the visual field had disappeared, we should be able to tell in which of the two hemispheres the information was being pooled, so as to yield actual conscious seeing.

Of course, people are hardly likely to allow themselves to be experimented on in this way. So we must look to patients who have either suffered accidental injury or else have undergone surgery that has a similar disabling effect on the corpus callosum. As a matter of fact, several patients have had an operation, known as *commissurotomy*, in which the corpus callosum is surgically severed; when this is done it is usually as a last-ditch measure to prevent or contain epileptic seizures, or else, more rarely, to remove a tumour. Such patients have been extensively studied, particularly by Sperry (1968a, 1986b) and Gazzaniga (1967). It turns out that if you present these patients with an object so positioned that light from it reaches only the left side of the retina, they will invariably say they can't see it. And this might seem to be a splendid vindication of the first of our two alternative hypotheses.

But it is no such thing; and indeed the whole line of reasoning that I disingenuously presented in the last paragraph but one harbours a gross fallacy. Once again, we must think about the matter in functional terms — though I cannot emphasize too strongly that 'functional' does not mean functionalist. The key point here is that the bulk of the areas concerned with language are known to be located in the left hemisphere of the brain (though the right hemisphere has a measure of language *comprehension*).

So if you ask people, regardless of whether or not they have an intact corpus callosum, what they can actually see, what they will then *say* is bound to be based on such information as is available to the left hemisphere. For commissurotomy patients, that can only be information about the right visual field, since, in the absence of the connections provided by the corpus callosum, there is no route by which the left hemisphere can gain access to information about what is impinging on the left side of each retina.

While the patients strenuously deny, verbally, that they can see anything that is placed in (what used to be) their left visual field, they continue nevertheless to perform successfully all manner of cognitive tasks for which conscious left-field vision would usually be thought to be a necessary prerequisite: they act, in most ways, as though they could see perfectly normally. This is because most sensorimotor tasks, in so far as they relate to the left side of the body and of the visual field, are under the control of the right hemisphere, which does have access to information from the left side of the retina. So the patients' denial that they can see an object, when light from it impinges only on the left side of their retinas, is largely contradicted by the way they act. Which speak louder, their words or their actions? Can they consciously perceive things to their left, or are the muscles on the left side of the body operating under the control of a kind of blind-sight?

The truth seems to be that there is no unambiguous answer to the question 'What do these patients see?' The patients' conscious lives have become internally dissociated to the point where all one can say is: there is a left-half visual field associated with the right hemisphere, and there is a right-half field that is associated with the left hemisphere, and corresponding to each hemisphere there is a subjective impression of seeing only the items in that half field. But the subjective impression associated with the right hemisphere is one which the patients are unable to articulate, simply because the means of articulating it are now functionally segregated from the cortical processes that underlie the impression. (Incidentally, this would appear virtually to put paid to the unorthodox theory, mentioned briefly above, that the seat of consciousness is in the brain stem. If that is where all visual information is ultimately, so to speak, delivered to consciousness, it is exceedingly difficult to see why commissurotomy patients should report that they are unable to see things which are projected on to the left side of the retina; for then the brain stem itself would effectively provide a route whereby visual information from both hemispheres could be transmitted to the speech centres.)

That there is this duality of phenomenal impressions seems to be the inescapable conclusion that emerges from experiments in which it is contrived that different images or incompatible instructions are projected on to the right and left sides of the two retinas. This is done by so-called *tachistoscopic* stimulation. Subjects are asked to fix their gaze on the midpoint of a screen; images are then flashed on to one side or other of the screen, long enough for the subjects to take them in, but not long enough for them to shift their gaze so as to expose both halves of each retina to the stimulus. Thus, an image of a toothbrush might be projected on the left side of the screen and that of a hat on the right. Subjects are then asked to select, from a pile of objects, the one that matches the image they saw on the screen. What happens is that the right and left hands sort through the objects independently; each hand selects the object which matches the image projected to the corresponding side of the subject's visual field, whilst ignoring or discarding the object matching the image projected to the opposite side of the field. If asked what they saw on the screen, subjects will say that they saw whatever was projected on to the right side ('hat' in the example given) – the information, that is to say, which is passed to the speech-controlling left hemisphere, which in turn controls the right hand.

Precisely how these extraordinary phenomena should be interpreted is a matter of intense controversy, amongst philosophers and scientists alike. But I shall not pursue these matters now. Rather, I shall postpone further discussion of 'split-brain' subjects until chapter 6, where we shall directly address the problem of the unity of consciousness.

5

Einstein and the Identity Theory

Materialism, as I defined it in chapter 2, is the theory that minds do not exist over and above material things and events. I also said that a – Descartes would have said *the* – characteristic feature of material things and events is spatial extension or location. (This would be consistent with regarding space itself as material, given that spatial points are located and spatial regions extended.)

There are various different versions of materialism, of varying degrees of sophistication and plausibility. But the simplest to state, albeit (as we shall see in subsequent chapters) far from simple to defend, is what goes by the name of the *identity theory*. According to the identity theory, mental states and processes, both conscious and unconscious, just *are* states and processes in the brain. Hobbes's remark, quoted in chapter 1, that 'sense . . . can be nothing else than a motion in some of the internal parts of the sentient' shows him clearly to have been an advocate of the identity theory. And its twentieth-century adherents have included Bertrand Russell (1927, 1949), Herbert Feigl (1967), J. J. C. Smart (1959, 1963, pp. 88–105) and David Armstrong (1968).

Contemporary proponents of the identity theory maintain that the identification of mental states with brain states is no different in principle from other such identifications that we should all accept as scientifically compelling; a favourite example is the identification of flashes of lightning with electrical discharges. The question, then, is whether the proposed identification of mental states with brain states really is, in relevant respects, like that between lightning and electrical discharges, say, or whether there may not be some crucial disanalogy. We can assume, since I see no reason to doubt it, that it would be possible in principle to establish the requisite correlations between mental events and states in the brain, so that the cases are alike to that extent.

Now as a matter of fact I think there are several crucial disanalogies;

this is implicit in much of what I have been saying in previous chapters, and much of what I shall be saying later. I want here to address just one supposed disanalogy of which much has been made in the philosophical literature; it is, for example, advanced both by Wittgenstein, in *The Blue Book* (1969, pp. 7–8) and by A. J. Ayer in his *Concept of a Person* (1963, p. 103). This is the alleged impossibility of assigning a spatial location to a mental event – or more precisely, of doing so independently of some prior *assumption* that it was identical with some brain event.

A flash of lightning and an electrical discharge, so it has been argued, as well as being assigned times of occurrence, may independently – that is, without assuming identity – be assigned spatial locations. So when the assigned times *and the assigned spatial locations* both turn out to coincide, we have a very strong motive for identifying them. As Ayer has elegantly put it in conversation, 'they are competing for the same space'. No such argument, it is alleged, is available for mental states in relation to brain states: the only grounds on which we could assign a spatial location to a mental state would be some prior decision to identify it with some physiological event the location of which was already known. There is no way in which we can first assign a spatial location to a given mental event and then use this as an argument for identifying it with whatever physiological happening turns out to have been going on at that place at the time in question.

Indeed, given that this independent assignment of a spatial location to a mental event seems to be an impossibility *in principle*, some philosophers go so far as to claim that to speak of such events as having a spatial location – of my twinge of anxiety, say, as occurring seven centimetres behind my left eye – is actually meaningless. This is Wittgenstein's position. (He also points out, however, that one could, if armed with an 'autocerebroscope' that allowed one to observe events in one's own brain, adopt a new 'language game' whereby such a form of words, meaningless in the context of our present linguistic practices, came to mean simply that this twinge of anxiety had a brain state correlate which was occurring in that region. Thus construed, it would still not, of course, commit the speaker to literal location as we currently understand it.)

I believe the foregoing argument to be mistaken. It is, I suggest, possible in principle to assign a spatial location to a mental event, independently of any prior identification with some physical event. Assume (1) that Einstein's special theory of relativity is correct. Now, according to special relativity, any two events that are temporally separated with respect to one frame of reference must be spatially separated with respect to some other frame. This goes back to the point – emphasized in chapter 1 as casting doubt on the idea that the future is, in contrast to the past, open – that different observers slice the space-time continuum at different angles, according to their instantaneous state of motion, thereby defining mutually incompatible simultaneity planes. If we assume (2) that mental events are located in time, in the same sense that physical events are, then it follows immediately, given special relativity, that they are also in space, since events could hardly be spatially separated without being spatially located.

(Incidentally, being spatially separated relative to a frame must not be confused with the property, which some pairs of temporally separated events possess and others do not, of having a *spacelike separation*. Two events are spacelike separated if the spatial distance between them, measured, say, in light seconds, is greater than the temporal interval, measured in seconds. The spatial distance is then said to *dominate* the temporal interval. Events in which the temporal interval dominates the spatial are said to be *timelike separated*. The properties of being spacelike or timelike separated are *frame-invariant*. Though spatial and temporal intervals differ from frame to frame, the four-dimensional spatio-temporal *interval*, given by the square root of the difference between the square of the spatial distance and the square of the temporal interval, is the same relative to all frames of reference. And the interval will be spacelike or timelike according as this spatio-temporal interval is *real* or *imaginary*: see below pp. 182–3.)

So far we have an argument for saying that mental events must be somewhere or other. But the argument does not, as it stands, provide us with a *criterion* of spatial location. It does not tell us how the (not overtly spatial) facts about a mental event go to determine, for that event, a specific place of occurrence. But if we make a few more assumptions, we shall have such a criterion. Assume (3), along with common sense, that physical events may cause mental ones, as when I sit on the proverbial pin and it punctures my skin, thereby causing pain, and (4) that mental events may cause physical ones, as when my pain causes me to wince or my embarrassment causes me to blush. These last two assumptions may seem too obvious to be worth stating, but there is nothing so obvious that a philosopher cannot be found to deny it. Finally (5), assume what is known technically, amongst physicists, as *causality*: the principle that causal influences cannot propagate faster than the speed of light. (Contrary to popular belief, this does not follow from special relativity alone; it is perfectly possible to postulate faster-than-light particles, *tachyons*, whose behaviour is entirely in accord with the so-called *Lorentz* transformation. But there is scant reason for believing them to exist in reality.)

We have need, here, of the concept of a *light cone* (see figure 5.1). The light cone associated with a given space-time point P is an imaginary

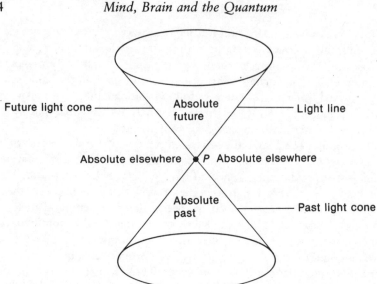

Figure 5.1 *A light cone, centred on the event* P.
Events in the region labelled 'absolute elsewhere' will, with respect to the event P, *be past relative to some frames of reference and future relative to others.*

structure defined by the spatio-temporal paths of all possible light rays passing through P. Relative to a frame of reference, P will correspond to a particular spatial point s and time t. Imagine a hollow sphere of light, with s at its centre, which closes on s, getting smaller and smaller until, at time t, it has contracted to a point, at s, whence it starts to re-expand, as a hollow sphere of light, still with s at its centre, getting larger and larger as the light passes away from s. The light cone is the four-dimensional structure to which this process corresponds, when one regards time as a fourth dimension perpendicular to the three spatial ones. If time is taken as the vertical axis, and one of the spatial dimensions is suppressed, then the light cone can be represented as what most non-mathematicians would think of as two cones arranged apex to apex, the point of contact representing the space-time point P. Each horizontal cross-section of the cone(s) will be a circle, which is a two-dimensional representation of the three-dimensional sphere of light referred to just now. The lower and upper cones correspond, respectively, to the 'imploding' and 'exploding' spheres.

The light cone divides space-time, relative to P, into three regions: the area outside the cone(s), sometimes known as the *absolute elsewhere*, the *forward light cone* or *absolute future*, and the *backward light cone* or *absolute past*. The absolute past and future comprise the events which all observers would agree to be respectively past and future with respect to

P. Assuming (5), only events in the backward light cone can influence what happens at *P*; and correspondingly, what happens at *P* can only influence events within the forward light cone.

This gives us all that is required to assign at any rate an approximate spatial location to some mental events. Let *A* be a physical event that causes a mental event *B*, which in turn causes a physical event *C*. If we know the time of occurrence and spatial locations of *A* and *C*, then we can at least place bounds upon the time of occurrence *and spatial location* of the mental event *B*: it must lie within the intersection of the forward light cone of *A* and the backward light cone of *C* (see figure 5.2).

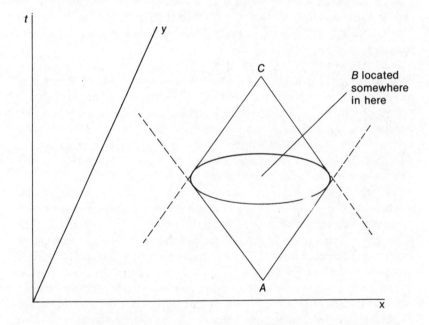

Figure 5.2 *Criterion for assigning an approximate location to a mental event* B. *On the assumption that it is caused by the physical event* A, *and causes the physical event* C, B *must lie somewhere in the region of overlap between the forward light cone of* A *and the backward light cone of* C. *(The z axis has been suppressed.)*

If it were now possible to find pairs of physical events, standing to *B* as cause and effect respectively, that were separated by ever smaller temporal intervals, then it would be possible to define the spatial location of *B* with any required degree of precision. (Possible, that is, in principle. I am not suggesting that this is a remotely *practical* method of assigning to mental events spatial locations precise enough to be of use to the neuropsychologist.) This is a very strong supposition, but I see no reason why someone who was disposed even to believe the correlational assumption behind the identity theory should be inclined to reject it. All causal processes that we know of are continuous, in the sense that cause and effect, when spatio-temporally separated, are found to be linked by some causal process that bridges the spatio-temporal gap.

I have put things this way because of possible difficulties surrounding the notion of assigning a precise time of occurrence to a mental event without correlating it with a physical one. Strictly, of course, it would suffice to find, for a mental event whose spatial location we were interested in, a physical cause *or* a physical effect – providing, that is, we had an independent fix on when the mental event occurred. For then the mental event would be known to be no further from the physical cause or effect than light could have travelled in the temporal interval separating them.

It may be worth pointing out that only the first part of the argument, the part designed to show that mental events must be located somewhere in space, makes essential use of relativity. Suppose one assumes that a certain mental event is somewhere in space, and that one can find other events, arbitrarily close to it in time, that are both spatially locatable and related to it as cause or effect. Then one does not need to invoke relativity, as such, to assign to that mental event, with an arbitrary degree of accuracy, a specific spatial location. All one needs is the premise that no causal influences can propagate faster than a certain given finite speed.

The only way I can see that one might get round the argument I have presented for the spatiality of mental events is by denying (2), the assumption that mental events are temporally related to physical events in the same way that physical events are related to each other. To be sure, it is part of our common-sense view of reality that mental and physical events have a shared chronology. But then it is independently obvious that the theory of relativity requires us to revise some, at least, of our common-sense preconceptions: common sense, in this area, is thus far from sacrosanct. What I would appeal to, in defence of the common-sense view, is the following principle: that two events can be causally related only if they are also temporally related. I am inclined to think that this is a conceptual truth; at any rate, I am confident that the prospect of having to deny it would strike most people as singularly unappealing. Given the scarcely deniable fact that mental events can both cause and be caused by physical ones, it then follows, by the above principle, that they do after all belong to the same temporal order. From which in turn it would follow that, if Einstein was right about space and time, they must belong to the same spatial order as well.

Someone might, however, say something like this. There are really two senses in which events may be held to be in time – a *primary* sense that applies directly to physical events, and a *derivative* sense that applies to any events that stand in a causal relation to events that are in time in the primary sense. (This line of attack was suggested by Peter Gibbins (1985).) A mind–body dualist might then insist that the correctness of the special theory of relativity implies only that events that are in time in the primary sense are also in space, whereas it has not been established that mental events are in time in anything but the derivative sense.

Interestingly enough, Robert Weingard (who first set me off on the line of thought developed in this chapter) explicitly considers a generalized form of the response just suggested, in an article of his own designed to establish, using relativity, the spatiality of mental events (though not *how* to locate them). Instead of 'causal relation' Weingard says 'non-temporal association'. What he says by way of rebuttal is the following:

> [I]t is a simple fact of our experience that we are aware of mental events directly bearing temporal relations to (non-mental) physical events, and not of (non-mental) physical events non-temporally associated with the mental event being temporally related to other (non-mental) physical events. When I am aware that I have a pain and that it is occurring before lunch, it is, I think, an obvious fact of experience that it is the pain itself that I am aware of occurring before lunch, and not that some (non-mental) physical event the pain is non-temporally associated with is occurring before lunch.
> (Weingard, 1977, pp. 283–4)

I ought to welcome this argument, inasmuch as it supports my case. But there is, I fear, something wrong with it. Suppose someone says, for example, 'When the train had pulled out, I suddenly felt very much alone.' Then what the speaker no doubt takes himself to have been aware of is that his feeling directly stood to the train's departure in the temporal relation 'very soon after'. For all that Weingard says, however, it is presumably open to the dualist to deny that what he was *in fact* aware of was that these events stood in the very same primary relation of temporal ordering as is to be found amongst physical events, and which enters into the mathematical statement of physical law. Compare someone who claimed that he was aware of a bright yellow after-image bearing to the lamppost the spatial relation 'to the left of'. Clearly, this awareness (or pseudo-awareness) does not license the attribution to after-images of spatial relations with respect to actual physical objects in the same (primary) sense in which physical objects may be said to stand in such relations to one another.

I do not think that there is, in fact, any knockdown way of refuting a very determined dualist who took the line suggested above. But his position runs wildly counter to common sense. For it is part of our common-sense view of reality that mental events do indeed stand in temporal relations in precisely the same primary sense as do physical events. Indeed, there seems to me to be something right about Kant's assertion that time is 'the form of the inner sense': what we are aware of within our own stream of consciousness serves as a kind of paradigm of temporal relatedness, which is then extended to the world at large. Of course the dualist might concede that his view conflicts with common sense in this respect; accepting, however, that the conclusion I have drawn regarding the spatiality of mental events follows logically from the stated premisses, he might regard the denial of premiss (2) as the only way of avoiding the offence to common sense involved in attributing spatial locations to mental events. But I should have thought that locating mental events in space was far less offensive to common sense than denying them a location, in the primary sense, in time.

Just how perverse would be the position of such a dualist becomes even more evident when one reflects that any set of events could, using the same strategy, be exempted from the strictures of special relativity. All one has to say is that such ostensible temporal relations as they stand in hold only in a derivative sense, grounded in the causal relations in which they stand to such events as are not so exempted. It is not, I think, merely the arbitrariness of such a move that offends. Rather, there is something deeply perplexing about so divorcing temporal relations, in their central, primary sense, from causal relations. Time and causality are, in our ordinary ways of thinking, intertwined and interdependent concepts.

Note

The material in this chapter is, in the main, drawn from three articles previously published in *Analysis* (Lockwood, 1984a, 1984b, 1985). Peter Gibbins (1985) drew my attention to the article by Weingard (1977), and also a remark of Russell (1927, p. 384) to the effect that the theory of relativity so mixes up space and time as to make it incoherent to suppose that mental events could be in time without being in space.

6

How Unified is Consciousness?

Descartes, as we saw in chapter 1, regarded the (ostensibly) all-or-nothing unity of consciousness as a decisive objection to any materialist conception of mind. His point was that, within the physical world, unity is invariably a matter of degree, depending as it must on spatial proximity, cohesion of parts, functional integration or causal connectedness, all of which are themselves a matter of degree. For him, therefore, only the entire physical universe, considered as a whole, is possessed of the absolute unity that belongs to each individual conscious mind. Strictly speaking, there is, for Descartes, only a single physical *substance*, in his sense, of which individual living human bodies are merely parts; but the conscious minds associated with these bodies are, all of them, fully distinct mental substances in their own right.

Not all philosophers, however, would accept that consciousness does possess any such absolute intrinsic unity as Descartes ascribes to it. In this chapter I shall consider an influential line of thought which is intended to cast doubt on this Cartesian unity; it is due to the contemporary American philosopher Thomas Nagel (1979a). In the first part of this chapter I shall give a summary of his argument, heavily embroidered with observations of my own. I shall then criticize his conclusions and suggest an alternative way of dealing with the difficulties that Nagel raises for the Cartesian view.

Nagel's views arise from reflection on the commissurotomy or 'split-brain' patients, briefly considered at the end of chapter 4. What we naturally want to ask about these patients is: how many (conscious) minds do they possess? If Descartes is right, this question should admit of a determinate answer: presumably 'one' or 'two'. But, argues Nagel, neither of these answers is satisfactory. That there are two minds here, two distinct streams of consciousness, is the position taken by Sperry, who pioneered the early experiments which first revealed such strikingly dissociated behaviour:

> Instead of the normally unified single stream of consciousness, these patients behave in many ways as if they have two independent streams of conscious awareness, one in each hemisphere, each of which is cut off from and out of contact with the mental experiences of the other. In other words, each hemisphere seems to have its own separate and private sensations; its own perceptions; its own concepts; and its own impulses to act, with related volitional, cognitive, and learning experiences. Following the surgery, each hemisphere also has thereafter its own separate chain of memories that are rendered inaccessible to the recall processes of the other.
>
> (Sperry, 1968a, p. 724)

A nice example of the kind of behaviour that has led Sperry to this view is given by Wilkes (1978, p. 186). To illustrate the superiority of the right hemisphere over the left, as regards 'Gestalt perception, spatial relations tests, and perceptuomotor tasks', she describes a film made by Sperry of one his patients, (shown at Princeton in 1971):

> The patient was asked to form a structure from a number of building blocks, using the right hand only; this was done in full view. The right hand was clumsy and slow, and the left hand moved in to help, brushing aside the right hand. The experimenter pushed away the left hand. A few moments later the left hand again attempted to take over; this time the patient, with his right hand, grasped the left wrist and pushed it away. But you cannot keep a good hand down; in the end the patient had to sit on the intrusive left hand, to prevent it from interfering further.

This astonishing behaviour is strongly reminiscent of the famous scene in the film *Dr Strangelove*, where the eponymous doctor's left hand battles with the right in an attempt to restrain it from making a Nazi salute. Here, the temptation to view the situation as involving two minds occupying a single body is virtually irresistible. Thus Sperry's position, as Nagel concedes, 'has much to recommend it'. But it fails, he thinks, to account satisfactorily for (what he claims to be) the thoroughly integrated manner in which these patients behave under normal, non-contrived conditions. Commissurotomy operations had been performed periodically for at least a decade before Sperry devised ways of presenting the two hemispheres with divergent information; but before Sperry's experiments the literature contains no reports of any behavioural dissociation in patients who had undergone such operations. Some people (for example Puccetti (1973)) have attempted to explain this integratedness, consistently with there being two distinct streams of consciousness, by suggesting that there were two distinct streams of consciousness even *before* the severing of the corpus callosum. According to this view, the two hemispheres are associated with distinct minds even in perfectly normal people; and the reason why the behaviour of commissurotomy patients exhibits, under normal circumstances, such a high degree of integration, is that these two minds, like an elderly and devoted married couple, have had a lifetime's practice in mutual cooperation! But the objection to that, as Nagel points out, is that it seems arbitrary. If the two hemispheres are to be assigned distinct streams of consciousness, even when they are joined by nerve fibres, then why should one not suppose that different centres within the same hemisphere are associated with distinct minds?

This last point of Nagel's may be bolstered by the following consideration. In the last chapter we concluded that it is possible in principle to assign to conscious events spatial locations within the brain. Now, in a normal individual, it is doubtless possible to find pairs of brain locations, situated in opposite hemispheres, that are spatially closer to each other, and which are (by any reasonable criterion) more intimately connected neurophysiologically, than are many pairs of locations that lie within the same hemisphere. It therefore seems likely that this is true, in particular, of pairs of spatial locations at which there are occurring simultaneous experiences (simultaneous, say, in the frame of reference within which the brain itself is at rest). So it clearly is, on the face of it, arbitrary to suppose that it is whether or not they occur in the same hemisphere that, in a normal brain, is the crucial determinant of whether two simultaneous experiences belong to the same stream of consciousness.

What, then of the suggestion that there is only a single stream of consciousness associated with the brain of a commissurotomy patient? This subdivides into two possibilities, which Nagel considers separately. First, there is the possibility that, both before and after the operation, it is, in normal people, only the left hemisphere that is conscious. This is the position taken by the eminent neurophysiologist John Eccles, and defended by him in a book written jointly with Karl Popper (Popper and Eccles, 1977). Eccles, actually, is a Cartesian dualist. For him the mind is a distinct entity, which interacts with the brain in a region, dubbed by Eccles the 'liaison brain', which he supposes to be located in the left hemisphere. But leaving aside the dualism, the idea that the left hemisphere has a monopoly on consciousness is hardly borne out by the known facts. There are people walking around whose left hemispheres have been totally destroyed. When this happens in adulthood, the patients usually never recover normal speech, and are generally of low intelligence; but they nevertheless give every appearance of being conscious. Moreover, children who suffer destruction of the left hemisphere in early infancy do, as a rule, learn to speak normally; the right hemisphere then seems to be capable of assuming most left hemisphere functions.

Perhaps Eccles thinks that in such cases the mind establishes relations with the right hemisphere, *faute de mieux* so to speak. But then there are also some people in whom there is relatively little lateralization – in whom, that is to say, such functions as language are performed more or less equally by both hemispheres, which are accordingly said to be *codominant*. What does Eccles think about them? As far as behavioural evidence goes, the mind would appear, in Eccles's terms, to be liaising equally with both hemispheres. If this is so in these unusual cases, it seems arbitrary to deny that it is true of the rest of us as well, seeing that hemispheric dominance is clearly a matter of degree. (It has even been suggested that, statistically, lateralization of brain function may be more marked in men than in women, though the most recent evidence seems not to bear this out.)

That brings us to the possibility that there is a single mind, encompassing both hemispheres, both before and after commissurotomy. The only person I know of who has defended this view is Wilkes (1978), whose paper was written in response to Nagel's. Anyone who takes this line is presumably prepared to give decisive weight to the integration exhibited under normal circumstances, regarding the dissociated behaviour evoked by the experiment as akin, perhaps, to the sort of scatter-brained (!) thinking and behaviour we all exhibit from time to time. A colleague told me how he once tramped home in the rain, wishing he had his car. On reaching his house, and seeing his car, he momentarily thought to himself: 'How splendid! Here's the car, now I can drive home.' Perhaps the bit of his mind that, recognizing the car and wanting to get home, had this mad thought, was fleetingly out of contact with the part of his mind which knew full well that he and his car *were* at home.

In addition to alluding to this sort of occurrence (to which philosophers are, perhaps, more prone than most people), Wilkes draws an analogy between the behaviour, in the experimental situation, of split-brain patients, and the mundane phenomenon of what she calls 'divided attention'. The example she gives is the familiar one of an experienced motorist driving while carrying on a conversation. Here we seem to have two disconnected, but within themselves highly integrated, cognitive activities going on in parallel with each other. Moreover, if asked, the motorist, assuming that he has been sufficiently absorbed in the conversation, may be totally unable to describe what, on the driving side, he has been doing over the past several minutes; and this may seem analogous to the commissurotomy subject's inability to say what is in the left side of his visual field.

But such analogies seem to me pretty lame. Cases of the sort related by my colleague can, surely, be fully and satisfactorily accounted for simply on the basis of one's having temporarily forgotten or overlooked something that should be, and normally would be, obvious: there is no need to suppose that at the moment of absent-mindedness there is *any* part of one's *conscious* mind that is aware of the consideration in question. Similarly with 'divided attention'. The key question is whether Wilkes's preoccupied motorist really is *conscious* of his driving, or whether he is doing it automatically. I would argue that cases of divided attention in normal subjects actually tend to fall into one of three categories, none of which implies any division within the subject's consciousness: (a) the subject is doing one of the things automatically, that is to say without giving it any *conscious* attention at all; or (b) he is constantly switching his attention from one to the other; or (c) a combination of (a) and (b) – sporadic conscious attention to each task, interspersed with automatism. That account seems largely to be borne out by the wealth of psychological evidence that, as regards our conscious activities, we tend to behave as 'single-channel' systems.

Some psychologists, indeed, have seen in this single-channel character a clue to the evolutionary role of consciousness. The brain, as we have seen, goes in for a great deal of processing of information in parallel. And parallel computers are prone to get into various forms of impasse, to which serial computers, for all their limitations, are immune. The best known such impasse goes by the picturesque name of the *deadly embrace*; it arises when each of two processors is waiting for information from the other, before it can proceed with its own appointed task, with the result that they are both frozen into inactivity. One way of avoiding such impasses is to have a serial computer sitting on top, providing a kind of global control, rather as the so-called *operating system* does in a conventional computer. That, so it is suggested by Johnson-Laird (1983, pp. 451–77), is precisely the role played by consciousness in relation to the largely parallel, but unconscious, activities of the brain. (This is an intriguing idea. But of course it remains obscure, on Johnson-Laird's account, why an *unconscious* serial computer wouldn't do just as well.)

To be fair to Wilkes, she herself nowhere claims that divided attention implies divided consciousness. Indeed, she is sceptical about the whole concept of the unity of consciousness and, like Nagel, thinks it unable to deal with the empirical realities. Where she differs from Nagel is in thinking that the sorts of dissociated behaviour exhibited by split-brain patients can be accommodated within a unitary concept of person, and perhaps even mind, when the latter is not equated with conscious mind. From our present point of view, however, that is neither here nor there. What we are concerned with precisely is the unity of *consciousness*, rather than that of a person or a mind. As regards that issue, split-brain patients remain problematic. And if Wilkes is right in seeing more familiar cases of absent-mindedness, divided attention and so forth as relevantly similar to the split-brain cases, then so far from solving anything, this just means that the problem begins closer to home than we had realized.

The only possibility now remaining is an unattractive variant of the one-(conscious)-mind view, according to which the experimental set-up induces a temporary division of a unitary consciousness into two streams, which subsequently reunite. That, as Nagel says, fails to take sufficient account of the fact that, during the experiment, the subject's behaviour can be highly integrated in some respects while being highly dissociated in others. Besides, it is difficult to believe that the experimental set-up could have such momentous effects as this view implies.

From the standpoint of our ordinary common-sense concept of a person, these possibilities would appear to exhaust the field. And yet none of them seems wholly satisfactory. What, then, should we conclude? Nagel argues that we should jettison our common-sense assumption (vigorously defended by Descartes) that the unity of consciousness is an all-or-nothing affair. In commissurotomy cases, there may, Nagel thinks, be no definite answer to the question how many selves, or conscious subjects, are present. He argues that such cases undermine the unity assumption implicit in our ordinary concept of a person.

I think there is a sense in which Nagel may be right here; and I shall attempt in a moment to formulate a principle which, though implicit in our ordinary thinking, is called into question by split-brain phenomena. Nevertheless, what Nagel himself actually goes on to say about commissurotomy patients seems to me to make no clear sense. His view, as I said, is that there is *no* definite number of conscious subjects present here. It is correct neither to say that there is just one self, just one stream of consciousness, nor to say that there are two. What we have is a situation intermediate between these alternatives, one for which ordinary language and thought about persons is effectively unprepared.

That, he admits, is on the face of it a deeply perplexing suggestion: on his account of the matter, it is, as he says, 'difficult to conceive what it is like to *be* one of these people' (Nagel, 1979a, p. 160). This difficulty he diagnoses thus:

> The fundamental problem in trying to understand these cases in mentalistic terms is that we take ourselves as paradigms of

psychological unity, and are then unable to project ourselves into their mental lives, either once or twice.

(Nagel, 1979a, p. 163)

Now there are two distinct ways in which it might be claimed to be impossible for some person to imagine, in some particular aspect, the mental life of another. One is if the person lacks the requisite phenomenal concepts. This, I take it, is what prevents the congenitally blind person from imagining the experience of seeing, and likewise – to take Nagel's own celebrated example – what prevents any of us from projecting ourselves into the sensory world of a bat. Nagel's account of commissurotomy patients seems to me, however, to imply a stronger kind of impossibility: if Nagel were right, then nothing, as far as I can see, would *count* as successfully imagining their mental lives. It isn't simply a matter of lacking the conceptual wherewithal; regardless of one's stock of phenomenal concepts, there are, on Nagel's view, no possible acts of projection that, jointly or individually, would do the trick.

But how can this be? Elsewhere, Nagel himself (1979b, anticipated by Sprigge, 1971) has argued – correctly, in my view – that the key criterion of whether something is conscious or sentient is whether there is a 'what it is like to be' that thing. Assuming that split-brain subjects are conscious at all, it follows that there must be at least one 'what it is like to be' associated with the brain of each such subject. If so, there must surely, given the right concepts, be something that would count as *imagining* what it is like to be such a subject; and by the same token, there will be an answer to the question how many distinct such imaginings – that is, acts of projection – are called for, in order to capture the 'inside story'.

So where do we go from here? Well, if, as it now appears, Nagel's own theory is ultimately incoherent, one might wonder whether one of the tentatively rejected alternatives was, after all, defensible. And, ostensibly, it is the two-minds theory that has the most going for it. Indeed, Nagel's arguments for rejecting this alternative are hardly decisive. Nagel places great stress on the apparent normality of split-brain patients when they are not in the experimental situation. But it is possible to explain this normality, consistently with there being two streams of consciousness. In the first place, the two hemispheres of a split-brain patient will, under normal circumstances, be receiving broadly the same information, and certainly consistent information. And secondly, these patients appear, in most cases, to be highly motivated towards behavioural integration. There is a wealth of evidence to support this. Split-brain patients, in the experimental situation, employ all manner of cunning stratagems to defeat the experimenter, by conveying information from one side to the other: signalling with the facial muscles and so forth. Moreover, in some experiments by the MacKays (1982), it was found to be impossible to get the two hemispheres to compete with each other, so to speak, in a simple game. Once again, each side of the body exhibited behaviour clearly designed, as it were, to give the other side a helping hand.

Quite apart from that, there is, contrary to what Nagel suggests, a certain amount of evidence for dissociated behaviour in split-brain patients, even outside the experimental situation. Sperry (1966) cites the case of a man who was seen to embrace his wife with one hand, whilst pushing her away with the other, and Puccetti (1973) mentions a rather similar case of a man one of whose hands pushed away a plate of food, whilst the other pulled it towards him. (Monkeys on whom commissuro-tomies have been performed have also been seen to pull at opposite ends of a nut, though only until they woke up to what they were doing.) Geschwind (1983) discusses a classic case (originally described by the neurologist Kurt Goldstein in 1908) of a woman who verbally disowned the left side of her body, describing it as 'evil', and whose left hand made repeated attempts to strangle her. On the basis of his examination of the patient, Goldstein diagnosed damage to the corpus callosum; and this was subsequently confirmed on autopsy. This is an extreme case; but a milder example of dissociation was described on British television, some years ago. A commissurotomy patient, being interviewed by Colin Blakemore, told him how she had gone to her wardrobe to get out a green dress and found, to her amazement, her left hand reaching out and taking a red one. It should be said, however, that the interpretation of these cases of dissociated behaviour is a matter of some controversy; and many workers in the field believe that they are to be attributed to brain damage additional to the commissurotomy. (Most commissurotomy patients _are_ suffering from additional brain damage, consequent upon repeated epileptic fits.) But still, we may reasonably ask: what precisely is affected by this additional damage? And the obvious answer is: the motivational system. The streams of consciousness associated with the two hemispheres may, therefore, be sharply divided even where there is no additional brain damage, the effect of the additional damage being only to reduce the drive towards cooperation.

That said, however, there remains something deeply unsatisfactory about a philosophical position that obliges one to impose this rigid dichotomy upon the experimental and clinical facts: either we have just one centre, or stream, of consciousness, or else we have two (or more), entirely distinct from each other. How, for example, are we to accommodate the fact that many commissurotomy patients gradually become less dissociated, even in the experimental situation, as time elapses after the operation? More precisely, how do we accommodate this gradual recovery, on the assumption that it is due to lower pathways, involving the brain stem, taking over some of the functions previously served by the corpus callosum. (An alternative possibility, put to me by Lawrence Weiskrantz, is that it is due to the right hemisphere's assuming left-hemispheric functions, such as speech and control over the left side of the body; that, clearly, would present no problems for the two-minds view.) Then again, what do proponents of the two-minds theory imagine would be the correct description of patients in whom the corpus callosum was gradually severed, one fibre at a time, always while the patients were fully conscious, over a period of several hours, days, months or years? Do they think that at some point in what was essentially a continuous process, a fully unified consciousness would instantaneously turn into two wholly distinct ones? This hardly seems plausible. (It may be worth pointing out in this context that a recent investigation by Weiskrantz and others revealed that, in a substantial proportion of commissurotomy patients, the corpus callosum turned out not to have been totally severed: there remained a significant number of intact fibres.)

Is there, then, after all, some way of matching up the spectrum of physiological possibilities – that is to say, degrees of neural connectedness of the two hemispheres – with a corresponding spectrum of possibilities at the level of consciousness? Can we do this without lapsing into the kind of incoherence to which, so I have argued, Nagel's account gives rise?

I believe we can. First, however, I think we must put aside some of the vague and metaphorical language we have thus far been using in talking about these patients, and the possible ways of construing their behaviour. Let us stop talking, for the moment, about streams of consciousness, centres of consciousness or even selves or minds or persons. Instead, let us talk in terms of *experiences*. 'Experience' here is to be understood in the philosopher's slightly technical sense of a conscious state, happening, or sequence of states or happenings, that is experienced *as a whole*. Thus a single note, or the corresponding auditory sensation, can be experienced as a whole, provided it is not too prolonged, and so, one might think, can a series of notes confined within the space of a second or less. These, then, would count as experiences; but the sequence of auditory sensations produced by several minute's worth of conscious attention to a symphony, say, would not. Rather, it would consist of a sequence of experiences. Thus understood, an experience can clearly have experiences as parts. An experience of a sequence of notes played in very quick succession may contain as parts experiences of the individual notes. And likewise, if I see a woman standing by a horse, I have a visual experience which contains as parts the experience of seeing the woman and the experience of seeing the horse. Likewise, I may have an audio-visual experience which contains, as parts, the experiences of seeing a man playing a trombone and of hearing the sound he is producing. (I am not denying, incidentally, that there is more to each of the larger experiences just cited than the parts I have mentioned; for example, I am also experiencing, in the first case, the temporal *relations* between the notes, and in the second, the spatial relation between the woman and the horse. Experiences are typically more than the sum of their experiential parts.)

It will be useful to have a term for an experience which does not form a part of any larger experience. I shall refer to this as a *phenomenal perspective* or a *maximal experience*. Intuitively, a phenomenal perspective or maximal experience encompasses the total contents of a given state of awareness. It will also be useful to have a term for the relation in which two experiences stand, when there is an experience of which they are both parts (understanding 'part' in the logician's sense in which, as a limiting case, anything may be regarded as a 'part' of itself). Let us say, following a number of other philosophers (for example Parfit, 1984, pp. 248–52), that they are *co-conscious*. With that, I am in a position to give precise statement to a key assumption which seems to me to govern our ordinary common-sense thinking about persons. It is this. *For any three experiences, a, b, and c, which are sufficiently close together in time, if a is co-conscious with b and b is co-conscious with c, then it follows that a is co-conscious with c.* Technically, this amounts to saying that, for experiences which are sufficiently close together in time, co-consciousness is a *transitive* relation. So I shall refer to it as the *transitivity principle*.

What, the reader may wonder, is the thinking behind the qualification, 'sufficiently close together in time'? Well, simply that it would be natural to regard experiences as temporally overlapping. If I hear a sequence of notes, say Do, Re, Mi, Fa, So, played at an appropriate tempo, then I may have the sequence of experiences, Do, Do–Re, Do–Re–Mi, Re–Mi–Fa, Mi–Fa–So, Fa–So, So. Thus the experience of Do would be co-conscious with the experience of Re, and likewise the experience of Re co-conscious with the experience of Fa, but the experience of Do not be co-conscious with the experience of Fa. The temporal dimension of experience is a matter to which I shall return later in the chapter, and which I shall discuss at length in chapter 16.

Now it goes without saying (given our understanding of 'part') that every experience is co-conscious with itself: in logician's jargon, co-consciousness is a *reflexive* relation. Furthermore, if a is co-conscious with b, then b must be co-conscious with a; that is to say, co-consciousness is also a *symmetric* relation. Now relations that are transitive, reflexive and symmetric are known as *equivalence relations*; and equivalence relations have a rather interesting property. Given an equivalence relation R, and a set of objects each of which bears the relation R to at least one object in the set (if only to itself), R has the effect of *partitioning* the set into mutually exclusive and jointly exhaustive subsets; the objects in each subset bear the relation R to all the other objects in the subset, but to no objects in the other subsets. 'Born in the same year as' is a good example of an equivalence relation. Given a group of school-children, the relation has the effect of partitioning the group into those born in 1979, those born in 1980, those born in 1981 and so on.

The point of this excursus into the theory of relations is that it enables us to give a precise rendering of what I take to be the common-sense view of consciousness, or rather co-consciousness, in relation to experiences that are sufficiently close together in time. According to common sense, such experiences may invariably be grouped into mutually exclusive and jointly exhaustive collections of co-conscious experiences: each experience belongs to one, and only one, collection. Since co-consciousness is undeniably reflexive and symmetric, the only contestable assumption upon which this conception rests is the transitivity principle. If one rejects that assumption, a remarkable possibility immediately opens up; that of simultaneous, *overlapping* phenomenal perspectives. And it is in these terms, I believe, that we should seek to understand the split-brain cases.

One widely cited experiment that has been performed on commissurotomy patients of both sexes involves projecting the picture of a naked person of the opposite sex on to a part of the retina that projects only to the right hemisphere, and which is thus inaccessible to the speech centres. Typically, the subject blushes and is visibly embarrassed, but is unable to say why. Nevertheless, it is clear that the whole subject experiences some emotional reaction. One male subject remarked: 'Wow, that's some machine you've got there!' Now much of the literature on split-brains seems to assume that consciousness is confined to the cerebral hemispheres. But without any real evidence. Indeed, the evidence, such as it is, would seem to me to point the other way. For example, emotion plays a major role in consciousness yet, as we saw in chapter 4, many of the brain centres that appear to be centrally involved with emotion, most notably the amygdala, lie below the cerebral hemispheres – and, *a fortiori*, below the level of the corpus callosum. That, no doubt, is why, in the experiment, both hemispheres have access to the embarrassment and/or sexual arousal, while only the inarticulate right hemisphere has access to the reason behind it.

It is convenient here to decompose an emotion, as psychologists and psychiatrists commonly do, into a cognitive and an *affective* component: roughly, a thought component and a feeling component. What I now wish to suggest is that the affective components of embarrassment and sexual arousal are, in whole or in part, literally *located* in the subhemispheric region of the brain. The conclusion of chapter 5 was that there are compelling reasons, stemming from relativity, for assigning physical locations to conscious states and events. And my suggestion is that the physical regions occupied by the affective components of states of consciousness lie, wholly or partly, in the diencephalon. If this is correct, then one would not expect commissurotomy alone to result in a complete fission within the consciousness of the subject. Co-consciousness, from the present point of view, would most naturally be construed as a relation between physically located states and events in the brain; and one that is, presumably – though no one yet understands how or why – a function of neural connectedness. Given these assumptions, the virtually inescapable conclusion is this. There are experiences located in the diencephalon of normal and commissurotomy subjects alike, that are co-conscious both with conscious events occurring in the left hemisphere and with ones occurring in the right. But the effect of commissurotomy is to render certain experiences, located respectively in the left and right hemispheres, non-co-conscious with each other. Thus, co-consciousness, within the commissurotomy patient, *ceases to be a transitive relation* – ceases, that is, to be transitive even in respect of 'simultaneous' experiences. In the experiment just described, the psychological reaction of the subject – embarrassment, sexual arousal or whatever – comprises, say, a left-hemispheric cognitive component which is co-conscious with an affective component in the diencephalon, which in turn is co-conscious with a right-hemispheric cognitive component; yet the left-hemispheric component is not co-conscious with the right-hemispheric component. Hence, we have a situation that can be represented schematically as in figure 6.1. We have two phenomenal perspectives, each occupying part of one cerebral hemisphere and extending down into the diencephalon, where they coincide.

This way of looking at things immediately solves the main problem that the Cartesian view seems to face us with, in relation to split-brain patients. With the rejection of the transitivity principle, we are no longer obliged to ascribe to commissurotomy subjects some integral number of *completely separate* centres or streams of consciousness; and we are in a position to allow for gradual change, or a spectrum of possibilities, representing degrees of connectedness. If we start by assuming that the transitivity principle holds true of normal subjects (an assumption that I shall presently question), then the effect of gradually severing the corpus callosum would, on the present view, be to cause the range of overlap between the associated sets of experiences gradually to diminish. That is to say, we should start out with all of the subject's experiences, within a sufficiently small time interval, being co-conscious with all the others. Then, as more and more fibres were cut, the proportion of experiences in one hemisphere that were not co-conscious with those in the other hemisphere would gradually increase, until finally, with no fibres in the

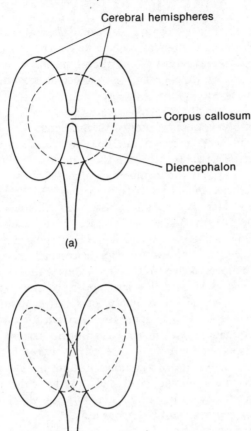

Figure 6.1 *A possible effect of severing the corpus callosum is to transform a single unitary state of awareness, represented by the dotted circle in (a), into two overlapping states, as in (b).*

corpus callosum remaining intact, it might be that no experience in either hemisphere was co-conscious with any experience in the other.

That is what is implied by figure 6.1. But I am far from confident that this is the situation in fact, since, as I mentioned earlier, the two hemispheres are also connected to each other via other lower pathways; and it is not improbable that these connections suffice to support some residual relations of co-consciousness which span the two hemispheres. In any event, after the operation, new relations of co-consciousness mediated by these lower pathways may well come into existence, as fibres in these pathways begin to take over some of the functions previously performed by the corpus callosum. That would certainly square with the behavioural evidence, though as I remarked earlier this behavioural evidence is equally consistent with the alternative theory that, when the hemispheres are disconnected, each begins to acquire cognitive skills that were previously the monopoly of the other.

Unlike Nagel's, the present view creates no problems in imagining what it is like to be a commissurotomy patient. On the simplest model of what is going on here, in my terms, there are just two sequences of phenomenal perspectives. To repeat: a single phenomenal perspective is composed of all and only the members of some set of experiences, such that every experience in the set is co-conscious with every other, and every experience which is co-conscious with every experience in the set is itself a member of that set. But, as we have seen, phenomenal perspectives, thus defined, may overlap. For this characterization of phenomenal perspectives allows for experiences that are not part of a given phenomenal perspective to be co-conscious with some experiences that are, provided only that they are not co-conscious with all the experiences that are contained within this perspective. So, in the simplest case, all that is required to imagine a given state of awareness of a commissurotomy patient is to imagine each of his current, overlapping phenomenal perspectives in turn. *Pace* Nagel, just two acts of 'projecting ourselves into the mental life' of a commissurotomy patient will suffice; it is no more problematic to imagine what it is like to be these patients, on the present view, than it is on Sperry's, according to which there are two completely separate streams of consciousness.

But what of the normal brain? Is the transitivity principle true, even of subjects with fully intact brains? I don't know the answer to this question. The only thing that can be said, at a philosophical level, is that it would be muddled thinking to take, as an argument for the truth of the transitivity principle in relation to ourselves, the fact that we don't *feel* disunified within ourselves. (Or not, at any rate, in any sense relevant to the present discussion – conflicting desires and the like are not germane here.) What is accessible to any act of introspection will invariably be the contents of a single phenomenal perspective. For that reason, commissurotomy patients aren't going to *feel* disunified either. The issue is just *how many* overall unified-feeling states of awareness – that is to say, phenomenal perspectives or maximal experiences – there are at any given point in the biography of such patients, or of ourselves. And that is a question that sheer looking within oneself can do nothing to answer. It would be more to the point to see whether it was possible, in normal subjects, experimentally to evoke anything like the kind of behavioural dissociation found in commissurotomy patients.

(Interestingly, there *is* some evidence (Hilgard, 1986) that such dissociated behaviour can be evoked, in normal subjects, under hypnosis. In one experiment, a hypnotized subject was asked to keep his left hand in a bucket of ice-cold water. Normally, one would find this unbearable after a while, but the subject, having been told that he would feel no pain, seemed capable of keeping it there indefinitely, and denied with every appearance of sincerity that it was causing him any discomfort. When given a paper and pencil, however, his right hand started writing that he was feeling terrible pain, and abused the experimenter for putting him through such torment!)

In any case, there is a clear sense in which the difference between normal subjects, and those commissurotomy patients who have been found still to possess a residue of intact fibres, is only a matter of degree, physiologically speaking. After all, brain cells are dying all the time. Moreover, it has been found recently (Innocenti, 1987) that the number of fibres in the corpus callosum is reduced by 70 per cent between birth and maturity. This is not a matter of the cells themselves dying, and probably has something to do with the learning or maturation process, which may be as much a matter of *eliminating* connections between cells as of forming new ones. Nor is it known whether the rate at which fibres disappear during the course of maturation in the corpus callosum differs from that in the brain as a whole: the corpus callosum was chosen simply because the fibres there are easier to count than in other parts of the brain. Nevertheless, this reduction in the number of fibres may have to do with the growing specialization of the two hemispheres as we mature. It is, after all, a well-known fact that in early life either hemisphere is capable of developing the functions usually served by the other, if that other hemisphere is damaged. Thus, we have already seen that infants whose left hemispheres (or the parts of the left hemispheres that in normal people subserve speech) are destroyed, usually learn to talk normally. And it is tempting to wonder whether this growing specialization, with attendant reduction in the number of fibres linking the two hemispheres, is not accompanied by a diminishing overlap in the associated phenomenal perspectives.

It is interesting, in this context to find Geschwind and Galaburda (1987) arguing, on neuropsychological grounds, that optimal functioning of the brain may require just the right degree of what they term 'fusion' between the two hemispheres. Commissurotomy patients, clearly, suffer from insufficient fusion. But there are some things they can do better than normal people – for example, brushing their teeth with one hand whilst combing their hair with the other. The ideal, these authors argue, is not total fusion but something intermediate between complete fusion and what we find in commissurotomy patients. Geschwind and Galaburda are neurologists, not philosophers, and nowhere do they explain precisely what they mean by 'fusion'. Moreover, their book was apparently written before the evidence of natural 'culling' of fibres within the corpus callosum. But the conception presented here allows us to give a precise meaning of 'fusion', at the level of consciousness – namely degree of overlap of phenomenal perspectives. So it is intriguing to find neuroscientists arguing, in effect, for less than total overlap, in normal subjects, on essentially empirical grounds. It is also intriguing to speculate that the phenomenal perspectives associated with the two hemispheres may progressively diverge in the course of normal maturation, and that this may serve a useful purpose.

Even if these speculations are mistaken, it still seems to me rather unlikely, on general grounds, that the transitivity principle could hold true, even of normal subjects, except to a close approximation. Indeed, the correct picture of my current state of awareness may be of a large number of phenomenal perspectives which approximately coincide, as schematically represented in figure 6.2(a). And perhaps the natural decay of the brain – with fibres disappearing all over the brain, and not merely between the two hemispheres – is associated with increasing failure of co-consciousness between experiences occurring in different regions of the brain, so that we get a picture something like that represented in figure 6.2(b). Is it too fanciful to suppose that this may be one of the things involved in progressive dementias, such as Alzheimer's disease, and also, to a milder extent, in the simple muddle-headedness that often comes with normal ageing? Of course, it is difficult to say anything with much confidence here, in the absence of a proper theory as to what the physiological basis of co-consciousness is.

It is time now to get back to Descartes. Do the foregoing considerations serve to defuse Descartes's anti-materialist argument, resting as it does on the supposedly all-or-nothing character of the unity of consciousness? Not altogether, it seems to me. To be sure, the assumption with which Descartes begins has come to seem very questionable; his own conception of (conscious) minds as independent substances, fully unified within themselves, and wholly distinct one from another, fails to do justice to the empirical facts. And even in the absence of those facts, it is surely a shortcoming of his view that it fails to accommodate the *logical* possibility of simultaneous, overlapping phenomenal perspectives. But Descartes could still argue that *co-consciousness* was an all-or-nothing affair. Given two experiences, there is invariably (according to the view I have been developing) a clear-cut answer to the question 'Are they, or are they not, co-conscious?', or, equivalently, 'Is there, or is there not, a phenomenal perspective which embraces them both?' What I want now

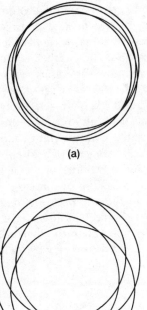

(a)

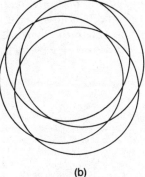

(b)

Figure 6.2 *Overlapping concurrent phenomenal perspectives, where any two points that lie within the same circle represent experiences that are co-conscious. In (a), which is intended to represent the situation with a normal healthy brain, the perspectives largely coincide; there may, in fact, be complete coincidence in this case. In (b), by contrast, there is a significant 'spread' or dissociation, which may conceivably be the situation that arises with progressive dementias, such as Alzheimer's disease.*

to consider, therefore, is whether it makes sense to construe co-consciousness as a matter of degree.

A consideration to which Nagel alludes, in defence of his own view, is the phenomenon of the gradual fading out of consciousness at what we sometimes refer to as the edges of awareness. One example is the way the visual field appears to have no clear-cut boundary. The size of our visual field is, of course, beyond our control; but I would argue that, in any case, we are only ever conscious of those parts of our visual field to which we are to some extent *attending*. And, once again, there are *degrees* of attention. But what are required to defeat Descartes are not degrees of consciousness but degrees of co-consciousness. The question, therefore,

·is whether it is possible to credit commissurotomy subjects with pairs of simultaneous experiences which are, considered individually, full-blooded conscious states or events, without being unambiguously either co-conscious or non-co-conscious – rather, something in between. What I am envisaging is a situation such as is schematically represented in figure 6.3. At any given time, there is a set of experiences associated with the left hemisphere, call it the left set, every member of which is unambiguously co-conscious with every other member of the set; and a set of experiences associated with the right hemisphere, the right set, of which the same can be said. But no pair of experiences consisting of a member of the left set and a member of the right set can be said to be unambiguously either co-conscious or non-co-conscious. Hence, there is no determinate answer to the question how many conscious minds the commissurotomy subject should be said to have. Resolve the ambiguity one way (transforming the broken line in figure 6.3 into a solid line), and the answer is two; resolve it the other way (deleting the broken line in figure 6.3) and the answer is one.

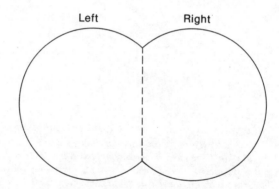

Left   Right

Figure 6.3 *A depiction of phenomenal perspectives, associated with the left and right hemispheres of a commissurotomy patient, which stand in a relation that is ambiguous as between coincidence and overlap: the experiences on the left of the broken line are neither determinately co-conscious nor determinately non-co-conscious with those on the right of the line.*

Superficially, this may seem, contrary to what I suggested earlier, to make perfectly good coherent sense. To see why it is problematic, however, consider now the following situation. Suppose we have a subject (or perhaps I should say 'subjects') with two series of phenomenal perspectives, the P stream and the Q stream, three successive temporal cross-sections of which are represented in figure 6.4. Initially (figure 6.4(a)), there is a pair of phenomenal perspectives, P_1 and Q_1, which

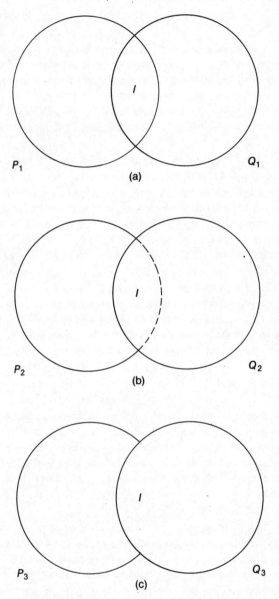

Figure 6.4 *A representation of a succession of situations, involving two streams of consciousness, a P stream and a Q stream.*

In (a) we have two phenomenal perspectives, belonging respectively to the P and Q streams, which overlap only in respect of the single experience I. In (b), it has become ambiguous whether I is co-conscious with those other experiences that unambiguously belong to the P stream. In (c), I is determinately non-conscious with the experiences in the P stream: the two streams are now unambiguously non-overlapping.

overlap solely in respect of the experience I which, to make matters concrete, we may imagine to be a persistent itch (unscratched during the relevant time interval) at the tip of the subject's nose. (In other words, every experience in P_1 is co-conscious with every other experience in P_1, and similarly with Q_1. But no experience in P_1 is co-conscious with any experience in Q_1, with the exception of I, which is co-conscious with every experience belonging either to P_1 or to Q_1.) We now imagine, in line with the supposition that co-consciousness admits of degrees, that the relation of co-consciousness holding between I and the remaining members of the P stream is gradually weakened, while the intrinsic phenomenal character of I remains unaltered. Eventually, when the relation has been weakened to vanishing point, we shall have the situation represented by figure 6.4(c). I has ceased to be co-conscious, to any degree, with any of the experiences in the P stream, and we have two disjoint (non-overlapping) phenomenal perspectives: I now figures only in the Q stream. Figure 6.4 (b) shows the intermediate situation, in which I is neither unambiguously co-conscious nor unambiguously non-co-conscious with the (remaining) members of P_2.

The question now is: how would this sequence of events appear, from the standpoint of the P stream? At stage (a) there would be an itch, I. At stage (c) the itch would appear to be gone. But how, subjectively, would the transition from (a) to (c) be experienced? Clearly, it would be inconsistent with the gradualness of the transition that I should be experienced as suddenly disappearing from the P stream. So the only coherent supposition open to us, as far as I can see, is that I is experienced, from the standpoint of the P stream, as *gradually* fading from consciousness. That supposition, however, seems palpably at odds with the assumption that I – whose intrinsic character we took to be unaltered over the period of the transition – is, throughout, genuinely the *same* experience, as it figures in the P stream and the Q stream. For, as it begins to fade from the P stream, the perceived character of I must surely become different as it figures in the two streams.

This would appear to be a *reductio ad absurdum* of the notion of degrees of co-consciousness. Co-consciousness must after all, it seems, be an all-or-nothing relation. In this sense, then, the unity of consciousness ostensibly returns to haunt the would-be materialist.

There is, however, another consideration which may suggest that there is more to be said on this issue. For there is a striking parallel between the situation just envisaged and a way philosophers and psychologists sometimes conceive of our perception of time. I have in mind the concept of the so-called *specious present*: the idea that states of awareness are tied, not so much to instants of time, but to brief temporal intervals. I remarked earlier that it would be natural to regard one's awareness as having a certain temporal span, since it would seem to be possible experientially to grasp *as a whole* any sufficiently brief sequence of events, or extended event: a word, of more than one syllable even, or a bar of music. Thus, to revert to the example given earlier in the chapter, one's awareness, in relation to the sequence of notes Do, Re, Mi, Fa, So, might successively comprise an experience of Do, followed by Do–Re, followed by Do–Re–Mi, followed by Re–Mi–Fa, and so on. Now if we think of Do, Re, Mi, etc. as single auditory experiences, then we have a situation, with regard to the specious present, that is parallel to that just envisaged, with regard to the itch. For the temporal boundaries of the specious present are themselves going to be fuzzy. Consequently, the note Fa, say, even if we ignore the fact that it is itself temporally extended, is not going *suddenly* to disappear from one's awareness, as the boundaries of the specious present move forward in time. Of some total state of awareness, or maximal experience, the question 'Does it contain one's experience of the note Fa?' must fail to admit of a clear-cut yes or no answer.

But then drawing this parallel, so far from helping vindicate the idea of degrees of co-consciousness, serves, arguably, only to tar the notion of the specious present with the same brush; for we get the same problem as before. Surely, the character of the experience, if it lies at the very periphery of one's awareness, so that one cannot be sure whether one is experiencing it at all, will be different from when it figures centrally and unambiguously in one's awareness? So how can it *be* the very same experience, as it figures centrally in one phenomenal perspective, and peripherally in a subsequent perspective? Doesn't this suggest that the whole concept of the specious present is a confused one, and that phenomenal perspectives are not, in reality, temporally extended at all? Must we not insist that experiences that are co-conscious correspond to states or events in the brain that are simultaneous (in some suitable frame of reference)? And wouldn't it then follow that the appearance of temporal extendedness, within a phenomenal perspective, is an illusion generated by the simultaneous co-presence within consciousness of current experiences and what, strictly speaking, are merely vivid *memories* of past experiences that are phenomenally very similar in character? What this would imply is that the neurophysiological correlate of our overall state of awareness, when we take ourselves to be experiencing, within a single phenomenal perspective, a temporally extended array of, say, auditory sensations, is in reality an instantaneous but *spatially* extended array of brain states that serves to *encode* a temporally extended sequence of sensations. Compare the way a teleprompter works. At any given instant, the speaker is faced with a screen, on which are represented, all at the *same* time, a sequence of words which, as spoken, extend over a *period* of time. On the view just envisaged, a given phenomenal perspective stands to a temporally extended stretch of consciousness much as do the instantaneous, spatially extended contents of the teleprompter screen to the corresponding sequence of utterances. (I shall be discussing this at length in chapter 15.)

Such conclusions may seem difficult to resist. Yet resist them I shall, for the present. What has clearly emerged, I think (and the discovery is an unexpected one), is that the concept of the specious present, and the concept of degrees of co-consciousness as between states and events that are unambiguously experiences, must stand or fall together. To assume outright, however, on the basis of the considerations advanced in the last few pages, that neither concept can be retrieved would, I suggest, mean placing excessive faith in the adequacy of the way we have thus far been conceptualizing these issues. We must beware, as Wittgenstein remarked in a different context, of allowing a certain picture to hold us captive. In due course, I want to suggest an alternative picture, an alternative way of thinking about these problems. But there are other matters that must be attended to first.

7

State Space

Let us briefly take stock. Evidence has been accumulating, in the last few chapters, for a form of materialism that is nonfunctionalist, and which equates mental states and events with states and events in the brain in the manner of the identity theory. We have found, in special relativity, a powerful argument for the identity theory, inasmuch as it implies that mental states must be in space given that they are in time.

The Achilles heel of functionalism was found to be the phenomenal qualities. And the considerations which led us to reject functionalism might at the same time be taken to suggest that it is the specific physical character of brain states, rather than their causal–functional role, that is responsible for the phenomenal character of the corresponding experiences. But I have given little indication as yet of just how phenomenal qualities might reflect the physical character of the brain states on which they supervene. There are, in fact, some extremely knotty philosophical problems here with which we have not yet properly come to grips. Before we do so, however, and in order to prepare the ground for much that I wish to say in the next few chapters, I want to inject a little more science into the discussion: specifically, to introduce a new key concept, that of a *state space*.

The concept of state space is one that has its origins in *classical dynamics* (where by 'classical' I now mean pre-quantum mechanics). The most widely encountered version is something called *phase space*. And I want to start with a discussion of classical mechanics, making use of this concept of phase space. The relevance of this to the philosophy of mind will not be immediately obvious, but I intend it to serve two main purposes. First, it will provide the reader with a clear and concrete example of a state space, one that can serve as a useful analogy for what I shall go on to say, later in the chapter, about phenomenal state spaces and the representation of information in the brain. Secondly, it will give us a platform from which, in chapter 11, we can embark on an explanation of quantum mechanics, which in its turn will be found to have a profound bearing on the place of mind within the material world. Properly to appreciate the revolution in thought which quantum mechanics involved, it is essential to have a clear conception of classical physics, as it was conceived in the early years of this century when the quantum revolution began.

To understand what is meant by phase space, in the context of classical dynamics, consider the following simple physical system (see figure 7.1). Imagine that you have a small weight, or *bob*, suspended by a spring. You pull the bob down and release it, whereupon it proceeds to move up and down with constant frequency and declining amplitude. This is an example of what physicists call a *simple harmonic oscillator*. Actually, it is a *damped* harmonic oscillator. This damping or attenuation of the motion is a consequence of friction with the air and dissipation of the energy through the not perfectly rigid support from which the spring is suspended. But let us idealize: imagine that the spring is suspended in a vacuum from a perfectly rigid (and rigidly fixed) bar, and that the bob is subject to no forces beyond that exerted by the spring itself and a downward gravitational pull, which is the same at all points on the

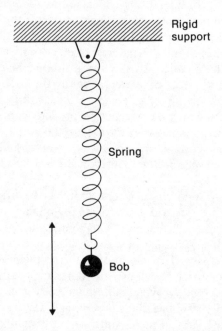

Figure 7.1 *Simple harmonic oscillator.*

vertical axis. The bob should then, in theory, continue to oscillate indefinitely, with constant frequency *and* amplitude.

Now classical mechanics is deterministic. What precisely does that mean, in the present context? Well suppose, first, we know how much force is exerted on the bob at each of the different points on its up and down trajectory: a mathematical relationship that allows us to calculate the force, given knowledge of where the bob is. And suppose, further, we know precisely what the bob is doing at some particular time *t*. Specifically, suppose we know its *position* at *t*, and its *momentum* at *t*, where its momentum is simply the product of its *mass* and its velocity. (The mass of an object is that property which causes it to be gravitationally attracted to other bodies and to resist attempts to change its state of motion; the greater the mass the greater this resistance or *inertia*. Mass must be distinguished from weight; astronauts in orbit may be *weight*less but their mass is no less than that of their earthbound colleagues.) Instead of taking the momentum we could take the velocity, since the momentum could then be calculated by multiplying it by the mass; but let's suppose that we're interested in accommodating a range of possibilities, in which bobs of different mass are suspended from the spring. Then the force law will allow us to calculate the position and momentum of the bob at any other time, earlier or later, within the period during which the system remains free from external interference.

Call the position of the bob at a time *t*, taken together with its momentum at *t*, the *state* of the system at *t*. Then the state may be thought of as a point in the abstract, two-dimensional space defined by a pair of axes, one of which represents position and the other of which represents momentum (see figure 7.2). This is a simple example of a *phase space*. It is customary to make momentum the vertical axis and position the horizontal axis, and to take the origin to be the point corresponding to the bob's hanging motionless, supported only by the spring. This *equilibrium position* is thus the conventional zero point on the position scale, relative to which other positions, according as they are to the right or left of this point on the vertical axis (which is to say, above or below the corresponding points in physical space), are represented by positive or negative numbers (of centimetres say).

If the bob is in motion, then the state of the system at any given time will, as I say, be represented by a point in phase space. But we can also plot the path *through phase space* which the bob describes as it moves up and down. This is called an *orbit*. Assuming there is no damping, this orbit will, true to its name, take the form of a perfect ellipse with the origin at its centre. (We can make it a circle by choosing an appropriate pair of units for position and momentum.) If there is damping, then the orbit will be a spiral that ends at the origin.

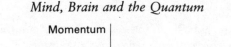

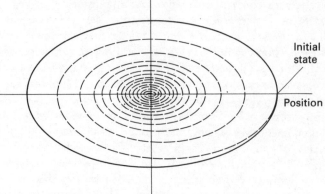

Figure 7.2 *Phase space for a simple harmonic oscillator.*
The solid line represents a typical phase space orbit. If one pulls the bob down and releases it, the state at the moment of release, the initial *state, will correspond to zero momentum and some positive value of the position variable. Thereafter, the bob travels clockwise around its phase space orbit, acquiring increasing momentum – initially negative, since it is travelling upwards in physical space. Then it slows, and starts moving downwards, so that the momentum again passes through zero as it changes from negative to positive. The dotted line represents the phase space orbit of a damped harmonic oscillator, which gradually spirals into the origin as its energy is dissipated.*

I have deliberately chosen a very simple example, in which the object in motion, the bob, is constrained to move in just one (the up–down) dimension. In general, a system consisting of just a single particle moving in a force field will need a phase space of six dimensions. This is because position and momentum are each three-dimensional *vector* quantities. That is to say, the specification of position and momentum each requires three numbers, corresponding to the position or momentum as measured with respect to each of, say, an x, y and z axis. Momentum, remember, is the product of the velocity and the mass, and velocity is speed in a given *direction*; and that's what vectors do: represent an amount in a direction. Likewise, position can be thought of as an amount (distance) in a certain direction from the origin. For this reason, the three-dimensional Euclidean space of classical physics, and many more abstract spaces as well, can be thought of as sets of vectors, rather than as sets of points; and that is how mathematicians generally think of them. But to go back to phase space: if there is more than one particle, then in general the dimensionality of the phase space will be six times the number of particles.

We have, remember, two versions of the vibrating bob. In the first (more realistic) one, friction and the like gradually drain the energy from the system; here the system is said to be *nonconservative*, meaning simply that energy *within the system itself* is not conserved. But, in our idealized version, where there is no friction with air or dissipation of energy through the support, the system is effectively *isolated*, free from outside influences; and seeing that energy is a conserved quantity, an isolated system is invariably *conservative*.

Corresponding to every isolated physical system, there is a mathematical object known as the *Hamiltonian* of the system. This is a *function*. A function can best be thought of as an input–output device. You pop in some numbers at one end, and out pops a number at the other, according to some precise rule. The +, −, × and so on of elementary arithmetic are all functions of two *variables*; that is to say they have two input slots; if you take minus, and pop five into the first slot and three into the second, out pops the number two. The Hamiltonian of a system is just the same sort of thing; its input slots correspond to the dimensions of the corresponding phase space. Thus, the Hamiltonian of our simple harmonic oscillator, the vibrating bob, will have just two input slots, one for position and one for momentum. And what pops out of the output slot of the Hamiltonian, its *value* for the given values of position and momentum, is the total *energy* of the system.

There is a simple graphic way of representing this. We can think of adding the value of the Hamiltonian as a third dimension to our original two-dimensional phase space, so as to yield a three-dimensional space, wherein the original two-dimensional phase space remains as the *phase plane*. For every point in the phase plane, there will then be a corresponding point, at a certain height above the plane, that represents the instantaneous energy that a particle (the bob) would have if its state occupied that phase space position. Taken together, these points comprise a parabolic-shaped surface – the Hamiltonian surface – that touches the phase space at the origin, where the energy is currently defined to be zero, and rises steeply as we progress away from the origin (see figure 7.3).

Thinking of the system this way, we can see that the requirement that energy is conserved, and thus remains constant, is equivalent to saying that the possible orbits in the phase space will be those that correspond to *contour lines*, so to speak: the projection, on to the phase plane, of lines of constant 'altitude' – that is to say, energy – on the Hamiltonian surface. The Hamiltonian for this simple system, constituting as it does a measure of the total energy, is simply the sum of two components: the *potential energy*, which is a function of the position, and hence the degree to which the spring is stretched or compressed; and the *kinetic energy*, or energy of motion, which is a function of the momentum. The bob is rather like a traveller who keeps crossing the English Channel, keeping

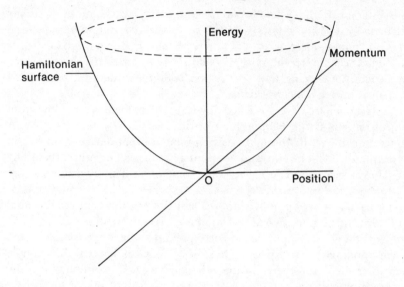

Figure 7.3 *The Hamiltonian surface superimposed on the phase plane.*
(What is depicted is simply a three-dimensional graph of the Hamiltonian function.)

with her a constant sum of money which she continually converts from pounds to francs and then back again. As the bob moves up and down, swinging around on its orbit in phase space, potential energy is constantly converted into kinetic energy and back again, with all the energy being in the form of potential energy whenever it crosses the position axis at the two extremities of the vibration, and all being held in the form of kinetic energy when it crosses the momentum axis or equilibrium position and its velocity is at its maximum.

For all kinds of reasons that I cannot go into here, this is an immensely fruitful way of looking at physical systems. Hamilton, after whom the Hamiltonian is named, discovered a marvellously elegant way of stating the laws of mechanics, using a set of equations equal in number to the dimensions of the corresponding phase space. Of our simple harmonic oscillator, these two equations respectively say the following (transposed into geometrical language). Let P be the point on the Hamiltonian surface directly above the point in the phase plane corresponding to the state of the system at a time t. Then the first equation says that the velocity of the bob at t is given by the slope of a line parallel to the momentum axis and tangent to the Hamiltonian surface at P. And the second equation says that the force acting on the bob at t is given by the slope of a line parallel to the position axis and tangent to the Hamiltonian surface at P. These two equations contain all the information one needs in order to express the state of the system at any arbitrary time, within a period during which it is free from outside interference, as a function of its state at any other time within this same period. (Technically, for the benefit of those who understand these things, what Hamilton did was replace a *second-order* differential equation, equating the force with the product of mass and acceleration in accordance with Newton's Second Law, by a pair of coupled *first-order* partial differential equations. See Gillespie, 1976, pp. 36–8.)

This, as I said, is all classical Newtonian mechanics in a new Hamiltonian dress. But it is from this Hamiltonian formulation that quantum mechanics has developed. In between the period when classical mechanics was in the ascendancy and the period when modern quantum mechanics came into being, there was an intermediate period (roughly corresponding to the first quarter of the twentieth century) in which was developed the so-called *old quantum theory*. This theory, in its mature form, was based on the principle that the *action* has to be *quantized*. The action is not, like energy, position or momentum, a property which a system has *at* a time. It is, rather, a property of a portion of the history of a physical system, that is to say, of the system considered over some specified time interval. Roughly, the action associated with a system over a given time interval is equal to twice the product of its average kinetic energy, over that interval, and the size of the interval in question. (In the jargon of calculus, it is equal to twice the time integral of the kinetic energy, taken over that interval.) Thus, it is measured in units of energy × time, which is equivalent to saying units of momentum × length. (How so? Well, energy is measured in units of mass × velocity squared, which is equivalent to momentum × velocity; and velocity is measured in units of length ÷ time. So action is measured in units of momentum × (length ÷ time) × time, which reduces to momentum × length.) These are the units in which one would measure the area of a given region of two-dimensional phase space. And indeed, the area of phase space enclosed by an orbit, in a one-dimensional physical system such as the simple harmonic oscillator, is equal to the action associated with one complete oscillation.

Action, in the old quantum theory, is quantized, in the sense that, for all periodic systems, the action associated with one complete period (the time it takes to make a single phase space orbit) is required to be equal to some positive integral (that is, whole number) multiple of a basic minimal unit of action, namely *Planck's constant*, h. With regard to our simple vibrating bob, the implication is that the only phase space orbits which are physically possible are those that enclose a region of phase space whose area can be expressed as a positive integral multiple of h. This in turn implies that the total energy of the system is confined to a range of discrete values: only certain 'contour lines' will now correspond to physically possible motions (Ehrenfest, 1967, p. 84).

If we return to our damped harmonic oscillator, a very curious picture emerges. As the system runs down, its phase space orbit will not now spiral into the origin. Rather, we have to think of the phase space as containing a discrete series of concentric grooves, to which the instantaneous state of the system is confined; there are no spiral grooves, as on a gramophone record. So the only way the system can come to rest is via a series of discontinuous hops from one groove to the next, giving up some of its energy, in discrete packets, each time. And it never does come *totally* to rest, since the lowest energy orbit is one in which the action is equal to h, rather than to zero. The only reason why we don't ordinarily notice any of this (so the story went) is that, for a massive object like a bob on the end of a spring, the grooves are so densely packed as to give step-by-step jumping the appearance of continuous motion, as in cinematography.

(A more familiar application of the old quantum theory is Niels Bohr's model of the hydrogen atom, first proposed in 1913, which has become a symbol of the atomic age. The hydrogen atom was envisaged as being made up of a single electron describing an elliptical path around a nucleus consisting of a single proton. This is essentially a higher-dimensional analogue of the simple harmonic oscillator. The instantaneous state of the electron may be equated with a point in a six-dimensional phase space; and the only permissible orbits will be those that lie on constant energy surfaces – the higher-dimensional counterparts of our 'contour lines' – which enclose a volume of phase space that is equal to a positive integral multiple of h^3. The upshot is that the allowed *spatial* orbits of the electron will form a discrete set. Periodically, the electron will absorb a photon and jump into a higher orbit – the original 'quantum leap'; and periodically, also, it will spontaneously emit a photon and fall into a lower orbit. But there will be a lowest orbit, corresponding to the zero-point energy, below which the electron cannot fall; Bohr's theory thus solved the problem of the stability of the hydrogen atom, by making it impossible for the electron ever to spiral into the nucleus, as classical electrodynamics said it should.)

Well, this theory is simple enough to state. But it never proved possible to make it wholly consistent internally. And besides, it made predictions that were in conflict with experiment. Although there is a sense in which it is true that the energy in periodic systems like an atom or a simple harmonic oscillator is quantized, one doesn't get an adequate picture of this quantization by thinking in terms of grooves in phase space. Moreover, the old quantum theory put the energy levels in the wrong place. In the modern theory, the energy levels correspond to $(n + \frac{1}{2})h$, *for n* = 0, 1, 2 . . .; thus the lowest energy level for the harmonic oscillator – the so-called *zero-point energy* – does not, after all, correspond to an action of h, but of ½h.

In order to grasp the principles of the new (post-1925) quantum mechanics, one has to start thinking about physical systems such as the simple harmonic oscillator in a radically new way, with a radically new kind of state space. But discussion of that must be postponed to chapter 11. For I now want to carry this notion of state space into the realms of psychology and neuroscience.

Janik and Toulmin (1973, pp. 143–5) argue persuasively that it was the concept of phase space that provided the inspiration for the notion of 'logical space', which figures prominently in the early philosophy of Wittgenstein. Wittgenstein remarks in his *Tractatus* (2.0131):

> . . . A speck in the visual field, though it need not be red, must have some colour: it is, so to speak, surrounded by colour-space. Notes must have *some* pitch, objects of the sense of touch *some* degree of hardness, and so on.
>
> (Wittgenstein, 1963, pp. 9–11)

Wittgenstein is clearly right to say that colours – that is phenomenal colours, which is what we're interested in (and what Wittgenstein appears to be talking about in this passage) – are embedded in a colour space; and as he says, we can think of such a space as being associated with every 'speck', or smallest discernible region, in the visual field. It will be a state space of at least three dimensions, because it must be capable of accommodating hue, saturation and luminance. A state space based on these parameters could be represented as a cylindrically shaped three-dimensional solid. Distance along the cylinder could be taken to represent luminance; and the hues could be arranged in a circle around the achromatic axis of the cylinder (running from black through all shades of grey to white), with the saturation of these hues increasing as one proceeds outwards from this central achromatic spine. This is essentially the scheme known (after its inventor) as the *Munsell colour tree* (see figure 7.4).

Edwin Land, however, has suggested an alternative state space for perceived colour. What he proposes is a cubically shaped *colour solid* based on a set of coordinates that correspond, respectively, to long, medium and short wave *reflectance*; or more accurately, *lightness*. (Just what is meant by that will be explained shortly.) The reflectance of a surface, at a given wavelength, is the proportion of light at that wavelength which it reflects back: white surfaces are ones that reflect back 80 per cent or more of the light at all visible wavelengths. Land's colour solid thus has black at the corner of the cube representing the

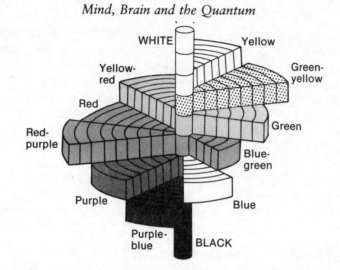

Figure 7.4 *Munsell colour tree*. (From *The New Encyclopaedia Britannica*, *Micropaedia*, vol III. Chicago: Encyclopaedia Britannica, Inc., 1984, p. 103.)

origin, where all three reflectances are at 0 per cent, and white at the opposite corner with respect to the long diagonal, where all three reflectances are at 100 per cent (see figure 7.5).

When I say that a given phenomenal colour *corresponds* to a surface with a given reflectance, I mean that it is the phenomenal colour that such a surface would elicit in a normal observer under suitably specified standard conditions of overall retinal illumination. It is a myth that the phenomenal colour that one sees in a given region of one's visual field is determined simply by the frequency of incident light on the corresponding part of the retina. Rather, the colour perceived locally within the visual field is dependent on the whole pattern of illumination of the retina in a way that Land himself seeks to explain by way of his *retinex* theory (Land, 1977). If a coloured surface is perceived in the context of a complex visual scene, as it normally would be, then according to the retinex theory, the perceived colour is the result of a comparison of the surface's long, short and medium wave reflectance (that is, the percentage of light it reflects back when illuminated by light of long, short or medium wavelength) with that of the surrounding scene. Thus, a surface will appear red if, relative to surrounding areas, it has high reflectance in long wave light and low reflectance in medium and short wave light. This comparative reflectance may be termed its *lightness* (not to be confused with luminance) with respect to long, short or medium wave light. But there are situations in which this method of associating phenomenal colours with perceived surfaces would result in a failure to discriminate between surfaces which had very different reflectances in different wavebands (that is, very different 'objective' colours). An extreme case is that of a coloured patch with a black surround. Here the lightness is going to be high for light of all wavelengths, given that the corresponding reflectances will all be high relative to those of the black surround. In such circumstances, the brain falls back on another, simpler method: it associates a phenomenal colour with the patch simply on the basis of the respective *absolute* long, medium and short wave reflectances, since there's nothing useful to compare them with.

This may seem an unnecessarily complicated arrangement, but in fact it makes very good practical sense. The overall distribution of wavelengths impinging on the retina is, statistically, a pretty good guide to the wavelength distribution within the light by which the visual scene is being illuminated. The method just described thus allows for the brain to compensate for the characteristics of the illumination, so that one can vary the wavelength characteristics of the illuminating light quite considerably without making much difference to the perceived colour of things. Life would be rather difficult if objects, for example, looked a radically different colour under the yellower light of late afternoon than they did in the whiter light of noon. (Evolution never had to contend, of course, with the even yellower light of electric light bulbs or, far worse,

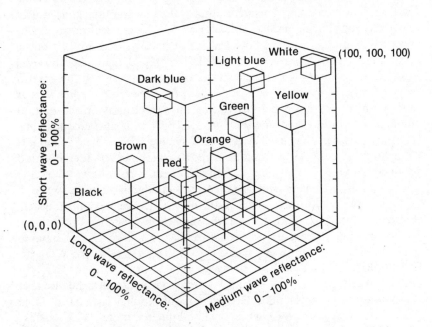

Figure 7.5 *Land's colour solid.* (From Churchland, 1986, p. 301.)

the monochromatic output of sodium street lights, where compensation is not possible. But it has unwittingly prepared us for tinted sunglasses, which make surprisingly little difference to perceived colours.)

So what can be said about these matters at the level of neurophysiology? Well, in chapter 5 I mentioned Zeki's work on monkeys. In areas V1 and V4 of the visual cortex, in rhesus and cynomolgus monkeys, Zeki (1983) has found three different types of cell that are wavelength-sensitive. Cells of one type, which Zeki calls *wavelength selective* (WL), respond to any area of colour provided it reflects enough light of their preferred wavelength. But, interestingly, Zeki has found another type of cell, which he calls *colour-coded* (CO), that responds in just the way that the retinex theory says we respond. Rather than having a preferred wavelength, a CO cell has what Zeki calls a preferred *natural colour*; it fires preferentially in, say, just such circumstances as a patch of colour would look to us to be red. Beyond that, neurophysiologists have not yet found any neurophysiological mechanisms corresponding to reflectance comparisons and the computation of lightnesses; but such mechanisms are now being actively sought.

Zeki also found a third type of cell that he called *wavelength selective opponent* (WLO). WLO cells have a base level of firing which goes up in response to light of one wavelength and down in response to light of a complementary wavelength. After-images are presumably generated by such an opponent mechanism: withdrawal of a stimulus that causes above base-level firing induces transitory below base-level firing and vice versa. After-images cannot, however, result in any direct way from the operation of such a mechanism in WLO cells and their ilk. This was neatly demonstrated by Zeki in a set of experiments designed to establish whether, when the wavelength of the light reflected from a patch was at odds with its perceived colour, it was the wavelength or the natural colour that would determine the perceived (phenomenal) colour of the after-image, when that itself was viewed against a black background. It turned out to be the natural colour: if the patch *looked* red, then it would produce a green after-image. And from this it follows that the phenomenon of after-images, like that, presumably, of perceived warmth and coolness, could only be the result of a high-level opponent system that comes into play after the sort of comparisons that Land postulates. We are looking, in short, for cells – let's call them COO cells – that stand to the CO cells in the same relation that the WLO cells stand to the WL cells.

I should have thought, by the way, that the joint presence of CO, WL and WLO cells in the areas V1 and V4 rather argues against the idea that this is where conscious colour perception in the monkey is actually taking place. For as Zeki neatly puts it, 'Unlike humans, these [WL] cells are able to "report" the presence of a wavelength without associating it with a colour' (Zeki, 1983, p. 761). Unless the CO cells are somehow segregated from the others, it is difficult to see how their firings could contribute constitutively to conscious perception when those of the WL and WLO cells manifestly do not (though, as I remarked earlier, it is possible that what makes a given brain event a conscious event is determined by the way it is causally linked to other brain events, rather than where in the brain it occurs.) I suspect that neurophysiologists will have come closer to the genuine 'seat' of conscious perception when they have succeeded in finding a cortical projection area in which COO cells reside.

To what extent the accumulating psychological and neurophysiological evidence for the correctness of Land's retinex theory should also be taken as evidence for the correctness of his colour solid (figure 7.5), as the appropriate phenomenal state space, is a moot point. It is, however, clearly superior to the colour cylinder idea that I floated a few paragraphs back. To the extent that any projected colour state space can claim some psychological reality, there must be a systematic correspondence between the distance separating any two points, and the overall perceived similarity or dissimilarity of the two corresponding colours. The colour cylinder obviously fails this test, since black and white are respectively represented not by points but by whole surfaces: the two ends of the cylinder. This fault can be corrected by squeezing each end of the cylinder to a point, whereupon the thing assumes a lozenge shape (like a rugger ball, or the ball used in American football, but with pointed rather than rounded ends). The two ends of the lozenge then correspond to the two opposite corners of the cube on the long diagonal. The cube and the lozenge could then be transformed one into the other by appropriate squeezing or stretching. And even this might not be necessary, if it turned out that only that part of the cube's interior corresponding to the lozenge corresponded to actual colour sensations. (There is a strong suggestion in Land's article that not all positions within his colour solid are realizable.) That aside, one might think that the issue was susceptible of empirical determination, simply on the basis of asking sufficiently many people with normal sight to judge, on a suitable scale, how similar two colours were, or, less subjectively, on the basis that the spacing of the colours should match the number of *just noticeable differences* – that is, the number of intervals corresponding to differences of colour that lay on the threshold of the average person's power to discriminate. (The latter might be preferable, since the other kind of question might not seem to make such sense unless a dimension of similarity were to be specified.) What Land in fact did was to scale the lightness, in each dimension, so that it matched people's judgements of degree of similarity. This means that the midpoint on each edge of the colour cube does not correspond to a reflectance of 50 per cent, but to the reflectance of a shade of grey that is perceived as half-way between black and white; and such a shade has a reflectance that is closer to 70 per cent.

Assuming that the state space satisfies the appropriate criteria of psychological accuracy, the question one then wants to ask is: what can we find in the brain that corresponds to this abstract state space? Given that, in conscious perception, colour is simply an integral part of a unitary visual field, what we should expect to find, in that part of the brain where conscious perception was actually going on (I take the argument of the last chapter to license this kind of talk), is a much more comprehensive state space, a distinctive subspace of which embodied information about colour. Consider, by way of analogy, our simple two-dimensional phase space for the harmonic oscillator. For certain purposes, one might wish to ignore spatial position and concentrate on momentum, which is to say different phase space locations with respect to the momentum axis. These comprise a one-dimensional subspace of the phase space. With respect to the phase space as a whole, position within that subspace represents momentum.

As far as conscious visual perception is concerned, one would expect to find a pattern of brain activity capable of varying along a very large number of dimensions, three of which defined a subspace that encoded for colour. One would expect, for example, at least the following: two dimensions to define position within the visual field, another to define depth with respect to each such position, and three to define colour with respect to each spatial position. (I'm not suggesting that these alone would be remotely adequate; what, after all, has become of all that wonderful information about edges, so painstakingly extracted by the striate cortex?) Within all that, one could then separate out the dimensions of brain activity that, taken together, specify colour, and regard them as defining a state space in their own right. (This would be analogous to the way physicists regard the axes in phase space that specify the positions of the particles described, and those that specify their momentum, as defining further state spaces: subspaces of phase space known respectively as *configuration* and *momentum* space.) Moreover, the procedure could be repeated; within the (neurophysiological) colour state space, we could, for example, discern a one-dimensional subspace corresponding to luminance.

Simply by considering colour, one sees that there are three distinct ways in which the concept of a state space enters the picture. Taking our cue from Wittgenstein, we developed the notion of a *phenomenal* state space for colour, where the *metric* of the space – the set of distance relations between state space points – reflects perceived degrees of similarity between colours. On the assumption that phenomenal colour is grounded in certain goings-on in the brain – presumably in some cortical projection area – the idea then arises of representing different patterns of neurophysiological activity as points in a multi-dimensional state space that mirrors the phenomenology of colour. This will then be a *physical* state space for the relevant brain subsystem, standing to this physiological activity as our two-dimensional phase space stood to the oscillatory activity of our spring-suspended bob.

That, however, is to ignore the *representational* dimension of colour. For we can also think of the neurophysiological activity and its phenomenal manifestations as conveying information about the state of the world, information about what is happening at the surfaces of perceived objects. In this sense, we can think of cortical projection areas as embodying or encoding state spaces for physical systems distinct from themselves. This last application of the concept of a state space has proved extremely fruitful in cognitive neuroscience. It is now widely believed that virtually every cortical projection area, and several subcortical nuclei too, are to be thought of, in the representational sense, as the neurophysiological embodiments of state spaces of one kind or another. And the reasons behind this belief do not lie purely within neuroscience itself, but also have a great deal to do with recent developments in computer science. It is to these ideas that we must now turn. (And let me here, in advance, express my indebtedness to a superb review article by Paul Churchland (1986).)

Once again, we must think about the brain in functional terms. What sort of cognitive processing is required of it, if it is to render possible the kind of behaviour of which animals are capable? Consider the game of stick-the-tail-on-the-donkey, a staple of children's parties, where one is blindfolded, turned right round once, and then asked to stick a tail on to a picture of a donkey. Whoever gets closest to the donkey's rump wins. It is, quite literally, a very hit and miss affair, so much so that it is more a game of chance than of skill. Remove the blindfold, however, and any child can do it instantly and effortlessly. How come?

Well, the following is a grossly oversimplified account of the matter. Specifically, I shall ignore two salient facts about this ability: first, that it isn't actually necessary to look directly at the relevant part of the donkey, in order to stick the tail in the right place, and, secondly, that the eye helps to guide the hand, while the latter is actually moving towards its destination. But if I may be allowed a degree of licence here, suppose first that the child fixates visually on the appropriate part of the donkey's anatomy; that is to say, moving head and eyes until light reflected from the donkey's rump falls on the fovea of each retina, and on the same part of the fovea. The eyes are appropriately converged on that part of the picture. How *that* is done I shan't attempt to explain, though I daresay I could hazard a guess if pressed. Now somewhere represented in the brain, let us suppose, is a seven-dimensional *eye-convergence* state space. This is defined by seven axes, all corresponding to angles, which, taken together, define the respective orientations of the two eyes and the head. The eyes, in effect, are mounted on universal joints, the position of each of which may be defined by two angles (measured, say, along a pair of imaginary arcs set at right angles to each other); the neck is also a universal joint, calling for another pair of angles; and we need a final angle to define the degree of rotation of the head. Represented somewhere else in the brain, probably fairly close by, is a six-dimensional *arm-position* state space, again defined by axes all of which correspond to angles. The first two serve to define the position of the upper arm with respect to the torso (the shoulder being yet another universal joint); the third defines the degree of rotation of the elbow; the fourth is the angle of the lower to the upper arm, the elbow being a simple hinge joint; the fifth defines the degree of rotation of the wrist; and the sixth the angle of the hand to the lower arm (the wrist also being a hinge joint). (For simplicity's sake, I ignore the thumb and index finger.) On each of these parameters there will be a particular angle that we can think of as the *resting angle*; in arm-position space, the angles will all have their resting values when the arm is hanging limply at the side of the body. (In eye-convergence space, the resting angles might be those that obtain when the person is looking straight ahead gazing into the distance; the 'resting' state may or may not be that which corresponds to maximum relaxation of the relevant muscles.)

Now the problem takes the following form. Given a point in eye-convergence space, find a corresponding point in arm-position space such that, with the arm in that position, the hand will be in the immediate vicinity of the point at which one's eyes are converging, with the arm as a whole minimally contorted. We are assuming that each of these state spaces is physically embodied in some array of brain cells, in such a way that a point in the state space is physically realized as some specific pattern of firing within that array. Given a pattern of firing in the eye-convergence array, what the brain needs to do is to effect what, in mathematical terms, is a *mapping* from one space to the other. It needs to find, and physically realize, what in mathematical language would be referred to as the *image point* in arm-position space of the given point in eye-convergence space. And the physical realization of this image point I assume to be a pattern of neural firing that automatically sets in train a series of muscular contractions that will lead the arm to the corresponding position in physical space.

The neural realization of a six- (seven-) dimensional state space may be thought of as comprising six (seven) batteries of neurons, each with a characteristic base level of firing that we can think of as representing the resting angle, with higher and lower levels respectively representing angles corresponding to displacement from the resting state in two directions with respect to some arc. In practice a given state would almost certainly be represented by the *average* rate of firing in each of the various batteries of neurons. (If the numbers of neurons in each battery are large enough, the proportion that are firing at any one moment will give a fairly accurate measure of this average rate of firing; as the jargon has it, the space average will give the time average. This, incidentally, means that, if the firing rate is to register in consciousness, it is not necessary for a phenomenal perspective to possess any temporal depth; there is no need, here,.to invoke a specious present.) But it will make no difference to any matter of principle if we assume that the value of each axis is determined by the rate of firing of just a single neuron – in other words that each 'battery' of neurons has just a single member. Then the problem of mapping a point in the seven-dimensional eye-convergence space into its image point in the six-dimensional arm-position space corresponds mathematically to that of mapping an arbitrary septuple (that is, seven-membered sequence) of numbers, giving the respective (angle-representing) spiking frequencies of seven neurons, $\langle a, b, c, d, e, f, g \rangle$, on to a sextuple (six-membered sequence) of numbers, the respective (angle-representing) spiking frequencies of another six neurons, $\langle u, v, w, x, y, z \rangle$. This would be effected mathematically by a seven (column) by six (row) array of functions, called a *matrix*. The seven functions in the first column of the matrix would be applied respectively to the seven numbers a, b, c, d, e, f and g, and the resulting values then summed to yield u; then the corresponding seven functions in the second column would be applied to a, b, c, d, e, f and g, and the results summed to yield v, and so on for the remaining columns.

This is a pretty tedious mathematical exercise, and as the number of dimensions of the 'source' and 'target' state spaces grows, can become very time consuming, even if carried out on a computer. *But in principle a neural network could do it in a matter of milliseconds.* Moreover, the time taken would be essentially independent of the number of dimensions of the state spaces involved: a more complex network, performing mappings between state spaces of higher dimensionality, need not, in general, take significantly longer than a less complex network performing mappings between state spaces of lower dimensionality. There are two key points here. First, the relationships between (axonic) input and (dendritic) output mediated by synaptic junctions physically realize, as they stand, a wide variety of different mathematical functions; and, given that fact, it will always be possible to build up more complicated functions from less complicated ones by suitable combinations of neurons and synapses. And secondly, though this is really just a special case of what I've already said, influences impinging at several different dendritic branches of the same neuron would naturally, in the ordinary course of things, produce an excitatory or inhibitory effect on the spiking frequency which was the mathematical sum of the effects each of the influences would produce on its own.

Figure 7.6 shows a schematic arrangement of neurons that would perform the required mapping. The parallel axonic fibres coming in on the left carry the spiking frequencies corresponding to the septuple $\langle a, b, c, d, e, f, g \rangle$; the axons emerging at the bottom correspond to the required sextuple $\langle u, v, w, x, y, z \rangle$. The synaptic junctions realize the required mathematical functions. Arrangements of essentially this sort have actually been found in the brain, by Pellionisz and Llinas (1985); specifically in the cerebellum, which seems to contain a great number. There is good reason to suspect that the major function of the cerebellum may precisely be to effect mappings between neural state spaces; this,

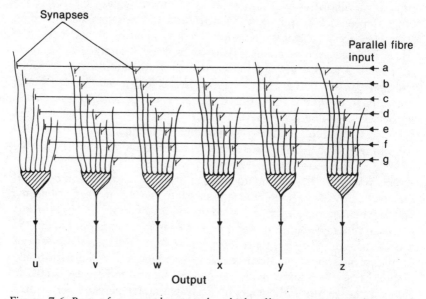

Figure 7.6 *Part of a neural network which effects a mapping from eye-convergence to arm-position state space.*

A point in eye-convergence space is represented by the respective spiking frequencies on the parallel fibres a–g (or rather, the average spiking frequencies within the batteries of fibres to which a–g respectively belong). The spiking frequencies on the output fibres u–z (or the average frequencies within the corresponding batteries of fibres) represent a point in arm-position space. (Adapted from Churchland, 1986, p. 297.)

concretely, may be what it is actually doing, for the most part, when it aids sensori-motor coordination and performs its other integrative functions. But it is a plausible speculation that a high proportion of the connections between cortical centres and subcortical nuclei in general are concerned, in one way or another, with performing mappings between state spaces.

This speculation receives indirect support from the latest thinking in the field of artificial intelligence. Until recently, the bulk of research in this field has been done using standard serial computers and by writing programs that embody a large number of explicit *rules*. (I have written such programs myself.) But the computer world has recently been taken by storm by a new approach, known as *parallel distributed processing* (PDP). (Actually, the central idea behind PDP was put forward by Hebb (1949); only relatively recently, however, have people found ways of implementing it effectively.) In PDP, sequential processing is abandoned in favour of so-called massive parallelism – vast arrays involving hundreds or thousands of very simple units arranged in parallel. And the units composing the array are linked by way of junctions that can be constantly modified from within the system. Such systems are sometimes referred to as *neural networks*, in honour of their supposed similarity to actual arrays of neurons; though systems of this general type have also gone by the name of *connection machines* and *Boltzman* computers. Most of them, in fact, don't exist as actual machines at all, but rather as simulations on conventional computers.

Suppose, now, one wants to teach such a system to recognize certain patterns. Then one part of the array is made to play the role of a state space for graphic information stored on a pixel-by-pixel basis, 'pixel' being computer jargon for minimal picture element. And another part of the array is set up to function as a state space for pattern information. The machine may then be said to be able correctly to identify patterns, within the range the pattern state space allows, when it can correctly map points in pixel-space on to the corresponding points in pattern space. A standard artificial intelligence program for doing this would involve building a whole set of complex rules into the system. But this system is set up in such a way that it can learn to get it right by trial and error. The machine is repeatedly presented with different pictures, by having its pixel space appropriately set up, and is then instructed to 'guess' what it is 'seeing'. That is to say, it is made to effect some sort of mapping into pattern space. It is then told whether it's right or wrong (or perhaps 'warm' or 'cold'). On the basis of what it is told, the machine constantly adjusts the *weights* of connections within the machine that link the two state spaces and physically realize the recognition mapping, in such a way that it gets better and better at the task. In the end it can, perhaps, perform flawlessly. Yet it still has no explicit rules; just the whole array of suitably modified connections.

The clever part of all this resides in the program for modifying the connections, and most of the current research is devoted to developing algorithms that are more powerful and also physiologically more realistic. A recently announced technique called 'recirculation' is currently attracting a lot of interest. One ostensibly very impressive demonstration, not of recirculation but of an older technique called 'back-propagation' (Rumelhart et al., 1986a), involved teaching a machine to form the past tense forms of English verbs when given, as input, the present tense forms. Now the way children learn to do this has previously been thought to provide some of the best evidence there is that learning grammar involves the successive postulation by the child, and subsequent modification, of hypothetical grammatical rules. This has been powerfully and influentially argued by Chomsky. The suggestion is, of course, that this is a largely subconscious process; otherwise one would be able to articulate the rules one is following, which most people clearly can't. And the way children learn is just what one would expect if Chomsky were right. They go through an initial period in which they tend to avoid the past tense, saying 'come' when they mean 'came'; then they start saying 'came'. But then after a while they stop saying 'came' and start saying 'comed'. This, so Chomsky's followers will tell you, is the point at which they have formulated a grammatical rule, generalizing in the obvious way from regular verbs. Then, finally, they go back to saying 'came'; the rule has been appropriately modified.

Amazingly, this – according to Rumelhart and McClelland (1986) – is exactly what an appropriately constructed neural network has been found to do, when it is 'trained' to inflect English verbs. It goes through all these stages. And it also has a tendency, fairly early on, to do something else that children do, that I didn't mention before; something which has no clear rationale on the Chomsky model. At a certain intermediate stage in the training process, it tends to come out with things like 'camed', sticking a regular past ending on to the irregular past form.

As a philosopher, I find this work immensely thought-provoking. It is far from clear that, at the end of such a learning process, the system could really be said to be storing *rules* of grammar at all. No doubt there's a sense in which the whole vast pattern of weights at the connections corresponds to a set of grammatical rules; but that's just to say that the system is such that it will *perform in accordance with* these rules. Equally, the vibrating weight that we discussed at the beginning of the chapter is acting *in accordance with* Hamilton's equations. That, however, doesn't mean that it contains a representation of these equations. (This is not an original point, by the way; Nelson Goodman once remarked, apropos of Chomsky's claim that there are neurophysiologically realized rules of depth grammar operating in all of us even before we learn to speak, that he saw no more reason to suppose that infants had rules of depth grammar inscribed in their brains than that stones thrown into the air had, somewhere inscribed in them, Newton's laws of motion.)

This research also sheds light on something which has long puzzled me. A large part of philosophy, as currently practised in what is called the *analytic tradition*, is concerned with the logical analysis of concepts; or equivalently, saying what certain sorts of word really mean. Knowledge is a good example. What conditions have to be satisfied for someone to know something? Everybody agrees that the something in question has to be true, and most people think that the person must in some sense believe it to be true (though this is disputed). But not every instance of true belief amounts to knowledge. So what further condition or conditions have to be satisfied? Well, in spite of the best efforts of a great many philosophers over a great many years (starting perhaps with Plato's *Meno*), no one has ever succeeded in coming up with a proposal that other philosophers were unable to refute. And this is a fairly typical example. The quest for an analysis of any concept, practically, takes the form of an endless tennis volley, in which one philosopher puts forward a definition, a second philosopher finds a counter-example, the first or perhaps a third philosopher modifies the theory to cope with the counter-example, in response to which another philosopher comes up with a new counter-example, and so on *ad infinitum*. I cannot, offhand, think of a single philosophically interesting concept that has been successfully and nontrivially analysed to most people's satisfaction. Conceptual analysis, in short, is fantastically difficult. And why is this? That's what I have always wanted to know. (And by the way, formulating exception-free grammatical rules for natural languages is equally difficult.) One possibility that suggests itself is that the concepts in question are exceedingly complicated. But that explanation has always struck me as very implausible, as it stands. For if the concepts are that complicated, how come even intellectually very ungifted people pick them up with so little difficulty? After all, in some sense we all know perfectly well what we mean by 'know'.

Now, perhaps, we have the hint of an answer to this riddle. The concepts in question *are* extremely complicated. And that is as much as to say that, if one set them out in the form of a set of explicit rules, the formulation might run to pages of densely packed text. But then how do we pick them up, and why should we have such complicated concepts? The answer to the first question is that we pick them up by continual

,modification of thousands, perhaps tens or hundreds of thousands, of individual connections in the brain, just as a connection machine does. Were one to state, *in the form of an explicit set of rules*, how a connection machine 'recognizes' a pattern, that too might well run to pages and pages of densely packed type. But why should one expect the information contained in such a vast array of distinct loci to be susceptible of neat encapsulation in a few choice sentences? The complexity of our concepts is no particular bar to learning them, precisely because this does *not* call for the mind to engage in any exercise of formulating rules to account for the data, in the way Chomsky thinks people learn grammar. And finally, the extreme complexity of our concepts is not necessarily inconsistent with their being, for us, very natural concepts to have, very natural ways of slicing up the cognitive terrain; this is why, in turn, we end up thinking about things in remarkably similar ways. For naturalness, here, need not be a matter of simplicity or logical elegance. Rather it is a matter of the concepts in question being appropriately attuned to the functional architecture of those parts of the brain that are involved in thought and other cognitive tasks. And the architecture of the cortex has, as we know, a complexity of almost astronomical proportions. Indeed, acquiring language or concepts may be more akin to progressively finer tuning of an instrument with a vast number of strings than it is to learning a set of rules. (Simmias, in Plato's *Phaedo* (85e–86d), may have been closer to the truth than he knew, when he compared the psyche to the 'harmony', attunement that is, of a lyre.)

There are a number of features that any theory of information storage within the brain must satisfy, if it is to be remotely adequate to the empirical facts, but which it has hitherto proved remarkably difficult physically to model. Three key such features are *content addressability*, *distributed storage* and *graceful degradation*. Content addressability means that memories can be accessed on the basis of what they are memories of, as opposed to how or where, in the brain, they are stored. This would be in contrast to most conventional computers, or computer programs, where access to memories is via an *address* which labels the physical location of the relevant byte(s). Content addressability is at work when you start with a vague thought like 'history teacher' and rapidly find yourself gaining access to a dossier on some particular history master at your school, some twenty years previously. Neural networks behave very much like this. Suppose, for example, that a set of pictures has been stored in such a network. Then if a pattern of activation corresponding to, say, a fragment of one of the stored pictures is imposed upon the system, the network can rapidly retrieve the entire picture, converging on the pattern of activation associated with whatever stored picture most closely resembles the input it is given. (Hopfield (1982) described a mathematically very elegant neural network model of human memory, with this feature of content addressability; and Windsor (1988) has written a simple simulation, capable of running on any home computer, which dramatically illustrates the Hopfield model in action.)

Distributed storage means that the physical representation of the information is spread out, or *distributed*, throughout a substantial part of the network, rather than being located in a small, well-defined region (again, as in a conventional computer). This feature is closely related to graceful degradation, in one of its aspects. For it has been known since the work of Lashley in the 1920s that the effect of minor lesions at specific locations within the brain is not (in general) to cause the sudden and total loss of specific memories or learnt skills, but rather, a diffuse and relatively minor decrement in a range of memories or skills. This is one example of *graceful degradation*: degradation in performance, in consequence of deterioration of the system, runs *pari passu* with the degree of deterioration, in physical terms. Slight, or gradual, physical deterioration is not, in general, associated with sharp, catastrophic changes in performance. (Such deterioration, as it occurs in us, might be anything from the temporary effects of alcohol, the changes in the synapses associated with gradual forgetting, or the physical decay of the brain that comes with age. or with progressive dementias such as Alzheimer's disease.)

Graceful degradation has other aspects to it as well; for example, the system can respond appropriately to degraded input. Minor mistakes, in the information one gives it, can produce behaviour which is either identical to that which would have been evoked had there been no mistake in the input, or else is just slightly degraded to an extent that matches the degree of input error. (Clearly, this is closely related to content addressability.) Here again, such behaviour is in sharp contrast to that of conventional computer programs, where a comma out of place can be a recipe for disaster.

Some recent work suggests that one may also be able to explain, on connectionist principles, how certain sorts of structure and specialization of function within the brain can form spontaneously, in response to appropriate sensory input. Modification of the strengths of the various synapses, based on such things as the degree of correlation between the firings or failure to fire of the neurons these synapses connect, may suffice – so it seems – to cause specialized modules of various kinds of take shape in the brain, given certain initial connections to the sense organs, muscles and so forth. Specific genetic pre-programming may not always be necessary.

These are fascinating developments, suggesting that we may be on the verge of a breakthrough in our understanding of brain function. Nevertheless, the whole approach is still hotly contested, and may yet turn out to be a blind alley. Rumelhart and McClelland's model of verb inflection, referred to earlier, has come in for much criticism, most notably by Pinker and Prince (1987). Indeed, it has become something of a key bone of contention in the current debate (see Johnson-Laird, 1987, and Devlin, 1988). Moreover, there are problems of *control* that the connectionist program has yet to address effectively. The approach to memory initiated by Hopfield (1982) lends itself not only to the storage, within a neural network, of static things such as pictures, but also to sequences of memories; or perhaps I mean memories of sequences (see Windsor, 1988, p. 18). Thus it can go some way towards explaining how we remember tunes, poems and what not. But human beings, of course, are not condemned to go through such sequences to the bitter end, much less cycle through them endlessly in their heads (though some tunes do, to be sure, have an infuriating tendency to make one do this!). We need something equivalent to a stop button, and a freeze frame, to accommodate such activities as searching for the right memory; and more complicated controls too, for things such as exercises of the imagination, or deliberate, directed thought. These 'controls' in their turn must be linked to complex recognitional skills, which have to be applied *to* patterns of neural activation (which is not inconsistent with the exercise of such skills amounting to patterns of neural activation in their own right). The speculations of Johnson-Laird's (1983), referred to in chapter 6, to the effect that parallel processing in the brain may take place under the overall control of a serial operating system, seem highly germane here. And, as Johnson-Laird suggests, it may be this operating system that is the proper domain of consciousness.

In any case, we must beware of getting carried away by all this (as I fear some philosophers have) to the point where we become blind to the fact that the fundamental philosophical mind–body problem is still as much with us as ever. It is to this that we must now return.

8

The Refutation of Physicalism

Paul Churchland – whose writings have done much to alert philosophers to the importance of this recent work in neurophysiology – is a materialist. As regards sensations, he inclines (as do I) towards an *identity theory*, defending the view that sensations just *are* states or processes in the brain. Reflecting on Land's three-dimensional state space for colour, his colour cube, and the way state spaces may be physiologically embodied in batteries of neurons whose respective spiking frequencies define a state space point, Churchland says:

> All of this suggests the hypothesis that a visual *sensation* of any specific colour is literally identical with a specific triplet of spiking frequencies in some triune brain system. If this is true, then the similarity of two colour sensations emerges as just the proximity of their respective state-space positions. Qualitative 'betweenness' falls out as state-space betweenness. And of course there are an indefinite number of continuous state-space paths connecting any two state-space points.
>
> (Churchland, 1986, p. 301)

Now I do not wish to insist that this is false. Nevertheless, I find it deeply mystifying. It is one thing to say that a specific kind of colour sensation is correlated with, or even caused by, a specific triplet of spiking frequencies, but quite another to assert an identity here. Presumably one set of action potentials, in one set of neurons, is qualitatively pretty much like any other. How are the three batteries of neurons within the colour system supposed to 'know' which is supposed to generate, nay constitute, which dimension of qualitative change? And are the spikings of neurons that code for sound qualitatively so different from the ones involved in visual discrimination that we can explain, on that basis, why sounds are

qualitatively so radically different from sights? Being told by Churchland
that all phenomenal qualities are constituted by suitable *n*-tuples of
spiking frequencies produces in me the same kind of feeling of intellectual
vertigo that the Pythagoreans doubtless induced in their hearers, when
they announced that everything was composed of numbers.

What someone might say at this point – a move suggested to me by
Peter Smith – is that it is not the spiking frequencies considered in
isolation that are to be identified with the phenomenal qualities, but the
spiking frequencies taken in conjunction with their functional role. On
this view, the intrinsic phenomenal character of a sensation depends both
on the intrinsic physical character of the corresponding brain state and
on its causal *interrelations* with other states of the brain. Thus, what
made a particular sensation one of phenomenal magenta as opposed, say,
to phenomenal ochre would be the particular combination of spiking
frequencies in certain batteries of neurons; but what made the firings of
these neurons sensations of colour at all as opposed, say, to auditory
sensations would be the way in which the activities of these neurons
slotted into the overall functional organization of the brain.

But it is difficult to see how this view can constitute any advance over
straight functionalism. For either functionalism has a problem accounting
for intrinsic phenomenal content (qualia), in terms of functional role, or
it doesn't. If it doesn't, then it is unnecessary to appeal to the intrinsic
physical character of brain states at all. If it does, then the same problems
will beset this mixed view, in regard to phenomenal qualities, as beset the
simpler functionalist view. I have in mind, of course, its essential
arbitrariness: the fact that it would seem possible, a priori, for any
functional role to be associated with any phenomenal content, or with
none.

The Pythagorean parallel, just alluded to, seems singularly apt when
we consider what Churchland goes on to say:

Evidently this approach to understanding sensory qualia is both
theoretically and empirically motivated, and it lends support to the
reductive position advanced in an earlier paper (Churchland, 1985)
on the ontological status of sensory qualia. In particular, it suggests
an effective means of expressing the allegedly inexpressible. The
'ineffable' pink of one's current visual sensation may be richly and
precisely expressible as a '95 Hz / 80 Hz / 80 Hz chord' in the
relevant triune cortical system. The 'unconveyable' taste sensation
produced by the fabled Australian health tonic, Vegemite, might be
quite poignantly conveyed as an '85/80/90/15 chord' in one's four-
channelled gustatory system (a dark corner of taste-space that is best
avoided). And the 'indescribable' olfactory sensation produced by a

newly opened rose might be quite accurately described as a '95/35/ 10/80/60/55 chord' in some 6-D array within one's olfactory system.

This more penetrating conceptual framework might even displace the common-sense framework as the vehicle of intersubjective description and spontaneous introspection.

(Churchland, 1986, p. 303)

Well, as Wittgenstein might have commented (how quaint this way of talking sounds today), one could of course play that language game if one so wished: it certainly gives a new twist to 'A rose by any other name . . .'! But one cannot eradicate a conceptual distinction simply by adopting a new vocabulary. If '95 Hz / 80 Hz / 80 Hz chord' is supposed to *mean* a triplet of spiking frequencies, then it cannot simultaneously *mean* some shade of phenomenal pink, ineffable or not. To invoke a familiar philosophical distinction, '95 Hz / 80 Hz / 80 Hz chord' may have the same *reference* as '(sensation of) phenomenal pink of such-and-such a shade' – they may designate the same objective state, but they clearly do not have the same *sense* or meaning; if they designate the same state, then, as the philosopher Frege put it (1966, p. 57), they do so under different *modes of presentation*. (In Frege's terms, 'Sir Percy Blakeney' and 'the Scarlet Pimpernel', in Baroness Orczy's novel, introduce what is in fact the same individual under different modes of presentation: as a foppish English aristocrat in the one case, and as an intrepid rescuer of people from the guillotine in the other. Hence one can know that the Scarlet Pimpernel is in Paris without knowing that Sir Percy is in Paris, even though the names have the same reference.)

Conversely, if '95 Hz / 80 Hz / 80 chord' really is being used merely to *describe* a particular, otherwise ineffable, shade of phenomenal pink – rather in the way well-practised interior decorators might come to use numbers indexed to a book of colour samples to designate precise shades of paint – then it can no longer have its literal neurophysiological sense, whereby it *means* a certain triplet of spiking frequencies. In short, one cannot have it both ways.

Churchland here seems to be confusing two questions. First, could the *vocabulary* of frequency *n*-tuples displace the *vocabulary* we normally use to describe phenomenal qualities? To which the answer is that it certainly isn't a logical impossibility that it should do so (though it seems to me that Churchland vastly overestimates the appeal and practical utility of such a scheme). But that is not the same as the question whether the *conceptual framework* of neural state spaces could supplant the common-sense framework that we bring to bear on phenomenal qualities. To that the answer is: no it couldn't, for the simple reason that they are not in competition with each other. Changing one's vocabulary, in the way Churchland has in mind, wouldn't involve throwing the common-sense framework overboard; it would just be a way of expressing finer distinctions *within* that common-sense framework. What would happen is that when someone said 'I'm having a 95/80/80 chord in area V4', you wouldn't be sure what he meant unless you knew whether he was just using a high falutin' vocabulary for saying he could see a particular shade of pink, or whether he meant to place a certain neurophysiological construction on the contents of his visual awareness. Were it to be used in the first sense, it would no more mean ditching one's common-sense conceptual framework than does saying that one's just had a 'brainwave'. It would all be a kind of elaborate, albeit very systematic, metaphor.

Perhaps, however, Churchland has in mind a far more profound change in our present practices, whereby we stop talking about visual sensations or phenomenal qualities, *as such*, at all. What we do is start talking about brain states and spiking frequencies instead. So when I say, albeit on the basis of introspection, that I'm having a 95 Hz / 80 Hz / 80 Hz chord in area V4, this isn't merely a way of *reporting* a visual sensation. Rather, it is exactly what it sounds like: saying that I'm having a certain sort of brain state. And the ultimate test of whether what I'm saying is true will be what shows up in a brain scan. It would be more like saying that I saw a rose than saying that my visual field contained a patch of red. For like the former, but unlike the latter, it would be going beyond what was phenomenally presented in order to make an assertion about the (with respect to the mind) 'external' physical world, an assertion with regard to which one would have no unique authority. Someone else, armed with some suitable instrument for scanning my brain, might be a far better judge of what was going on in area V4 than I. But he couldn't, one would think, be a better judge of whether I was *experiencing phenomenal pink*.

Churchland would concede, of course, that statements about *n*-tuples of spiking frequencies and the like are very different in meaning (that is, sense) to anything we could say using our ordinary psychological vocabulary. Nevertheless, he would insist that there is no *fact* about conscious states or phenomenal qualities which is incapable of being captured using neurophysiological descriptions instead of our common-sense ones. It is that claim which it is the purpose of this chapter to refute.

Putting it very crudely, one could say that a materialist is someone who believes that there are only material things, and a physicalist is someone who believes that there are only physical facts. In terms of this definition, Churchland is a physicalist; he believes that there are, in some sense, only physical facts. But he would not accept the criterion, proposed in chapter 2, for what it means to say that there are only physical facts. Take the statement that there is currently a patch of (phenomenal) pink in Angela's visual field; and assume that it is true. The question, then, is whether this is a fact over and above all the physical facts that there are.

Now it would be all too easy, at this point, to get led into a digression about what exactly is meant by 'facts' in this context. Someone might ask whether, in terms of the distinction invoked just now, facts are to be thought of as belonging to the domain of sense or of reference. (For example, should the statements that Sir Percy Blakeney is in Paris and that the Scarlet Pimpernel is in Paris be thought of as expressing different facts, or the same fact under different modes of presentation?) This is a question which I shall address very briefly towards the end of the chapter. It seems to me, however, that the present issue does not really hinge on what is, or should be, understood by 'facts', but on what is the appropriate concept of *reduction*. That is something we discussed at length in chapter 2. There I argued that a domain of discourse D should be regarded as reducible to another domain E just in case any true statement belonging to the domain D could be logically deduced from some set of true statements in the domain E by someone who possessed the concepts appropriate to the domain D and had sufficient ratiocinative power. That, I argued in effect, is what someone means, or ought to mean, when he says that there are no D-facts over and above E-facts, or that, as regards the domains D and E, E-facts are all the facts there are. The point is that if such statements are understood in terms of my criterion of reducibility, the reference to 'facts' here is inessential; one could always express oneself, albeit more long-windedly, without using the term 'fact' at all. And that in turn means that use of the term 'fact' can be regarded, in this context, simply as a harmless *façon de parler*.

Let us return, then, to Angela, and the question whether the fact that she has a patch of phenomenal pink in her visual field is or is not a fact over and above the physical facts about Angela. In terms of my criterion of reducibility, the appropriate test is this. Would someone who knew all the relevant physical facts about Angela (that is, knew the truth of all the relevant statements, expressible in the language of physics, chemistry or physiology), *and who was in a position to understand the statement that she was experiencing a patch of phenomenal pink*, be, in principle, in a position to deduce its truth. To understand the statement, one would of course have to possess the *concept* of phenomenal pink. Philosophers who have adopted what is in essence the same criterion as mine have not always made the italicized qualification, the need for which Churchland implicitly acknowledges:

[W]e can legitimately ask of a putatively correct theory of a given objective domain that it account for the phenomena (= function successfully) in that domain. But we cannot insist that it also be able to predict how this, that, or the other conceptually idiosyncratic human culture is going to *conceive* of that domain.

(Churchland, 1985, p. 13)

That is, of course, absolutely right, and is the reason why in chapter 2, I chose to define physicalism in terms of weak reduction, in my sense, rather than some stronger notion. But now Churchland would think that, even with this qualification, the criterion I have given is too strong. His reasons for this are as follows:

[H]owever much one bends and squeezes the molecular theory concerning H_2O, one cannot deduce from it that water will be *blue*, but only that water will scatter electromagnetic radiation at such-and-such wavelengths. And however much one wrings from the mechanics of molecular motion, one cannot deduce from it that a roaring hearth will be warm, but only that its molecules will have such-and-such a mean kinetic energy and will collectively emit *EM* radiation at longish wavelengths.

(Churchland, 1985, p. 12)

Now the crucial point here, to the extent that what Churchland says is true, is that one would not, seemingly, be able to make the deductions *even if one had the concepts of warmth and of blue*. So even my 'weak' concept of reduction turns out to be strong enough to disqualify from being genuine reductions scientific advances that would normally be thought of as paradigms of successful reduction. If even the equation of heat with molecular motion is not allowed to count, in my sense, as genuine reduction, then all that shows, one is tempted to say, is that 'weak' is a bit of a misnomer for the concept of reduction that I have been operating with, and that the appropriate concept, for our present purposes, must be something weaker still.

That is the moral that Churchland himself draws from this and other considerations I have not mentioned; and on this basis he offers a *far* weaker criterion of reducibility, with respect to which it is reasonable to suppose that statements about phenomenal qualities, and indeed folk psychology in general, are, in principle, reducible to physiology, and ultimately to physics. The details need not concern us, since my only purpose here is to defend my original criterion of weak reduction against a line of attack which may seem to have considerable initial plausibility.

It seems to me that Churchland has drawn precisely the wrong moral here. What he should have asked himself is *why* the deduction fails. To the extent that it does, that is: I think there may, after all, be a weak sense in which even an alien could know that the water was blue or the hearth warm. 'Warm' connotes a physical property via a certain mode of presentation: namely, as whatever physical property it is that causes, amongst other things, such-and-such a sensation in normal human observers. The weak sense just alluded to is that in which one could be said to know that something was warm if one knew that it had the relevant property, even though one didn't know this property under that description – as is required for knowing that the hearth is warm in the stronger sense. The reason, then, why the deduction fails is that knowing (in the strong sense) that something is warm or blue logically requires one to know, with respect to some sensation that one can imagine or otherwise identify, that the thing is in a state that would engender such a sensation in a suitably situated normal human observer. Understanding the statements that way, it will indeed be impossible to deduce them from descriptions couched purely in the language of physics, even if one has the relevant concepts. But that's because the statements, thus understood, have a partly psychological content to begin with; they aren't *just* statements about physical reality.

There is a splendid irony here which deserves to be savoured. Facts that Churchland cites by way of defending physicalism, in order to justify the adoption of a weaker criterion of reducibility than is usually offered, turn out upon closer examination to be ones whose truth, in so far as they are true, is due precisely to the ostensible falsity of physicalism!

But it probably isn't immediately clear to everyone *why* I say that, from a description couched in the language of physics, it would be impossible to deduce, even if one had the relevant concepts, that the hearth was warm. The point here is that when judging that something is warm *we are drawing on information that goes beyond what is involved either in having the relevant concepts or in knowing the truth of the scientific description.* We are drawing on a fact of our experience that the description at the level of molecular motion and so on ostensibly fails to capture: namely the fact that our *sensation* of warmth is correlated with a certain level of molecular motion.

This is a different way of approaching the question of reducibility in the mind–body case than that usually encountered in the philosophical literature. What philosophers usually do is construct cases where, in spite of knowing all the relevant facts, couched in the language of physics, physiology or whatever, someone is patently unable to tell what it is like to be having such-and-such a set of experiences. Therefore they conclude that there must be more to having these experiences than the physiological description is capable of conveying. In short, there are facts over and above the physical/physiological facts. There are many examples of this strategy in the literature. One is Nagel's claim that we cannot, no matter how much we learn about the physiology of these animals, know what it is like to be a bat (Nagel, 1979b). Another is Frank Jackson's (1982) case of a brilliant neurophysiologist who has reached near-omniscience in her field and is able to scan people's brains by remote sensors, computer links and black-and-white television monitors. But she is confined to a room without windows and which is decorated exclusively in shades of grey. She herself has grey eyes, grey clothing, and has never in her life seen the colour green. She has everyone's neurophysiology off to a tee. Yet there's something she does not know and cannot tell: namely, what it is they experience when, for example, they gaze at a garden lawn. (A similar thought-experiment, involving a deaf neurologist, is to be found in Robinson, 1982, p. 4.)

Well *I* find these cases pretty convincing against physicalism. Nevertheless, this sort of example leaves a loophole for the reductionist. For he is able to claim that it is lack of the relevant conceptual resources, not lack of factual knowledge as such, that makes it impossible for thus-and-so situated individuals to make certain sorts of deductions from the scientific information at their disposal, no matter how comprehensive, in its own terms, it is. Why, after all, does Nagel take the case of a bat rather than another human being? It is because he takes the bat's conscious life to possess essentially *alien* features. In particular, its echo-locatory sense is, he suspects, associated with phenomenal qualities that do not figure in our conscious lives at all, and which we are correspondingly unable to imagine (Nagel, 1979b, p. 168). In short, we do not possess the relevant psychological *concepts*, just as Jackson's neurophysiologist lacks the concept of phenomenal green. It is surely unreasonable to regard, as an obstacle to reductionism, the impossibility of deriving certain conclusions from the physical descriptions when one lacks the requisite higher-level concepts. For that would have the effect of rendering it impossible ever to carry through a successful scientific reduction.

Well, I think myself that these particular examples could be successfully defended against that line of criticism. But the general point clearly has some force. (Certainly, Churchland exploits it to the hilt.) So my own inclination is to say: forget about exotic cases in which, for some reason or another, our conceptual resources are inadequate to the task of formulating to ourselves a conception of what it is like to experience this or that. Simply reflect on any common or garden case of knowing what someone else is experiencing.

There is a marvellous scene in the film *The Front* where the character played by Woody Allen is hauled up before Senator Joe McCarthy's notorious Committee on Un-American Activities. One of McCarthy's lawyers asks the Woody Allen character: Do you know so-and-so? To which he replies: 'Ah, can any human being ever be said really to *know* another human being?' – continuing in this philosophical vein until he is finally hauled off to gaol for contempt.

The allusion is to what is known in philosophical circles as the *problem of other minds*. The question of whether and to what extent one *can* know what is going on in another person's mind is not really to the point in the present context. What is very much to the point, however, is the predicament that gives rise to the problem. And this is the logical gap between the publicly accessible facts and the construal that we normally place upon them, whenever we draw conclusions about what another person is thinking or experiencing. Now in the normal way of things, the only publicly accessible facts about the person that we have at our disposal are facts about their outwardly perceptible physical circumstances, and their behaviour. But suppose we had, in addition, the benefit of a comprehensive physical description, and unlimited intellectual powers. Would we then be able to know what they were experiencing? Would we know them in Woody Allen's sense of knowing exactly what it was like to be them?

The answer, clearly is that we would not. For we would not know how to interpret the physical facts. The only way a physical description could help us would be via a correlation, direct or indirect, with our own states of mind, as we ourselves introspect them. By 'direct' I mean correlating a particular kind of neural state type, as it occurs in oneself, with a certain conscious state type, and then inferring the existence of a token of that conscious state type in the other person on the basis of knowing that that person was in a neural state of the corresponding type. (For this, of course, one would also need a sufficiently comprehensive physical description of oneself.) By 'indirect' I mean correlating neural state types, in the other person, with types of behaviour or of outwardly perceptible physical states that, in one's own experience, have been found to correlate with certain conscious state types. To the extent that one is allowed to draw on these correlations, a comprehensive physical description of the other person could, assuming the soundness of the methodology, yield rich insights into that person's inner life.

But the point is that *to do that is to draw on information that goes beyond that contained in the physical descriptions themselves.* No one drawing conclusions on that basis could claim merely to be deducing it from the physical descriptions alone. In fact it isn't strictly being *deduced* at all, since if it were a deduction, in the logician's sense, the combination of the premises with the denial of the conclusion would yield a contradiction, which manifestly it does not. Essentially involved here is an inherently fallible step of scientific generalization. But waiving that point, it isn't even true that the conclusion is in any sense being inferred purely from the given *physical* facts. What it is being inferred from is a combination of physiological and other physical facts and certain psychological or experiential ones, namely facts about oneself. And these latter are plainly indispensable to the inference, as indeed they are to our ordinary ascriptions of experiences to others.

On the face of it, this seems amply to demonstrate that physicalism, as I have defined it, is false. For it appears to follow inescapably that these facts are ones that a description couched purely in the language of physics, chemistry or physiology leaves out of account.

Is there any way in which the physicalist might attempt to resist this conclusion? One way might be along the lines suggested by Michael Tye (1986). Tye's arguments are explicitly addressed to examples like those of Jackson and Nagel. But they apply equally to the sort of case just considered. Suppose that I have a physical description of what was going on in Harriet's brain, at a specific time *t*, sufficiently comprehensive to encompass all facts that could conceivably, from the physicalist's standpoint, be constitutive of Harriet's mental life, and (implausible though this would be in practice) that I understand this description. And suppose that I am wondering whether, at time *t*, Harriet was in any pain or discomfort, and if so, what form that took, phenomenally speaking. I have not yet got round to correlating physiological states of my own brain with phenomenal qualities as revealed by introspection. So I am not yet, seemingly, in a position to know what in the relevant respects it was like to be Harriet at *t*. It would appear, then, that there is something I don't yet know, in spite of having been given, and having inwardly digested, all the relevant physiological facts.

That there is indeed something I don't know, would seem to be confirmed by the following consideration. Suppose I do then go ahead with the exercise of matching up her physiological states with my own, and discover that she was in a state which is similar, and similar in what look to be relevant respects, to that which I am in when and only when I am experiencing a throbbing headache. I, who have not infrequently experienced throbbing headaches (especially when doing philosophy), would then appear to have found out a new fact I didn't previously know, and (as I stressed a few paragraphs back) couldn't possibly have learned from any amount of studying the physiological description by itself: I would then know approximately what, in the relevant respects, it felt like to be in Harriet's shoes at *t*.

But Tye denies this. He doesn't deny that I have learned something. But he does deny that what I have learned is some fact that I didn't know previously – or rather some new nonrelational fact about Harriet's state. (For of course I have, from any point of view, learned a relational fact to the effect that Harriet's state at *t* resembled, in certain respects, certain past states of myself.) What Tye says is that, rather than learn a new fact about the intrinsic (nonrelational) character of Harriet's state at *t*, what I have done is come to know an old fact in a new way. Previously I knew the facts about Harriet's conscious state at *t* only via the physical description; now, as a result of the correlation exercise, I know them in a new way. In the light of my knowledge of my own states derived from introspection and experiential memory, I can identify the (type) state she was in at *t* in a way that I couldn't previously. Thus I can *do* something that I previously could not. But this new ability does not, at any rate as regards what state Harriet was in at *t*, give me new factual knowledge, any more than learning how to balance a pencil on the end of my nose *need* carry with it knowledge of any new facts. (This is Tye's analogy.) Tye would say the same about a congenitally blind neurophysiologist who is in possession of all the physical facts relevant to a determination of what people see when they look at a ripe tomato. Supposing her then to gain her sight, Tye says that she does not learn any new facts about what goes on when people view a ripe tomato; what she learns is a new way of identifying states that involve experiencing phenomenal colours. She can now do this by way of introspecting such states in herself.

This is a bold proposal. But it won't wash, it seems to me. Tye is of course quite right to say that learning new things need not amount to learning new facts; learning *how* to do something, for example, is not in general a matter of learning *that* it is done in a particular way. (If it were, one could learn to type by reading, and inwardly digesting, the contents of a suitable manual, without ever touching a keyboard.) That this, however, despite what he says, *is* a case of learning a new fact is decisively demonstrated by the following consideration. Suppose that I am wrong about Harriet's conscious state at *t*. Let us suppose that my analogical reasoning has led me astray; I was right about her physiological state, but wrong in thinking that, in her, it correlated with a headache, throbbing or otherwise. Then I have surely come to believe something false: I am now factually mistaken as to Harriet's conscious state at *t*, in spite of having all the relevant *physical* facts. Where there is falsity, there is surely also potential truth; and where there is truth there is a *fact*. If I was factually misled in this case, then surely I must, after all, have *learned* a fact in the other case.

(Of course, a sufficient knowledge of Harriet's physiology might enable me to know that, when stimulated with the sentence 'What are you feeling?', she would emit the sentence 'I've got a throbbing headache'. But that's compatible with her not really having one; not because she's lying, but because, say, she mistakenly thinks that the unpleasant sensation associated with her head that she *is* feeling is what other people mean by 'throbbing headache'. There are more radical possibilities too, which cannot *logically* be ruled out – such as that she is not conscious at all, but is just behaving as though she were.)

But there's a final move open to Tye. He might insist that the fact that Harriet had a throbbing headache at *t* was, after all, the same as some fact or set of facts already included in the physical description. Yet I didn't realize these were the same fact. Now I argued earlier that talk of facts in this context is, strictly speaking, otiose. What it really boils down to is whether someone with sufficient ratiocinative power, who knows the truth of certain statements, and possesses the concepts required for understanding certain others, would be in a position to deduce the truth of these other statements. Thus, if no one could deduce that Harriet had a throbbing headache at *t* from any amount of physiological or physico-chemical facts, in spite of possessing all the relevant concepts, no matter how great his or her powers of logical deduction, then it would seem, in any case, that reducibility fails, and physicalism must be false.

That, indeed, is what I believe. But one could interpret the query about facts as being designed precisely to undercut this criterion of reducibility. (Again, I owe this point to Peter Smith.) It is surely possible, someone might insist, to know a fact under one mode of presentation, but not know it under another. Consider, once again, the example of Sir Percy Blakeney and the Scarlet Pimpernel. Someone might argue as follows. 'The statement that Sir Percy Blakeney is in Paris must express the same fact as the statement that the Scarlet Pimpernel is in Paris; for the fact, here, surely just consists in a certain person bearing a certain relation to a certain city. Same person, same relation, same city adds up to same fact.'

Well, of course, one could if one wished use the term 'fact' in this way. I would have no objection to that. What I would baulk at, however, is the idea that, in terms even of this concept of fact, one could be said to be aware of the fact that Harriet was experiencing a throbbing headache at *t* (or that Angela was aware of a patch of phenomenal pink) when the only true statements about Harriet (or Angela) that one knew were statements couched in the language of physics, chemistry or physiology. For any sensible concept of fact must, I would argue, be subject to the following principle. Suppose that one knows a fact under one mode of presentation (that is, as the fact expressed by a particular statement or proposition) but does not know it under another, or knows a fact under each of two modes of presentation without knowing that they are the same fact (for example, knows the truth of the statement that Sir Percy Blakeney is in Paris and the truth of the corresponding statement regarding the Scarlet Pimpernel, but thinks that these two statements express different facts); *then one's not knowing that it is the same fact that corresponds to each mode of presentation (statement or proposition) must be attributable to one's failure to know some further substantive fact or facts, under any mode of presentation* (that is, as expressed by any statement or proposition). I say *substantive* fact, in order to avoid the trivialization of the principle that would result from allowing the 'further fact' simply to consist in the fact that each of two statements expresses the same fact. By 'substantive fact', I mean one which is expressible without reference to statements, propositions, concepts, modes of presentation and the like (assuming these not to be what the original fact was about). Thus, the only way one can know the fact that a certain person is in Paris, under the mode of presentation 'the Scarlet Pimpernel is in Paris', but fail to know it under the mode of presentation 'Sir Percy Blakeney is in Paris', is by failing to know, under any (appropriate) mode of presentation, such facts as that one and the same person combines the attributes of being an English aristocrat and so forth, and of carrying out brilliant and daring rescues of people condemned to the guillotine.

Assuming the above principle to be correct – and it scarcely seems possible to deny it – it follows that there must, after all, have been *some* fact about Harriet that I didn't know, so long as I was unable to deduce from my physiological knowledge about her the truth of the statement that she was experiencing a throbbing headache at *t*. And that fact, which I subsequently learned, cannot itself be a physical fact about Harriet, since *ex hypothesi* I already knew all the relevant physical facts about her. So it turns out, in the end, that nothing is gained by consigning facts to the domain of reference, rather than of sense.

Thus far, we have been assuming only that I know all the relevant physical facts about Harriet (that is, that I know the truth of all the relevant statements, couched in physico-chemical and physiological vocabulary). But suppose that I had all the relevant physical facts about myself as well, now and in the past. Would that have sufficed, by itself, to enable me to deduce that Harriet had a throbbing headache (or that the corresponding statement was true)? Clearly not. Those facts, by the way, taken together with the physical facts about Harriet, ought to include that relational fact that I do, even from Tye's perspective, learn – namely that her state at *t* resembled in a particular phenomenal respect previous states of my own. But clearly it doesn't; and this is yet another problem for Tye. So one way or another there must be facts that the physical descriptions omit. Tye's position is hopeless.

Thus, our original conclusion is sustained. A description couched purely in the language of physics, chemistry or physiology does after all leave something out. There are facts beyond the ken of physics and physiology, which nevertheless have somehow to be accommodated within a philosophically integrated world view. How this might be done is the subject of chapter 10. The discussion there, however, presupposes a certain, somewhat unfashionable, view of the nature of perception, which I shall now attempt to defend against its contemporary critics.

9

The Problem of Perception

Ordinary, philosophically unreflective men and women, so philosophers are fond of telling us (as if they would know!), believe that in perception the mind is in direct cognitive contact with external physical objects. What we are immediately aware of are the objects themselves: specifically, in vision, touch and taste, parts of their surfaces. Words like 'direct' and 'immediate' have proved very troublesome in this context; and attempts at defining them positively are liable to land us in a maze of difficulties. But for present purposes, an essentially negative definition will suffice. First, let us say that two things are *nonconstitutively* related to each other, if they are so related that the one is neither the same thing as, nor a part or aspect of, the other thing. Then we can say that a person, Harriet, is directly or immediately aware of a jub-jub, if and only if (a) she is aware of the jub-jub, and (b) there is not some other thing, call it a bula-hula, which is nonconstitutively related to the jub-jub, and is such that Harriet's being aware of the jub-jub simply *consists in* her being aware of the bula-hula and the fact that the jub-jub stands in some specific (nonconstitutive) relation, for example a causal relation, to the bula-hula.

For an uncontroversial example of indirect awareness, consider seeing something on television. I vividly remember, in the summer of 1973 in la Jolla, California, watching the Sam Ervin hearings live on television at the moment when Alexander Butterfield first revealed to an astonished public the existence of the Watergate tapes. According to the definition just given, I was not then directly aware of Butterfield. For there was something else that I was aware of, such that my being aware of that, and its being appropriately causally related to Butterfield himself, was what constituted my being aware of Butterfield. I mean, of course, the image on the television screen, which was clearly nonconstitutively, and indeed causally, related to Butterfield himself.

There is, however, a crucial distinction that must be made here, one that is stressed by Wittgenstein in his *Philosophical Investigations* (II, xi), where he distinguishes *seeing* and *seeing as* (Wittgenstein, 1963, pp. 193–208). (His own example is the famous 'duck-rabbit': a line drawing which admits of being seen either as a duck or as a rabbit.) The distinction generalizes naturally to awareness in general. Some might object to my saying, in the last paragraph, that I was aware of the image on the television screen. 'On the contrary,' they might insist, 'assuming that you were absorbed in the hearings – and not, say, wondering why there was that irritating flicker and whether you should adjust the horizontal hold – you wouldn't have been aware of the *image*, but merely of the persons and events that the image revealed.' This response, though natural enough, is nevertheless incorrect, it seems to me. I *was* aware of the image, and indeed it was precisely *because* I was aware of the image that I was aware of Butterfield himself. But it is, to be sure, quite likely that I was not, at least at that instant, aware of the image on the screen *as* an image on the screen.

Now according to what was the dominant tradition in modern philosophy, from Descartes and Locke right up to the middle of the twentieth century, not only could I not, in this situation, have been said to have been directly or immediately aware of Butterfield; I could not have been said to have been directly aware, either, of the image on the screen, or indeed of any external physical object or phenomenon. For, according to this dominant tradition, the only things one can be said ever to be directly aware of are purely mental items; the conscious mind is directly and immediately aware only of states of, and happenings within, itself. When I look at something, what I am directly aware of (in the sense above defined) is not the object itself but a phenomenal item whose presence within my visual field is caused by the physical presence of the object: a constellation of phenomenal qualities or qualia. Needless to say, I am not in the ordinary course of things aware of them *as* that. Rather, I see 'through' what is phenomenally presented to a physical object, just as I saw 'through' the image on that television screen to Alexander Butterfield. But that's merely a metaphorical way of saying that my awareness of what is immediately present to consciousness is an awareness of it *as* interpreted in a certain way, namely as a presentation of some particular person or physical object; it is this interpretation that governs my mental focus.

It is, incidentally, this mental focus that distinguishes ordinary perception from introspection. The very word 'introspection' evokes the metaphor of the inner eye: a sixth sense that is turned inwards rather than outwards. And the implication is present, even more blatantly, in Kant's talk of the 'inner sense'. But this way of looking at the matter is, from any point of view, profoundly misleading. Gareth Evans quite rightly inveighs against this conception in his book *The Varieties of Reference*:

> [A]ny informational state in which the subject has information about the world is *ipso facto* a state in which he has information about himself . . . available to him. It is of the utmost importance to appreciate that in order to understand the self-ascription of experience we need to postulate no special faculty of inner sense or internal self-scanning.
>
> (Evans, 1982, p. 230)

Evans is (or rather was: he died tragically in 1980 at the age of 34) no friend of the Cartesian conception that I am defending here. But on this at least we can agree: when I ascribe to myself the having of a particular kind of subjective visual impression, that is, the presentation of certain phenomenal qualities, I am not employing a sense *distinct* from that which I employ when I say that I see a squirrel. I am merely bringing to bear on the very same visual sense a different set of concepts: I am shifting my mental focus.

As I said, the view I have been presenting has, until comparatively recently, been the dominant tradition in modern philosophy. But it is so no longer. There are many philosophers nowadays who would insist that the (supposed) common-sense position is right after all, and that the arguments for denying that in perception we are directly aware of physical objects themselves do not withstand close scrutiny. Indeed, they might well go further, holding that the conception I have just presented is actually logically incoherent.

Now it is indeed far from obvious that what I shall henceforth call *common-sense realism* is false. The principal argument for saying that it must be false runs as follows. Whatever my conscious state when I see, for example, a patch of green paint on an otherwise white wall, I could have been in a subjectively indistinguishable state in which I was not really seeing a patch of green paint at all. Suppose I have been sitting in the car staring at a red traffic light waiting for it to change, and have then transferred my gaze to what is in fact a uniformly white wall. What I am actually experiencing is a green after-image; and were I to close my eyes, I would find that it was still there. Clearly, the patch of green that I am immediately aware of in the second case is not part of the surface of the wall. It is not anything that belongs to the external world at all (though of course I am also, so long as I keep my eyes open and directed at the spot, seeing a part of the surface of the wall, illusorily coloured by the green after-image).

But, as regards its conscious aspect, what I am experiencing in the two cases is the same. So if I am not directly or immediately aware of a green surface when I am having an after-image experience which is subjectively indistinguishable from really seeing a green surface – as obviously I am not, no green surface being there for me to be aware of, either directly or indirectly – then even when I really am seeing a green material surface, it cannot be *that surface itself* that I am immediately aware of. This invites the conclusion that in general visual perception is to be regarded as comprising (a) a material something, the thing seen in the ordinary sense of that term, (b) an appropriate phenomenal impression, and (c) an appropriate causal relation between the two. This view, the classic statements of which are to be found in the writings of Descartes, Hobbes and Locke, I shall henceforth refer to as *causal realism*. In the case of the after-image, only one of the three elements requisite for genuine perception of a material green patch is present, namely (b); (a) and hence also (c) are missing.

That, then, is the argument. But it is hardly compelling, as it stands. For it evidently rests on the tacit assumption that if some seeming, but not genuine, X is subjectively indistinguishable from a genuine X, then the genuine X must itself consist of a seeming X (or at any rate that component in seeming Xs which makes them seem Xish), together with some *additional* components, the presence of which serves to render it a genuine X. But in general that is not so. To an untutored palate mock turtle soup may be indistinguishable from true turtle soup; but from that it does not follow that there is anything one could conceptually *subtract* from genuine turtle soup which would leave one with mock turtle soup; rather, the two are, through and through, qualitatively distinct, albeit superficially similar in taste and appearance.

Thus one is not logically debarred from saying, in the perceptual example just discussed, that where one is really seeing a patch of green paint, that physical patch is what one is immediately aware of, but that where one is experiencing an after-image, it is that after-image, and not some external physical object, that one is immediately aware of. What one is immediately aware of, when genuinely seeing a material object and when merely seeming to, are, respectively, radically different sorts of thing, in the one case an external material object and in the other case not. To suppose that normal genuine perception somehow *incorporates* the non-external object of immediate awareness that figures in such experiences as after-images and the drunkard's proverbial pink rats is like supposing that whatever it is that makes mock turtle soup taste turtlish and what makes genuine turtle soup taste turtlish, is some single ingredient that is common to the two types of soup.

Well, one could take this line, it seems to me. But why would one wish to? Why should it be thought desirable, from a philosophical perspective, to resist the conclusion that, in genuine cases of perception, the external objects that are in the ordinary sense what it is we perceive are not what we are directly or immediately aware of? The main reason is that the view I earlier referred to as causal realism has historically been thought to lead to *scepticism* about the external world. It's all very well saying that these mental items, of which I am alone directly aware, are caused by external objects in such a way as to validate my ordinary perceptual judgements. But if the mental items themselves are, ultimately, all I have to go on, how I am supposed to know this?

Now of course what one could do at this point is try to show how such scepticism can be allayed, even assuming the correctness of the kind of Cartesian view that I am here trying to defend. But to adopt that strategy, it seems to me, would already be to concede too much to the common-sense realist. The correct response is to point out that, to the extent that this kind of scepticism is a problem at all, it is quite as much of a problem for the common-sense realist as it is for the causal realist. For, on reflection, it is surely perfectly clear that, for any doubt that can be raised in the context of causal realism, a precisely parallel and no less disturbing doubt can be raised in the context of common-sense realism. The causal realist says: 'What I am directly aware of is not an external material object anyway; so, given that all I have to go on is the phenomenal presentation, how can I be sure that it is being caused by a corresponding material object?' But equally, the common-sense realist can say: 'If this is a case of genuine perception, then what I am now directly aware of is (part of the surface of) an external material object. Given, however, that the state of awareness I should be in, were I not directly aware of a material object but were instead suffering from some form of perceptual illusion, might be subjectively indistinguishable from my present state, how am I supposed to know whether this really is a direct awareness of a material object?'

From this perspective then, there would seem little reason for preferring common-sense to causal realism. And besides, common-sense realism is faced with the unenviable problem of accounting for the subjective similarity of genuine perception of a green surface and the experience of, say, an after-image: that is, explaining it without postulating a common immediate object of awareness. To the best of my knowledge, no philosopher has succeeded in coming up with even a half-way plausible analysis that does this. It is no good saying that what they have in common is a belief that one is seeing a green surface; for that need not be true. I may be perfectly well aware that what I am experiencing is only an after-image, or conversely believe that what I am experiencing is merely an after-image when the truth is that I am seeing a material surface that is painted green. Nor need it be true (contrary to what some philosophers have suggested) that when I am experiencing an after-image I have the slightest *inclination* to believe that I am actually seeing a material green surface. It is, to be sure, *as though* I were seeing a green surface; it is *like* seeing a green surface. But these idioms do not admit of being defined in terms of belief, nor indeed in terms of anything other than phenomenal impact.

There is, however, another way of viewing these matters. I do not, in the end, think that it is the *right* way, but the line of thought I have in mind is quite simply too important to ignore. It owes more to John McDowell than to any other single philosopher. Suppose someone were to say: 'You've been in my thoughts lately'. We (meaning by 'we' the vast majority of philosophers) would tend to interpret this as simply a vivid metaphor. One person's thoughts, we would insist, cannot literally have someone else, or indeed any extra-mental item, as a component. What the person who says this must mean, or at least all that he has any right to mean, is that he has been having thoughts that *referred to*, thoughts that were *about*, the person being addressed. And this is a matter of certain mental occurrences being appropriately *related* to something, or in this case someone, external.

Now there is an instructive parallel here with the Cartesian picture of perception. There also the thought is that what is immediately before the mind is not the external object seen, but some inner experience whose status as a perception of that object is dependent on some suitable relation's holding between the external object and the mental occurrence. In both cases there is a problem. Rather than being, so to speak, right up against the world, the mind is conceived as being set back, or set apart from it. And the philosophical problem is that of how, given its predicament, the mind can establish contact with reality: *epistemic* contact (a knowing relation) if we are thinking of perception, *semantic* contact (a meaning relation) if we are thinking about reference. Moreover the problem of how the mind is to establish semantic contact with the world is actually a far more serious problem than the traditional sceptical problem of how it can *know* what is going on outside the mind. For it is only in regard to what can already be thought that the question how we can know it can even be intelligibly raised. The traditional Cartesian picture, so this line of thought proceeds, does not just threaten loss of certainty in regard to the external world; it threatens 'loss of the world' altogether. It places the world where the mind cannot reach it even in thought. Kant here might be instanced as a philosopher who saw this very clearly. For him, taking as he does the Cartesian position to its logical conclusion, the objective external world becomes an unknowable and unthinkable *Ding-an-Sich*, a practical irrelevance; and what is left is a construction of the mind.

According to McDowell, a key feature of theories of mind that are in a broad sense Cartesian – and this will include functionalism, for example – is that they effectively construe mind, in relation to the world, from a perspective that, were their theories correct, would be unavailable to the mind itself. Perception, for example, is construed as a linear chain of causes, with the object of perception at one end, and a 'percept' in the mind, at the other. But this is to represent perception in a sideways-on perspective, so to speak. If the only part of this process that is supposed to register in consciousness is the terminal link, the 'percept', then it would seem that the only perspective available to the mind itself is an end-on perspective. And how, from that, are we supposed to derive a conception of the senses as bringing us into touch with extra-mental reality? Isn't it a condition of adequacy of any philosophical conception of what happens when we perceive, that the conception in question be one that is available to the mind itself in the act of perceiving? Something parallel, clearly, could be said about meaning: what gives my thoughts the reference they have must itself be available to thought, if we are to know what it is we are thinking.

If one adopts the Cartesian picture as one's starting point, then the task of showing how knowledge or reference is possible becomes, as McDowell puts it, a gap-filling exercise. Perhaps the correct response to either problem is not to attempt to fill this alleged gap, but rather to challenge the assumption that there really is a gap to be filled, to insist that this supposed gap is simply the product of a radically mistaken conception of mind. Let's go back to that remark: 'You've been in my thoughts lately'. Is it, after all, so obviously *just* a metaphor? Why does it seem to us that it must be? Very crudely, it is because we think of thoughts as being in the head; and the things we think about obviously can't be, in general. At this point, proponents of the view I have in mind make a move of quite startling audacity. *Perhaps thoughts aren't in the head either.* Well, Descartes himself didn't think that thoughts were *literally* in the head, because he didn't think that they were spatially located at all. (I have already argued that this is a mistake on his part.) But the proposal is that we should reject the assumption that the mind is set back from its would-be objects, trying somehow to *reach out* to the world. Indeed, we should stop thinking of material objects as essentially *external* to the mind.

A trend in this direction is already evident in the work of Gareth Evans, who argues that there is a kind of thought – he calls such thoughts *Russellian* – that requires for its occurrence the existence of an appropriate object, with which the thinker is acquainted. Someone looks up into a tree – this is an example I once heard him give in a lecture – and says to himself: 'That bird's a chaffinch'. But actually there's no bird there; he's been deceived by a trick of the light. If there is no such bird, Evans argues, then there is no such bird for him to be having a thought about. It is, for him, *as though* he is having a thought of a certain kind, but he is not in fact having such a thought; though he may indeed be having various ancillary thoughts, such as the thought that he is seeing some bird or other. Evans draws a parallel here with common-sense realism in regard to perception. A 'cause of resistance' to his thesis is, he says,

> an adherence to a conception of the mind as a repository whose contents are unmistakably accessible to us – like a theatre whose actors are incorrigibly known to us. But we must reject this picture. It is already rejected when one acknowledges that if in perception anything is before the mind, it is the public objects themselves, not some internal representation of them. The thesis we have been considering is really no more than a corollary of that realism.
>
> (Evans, 1982, p. 199)

I think there are Russellian thoughts, in Evans's sense. What he has described is, I believe, a perfectly genuine case of a kind of cognitive illusion, parallel to, and indeed in the example given consequent upon, a perceptual illusion. There is no genuine thought here, because there is no proposition, and there is no proposition because there is nothing for such a proposition to be about; its putative subject is absent. This is parallel to the fact that there can be no genuine perception if there is no appropriate object of perception; only visual experience. But the analogy with perception cuts both ways. Anyone who is disposed to believe in causal realism, in relation to perception, will likewise believe in something like a causal theory of reference in regard to Russellian thoughts. My thinking of a certain bird, where there really is a bird there, is, he will argue, mediated by visual and memory impressions that are appropriately causally related to the bird in question, in a way parallel to my seeing the bird. And it is those impressions that are immediately before the mind.

In the place of the traditional Cartesian picture, McDowell offers us another one. The mind is to be thought of as tracing a path through reality. And the objects and occurrences therein should be thought of as set out, potentially, in two abstract spaces (in addition to their concrete positioning within space and time). There is the space of *causes*, under which aegis things are the object of scientific inquiry, and the space of *reasons*. Mental states and occurrences belong *ab initio* to both spaces: desires, for example, are at once causes and reasons for action. But perception is, *par excellence*, a transaction, an *encounter* with reality that allows the mind to take elements of reality and place them in the space of reasons, thus rendering them accessible to thought: available both to practical and to theoretical reason, in Aristotle's sense.

How, then, are we to think of perception in relation to the various neurophysiological goings-on in the brain? And what, from this perspective, is the right thing to say about after-images and the like? Well, proponents of the view I have been presenting will argue that perception is *supervenient* upon the sum total of physical goings-on, from the scattering of photons at the surface of physical objects right through to the progressively more sophisticated neuronal analyses conducted in the cerebral cortex. But they would reject the idea that perception can be simply *equated* with this process, or that the experience of perceiving something is to be equated with some key part of it, whether in the head or out of it. What they would say here is, I imagine, something very similar to what we find Gilbert Ryle saying in his book *Dilemmas*:

> From some well-known facts of optics, acoustics and physiology it seem[s] to follow that what we see, hear or smell cannot be, as we ordinarily suppose, things and happenings outside us. Where we ordinarily speak confidently of seeing other people's faces, we ought, apparently, to speak instead of seeing some things going on behind our own faces, or else, more guardedly, inside our own minds. Where we ordinarily suppose that we cannot see inside our own heads, and that only unusually situated surgeons could possibly get a look at what exists and happens there, we ought instead to allow that all the sights, sounds and smells available to us are literally or else metaphorically internal to us . . .
>
> One source of this dilemma is . . . the natural but mistaken assumption that perceiving is a bodily process or state, as perspiring is; or that it is a non-bodily, or psychological process or state; or, perhaps, that it is somehow jointly a bodily and a non-bodily process or state. That is, we have yielded to the temptation to push the concepts of seeing, hearing and the rest through the sorts of hoops that are the proper ones for the concepts which belong to the sciences of optics, acoustics, physiology and psychology.
>
> To say this is not to disparage the admirable conduct of the concepts of optics, acoustics or physiology . . . There are all sorts of important connexions between the things that we all know, and have to know, about seeing and hearing and the things which have been and will be discovered in the sciences of optics, acoustics, neurophysiology and the rest.

(Ryle, 1954, pp. 109–10)

These remarks of Ryle's might be illuminatingly recast in terms of McDowell's analysis. The attempt to force mind generally, and perception in particular, into the mould of the sciences fails because it is an attempt to confine within the space of causes something that properly belongs both to the space of causes and to that of reasons. This at once explains why it is hopeless to try to extend supervenience upon the scientific facts into an identity. Nevertheless, we can quite properly invoke the physiological facts by way of *explanation* of various aspects of perception. Thus, what is going on in the cerebral cortex when one has a green after-image is presumably, in certain key respects, identical with what goes on when one sees, say, a patch of green paint. And that can certainly be cited in explanation of why the two experiences seem so similar. But there is nothing here to license the conclusion that it is those cortical goings-on, and those alone, of which one is immediately aware. These cortical processes cannot be seen as a common component of the experiences of having a green after-image and seeing a patch of green paint; for they are not *components* of these experiences at all, albeit that they are physiological processes on which the occurrence of both experiences is partially supervenient.

I have set out these views at some length, and with all the persuasive force I can muster. Not, however, because I have the least inclination to go along with them; but rather because of their intrinsic interest and importance, and also in order to reassure readers who are *au fait* with these recent developments that my adherence to the Cartesian viewpoint is in no way due to my ignorance of these anti-Cartesian trends, or to a failure to appreciate the strength of the associated arguments.

Why, then, am I not an enthusiast for this approach? Well, first, like any version of common-sense realism, McDowell's view has, for the reasons given earlier, no advantage over causal realism with regard to the traditional sceptical problem regarding perception. So there is a lot riding on its claims to superiority in regard to the problem of meaning or reference. Now it is my belief that these claims to superiority are largely spurious. I would not deny for one moment that there *is* a problem of reference, and that this is a problem to which causal realists such as Descartes and Locke paid insufficient heed. But I would argue that this, like the traditional sceptical problem, is no less problematic for those who would deny the existence of a gap between mind and its objects. Even if the mind is, so to speak, tucked up in bed with its objects, still it seems to me a mystery how its thoughts come to be *about* those objects. Making the object which a thought is about literally a component of that thought obviates the problem of reference only if one somehow thinks it unproblematic that an object should, as it were, *mean itself*. (Kant comes close to making the same point in his *Prolegomena*, sec. 9.) What is mysterious here, as I indicated in chapter 1, is how any state or process can be intrinsically meaningful, regardless of what it is about, or the relation in which it stands to what it is about.

In short, whether there is a gap between mind and its objects is, as things stand, largely beside the point. It could only conceivably become relevant if we had some theory of meaning which made literal presence in thought a precondition of genuine reference – reference, that is, that was suitably transparent to the thinker. But as far as I can see, we have no such theory. What we have is merely an uncashed and at present uncashable metaphor of the mind, through its direct encounters with objects in perception, being enabled to place them in the 'space of reasons' where they become available as components of thoughts. The picture is neither articulated nor argued for to the point where any sensible answer could be given to the question: 'Why won't *indirect* encounters, in the manner of Descartes or Locke, do just as well?'

Thus far, the situation looks like a stand-off; but I should have thought that the more traditional causal realism has one key advantage over common-sense realism, in any of its forms. And that is that it admits of relatively literal articulation – even more so if one is able to place our perceptual experiences, as I have argued that one can (and perhaps must), quite literally in the head. McDowell's work, like that of Ryle before him (albeit that McDowell's is the subtler mind), belongs to a philosophical genre that seems to me to place excessive reliance on suggestive metaphors and analogies. I do not deny that these metaphors and similes are often very engaging and illuminating ones. (Listening to a talk by McDowell is an aesthetic experience quite as much as it is a philosophical one.) But the currency of metaphors and similes needs to be backed by the gold of plain speaking if it is ultimately to inspire much confidence. And science, *par excellence*, is the art of saying precisely and literally how it is with the world. I do not consider it a virtue of the approach adopted by Ryle and McDowell that it effectively places mind and perception in a region where natural science has but limited jurisdiction. What starts as a defence of common sense ends, it seems to me, in obscurantism.

That said, I think there is an element of truth in the line of thought that we have been exploring. I can see, in the end, no good grounds for holding that a causal theory of perception threatens loss of the world in the sense of its being incompatible with our ability to conceive of or refer to material objects at all; just what this ability depends on is a question that we shall be addressing in chapter 16. But I do think that a causal theory places certain constraints on *how* we can conceive of them. And that, I believe, is a consideration of great relevance to our present enterprise. If we are not quite as closely in touch with the external world as common sense and its philosophical champions would have us believe, that may actually *facilitate* the task of carving out a place in the material world for mental phenomena, including perception itself.

10

Berkeley, Russell and the Inscrutability of Matter

We discussed in the last chapter the idea that causal realism threatens loss of the world, in McDowell's phrase. This is not a new idea, but is precisely what we find Berkeley arguing in the eighteenth century, with Locke's *Essay Concerning Human Understanding* as his intended target. If the material world, both in itself and in relation to mind, were as Locke represented it – something that lies behind our perceptions, as their putative cause – then it would not, according to Berkeley, be available to us even in thought, let alone as an object of knowledge. This Berkeley takes to be a *reductio ad absurdum* of Locke's conception of matter. It may prove instructive, therefore, to examine Berkeley's views.

The enduring appeal of Berkeley's thought bears witness to the fact that, in order to be counted a great philosopher, it is not always necessary to arrive at believable conclusions. Berkeley's importance, like that of Hume and Descartes, lies in his ability to puncture our complacency, forcing us to re-examine the foundations of our common-sense beliefs about appearance and reality. That said, Berkeley's own manner of exposition is often such as to obscure his insights. What follows is thus in the nature of a rational reconstruction of Berkeley's argument for *idealism*: his notorious doctrine that the material world is constituted wholly of *ideas of sense* or 'perceptions' in the mind, sustained ultimately by God.

Berkeley, like Locke, was an *empiricist*. Empiricism is not just a theory of knowledge; it is also a theory of meaning. Empiricism, as understood by Locke and Berkeley, circumscribes what may intelligibly be thought, just as it circumscribes what we may properly be supposed to know. For the seventeenth- or eighteenth-century British empiricist, our minds are confronted, in perception and introspection, with a 'given' that not only provides the only data from which we can derive knowledge of the world, but also provides the raw material from which all meaningful thought, all the concepts we bring to bear on reality, must ultimately be fashioned.

From this perspective, Berkeley's main charge against Locke is that, although he proclaims an allegiance to empiricism, thus construed, his substantive doctrines are impossible logically to reconcile with this empiricism. It is not merely that Locke can provide no empirically acceptable grounds for claiming to *know* that there are material substances, as he understands that notion. If that were all (as has frequently been pointed out), a supporter of Locke might retort that Berkeley's claim to knowledge of a 'supreme spirit' was similarly bereft of empirical support. No; far worse, Locke's conception of matter is, from the standpoint of his very own theory of meaning, simply incoherent: one can show a priori, Berkeley thinks, that the raw material that the empiricist allows himself simply does not admit of the construction of such a notion as Locke claims to have.

The following beliefs are, I contend, axiomatic for Berkeley:

1 All meaningful concepts must either be definable by reference to what we are immediately aware of (in the sense introduced in the previous chapter) or be capable of being constructed from these by the exercise of reason. I see a very close similarity here between the theory of meaning presupposed by Berkeley and that advanced by Bertrand Russell in his celebrated 1910 article 'Knowledge by acquaintance and knowledge by description'. The way Russell states his own principle is: 'Every proposition which we can understand must be composed of constituents with which we are acquainted' (Russell, 1963, p. 159). Waiving a certain confusion here between constituents of propositions and the reference of such constituents, and the fact that Berkeley would have thought of concepts, rather than propositions, as the primary objects of our understanding, I take this to be exactly Berkeley's position.

2 The objects of immediate awareness comprise only such things as thoughts, 'volitions' (acts of will), memories, 'perceptions' (sensory impressions), and so on, their phenomenal qualities and relations; and finally the self that is aware of all these and the originator of some of them. Here too we have a similarity with Russell, who in 1910 was still of the opinion that an irreducible self, or subject of experiences, was to be numbered amongst the things with which we are immediately acquainted.

3 Everything has a cause.

(Someone might challenge – one reader *has* challenged – my assertion that Berkeley thought of the self as an object of immediate awareness, on the grounds that Berkeley repeatedly insists that 'properly' or 'strictly' he has no *idea* of himself (for example, *Treatise Concerning the Principles of Human Knowledge* I 27). Correctly understood, however, this does not conflict with my interpretation. Berkeley says explicitly (*Three Dialogues Between Hylas and Philonous* III 233): 'I am conscious of my own being'. He says also (231): 'My own mind and my own ideas I have an immediate knowledge of'. What Berkeley wishes to deny is that 'the mind, spirit or soul' – the phrase shows that he uses the words as synonyms – is an object of *perception*, as he employs the term: 'I know what I mean by the terms *I* and *myself*; and I know this immediately or intuitively, though I do not perceive it as I perceive a triangle, a colour or a sound' (*Dialogues* III 232). The same, in his view, goes for the operations of the mind, including volition, and relations between ideas: he says of all of these that we have 'notions', but not ideas of them. Again, the parallel with the early Russell is exact: Russell regards the self as one of the things with which he is immediately acquainted, but would deny that he has a 'sense-datum' of the self.)

The three principles, (1)–(3), Berkeley took to be self-evidently true and also to have been shared by Locke. (To what extent Berkeley was correct in his interpretation of Locke is a question into which I shall not here enter.)

So how does Berkeley get from these principles to idealism? Well, first, by (3), all my 'ideas' must have some cause or other. What, then, can we intelligibly suppose the cause to be? By (1), we can only suppose that the cause of our perceptions is X if the concept of X can be constructed out of conceptual components that are grounded in immediate awareness. Now according to Locke, the cause of our perceptions lies in externally existing material objects, which, by (2), we are not immediately aware of. So how can we have a concept of them? Locke says (*Essay* II.viii.15) that they are 'resemblances' of the perceptions to which they give rise, in respect of their primary qualities. But we cannot coherently suppose something which is not itself an object of immediate awareness to resemble something that is an object of immediate awareness in respect of the 'sensible' (that is, phenomenal or introspectible) qualities of the latter. That would be an example of what Ryle calls a *category mistake*: as Berkeley says (*Principles* I 9), 'an idea can be like nothing but another idea', in respect of its sensible qualities.

It follows that if we are to conceive of matter at all, we can only have, at best, what Berkeley (*Dialogues* I 197) calls a '*relative*' conception of it. In Russell's terms, we can only think of it '*by description*' – as that which stands in a certain relation R to our perceptions. Moreover, the relevant relation R, if it is to make empirical sense, must itself be grounded in immediate awareness. Now presumably, R here must either be, or at any rate include, the relation *causes*. But the only causation of which we are immediately aware is volitional causation: specifically, the inducing of events in our awareness by way of directly willing them (as in exercises of imagination). The concept of volitional causation is therefore alone capable of being grounded in immediate awareness; accordingly, it is the sole concept of causation that is empirically intelligible. This, however, is a concept which is meaningfully applicable only to conscious subjects, or what Berkeley calls '*spirits*'. We can no more suppose material objects, which by definition are not spirits, to cause our perceptions, in this sense of 'cause', than we can suppose them to resemble our perceptions in respect of the latter's sensible qualities.

In summary, then, we cannot conceive of what matter is like in itself, nor can we conceive it in an appropriate relation to anything else of which we can have a conception, such as our own perceptions. Hence we can have no conception of matter at all. It is a vacuous notion. As Philonous (representing Berkeley himself) says to Hylas (the champion of matter) in the Second Dialogue (220):

> Do you not . . . perceive that in all these different acceptations of *Matter*, you have been only supposing you know not what, for no manner of reason, and to no kind of use?

Or a little later (225–6):

> Now in that which you call the obscure indefinite sense of the word *matter*, it is plain, by your own confession, there was included no idea at all, no sense except an unknown sense, which is the same thing as none. You are not therefore to expect I should prove a repugnancy between ideas when there are no ideas; or the impossibility of matter taken in an *unknown* sense, that is no sense at all. My business was only to shew, you meant *nothing*; and this you were brought to own. So that, in all your various senses, you have been shewed either to mean nothing at all, or if anything, an absurdity. And if this be not sufficient to prove the impossibility of a thing, I desire you will let me know what is.

That is a purely negative conclusion, but the foregoing considerations immediately give rise to a positive conclusion. Given that our ideas have some cause (*Principles* I 26), and that volitional causation is the only kind of causation of which we can, consistently with an empiricist theory of meaning, make any sense, the only conclusion open to us is that the sole cause of our perceptions is spirit, since only spirits may intelligibly be supposed to cause anything volitionally – that is by willing. Now each of us knows from immediate introspection that he himself does not will his perceptions, nor his ideas of sense. We can choose whether to have our eyes open or shut, or in which direction to look, but given such a choice, it is not up to us what visual impressions we receive. It follows, therefore, that the ideas of sense must be caused by some other spirit or spirits (*Principles* I 29). (Note that for Berkeley the concept of spirit in general may itself be derived from our direct acquaintance with ourselves.)

This brings us to within an ace of Berkeley's desired conclusion. He needs some further argument, of course, to render plausible the proposition that there is just one spirit behind our perceptions rather than a number of distinct spirits. Here he appeals to the harmony within our experience, which he takes to be inconsistent with the operation of several independent wills. Even granted that there is just one spirit involved, further argument still, of course, would be required (argument that Berkeley never seriously attempts to provide) to render plausible the ascription to this spirit of the attributes of the God of Christian theology. But I shall ignore these later steps. The important point is that, given Berkeley's assumptions, which are essentially Locke's, his own theory is at least intelligible, in a way that Locke's is not. The concept of a self that wills our perceptions appears to be comprised of elements, all of which may be grounded in immediate awareness, in a way that the concept of a material cause of our perceptions seemingly cannot be.

I am not, of course, suggesting that this argument should, in the end, be regarded as valid. Only that it is an argument that deserves to be taken seriously. It contains no *blatant* fallacies. Considering the argument simply in its negative aspect – in respect of its attack on the intelligibility of matter – I suppose its major weakness would seem to lie in its treatment of causation. One can articulate the central problem in the form of a dilemma for Berkeley. Either he cleaves to a rigidly empiricist theory of meaning (in the eighteenth-century mould) or he doesn't. If he does, then he will be obliged to construe causation along essentially the lines proposed by David Hume (*Enquiry Concerning Human Understanding*, sec. VII). That is to say, he must take it to consist essentially of some sort of association or regularity. If that is all that can properly be understood by causation, then there is obviously nothing incoherent in the supposition that, in this sense, things which are not spirits may cause our perceptions. Moreover, as Hume himself pointed out (*Enquiry*, sec. VII, Pt I, paras 51–3), it is, from this perspective, a mistake to suppose that immediate awareness of the operation of our own wills reveals a relation of anything more than constant conjunction as holding between our acts of volition and subsequent actions.

If, on the other hand, Berkeley is prepared to relax these empiricist constraints, to the degree required in order to accommodate our ostensibly more full-blooded common-sense concept of causation, then again it seems to me that he has no principled grounds for confining its application to the volitional sphere. In my view, it is this second horn of the dilemma that Berkeley ought to have embraced. I would argue that we can and do attach a perfectly intelligible content to the word 'cause' which goes substantially beyond constant conjunction; and consequently that any theory of meaning according to which we cannot intelligibly mean more than that must simply be incorrect. It is tempting, indeed, to see the concept of causation as a product of reason rather than of perception or introspection: something that reason brings to bear on the data of sense, by way of imposing an explanatory order on them. A cause of X is essentially something that constitutes an answer to the question 'Why did X occur?' It is not just an accompaniment to X; it is the *reason* why X occurred. Also, in more pragmatic vein, to regard Ys as in general causing Xs is to regard bringing about a Y as a way of bringing about an X. If I want an X, then to believe that Ys cause Xs is *ipso facto* for me to have a reason to bring about a Y.

Of course, Berkeley himself allows reason a substantial role in concept formation, as does Russell. But there is reason and reason. For Berkeley, for Hume and for the early Russell, reason is a mere organizer of the data which the senses supply. It can fashion the raw material of sense, it can perform upon it various logical operations, create logical constructions out of the given material. But it is not itself a source of material – of substantive conceptual content. If reason is to be seen as the source of a more full-blooded concept of causation than Hume allows, then reason itself, I would contend, has to be construed as more full-blooded: as a potential provider of content as well as logical form – albeit content at a very high level of generality. And this is the key point. Notions such as that of a reason why something occurs, or of a *sufficient* or *necessary* condition of something's occurrence (respectively, a condition on which it must occur, or a condition without which it will not), are essentially *transcategorial*. Once grasped, they are applicable to anything, or at any rate anything that occurs in or persists through time. If such notions make sense at all, then it makes perfectly good sense to apply them indifferently to the operations of our own wills and to hypothetical events in which 'spirit' has no hand.

Berkeley may still be right, incidentally, in thinking that we could not come by such a full-blooded concept of causation were it not that we are agents. A mere passive recipient of sense impressions might be unable to form anything beyond a Humean concept of causation. But agents, faced with an apparent constant conjunction between X and Y, can always experiment – bring about an X and see if a Y still occurs. And even if they don't actually experiment, they can contemplate such experiments in their imagination. Perhaps, then, such notions as those of necessary and sufficient conditions, and counterfactual considerations of what *would have* happened *if* are, in some way, grounded in awareness after all, but awareness of ourselves as active interveners in the world rather than mere passive spectators of it. (This is the line taken by Flew, 1961, pp. 127–39.) Be that as it may, what emerges is a concept which, whatever its genesis, is free from any essential logical tie to agency.

If Berkeley is wrong about causation, as I believe him to be, does it follow that all his conclusions must be rejected? No. One central claim remains intact. I quote from the *Principles* I 87 (the italics are Berkeley's):

> Colour, figure, motion, extension, and the like, considered only as so many *sensations* in the mind, are perfectly known; there being nothing in them which is not perceived. But, if they are looked on as notes or images, referred to *things* or *archetypes existing without the mind*, then we are involved all in scepticism. We see only the appearances, and not the real qualities of things. What may be the extension, figure or motion of anything really and absolutely, or in itself, it is impossible for us to know, but only the proportion or relation they bear to our senses.

What Berkeley is driving at here is, I maintain, perfectly true. Of course it is easy to object pedantically to what he says. In the ordinary, common-sense, acceptation of the words 'see', 'real' and 'quality' we do, no doubt, see the real qualities of things: if the ball really is red and I see it as red, then (assuming we are not driven to adopt an error theory of colour) it follows that I see a real quality of the ball. But the truth of that truism is beside the point. The question is: if causal realism is correct, what exactly is it that I can take myself to know, in knowing that the ball is red – or rolling, come to that, for in the present context primary and secondary qualities are, as Berkeley points out, in exactly the same boat?

Berkeley reasons as follows: for the causal realist, it can only ever be possible to have a 'relative' conception of an object's intrinsic attributes. Ultimately, we can know objects only by their sensory effects. Believing in external causes, we credit material objects with systematic causal powers to produce certain sorts of sensation in us. And the words 'red' or 'round' signify those intrinsic attributes, *whatever they may be*, which ground the powers or causal dispositions of an object to produce in us visual sensations of redness or visual and tactile sensations of roundness. In one clear sense, we do not, and indeed cannot, know what external objects are like in themselves. We know, or take ourselves to know, the causal structure of the world; but we do not know how this causal structure is qualitatively fleshed out. And, *pace* Locke, this goes just as much for so-called primary qualities as it does for secondary qualities. We know nothing of motion, shape or size except that they occupy certain slots within an abstract causal schema that is ultimately grounded in our own perceptions. If in our daily lives we are intuitively unaware of our essential ignorance of the inherent qualities of things, it is because of what Hume referred to as the mind's 'great propensity to spread itself on external objects, and to conjoin with them any internal impressions which they occasion' (*A Treatise of Human Nature*, bk I, pt III, sec. XIV). In our imagination we colour in the world with the qualities of our own sensory impressions; we project these on to the external reality.

In no way are we entitled to say, as does Locke, that external objects 'resemble' the sensory images to which they give rise, even in regard to their primary qualities. As Berkeley says, it is doubtful whether it even makes sense to suppose that a material object could resemble our idea of it. But even if it did make sense to say that, we could have no positive reason for believing it to be true. It would, so to speak, be a mere happy accident if the ball intrinsically resembled our visual image of it, in respect of the latter's geometrical aspect. For, to repeat, the intrinsic character of things is, in the very nature of the case, hidden from us. If causal realism is true, the material world is, in a sense, *inscrutable*.

This is what Berkeley thinks follows from Locke's assumptions. As we have seen, Berkeley does not believe that even such a 'relative' conception of an external world is available to Locke, since the causal relation that he requires is not one that he can intelligibly deploy in this context. But could this objection be overcome (*per impossibile*, Berkeley would add), then what I have just described is, according to Berkeley, the view that we should be left with. What I am suggesting here is that the objection can be overcome, that the form of causal realism that results is true, and that, in consequence, the epistemic predicament that Berkeley so eloquently describes precisely *is* the predicament which we are all of us in, albeit few of us realize it. In one sense, Berkeley and McDowell are right in their claim that the Cartesian picture implies a loss of the world. Where they are wrong is in taking this to be a *reductio ad absurdum* of causal realism. For, if I am right, what is 'lost' here is something that we never had to begin with. This is what Kant saw and Berkeley did not.

I have drawn attention, at several points in this chapter, to the close similarity between many of Berkeley's views and those of Bertrand Russell, albeit that Russell was, for the major part of his life, a firm adherent of causal realism. Russell, it seems to me, has taken this inscrutability of matter (a phrase I owe to John Foster (1982)) more closely to heart than any other major contemporary philosopher. (The unknowability of the intrinsic nature of external objects was, however, axiomatic in Kant's philosophy.) I shall devote the remainder of this chapter to developing a speculation of the later Russell's, regarding the mind–body problem, that arises directly out of Berkeley's insight. But before I come actually to state Russell's views, a few preliminary remarks may be in order.

In Russell's *My Philosophical Development*, we find the following rather plaintive passage:

> I have found . . . that by analysing physics and perception the problem of the relation of mind and matter can be completely solved. It is true that nobody has accepted what seems to me the solution, but I believe and hope that this is only because my theory has not been understood.
>
> (Russell, 1959, p. 15)

There are several things to be said in response to this. First, the vast majority of contemporary philosophers have probably never read Russell's writings on this issue. (The tendency has been to concentrate on Russell's early writings, especially those on logic and the philosophy of language, and virtually to ignore the rest.) But of those who *have* read the relevant texts, it is perfectly true that most have failed to see what Russell was driving at; I have explored elsewhere (Lockwood, 1981) the extraordinary misapprehensions that have prevailed amongst Russell's leading philosophical commentators. Russell is, in many ways, a non-philosopher's philosopher whose greatest appeal has always been to the philosophical amateur (as indeed was I, when I first read Russell as an impressionable teenager). In Russell's own lifetime, his writings were, for example, widely read and admired by scientists, including Einstein. The physicists Sir Arthur Eddington (1935, pp. 269–70) and Sir James Jeans (1934, pp. 295–6) read, understood and agreed with Russell's views on mind and body. Professional philosophers, however, read his exposition of these views, if at all, through the distorting lenses of their own philosophical preconceptions and have mostly made nonsense of them (and, depending on their degree of charity, have concluded either that what he is saying *is* nonsense, or that his words somehow belie his intended meaning).

That said, however, I think Russell was deceiving himself if he thought that widespread comprehension, on the part of his philosophical colleagues, would have brought comparably widespread acceptance. On the contrary, I think his theory would strike many philosophers as too fantastic to merit serious consideration. And even the most sympathetic philosophically trained reader of Russell could hardly but regard his claim to have 'completely solved' the problem of the relation between mind and body as a grotesque exaggeration. The most that could reasonably be said of his theory is that it is a gesture in the direction of a possible solution. Such is my own view and, I think, that of the only other contemporary Russell sympathizers that I have come across, Herbert Feigl and Grover Maxwell (1978). (Feigl, incidentally, wrote an extended defence of a Russellian view of mind and body (reprinted in Feigl, 1967) which was first published a year before the book by Russell from which I have just quoted; one wonders whether Russell was ever aware of it.)

So what, after all that, *is* Russell's theory? Well, let us again approach him through Berkeley. In the *Dialogues*, Hylas is represented as a mind–body dualist. This allows Philonous to embarrass his adversary by asking him how matter can be supposed to interact with mind – something that, again, is no particular problem for a post-Humean conception of causation. By contrast, Alciphron, in the dialogue of that name, is represented by Berkeley as a proponent of the identity theory. The soul, he suggests, 'may be no more than a thin fine texture of subtle parts residing in the brain' (*Alciphron* IV 4). Elsewhere, defending determinism, Alciphron says (VII 16):

Corporeal objects strike on the organs of sense, whence ensues a vibration of the nerves, which, being communicated to the soul or animal spirit in the brain or root of the nerves, produceth therein that motion called volition: and this produceth a new determination in the spirits, causing them to flow into such nerves as must necessarily by the laws of mechanism produce certain actions.

To this Euphranor objects: 'it seems plain that motion and thought are two things as really and manifestly distinct as a triangle and a sound.' This has always been a stumbling block for materialism. What Russell realized, and very few other philosophers have, is that these objections to materialism are implicitly predicated on the assumption that we are, after all, transparently acquainted in perception with the inherent or intrinsic nature of material reality – and, being so acquainted, see it to be radically different from the reality of our own mental lives. Rather than caving in before Euphranor's objection, what Alciphron should have said is something like this:

Perception does not tell us, Euphranor, what motion is like in itself, either directly or in the particular case of the subtle and complex motions of the animal spirits in the brain. For, in perception, we know the appearances of things only; we know only their remote effects in our own minds. But I know my own thoughts immediately and as they are in themselves. Those qualities which are revealed when I reflect upon the operations of my own soul are, I hold, the very same (or some of the very same) qualities that inhere in those subtile motions in the brain, but are hidden from view in outward perception.

Consciousness, in other words, provides us with a kind of 'window' on to our brains, making possible a transparent grasp of a tiny corner of a material reality that is in general opaque to us, knowable only at one remove. The qualities of which we are immediately aware, in consciousness, precisely *are* some at least of the intrinsic qualities of the states and processes that go to make up the material world – more specifically, states and processes within our own brains.

This was Russell's suggestion. Much fun has been made of his notorious assertion (Russell, 1927, pp. 320, 383) that what a physiologist really sees when he examines someone else's brain is a part of his own brain. The point of that misleadingly phrased remark should now be clear, however. If matter is, on a causal theory of perception, essentially inscrutable, then the way is clear to explaining the apparently irreconcilable nature of mental events and physical events, even those in the brain, as an illusion fostered by the radically different ways in which the very same brain events might be known – on the one hand by perception, aided perhaps by modern instruments; and on the other hand by self-awareness: knowing certain brain events by virtue of their belonging to one's own conscious biography, knowing them, moreover, in part, *as they are in themselves* – knowing them 'from the inside', by living them, or, one might almost say, by self-reflectively *being* them.

These considerations do, I believe, remove what has historically always been seen as the main obstacle to identifying mental events with events in the brain. They show how an identity theory can be true, an identity theory, moreover, which in no sense *reduces* mind to matter. Rather, such a theory represents the physical world as infused with intrinsic qualities which, in conjunction with natural laws, constitute the basis of its causal powers and which include immediately introspectible qualities in their own right. It takes the mental seriously, in a way that functionalists, and physicalists generally, simply do not.

J. J. C. Smart (though I think he may now have abandoned this approach) once sought to accommodate phenomenal qualities within a physicalist scheme by construing them as *topic-neutral*:

> The man who reports a yellowish-orange after-image does so in effect as follows: '*What is going on in me is like what is going on in me when* my eyes are open, the lighting is normal, etc., etc. and there really is a yellowish-orange patch on the wall'.
>
> (Smart, 1963, p. 94; his italics)

Since the respect of likeness is not specified this allows one to hold that what is actually being reported is a brain process, the intrinsic nature of which can be fully captured in purely physical vocabulary. What Smart means by a 'topic neutral' conception is thus precisely what Berkeley means by a 'relative' conception. Smart is denying, implausibly, that awareness provides us with what Foster (1982, p. 62) would call a *transparent* grasp of phenomenal qualities – a grasp, that is, of their intrinsic character. ('Transparent', in this sense, is not to be confused with what Quine calls 'referential transparency'; it is simply the opposite of 'topic neutral'.) The reason why Smart's view seems so repugnant to common sense is that, in reporting the phenomenal colour of an after-image, one would normally take oneself precisely to be *specifying* thereby the respect in which my experience resembles that of seeing a yellowish-orange patch on the wall. Indeed, it is, on the face of it, only by registering its intrinsic phenomenal character that I am enabled to see that it resembles other experiences. If Smart were right, actually experiencing yellowish-orange after-images and seeing yellowish-orange patches on walls, would give me no knowledge beyond that which a congenitally blind person could acquire simply by being *told* that these experiences were similar.

Now the Russellian position that I am here concerned to defend effectively turns Smart's view on its head. I am suggesting that it is the *physical* characterizations that are topic-neutral, in Smart's sense. It is they that represent physical attributes only in the mode of whatever it may be that satisfies certain descriptions, as whatever it is that occupies the relevant positions within a certain causal structure. And the structure itself is saved from being purely formal (contentless) only by virtue of our ability causally to relate, within it, physical items with mental events of which we have a more than merely topic-neutral grasp.

Anyone who wants to argue, as do I, that the phenomenal qualities presented in perception, and other so-called 'raw feels', are amongst the intrinsic attributes of certain physical states in the brain, obviously has to confront the problem of how one is to conceive of the intrinsic nature of physical states that are not associated with awareness. (On this issue, Russell himself is exasperatingly – and uncharacteristically – vague and ambiguous.) Now there is a well-established philosophical tradition, according to which the concrete realization of phenomenal qualities is logically inseparable from their being objects of awareness. Some philosophers, indeed, refer to them as qualities *of* awareness, as though our awareness were a persisting entity of some kind, that took on such attributes (rather like a chameleon changing its colour) in response to various influences such as the stimulation of sensory receptors. Other philosophers would have it that these qualities are (or else are attributes of things that are) the internal objects (or 'accusatives') of acts of sensing.

On either view, phenomenal qualities are *realized* – that is to say, instances of them come into being – by way of their being sensed. More recently, however, Foster (1982, pp. 103–7) has made the bold suggestion that this gets things back to front. According to him, phenomenal qualities are inherently and essentially *self-revealing*; and they are sensed by being realized. It is the realization of such a quality, together with its essentially self-revealing character, that accounts for its being sensed, not conversely. This way of looking at the matter has, Foster thinks, two principal merits. First, it avoids the difficulty, associated with the internal object view, of explaining why a mental act of sensing a phenomenal quality carries with it the realization of this quality, while a mental act of merely conceiving the same quality does not effect a realization of it. Secondly, it explains why having a transparent conception of a phenomenal quality is logically inseparable from the ability to conceive (transparently) what it is like actually to sense that quality. Hence it explains why the congenitally blind person's inability transparently to conceive what it is like to have a visual impression of phenomenal blue, say, prevents that person from having a more than topic-neutral grasp of the phenomenal quality of blueness itself.

Foster argues further that one cannot have a transparent grasp of any (nonformal) attribute, other than by way of knowing what it would be like to sense, or be immediately aware of, that attribute. Only self-revealing attributes admit of being transparently conceived. His view thus has the consequence that, unless the intrinsic character of the physical world were itself mental, there would in principle be no way of having a transparent grasp of what it was like in itself. It is not just that one would have no way of *knowing* what it was like in itself. Rather, nothing would *count* as having a true conception of its intrinsic nature. Even a God could have no grasp of the intrinsic character of the physical world. It is, in Foster's judgement, far from clear that the idea of a physical reality whose intrinsic nature thus eluded, in principle, any possibility of transparent conception, is even a coherent one. But even if coherent, it is, he thinks, distinctly unappealing.

I used to think that one should simply grasp the nettle here, and embrace this conclusion, unattractive though it is. For the alternative of accepting what Foster calls *mentalistic realism* – according to which the causal powers of things are all grounded in states of awareness, the universe being mental through and through – struck me as even less attractive, not to say preposterous. It seems to me now, however, that the traditional 'sense-datum' view, according to which phenomenal qualities depend for their realization on being sensed, is just a dogma and should be rejected. The alternative conception that I propose is what I shall call the *disclosure* view.

The disclosure view might be thought of as a kind of *naive realism* with respect to phenomenal qualities. Naive realism is an extreme version of what I have been calling common-sense realism. The naive realist with respect to material objects holds that we have an immediate and transparent acquaintance, in perception, with certain material objects and certain of their attributes. Furthermore, he holds that the objects and attributes which are presented in perception are in no way dependent for their existence on being perceived; nor is there any mystery about what objects are like when we are not perceiving them. Even when unperceived, they are essentially as they appear when they *are* being perceived (under favourable conditions). Perception serves merely to *disclose*, in part, the inherent nature of things.

Naive realism regarding perception in relation to the external world is, it seems to me, certainly false, and probably logically incoherent. (Russell remarks, in his *Inquiry into Meaning and Truth* (1962, p. 13), with somewhat eccentric logic, 'Naive realism leads to physics, and physics, if true, shows that naive realism is false. Therefore, naive realism, if true, is false; therefore it is false.') But there is, as far as I can see, nothing to prevent one's being a naive realist about *sensing* in relation to phenomenal qualities. Why should one not think of awareness precisely as *disclosing* certain intrinsic attributes of states of, or events within, our brains – intrinsic attributes, moreover, which do not, in general, depend for their existence on their being sensed? According to this view, phenomenal qualities are not qualities *of* awareness. On the contrary, awareness is *of* them (though, of course, in a different sense of 'of'). Nor are they (qualities of) *internal* acts of sensing. Nor is it the case, as Foster argues, that they are inherently self-revealing; on the view I am proposing there is no such thing as a self-revealing quality. What we think of as phenomenal qualities are not inherently different from any other intrinsic attributes that are realized in nature. They are distinguished merely by the contingent fact that we are periodically aware of them. Any physically realized quality can be thought of as a *potential* object of immediate, transparent awareness for some conceivable sentient being. Whether a given quality is a potential object of such awareness for me, depends on whether the relevant part of my brain is so constructed that this quality is realized within it, and whether my awareness is such as to be capable of disclosing it, if it is so realized.

To repeat, phenomenal qualities are, on the disclosure view, simply intrinsic attributes *as* disclosed by awareness. They are not self-revealing; it is awareness that reveals them. They are revealed by conscious activity of the appropriate kind. Direct your gaze at something, and then let your mind (but not your gaze) wander. The phenomenal qualities associated with different parts of your visual field will then figure only sporadically in consciousness. The traditional view would have it that a given quality ceases to be realized in one's visual field, when one ceases to be conscious of it (even dimly). That, however, is precisely what I wish to dispute: I find it plausible to suppose that the phenomenal qualities themselves are less fickle than one's attention, and may persist even when one's awareness of them lapses. On this view, phenomenal qualities are neither realized by being sensed nor sensed by being realized. They are just realized, and sensed or not as the case may be. The realization of a phenomenal quality is one thing, I contend; its being an object of awareness is something else, albeit something for which its realization is a necessary condition.

As a first approximation, one could think of awareness as a kind of searchlight, sweeping around an inner landscape. (Literally inner: in the brain.) The searchlight may be thought of, in part, as revealing qualities that were already part of the landscape, rather than as bringing these qualities into being. But this is only a first approximation; for there is no reason to suppose that the intrinsic character of a brain state is, in general, unaffected by our becoming aware of it – especially if one believes that awareness is itself realized as neural activity of some kind.

At first hearing, the present proposal may seem wildly eccentric. In fact, however, it represents no more than a natural extrapolation from entirely commonplace facts about the phenomenology of perception and sensation. Consider a situation similar to that which we briefly considered in chapter 4. A person has the impression of a lot of black dots on a white background. (Such an impression might, in principle, be the result of direct stimulation of the visual cortex.) The subject may be aware that there is, *simply as regards the phenomenal character of what is being experienced, some* exact number of dots. And yet the removal of one of them may (contrary to what we envisaged in chapter 4) fail to make any conscious impact. Similarly, a subject may fail to discern any difference between two simultaneously presented arrays of dots, identical save for the presence in one of the arrays of a dot absent from the other. (Think of those pairs of puzzle pictures where one is asked to spot the differences.)

In such cases, of course, the difference will become apparent if the subject's gaze and attention are focused appropriately. But now consider the following example. Suppose we have three colour patches projected close together on to a screen; call them L (left), M (middle) and R (right). Suppose, further, that in the absence of R, L is indistinguishable from M, and that in the absence of L, M is indistinguishable from R. L, however (in the presence or absence of M), *is* distinguishable from R. Clearly, it cannot be true of the corresponding *phenomenal* colour patches that the left is qualitatively identical with the middle, and the middle with the right, but that the left is qualitatively distinct from the right. So what are we to suppose happens if we start with a screen containing only L and M, which are *ex hypothesi* indistinguishable, then add R, so that all three patches are present, and finally remove L, leaving M and R, which are likewise indistinguishable?

There are only two possibilities, surely. By far the more plausible, to my mind, is that the phenomenal colours corresponding to L and M are distinct, even in the absence of R: there *is* a phenomenal difference here, but one which is too small to register in consciousness, no matter how closely the subject attends. Adding together two phenomenal differences of this magnitude does, however, produce a difference that registers in consciousness; hence the subject's ability to distinguish L from R. The only alternative is to suppose that the effect, either of adding R or of removing L, is to induce a qualitative change in the phenomenal colour corresponding to one or other of the remaining patches. But it surely won't *seem* to the subject that this is what happens. So on this supposition too, there would be phenomenal differences – or at least, phenomenal *transitions* – that defied conscious detection.

Not only, in such perceptual cases, does the phenomenal character of what one is immediately aware of outrun one's awareness of it; it actually *seems* so to do. This kind of consideration has always been a thorn in the side of those sense-datum theorists who would have it that our sense-data are, of necessity, possessed of all and only the phenomenal qualities that they appear to have. That notion of a sense-datum is, I think, ultimately unintelligible: there is not, and could not be, anything that answered to such a conception. What I am suggesting, in effect, is that we should allow phenomenal qualities quite generally to outrun awareness. Those who think they understand what it is for phenomenal qualities to inhere in portions of their visual field of which, through inattention, they are not currently conscious, now have a model for what, according to the disclosure theory, the unsensed portion of the physical world is like in itself, quite generally – even in regions beyond the confines of the brains of sentient beings, where awareness, as far as we know, never intrudes.

One bad argument that Berkeley adduces for his doctrine that the *esse* of objects of perception is *percipi* (that to be is to be perceived) is that it is impossible to abstract the idea of the tree that one perceives from the idea of one's perceiving it (*Dialogues* I 200). (I have, I hope, established that Berkeley has much better arguments for his idealist conclusions.) Berkeley, notoriously, fails to provide any real grounds for judging such an act of abstraction to be impossible. But if this is a bad argument –

something that few philosophers seem inclined to dispute – then one cannot argue either, it seems to me, that we are incapable of abstracting the idea of a phenomenal quality, as it is presented in awareness, from the idea of our being aware of it. Whatever can be said by way of criticism of Berkeley's argument will, *mutatis mutandis*, apply to the latter argument also. To be sure, there is one salient disanalogy here. Someone might grasp the concept of a tree without being able to conceive what it was like to perceive a tree; but no one could grasp the concept of phenomenal red without grasping what it would be like to be aware of phenomenal red. That disanalogy, however, merely reflects a difference in the nature of what one is required to grasp in each case: the concept of a tree is topic-neutral in a way that the concept of phenomenal red is not.

If that is right, then the intrinsic character of the physical world is not, *pace* Foster, required to be mentalistic in order to admit of being transparently conceived. For any intrinsic attribute, there will, according to the disclosure theory, be an answer to the question what it would be like to be immediately and transparently aware of it, whether or not we are contingently in a position to *know* what it would be like.

The foregoing speculations have an obvious and immediate bearing on the status of *subconscious* mental states. Freud makes a useful distinction between the *conscious*, the *preconscious* and the *unconscious* minds. The preconscious comprises those mental states and processes which we are not currently aware of, but which can be brought into awareness at the immediate bidding of our will. Parts of the visual field to which we are not consciously attending thus belong to the preconscious, in Freud's sense. The unconscious, for Freud, comprises those mental states and processes which cannot be brought into consciousness at will. To render them accessible to awareness is the aim of psychoanalysis. I shall use the adjective 'subconscious' as a collective term for those states and processes of which we are not currently aware, regardless of whether we are capable, by a simple act of will, of rendering ourselves aware of them.

Now there is a very important point about subconscious mental states and processes which Richard Swinburne has recently impressed upon me (Swinburne, 1987, pp. 44–6). It is this: any explanation, of behaviour say, that is couched, like Freud's, in terms of subconscious mental states and events, must be of the same general form as a corresponding explanation couched in terms of conscious mental states and events. A conscious mental state and its subconscious counterpart must be able to cause and hence explain behavioural or mental events in the same sort of way. Otherwise the whole notion of subconscious mental states would be no more than a thoroughly misleading metaphor. But how could this requirement possibly be met, on the traditional view of phenomenal qualities? For, unless one is to be an *epiphenomenalist* – someone who thinks that conscious states are a causally inefficacious by-product of brain function – it seems impossible to deny that the phenomenal qualities associated with conscious states and events are, in general, essential to an explanation of why they give rise to the behavioural and mental consequences that they do. But anyone who takes the traditional view of the status of phenomenal qualities, according to which they are inseparable from our awareness of them, is obliged to hold that subconscious mental states are totally devoid of phenomenal qualities! So how *can* these states cause behaviour in the same sort of way that their conscious analogues do?

This latter consideration seems to me to weigh decisively in favour of the view I have been advocating. It is enough, here, to reflect on the preconscious mind. Consider once again the familiar example of the motorist, briefly discussed in chapter 6. Experienced drivers, it seems to me, are perfectly capable of driving competently whilst being, much of the time, largely unconscious of what they are doing. And amongst the things that they may do, while their conscious minds are preoccupied with other matters, is moving the steering wheel in response to perceived bends in the road. Now no one, surely, could deny that when motorists are *conscious* of such bends, the phenomenal character of the associated patterns in their visual field plays an essential role in the psychological explanation of why seeing those bends causes them to adjust the steering wheel in the way they do. But granted that, anyone who takes the traditional view of the status of phenomenal qualities is going to be totally debarred from giving a parallel explanation of why motorists who are *not* consciously aware of what they are doing are nevertheless able to respond in the same way. Perhaps an advocate of the traditional view might insist that such motorists must still be dimly conscious of the relevant part of their visual field. But that seems to me just empirically mistaken; there is, as a matter of brute fact, no need for that to be the case. (Another possibility that may occur to the reader is that motorists with their minds on other things are operating by blind-sight. This can be ruled out, I think. For blind-sight, as far as one can judge from the experimental evidence, comes nowhere close to providing the fineness of discrimination requisite for steering a car.)

This is a long way removed, of course, from the use Freud makes of explanation in terms of unconscious mental states. But the same general considerations seem to me to apply to, say, anger. When one is consciously angry with someone and responds accordingly, the phenomenal character of the emotion will surely figure essentially in any fully adequate psychological explanation of why that anger caused one to behave in the way one did. Once again, it would seem to be a precondition of unconscious anger being able to cause behaviour in the same general sort of way that it can retain, in part, its phenomenal character, as anger, even when it is successfully repressed and therefore hidden from awareness. The disclosure view allows for that; the traditional view does not.

If the general form of a psychological explanation can be indifferent to the question whether the mental states and processes which it invokes are or are not conscious, it may seem that awareness itself becomes a causal irrelevance – a kind of epiphenomenon. But that does not follow. Nothing that I have said implies, or is meant to imply, that awareness is causally inefficacious, or that it never makes any difference whether or not one is conscious of something that is phenomenally presented. On the contrary, when people *are* conscious of certain sensory or perceptual stimuli, the fact that they are will often (though not invariably) figure essentially in a psychological explanation of why they then respond in the way they do. For awareness is, in general, a precondition of flexible and rationally appropriate response to sensory and perceptual input of an unfamiliar or unpredictable kind. Awareness, if you like, is a channel through which *thought*, of the appropriate kind, may be brought to bear on the phenomenally given (which of course is not to deny that there are subconscious thoughts). There may, incidentally, be an affinity between this, fairly commonplace, observation and Freud's doctrine that to bring previously unconscious mental states within the purview of consciousness is *ipso facto* liberating, inasmuch as it brings them under what he calls 'ego control'. There is also the point, mentioned earlier, that the phenomenal character of, for example, our visual field is clearly affected by the way we interpret its contents. Witness the way we can cause the phenomenal character of a Necker (skeleton) cube to shift discontinuously by a conscious decision to impose upon it a different perspectival construal.

But awareness, someone might insist, encompasses more than phenomenal qualities. Well, perhaps so. One must tread warily here, however. What is certainly true is that the concepts we bring to bear on the phenomenally given invariably import a large measure of interpretation, inference or theoretical elaboration. This is obviously true, in the way we interpret perceptual data in terms of externally existing material objects and events. Equally though, it seems to me to be true of such *psychological* concepts as those of belief, desire, intention, thought and so forth, that they import a large measure of interpretation and theoretical elaboration. Even as applied to ourselves, their application does more than merely report what is phenomenally given. Just as our cognitive responses to perceptual qualities are governed by a theory of the material world, so our cognitive responses to phenomenal qualities generally are governed by a theory of mind.

Failure clearly to appreciate this has, historically, led to two complementary kinds of philosophical mistake. The first sort of mistake starts with a philosopher identifying the mental with the phenomenally given. Since beliefs, memories, desires, thoughts, emotions and so forth are mental, the philosopher then proceeds to proffer an analysis of these in what purport to be purely phenomenal terms. Two well-known examples are Descartes's analysis (in his Fourth Meditation) of a belief as an idea accompanied by a volition, and Russell's analysis of a memory as a mental image accompanied by a feeling of familiarity (Russell, 1949, pp. 161–2). The opposite and complementary mistake is to argue from the manifest hopelessness of such an enterprise to the conclusion that there is more to what is immediately presented to consciousness than the phenomenally given. That, however, whilst almost certainly true for independent reasons, doesn't follow either. All that follows is that many of our psychological concepts go beyond what is immediately present to consciousness, in just the same way that the concepts associated with an external world do; and that, correspondingly, there is, in our conception of the mind, more to mind than what surfaces in immediate awareness. But we knew that anyway.

Berkeley may have been more sensitive to this point than other philosophers of the Enlightenment. He uses the term *ideas* to apply indifferently to what is phenomenally given and the corresponding, phenomenally defined, concepts. But, recognizing perhaps that a purely phenomenal construal of much that we would consider mental is implausible, he says of many mental items (as we saw earlier) that we have *notions* rather than ideas of them (*Principles* I 27). What Berkeley fails sufficiently to appreciate is that it is the theoretical element in many psychological concepts that distinguishes them from his 'ideas'. Nor does he recognize the inconsistency in admitting notions in the psychological realm while banishing them from the physical realm (and thus, in effect, banishing the physical realm itself). The concept of matter is, it seems to me, a notion in Berkeley's sense. Another way of putting this would be to say that Berkeley's contrast between ideas and notions approximately corresponds to the distinction between what we have a transparent conception of and what we have a wholly or partly topic-neutral conception of. Precisely because we are unable to give a purely phenomenal construal of, say, belief, we cannot, it seems to me, be said to have a fully transparent grasp of the concept of belief. One thing that is right about currently fashionable 'holistic' approaches to the analysis of psychological concepts (Davidson, 1980; Peacocke, 1979), is the recognition that our grasp of many psychological concepts is inseparable from seeing them as thus-and-so situated within a certain theoretical scheme. But once again, it is our ability to locate, within this scheme, certain items of which we do have a transparent grasp that lends substance to the scheme as a whole.

In any case, considerations of this kind pose no difficulty for my thesis. To the extent that we do have a transparent grasp of the concepts that we bring to bear on our mental lives, those concepts may be seen as capturing certain intrinsic attributes of brain states. To the extent, however, that they are topic-neutral, they represent no obstacle to an identity theory anyway. Moreover, *this goes for the concept of awareness itself*. For it seems to me that we cannot be said to have a transparent conception of awareness. (Can one see the eye with which one sees?) To return to the searchlight analogy, what we see are the objects that the searchlight illuminates for us. We do not see the searchlight. Nor do we see the light: merely what the light reveals. (Compare Hume's observation in his *Treatise* (bk I, pt III, sec. XIV) that he could find no impression of the self, or Kant's insistence in his *Critique of Pure Reason* (A 398–9) that the 'I' of consciousness was purely formal, and did not carry with it any positive conception of the self as substance.) If that is right, then it follows that there can be nothing in our concept of awareness, such as it is, that could debar us from identifying awareness with some kind of physical process in the brain – albeit that it remains profoundly mysterious, in physical terms, what form such a process could possibly take.

Historical note

Russell was by no means the first philosopher to formulate such a view as I have been discussing in this chapter (though he may have thought he was). A number of nineteenth-century followers of Kant can be found saying much the same thing. Schopenhauer (*World as Will and Representation*, esp. vol. I, bk 2, para. 18) is perhaps the earliest such writer; the mathematician W. K. Clifford (1964), who gives priority to the psychologist Wundt (amongst others), is possibly the most lucid. Kant held that ordinary sense perception fails to reveal the intrinsic character of the external world, that the 'things-in-themselves' or *noumena* lie hidden behind their representations in experience, as an unknowable objective ground of the latter. There is a close similarity, clearly, between this view and Russell's, that we have only causal–structural knowledge of the external world, and that perception fails to reveal the intrinsic character of external states and events.

Now officially, Kant thought the same about our introspective acquaintance with our own minds, which he held to be likewise mediated by a veil of representations. According to Kant, we are, in this sense, opaque to ourselves. But it occurred to Schopenhauer, Wundt, Clifford and others to question this assumption. On the contrary, introspection – Kant's *inner sense* – may, they suggested, be giving us a glimpse, in respect of our own brains, of that very noumenal reality which Kant quite properly denies that the outer senses can ever convey. This noumenal reality, which is to be thought of as underlying all the appearances of outer sense, is labelled by Clifford 'mind-stuff', and by Schopenhauer 'will'. Schopenhauer, in effect – strikingly anticipating modern physics – conceives the physical world, in its phenomenal aspect, as consisting, in its entirety, of a flux of energy. And what we know through introspective awareness as *will* is, he thinks, a partial manifestation of the noumenal reality that underlies this phenomenal flux. I say 'partial', because for Schopenhauer, as for Kant, reality as it is in itself is neither spatial nor temporal, space and time being mere 'forms of intuition'. The inner sense, Schopenhauer thinks, brings us closer to this noumenal reality than can the outer senses, as is evidenced by the fact that the objects of inner sense are not, in general, presented as being in space. But, in so far as the objects of inner sense are still presented as being in time, we do not, even in introspection, perceive reality quite as it is in its own nature (*The World as Will and Representation*, vol. II, Supplements to bk I, ch. XVIII). (Speaking for myself, of course, I can see no good reason for following Kant in supposing that reality is, in its own nature, atemporal; though temporality, if it is plausibly to be regarded as an intrinsic feature of 'noumenal' reality, must obviously be understood in a sense that is appropriately respectful of relativity.)

The line of thought pursued by Schopenhauer, Clifford and others is one that receives some encouragement from Kant himself. In a passage in the first edition of his *Critique of Pure Reason* (A 358–9: in the section entitled 'the Paralogisms of Pure Reason'), Kant suggests that the noumenal reality underlying the representations of outer sense might be mental: that is to say, similar in its intrinsic nature to what is revealed by the inner sense. The fact that the inner sense is not, for Kant, supposed to reveal the intrinsic nature of anything, any more than is the outer sense, is probably the main consideration that led him to excise this passage from the second edition of the *Critique*.

Kant's suggestion seems to be overtly panpsychist. But it might be thought that Schopenhauer's and Clifford's views, and perhaps Russell's too, are at least implicitly so. And, as I pointed out earlier, the fact that it enables one to halt this slide into panpsychism is, from our present point of view, the major advantage of holding that phenomenal qualities can exist unsensed. This is not a new conception either (though, forgetful of the history of my subject, I mistakenly believed it to be when I first formulated it). G. E. Moore (1942, pp. 629–31; 1953, ch. II), who first coined the term 'sense-datum' around 1910, remained to the end of his life open-minded on the question whether there could be sense-data of which no one was conscious, as also on the question whether they might have attributes beyond those they appeared to have. C. D. Broad went even further, judging it likely that there *were* unsensed sense-data, and that they were probably differentiated beyond our powers of conscious discrimination (Broad, 1919, p. 218; 1969, p. 265). A. J. Ayer (1954) castigated Moore and Broad for employing the term 'sense-datum' in a way that allowed such possibilities to be entertained. So too did the American philosopher C. I. Lewis (1956, pp. 61–5), who felt that sense-data, as understood by Moore and Broad, were entities of ambiguous ontological status, which hovered uneasily between phenomenal appearance and material reality; he said of them that they were 'neither fish, flesh nor good red herring' (p. 64). It was Lewis who, partly in order to dissociate himself from Broad, introduced the term *quale* (plural *qualia*), for experienced qualities that are 'directly intuited', 'purely subjective', and known completely and beyond possibility of error, because for them seeming is being (Lewis, 1956, pp. 121 ff). That is the reason why I have largely avoided the term 'qualia' in this book. For, in this now largely forgotten dispute, I side with Moore and Broad, rather than with Ayer and Lewis. Phenomenal qualities, as I use the term, are, by definition, those qualities with which we are immediately acquainted in experience. But the ontological status of these qualities seems to me, as it seemed to Moore and Broad, to be a substantial matter of fact; not something to be decided, as Ayer and Lewis would have us believe, simply by linguistic fiat.

11

States and Observables

The discussion in the last chapter was, in a sense, highly abstract. The idea that physical descriptions are topic-neutral, in Smart's terms, opens the way to regarding the phenomenal, as revealed in consciousness, as that which concretely realizes certain physical descriptions of the goings-on in our brains. (Compare the way in which the doings of certain strands of DNA concretely realize the hitherto topic-neutral description of the mechanisms of heredity embodied in talk of 'genes', 'alleles' or 'Mendelian factors'; though of course, if the present suggestion is correct, physico-chemical descriptions of the DNA strands are themselves topic-neutral with respect to some underlying intrinsic characterization.) But our discussion was largely silent on the question just how the physical might be realized by the phenomenal.

Take some range of phenomenal qualities. Assume that these qualities can be arranged according to some abstract n-dimensional space, in a way that is faithful to their perceived similarities and degrees of similarity – just as, according to Land, it is possible to arrange the phenomenal colours in his three-dimensional colour solid. Then my Russellian proposal is that there exists, within the brain, some physical system, the states of which can be arranged in some n-dimensional state space, just as the states of the simple harmonic oscillator discussed in chapter 7 can be arranged in a two-dimensional phase space. And the two state spaces are to be equated with each other: the phenomenal qualities are identical with the states of the corresponding physical system. They are the realities that underlie, and render true, the corresponding topic-neutral state descriptions, couched in the language of physics, chemistry or physiology. This, at any rate, is what it would be appropriate to say, on the assumption that classical physics is true – which it is not. We shall shortly be re-examining the matter in the light of quantum mechanics.

There is a superficial similarity here between my view and that of

Churchland, who also wishes to equate phenomenal qualities with points or vectors within physical state spaces, and who likewise speaks of the 'direct introspection of brain states' (Churchland, 1985). But there are two crucial differences. In the first place, Churchland does not believe that we are *directly* and *transparently* acquainted with our own brain states in the sense in which I have been using these terms. On the contrary, Churchland enthusiastically endorses the Kantian view that

> the world of inner sense, the world of sensations and thoughts and emotions, is . . . a 'constructed world'. As with its access to the 'external' world, the mind's access to itself is equally mediated by its own structural and conceptual contributions. It has access to itself only through its own self-representations.
>
> (Churchland, 1984, pp. 84–5)

He goes on to say:

> The idea that one can have some suprascientific knowledge of the self, some special form of knowledge other than through the medium of constructive, objectifying conceptualization . . . goes against the modern psychological evidence that one's introspective judgements are on all fours with perceptual judgements generally, and provide knowledge that is in no way distinguished by any special status, purity, or authority.
>
> If *all* knowledge is inevitably a matter of conceptual construction and speculative interpretation . . . then it would seem that the 'special access' to the 'essential nature' of mind . . . is but a dream, and that the standard methods of empirical science constitute the only hope the mind has of ever understanding itself. This need not preclude admitting introspective judgements as data for science . . . , but it will deny [them] any special or unique epistemological status.
>
> (Churchland, 1984, p. 87)

This is marvellously eloquent. And profoundly mistaken. Of course introspection involves bringing a host of concepts to bear on the data of sense. But to have a concept is simply to have a certain cognitive *capacity*: a power of discriminating, classifying, interpreting, and so forth. Churchland (and Kant too in his worst moments) talks about concepts and 'representations' as though they were akin to patches of mental fog that hovered between consciousness and its objects, preventing one from getting a clear view, or to surrogates for the objects proper. But they're simply not like that. They're not mental substitutes for the objects. And they don't obscure – they may even facilitate – our apprehension of sensations and the like (or at least *clear* concepts may). And, anyway, they don't stand *between* the mind and anything else; they aren't objects of consciousness in that sense at all. Hence, they in no way detract from the immediacy of our awareness of our own sensations and so forth. However embarrassing it may be to Churchland's reductionist ambitions, 'special access', in this regard, is an inescapable fact of conscious life.

The second respect in which the view I am here concerned to defend differs from Churchland's, is that the *candidates* he offers for the relevant physical state spaces seem to me very implausible. This point is related to the first. I just don't see how a three-dimensional physical state space, whose coordinates correspond to spiking frequencies, can be capable of harbouring the *qualitative* diversity that we find within the realm of, say, phenomenal colour. (That goes back to what I was saying at the beginning of chapter 8.) It is for this kind of reason, presumably, that Churchland thinks it necessary to suppose that the perceived quale of, for example, shocking pink, is the *construction* that the mind places on some austere triple of spiking frequencies. But the futility of this move becomes evident, immediately we ask how one is supposed to account for the qualitative diversity within the supposed 'constructions' or 'representations' themselves.

Only by going to the lengths of embracing some form of eliminative materialism is one enabled, it seems to me, to dismiss this diversity as simply a fiction. But if it is not a fiction, and if materialism is true, then it follows inescapably that the material world itself must be correspondingly qualitatively diverse, in its inherent nature. And whatever physical state space is to be equated with, say, phenomenal colour space, *the dimensions of that space must represent what are, as regards the intrinsic character of the corresponding ranges of possible attributes, qualitatively distinct dimensions of diversity within that portion or aspect of the material world to which the physical state space applies.* Churchland's triples of spiking frequencies clearly fail to satisfy that requirement, on the plausible assumption that one neuronal firing is qualitatively much like any other.

My own tentative conclusion, therefore, is that it is not any neuronal firings *per se* that are registered in consciousness as phenomenal qualia, but something else that has an intimate causal connection with certain such firings. One way of looking at the electrochemical mechanisms that lead up to the transmission of an action potential along a nerve axon, is as a kind of analogue-to-digital conversion. What we start with is something that can vary along a continuous spectrum, the concentration, say, of certain chemicals or ions; and when that concentration crosses a certain threshold, we get a sudden, catastrophic change in the voltage gradient across the cell wall, that is transmitted along the axon as the action potential. Something essentially continuous is thus converted into something essentially all-or-nothing: either the cell is firing or it isn't. Then, at the other end, we get the reverse process: the all-or-nothing firing of the cell emits transmitter substances which, along with contributions from other cells, enter the electrochemical pool in which the neurons are suspended. Here the conversion is all-or-nothing to continuous: digital-to-analogue, so to speak.

My own feeling is that it is on the analogue side of this divide that we are more likely to find the qualitative diversity that we are seeking. It is, I suspect, some facet of such brain activity as surrounds the action potentials, rather than the spiking itself, which possesses the attributes that we register in consciousness as phenomenal qualities. Whether it is inside or outside the neurons, or on the semi-permeable membranes which form the interface between their external and internal environments, that the relevant activity is to be found, I have no idea. The psychologist Pribram (1971, p. 432) has made an interesting attempt to revive an idea originally put forward around the turn of the century by the Gestalt psychologists: namely that it is certain *fields*, in the physicist's sense, within the cerebral hemispheres, that may be the immediate objects of introspective awareness. Pribram suggests that these might be used to store information in a form analogous to a hologram (an idea that is cited by Maxwell, 1978, p. 399, as a possible way of putting flesh on the bare bones of Russell's theory). I am hardly competent to assess this speculation as a piece of serious neuroscience. What it would amount to, in terms of the present proposal, is that we have a 'special' or 'privileged' access, via some of our own brain activity, to the intrinsic character of, say, electromagnetism. Put like that, the idea sounds pretty fanciful. But make no mistake about it: whether about electromagnetism or about other such phenomena, that is just what the Russellian view ostensibly commits one to saying.

There are, however, two things that must now be emphasized. In the first place, it is a clear implication of the Russellian view that the material world, or more specifically, that part of it that lies within the skull, cannot possess less diversity than is exhibited amongst the phenomenal qualities that we encounter within consciousness. I am inclined to doubt whether the stock of fundamental attributes countenanced within contemporary physical science is, in principle, adequate to the task of accounting for the qualitative diversity that introspection reveals. The current trend, within physics, is towards ever greater unification of the fundamental forces, and so on. Now of course the material world must hang together in some harmonious fashion. But to take the Russellian view is to see introspection as to some extent reining back these unificatory ambitions. A theory that, at the most fundamental level, completely ironed out all qualitative diversity within the material world, could not, I am suggesting, be complete as an account of the underlying material reality. To the extent that such a theory was, as far as it went, correct, we should, from the present point of view, have to make one of two assumptions: either that there was a whole realm of material goings-on that the theory completely neglected; or else that behind the façade of what, at the level of physical theory, was a single (topic-neutral) description, there must lie a whole spectrum of so far unsuspected qualitative differentiation.

In short, I am suggesting that introspective psychology might have a contribution to make to fundamental physics. If mental states are brain states, then introspection is already, it seems to me, telling us that there is more to the matter of the brain that there is currently room for in the physicist's philosophy.

The second, equally crucial, point is one that may represent something of a departure from Russell's original vision. But, if so, it is one that simultaneously renders it more plausible and also brings it closer into line with current thinking both within physics and within philosophy. I think we must acknowledge that there is an irreducibly *perspectival* character to what is revealed in consciousness. We should still, I suggest, conceive of awareness as acquainting us with the intrinsic character of certain brain states. But the acquaintance is inescapably one that is tied to a point of view. What one must resist here is the fallacious notion that acquaintance with something from a certain point of view is somehow at odds with the objectivity of what is thereby grasped. Although what we apprehend, in apprehending a phenomenal quality, is irreducibly an attribute of a brain state *as it appears to a consciousness thus-and-so embedded in reality*, there is, I am suggesting, no gap here between appearance and reality. What appears to consciousness *is* the reality, or at least a part or aspect of it.

Just how objectivity and subjectivity are to be reconciled, how it is possible to make a place for subjective points of view, or what I have been calling phenomenal perspectives, within a conception of what the world is objectively like, has been a perennial problem for philosophy. One very radical response to it has been to construe 'objective' reality as actually being composed of points of view. If all these constituent points of view are regarded as being conscious, then the result is a form of idealism, or panpsychism. If, on the other hand, only some of these points of view are equated with centres of consciousness, we get a view such as was held by Leibniz in the eighteenth century, with his system of *monads* (described in his *Monadology*). A major obstacle to such a view is that its ontology and manner of conceptually carving up the universe seem so radically at odds with those of physical science. Russell, who held a view which (as he himself acknowledged) was closely akin to that of Leibniz, attempted to equate the counterparts, in his own theory, of Leibniz's monads, with something like the point-events of relativity: minimal spatio-temporal regions, at which lines of causal influence converge. There is, however, a displeasing arbitrariness about this: how small is 'minimal'? And anyway, why should there be any unique association between minimal space-time regions (whatever that means) and points of view, such as would justify our equating the two? On the assumption that a phenomenal perspective is directly sensitive to the physical goings-on in some spatio-temporal region of the brain, the evident *selectivity* of consciousness in relation to these goings-on remains to be accommodated within any such Leibnizian conception. This brings us back to the so-called grain problem, referred to in chapter 2: the fact that mental states seem to be less *structured* than any physical states with which they could be plausibly correlated. There is more to a point of view than relativization to a spatio-temporal location; there is also the question of what, at or relative to that location, is to be registered, measured, observed or perceived, and under what principles of ordering. (Compare the way a physicist can choose to diagram a system of particles according to their distribution in configuration space, or according to their distribution in momentum space.)

Given these difficulties, I intend, in the remainder of this book, to pursue a different strategy from Russell's, taking my cue from quantum mechanics rather than relativity. It seems to me that there is a way of interpreting quantum mechanics which leads quite naturally, and independently of any extraneous philosophical considerations, to a conception of the world as, in some sense, a sum of perspectives. (Indeed, almost literally a sum, seeing that the mathematical operation of vector addition is at the heart of the quantum-mechanical conception I have in mind.) And, in this conception, the inevitable selectivity involved in a point of view is automatically accommodated, via the idea that consciousness is tied to one amongst a potential infinity of what, in the context of quantum theory, are known as *representations*.

But none of this will make sense without the requisite scientific background. Thus, the time has now come to provide the reader with an introduction to quantum mechanics: the real McCoy, rather than the unstable half-way house between classical and quantum physics that was represented by the old quantum theory, briefly discussed in chapter 7. There is a widespread belief about quantum mechanics, as also about relativity, that it is something that one is entitled to ignore for most ordinary philosophical and scientific purposes, since it only seriously applies at the microlevel of reality: where 'micro' means something far smaller than would show up in any conventional microscope. What sits on top of this microlevel, so the assumption runs, is a sufficiently good approximation to the old classical Newtonian picture to justify our continuing, as philosophers, to think about the world in essentially classical terms.

I believe this to be a fundamental mistake. What I shall be urging in the next few chapters is that the world is quantum-mechanical through and through; and that the classical picture of reality is, even at the macroscopic level, deeply inadequate. It is true that the bulk of macroscopic phenomena admits, to a high degree of approximation, of being analysed in classical terms. But quantum mechanics is not to be regarded as just another scientific theory. To the extent that it is correct, it demands a complete revolution in our way of looking at the world, more profound than was required by any previous scientific breakthrough: this is what makes it so exciting philosophically. Moreover, it embodies within itself, as no other scientific theory does, a radically new conception of the relationship between observation and reality. Where previous physical theories have effectively taken for granted people's capacity observationally to lock on to the states of physical systems with which they dealt, quantum mechanics, in effect, incorporates a physics of observation or *measurement* as an integral part of the theory itself: one that strikes at the heart of our common-sense conception of what happens when one observes or measures something. The concepts that are involved in this theory are of a degree of abstractness and generality that permit their application to observation right across the board, regardless of the extent to which there is anything distinctively quantum-mechanical about what is being observed. They will, in due course, allow us to recast the Russellian ideas that we have been exploring in a more fruitful and illuminating way.

Before I embark on an exposition of this theory, I must enter one very important caveat. Readers must put completely out of their minds anything they may have heard about the uncertainty principle, and so forth, being attributable to the necessity of firing photons at things, in order to observe them, with the consequence that the objects of our observations are disturbed in an unpredictable fashion. This is a thoroughly confused and misleading attempt to force observation, as understood within quantum mechanics, into an essentially *classical* conceptual framework. Such crude travesties of the truth can only obstruct a clear grasp of what the theory is really saying, which is at once something far more astonishing and something that can be fathomed only by way of a fundamental adjustment in one's way of thinking about appearance and reality. I am not denying, by the way, that the act of observation *may* involve physically interfering with the system. But it need not do so; or, at least, not in any ordinary sense of 'physically interfere'. And even where it does involve physically interfering with the system, that interference has nothing whatsoever to do with the peculiar properties of quantum measurement (see Brown and Redhead, 1981). It is customary, within quantum mechanics, to distinguish between *perturbing* and *nonperturbing* measurements, on a physical system, according to whether the measurement interaction does or does not bring about a change in the attribute that is being measured. What I shall have to say in this chapter about observation will apply equally to both.

I said at the beginning of this chapter that, on a Russellian view, an *n*-dimensional phenomenal quality space is to be thought of as being identical with some *n*-dimensional physical state space. That indeed, it seems to me, is what a Russellian view would effectively commit one to, *classically* speaking. But it cannot, I suggest, be what a Russellian view would commit one to from the standpoint of a quantum-mechanical theory of measurement. Just what it *would* commit one to is something that I shall be in a better position to explain, after having conveyed the broad outlines of quantum mechanics itself.

In chapter 7, I offered an analysis of a simple physical system, a bob suspended by a spring, in terms of its two-dimensional phase space. Without going very deeply into the whys and wherefores of the matter, I want now to give an account of this same system as seen in the light of quantum mechanics. We have already mentioned the modification of the classical picture that was required by the old quantum theory. Briefly, the possible *energy levels* of the system came to be thought of as no longer lying along a continuous spectrum. Rather, they were conceived as being confined to certain discrete values, just as, on Bohr's theory, were the electron orbits in a hydrogen atom. Now what, in effect, Heisenberg did in 1925 – though this precise way of looking at the matter was not arrived at until a year or so later – was to redescribe the simple harmonic oscillator (and by implication other periodic systems, such as atoms) in terms of a new kind of state space with an *infinite* number of dimensions. This new space is known as a *Hilbert space*. And its dimensions, in this so-called *energy representation*, correspond one to one with the discrete energy levels (except, as remarked in chapter 7, for the fact that the levels in the new theory do not precisely correspond to those of the old). Consider the analogy of the *x*, *y* and *z* axes used in the mathematical description of ordinary space. Each axis corresponds to a distinct *direction* in space. Analogously, in the energy representation, each axis of the quantum state space for the simple harmonic oscillator corresponds to a distinct, discrete energy level.

Now we come to the first key feature of quantum mechanics that renders it so perplexing, and such a radical departure from the common-sense way of looking at the world. Once again, consider the three axes, *x*, *y* and *z*, as applied to ordinary three-dimensional space, and associate with each of these a *unit vector*: that is to say an arrow, one unit long, in whatever spatial units (centimetres, say) one is employing, lying parallel to the corresponding axis. These unit vectors are conventionally represented as $\vec{x}$, $\vec{y}$ and $\vec{z}$. Given an $\vec{x}$, $\vec{y}$ and a $\vec{z}$ vector, thus defined, it is possible now to combine these mathematically so as to generate a vector of any desired length and direction. Draw the desired vector, with its tail at the origin, drop perpendiculars from the tip of the vector on to each of the *x*, *y* and *z* axes. Let the points at which the perpendiculars join the axes correspond to the numbers a, b and c. Then the desired vector may be expressed as $a\vec{x} + b\vec{y} + c\vec{z}$ (see figure 11.1). It is said to be a *linear combination* of the vectors $\vec{x}$, $\vec{y}$ and $\vec{z}$.

(Multiplying a vector by a number produces a new vector, parallel to the original vector, but with a length that is the product of the original length and the number in question. Multiplying it by a negative number has the effect of reversing its direction. Vector addition may be understood geometrically, according to the so-called *parallelogram rule*.

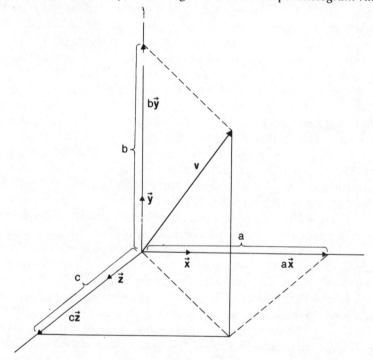

Figure 11.1 *An arbitrary vector* v *represented as a linear combination of the basis vectors* $\vec{x}$, $\vec{y}$ *and* $\vec{z}$.

If you want to add two vectors, arrange them with their tails touching, then, starting at the tip of each vector, draw a line parallel to, and of the same length as, the other vector. The result will be a parallelogram. Now draw a vector from the tails of the original vectors to the point where these two new lines meet, at the opposite corner of the parallelogram (see figure 11.2). This will be the vector that is the sum of the two vectors one started with.)

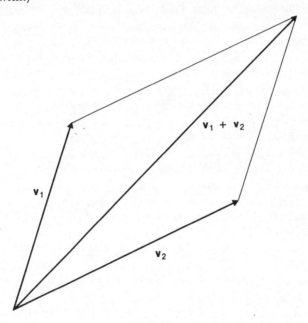

Figure 11.2 *Vector addition.*

This makes good, unproblematic sense. Now consider the corresponding operation with regard to the infinite-dimensional Hilbert space for the harmonic oscillator, briefly described above. In the energy representation, a vector parallel to one of the axes represents the state that the harmonic oscillator is in when it occupies the corresponding energy level. The unit vectors parallel to these axes are known as the *basis vectors* of the energy representation (just as the $\vec{x}$, $\vec{y}$ and $\vec{z}$ vectors are the basis vectors of the so-called *Cartesian representation* of ordinary Euclidean space). But equally, any vector is supposed to correspond to a possible state of the system. As a matter of fact, in quantum mechanics, all vectors parallel to a given vector correspond to the same state. So how are we supposed to interpret a vector that does not lie parallel to any of the axes corresponding to one of the discrete energy levels? The answer is that we are to interpret it as a state of *indeterminate* energy.

Let's be clear. According to the *standard interpretation* of quantum mechanics, a state of indeterminate energy is not an indeterminate state. We are not, on the standard interpretation, talking here about a situation in which the oscillator *has* some precise energy, but we are in a state of uncertainty as to what it is. On the contrary, this is supposed to be a fully determinate state in which the energy of the system is represented by a vector which is a linear combination or *superposition* of the basis vectors corresponding to determinate energy states. Take any arbitrary set of possible states of a physical system, represented by vectors in Hilbert space, multiply the vectors by any numbers you like, and add the corresponding vectors together. Then, provided the result is a vector with a finite length, it in turn will represent a physically possible state of the system. This is known as the *superposition principle*.

We should pause to reflect just how extraordinary this is. My having my jacket on is a possible state. My having my jacket off is a possible state. According to the superposition principle, then, two-and-three-quarters times jacket on plus six times jacket off is also a possible state. Actually, it gets worse. What I have so far neglected to point out is that Hilbert space is a so-called *complex* vector space. That is to say, when we represent an arbitrary vector as a linear combination of the basis vectors, the corresponding coefficients, that is to say numbers by which the basis vectors are multiplied, are in general *complex* numbers. A complex number is one of the from a + bi, where a and b are ordinary *real numbers* (such as 51, 6.25 or π) and i is the square root of minus one, multiples of which are known as *imaginary numbers* (see figure 11.3). So six times jacket on plus eight times the square root of minus one times jacket off is also a possible state.

We shall be considering, in the next chapter, the implications of quantum theory for macroscopic objects like people and jackets, as also the question whether the standard interpretation of the theory is correct. But for the moment, let us return to the simple harmonic oscillator, and consider a state corresponding to a specific energy level, in which the state vector is, accordingly, parallel to one of the axes. Note that nothing has yet been said about the position and momentum. The point here is that, according to the standard interpretation, if the system is in a fully determinate energy state, nothing beyond a specification of its energy level is required for a *complete* specification of its state. That again sounds crazy. From a classical standpoint, a given value of the total energy corresponds to an entire phase space orbit. And we shan't know the precise state of the system, at a given time, unless we know where in its orbit the system is. But, according to the standard interpretation, a state in which the energy is precisely defined is a *stationary state* in which, so long as the system is not interfered with, the position and

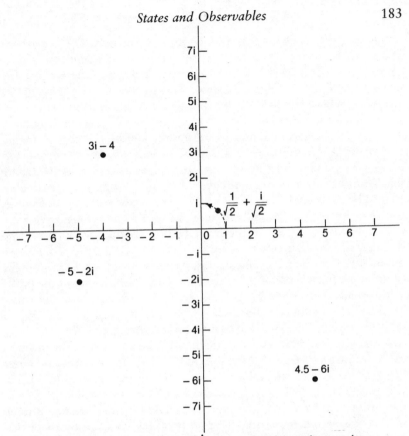

Figure 11.3 Argand diagram, *showing real and complex numbers.*

One commonly thinks of the real numbers as points on an infinite horizontal line, with zero in the middle, the positive numbers extending to the right, and the negative numbers extending to the left. In terms of this model, imaginary numbers may be thought of as points on a line perpendicular to this horizontal line, with positive imaginary numbers extending upwards from zero, and the negative imaginary numbers extending downwards. This makes good sense when one sees that a real number can be uniquely associated with a vector, so positioned that its tail is at the zero point and its tip is at the point on the line corresponding to the number in question. Multiplication of a number by another number may then be thought of as a matter of rotating and/or changing the length of the corresponding vector. Thus, multiplying by 2 doubles the length of the vector, multiplying by -1 rotates it through 180 degrees, and multiplying by -2 both rotates the vector through 180 degrees, and doubles its length. From this point of view, the operation of multiplying by i, the square root of -1, corresponds to an anticlockwise rotation of 90 degrees; and multiplying by $-i$ corresponds to a clockwise rotation of 90 degrees. The fact that (by definition) squaring i, or $-i$, gives -1 then corresponds to the fact that two 90-degree rotations, in the same direction, are equivalent to one 180-degree rotation. Adding a real to an imaginary number gives a complex number; and the complex numbers correspond to all possible operations of changing the length of a vector and rotating it (through any angle). The complex number $1\sqrt{2} + i\sqrt{2}$, for example, corresponds to a 45-degree anticlockwise rotation.

momentum do not change from one moment to the next. They are frozen in an unchanging, and precisely defined, state of indeterminacy.

For every energy level, there is a corresponding *wave function*. For any given place, P, that might be occupied by, say, the centre of mass of our vibrating weight, where P is defined by a value of the x coordinate of the phase space, the wave function yields a corresponding complex number. Now, given a complex number of the form a + bi, the corresponding number a − bi is referred to as its *complex conjugate*. And the product of a complex number and its complex conjugate is known as its *square modulus*; it's just $a^2 + b^2$. The square modulus of the complex number yielded by the wave function, for a given value of the position coordinate, is proportional to the probability that one would find the centre of mass of our vibrating weight in the immediate neighbourhood of P, if one carried out a measurement of its position. (More precisely, for those familiar with the language of calculus, the integral of the square modulus of the wave function over an interval on the spatial, x, axis of the phase space, yields the probability that the result of such a position measurement will lie within that interval.) The wave function is thus said to define a *probability density* over the position coordinate, x.

In the classical picture of the simple harmonic oscillator, the position of the (centre of mass of the) bob, and likewise its momentum, varies between two extreme values (which define the *amplitude* of the vibration). Thus, classically, if one chose a time at random, and measured the position of the bob at that time, one could be sure of finding it to lie somewhere within the spatial interval that was bounded by these two extreme values. But the corresponding wave function has non-zero values for some regions that lie outside this interval. And this means that, upon measuring the bob's position, one may find it somewhere that, classically speaking, it has insufficient energy to reach! Rather than being spread out evenly along the spatial interval that, classically, the bob is to be thought of as perpetually traversing and retraversing, the probability density oscillates, over the interval, with varying frequency and amplitude, between zero and some positive quantity, in a way that extends beyond the classical extreme values (see figure 11.4). As one considers higher and higher energy levels, the spatial frequency of these oscillations increases, and the average value, within any small region, comes increasingly to match the classical probability of finding it within that region, if one chooses a time *at random*. By contrast, the quantum-mechanical probability for finding the bob within a given spatial region, when the system is in a stationary state, holds good for any time one chooses. (Classically, one is more likely to find the bob, at a randomly chosen time, in a spatial interval closer to its extreme values, since it is then moving less rapidly; accordingly, it spends more of its time in these outer regions.)

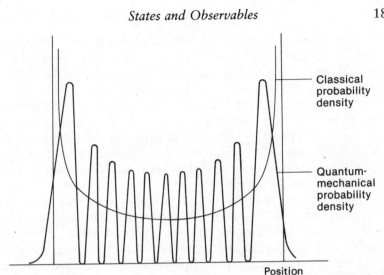

Classical probability density

Quantum-mechanical probability density

Position

Figure 11.4 *Here the classical probability density for the simple harmonic oscillator is superimposed on the quantum-mechanical probability density, for the case in which the energy is equal to $10\frac{1}{2}h\nu$, where h is Planck's constant and ν is the frequency of oscillation. The vertical lines mark the limits beyond which, according to classical mechanics, one would never find the bob. (After* Arthur Beiser, Perspectives of Modern Physics. *Singapore, McGraw-Hill, 1981, p. 189.)*

What I have just been describing is the *position* wave function; there is also a corresponding *momentum* wave function, of which similar things may be said. I remarked that there are such functions for every energy level. But, in fact, there is a position wave function and a momentum wave function for every possible state, regardless of whether it is a stationary state – one, that is, in which the energy is fully determinate. Position wave functions, and likewise momentum wave functions, correspond one to one with state vectors. Indeed, we can, if we like, *equate* the state vectors with the corresponding position or momentum wave functions. Hilbert space, in fact, was originally conceived, prior to the advent of quantum mechanics, as an abstract space whose elements were such complex functions. And it was in terms of these functions that Schrödinger represented quantum states in his *wave mechanics*. (It was not immediately appreciated that his formulation and Heisenberg's were essentially equivalent, mathematically.) This correspondence allows us to speak of state vectors and wave functions more or less interchangeably.

I have given some indication in the last few pages of how we are to think of states of physical systems, from the standpoint of quantum mechanics. Now in classical physics, an attribute such as position or energy is simultaneously to be regarded as an aspect of the state of a physical system, and something that can be measured or observed. In quantum mechanics, however, a sharp distinction is made between *states* of physical systems and physical *observables*. It is precisely this crucial distinction that our previous formulation of the Russellian view of phenomenal qualities failed to take into account.

States, as we have seen, are represented within the formalism of quantum mechanics by Hilbert space vectors. Observables, by contrast, are represented by certain Hilbert space *operators*. An operator in this sense is a function which, unlike an ordinary numerical function, takes vectors as input and issues corresponding vectors as output, according to some precise rule. In general, the effect of applying a Hilbert space operator to a vector will be to produce a new vector which differs from the original vector both in length and direction. But for certain vectors, known as the *eigenvectors* of the operator, the effect of applying the operator is to produce a new vector parallel to the original vector: the input and output vectors will differ, if at all, only in length. And the factor by which the length is changed is referred to as the *eigenvalue* corresponding to that eigenvector. Thus, if application of the operator to one of its eigenvectors results in a new vector twice the length of the original vector, then the corresponding eigenvalue will be two; if, to take another example, it has the effect of producing a vector identical to the original, save that it points the opposite way, then the corresponding eigenvalue will be minus one.

I pointed out earlier that Hilbert spaces are *complex* vector spaces: the length of a Hilbert space vector is, in general, a complex number. By the same token, the eigenvalue associated with a given eigenvector of a given Hilbert space operator will in general be a complex number also. But there is a class of operators, known as *Hermitian* operators, which have the property that all their eigenvectors are associated with *real* eigenvalues. These Hermitian operators correspond to quantum observables. The range of eigenvalues, or *spectrum*, of such an operator comprises all the possible results of measuring the corresponding observable: position, energy, momentum or whatever. The point here is that physical measurements invariably yield ordinary real numbers; no clear sense could be attached, say, to a measured length of six times the square root of minus one centimetres, or a measured energy of two-and-a-half plus pi times the square root of minus one ergs.

Let me emphasize that the *act* of measuring an observable on a physical system in a given state is not here being equated with the *application* of the corresponding operator to the state vector. Just how we are to conceive the act of measurement is a matter which we shall be considering presently. No; the Hermitian operator is simply a mathematical object that is used to *represent* a quantum-mechanical observable, just as a Hilbert state vector is used to represent a quantum-mechanical state.

Between them, the observable operator and the state vector can be used to calculate the probabilities of getting certain results when measuring an observable on a system in a given state, and also the so-called *expectation value* of the observable relative to that state. This expectation value is the average value one would get, if the observable were to be repeatedly measured on systems prepared in that same state.

Consider the analogy of rolling a die. There are six faces, bearing one to six spots. The act of rolling the die may be thought of as analogous to measuring an observable. And the possible numbers of spots on the uppermost face, when the die comes to rest, may be thought of as analogous to the eigenvalues of the corresponding observable operator; these will simply be the numbers one to six. Assuming the die to be unbiased, each of these 'eigenvalues' will be associated with a probability of one-sixth. In terms of this analogy, seeing that all the 'eigenvalues' are associated with equal probabilities, the expectation value is the total number of spots, namely twenty-one, divided by the number of faces, six, which is to say three and a half.

How, then, in the quantum-mechanical case, are these probabilities and expectation values calculated? Well, to explain that we need to introduce the concept of the *inner product* of two Hilbert space vectors. In ordinary Euclidean space, the inner product (v_1, v_2) of the vectors v_1 and v_2 is defined as the length of v_1 times the *projected length of* v_2 *on* v_1. Place the two vectors with their tails touching, then drop a perpendicular from the tip of v_2 on to v_1, or, if that is impossible, on to a straight line that coincides with v_1 but extends beyond it in the appropriate direction to the required length. The length of the line from the tail of v_1, to the point where it is touched by the perpendicular, is the projected length of v_2 on v_1 (see figure 11.5). This projected length will be a positive or negative number according as the line extends, from the tail of v_2, towards or away from the tip, which will depend on whether the angle between the two vectors is less than or greater than ninety degrees.

The inner product of two Hilbert space vectors – though I shall not here give a definition – may be thought of by analogy with its Euclidean counterpart. Note that when two vectors, in Euclidean space, are at right-angles to each other, it follows from the above definition that their inner product is zero. Such vectors are said to be *mutually orthogonal*. And this generalized notion of orthogonality, understood as the vanishing of the inner product, carries over to Hilbert space as well (as indeed to any vector space for which an inner product can be defined). There is, however, an important disanalogy between the inner product in Euclidean space and its Hilbert space counterpart. In ordinary Euclidean space, the inner product (v_1, v_2) is-invariably equal to the inner product (v_2, v_1); order is immaterial. This is not so in general, with the inner

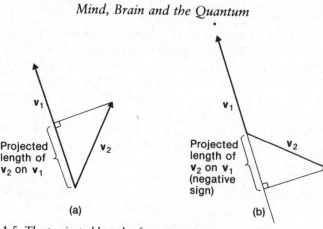

Figure 11.5 *The projected length of a vector* v_2 *on a vector* v_1, *for the cases (a) in which the angle between the two vectors is less than 90 degrees, and (b) in which it exceeds 90 degrees.*

product of two Hilbert space vectors ψ_1 and ψ_2. Here the inner product (ψ_2, ψ_1) is equal to the complex conjugate of (ψ_1, ψ_2). Only where the inner product is a real number, therefore, will its value be unaffected by transposing the order of the vectors.

Given an arbitrary vector, the *components* of that vector, with respect to the chosen basis – that is to say, the coefficients by which the basis vectors are respectively multiplied, when the vector is expressed as a linear combination of the basis vectors – are simply the respective inner products of the basis vectors and the given vector (taken in that order). The coordinate axis corresponding to a specific basis vector may be thought of as the set of all vectors parallel to the basis vector; and the various coordinate *values* will be the corresponding lengths of these vectors.

The inner product of a vector with itself is known as its *norm*, and is always a positive real number. I remarked earlier that all vectors parallel to a given vector, in Hilbert space, correspond to the same quantum state. For the purposes of computing probabilities, however, it is convenient to represent states by vectors with a norm of one; these are known as *normalized* vectors. In what follows, I shall assume that the vectors we are talking about are normalized.

Now suppose we have a physical system that is in the state represented by the (normalized) Hilbert space vector ψ. (Rather than constantly speaking of the state represented by the vector ψ, or the observable represented by the operator A, I shall henceforth speak simply of the state ψ and the observable A; such conflation of states and observables with the corresponding Hilbert space ·vectors and operators is essentially harmless, and makes for more concise prose.) Suppose, further, that we wish to know the probability of getting the eigenvalue a, when we measure the observable A; and assume that no two eigenvectors of A are associated with the same eigenvalue. Then if α is the (normalized) eigenvector corresponding to the eigenvalue a then the probability of getting the value a, when we measure A, will be equal to the square modulus of the inner product (α, ψ).

Suppose, on the other hand, we want to know the expectation value of A, when the system is in the state ψ. That expectation value is equal to the inner product $(A\psi, \psi)$, $A\psi$ being the state vector one gets by applying the observable operator A to the state vector ψ. Given that A is a Hermitian operator, $(A\psi, \psi)$ must be equal to $(\psi, A\psi)$. And that, as it happens, is the definition of a Hermitian operator: an operator, A, is Hermitian if and only if, for all vectors ψ, $(A\psi, \psi) = (\psi, A\psi)$.

A good example of an observable operator is the *Hamiltonian operator*, which for a conservative system, such as the undamped simple harmonic oscillator, is the operator that corresponds to the energy observable. Classically, as we saw in chapter 7, the Hamiltonian corresponding to the simple harmonic oscillator is a function that takes position and momentum as inputs and yields the energy as output. In quantum mechanics, this function becomes transmuted into a Hilbert space operator. This operator has, as its eigenvectors, those Hilbert space vectors that represent stationary states, states of determinate energy; and as its eigenvalues, it has the numerical values of the corresponding energies. These stationary states are, accordingly, also known as *energy eigenstates*.

The energy observable, represented by the Hamiltonian operator, is an example of what is known as a *maximal* or *nondegenerate* observable. This goes back to what I was saying earlier about the attribution of a determinate energy to the simple harmonic oscillator amounting to a complete specification of its state. The knowledge one has about a system, having carried out a (precise) measurement of its energy, constitutes a state of maximal information, one that cannot be improved upon by carrying out any further measurements. In our explanation of how to calculate the probability of getting a certain result when carrying out a measurement, we made, as the reader may remember, the simplifying assumption that no two eigenvectors of the measured observable were associated with the same eigenvalue. This, in fact, is the definition of a maximal observable, that distinct eigenvectors are associated with distinct eigenvalues.

The Hamiltonian operator may still, incidentally, be thought of as a function of position and momentum. That is to say, one can express it as a mathematical function of position and momentum observable operators. Considered as operators, position and momentum have, as their eigenvalues, all the possible values of the position and momentum coordinates, respectively. (This treatment of position and momentum as observables is, however, an idealization. Strictly speaking, position and momentum cannot be represented by Hilbert space operators, seeing that there is no such thing as a precise measurement of, say, an object's position. In the case of our vibrating weight, for example, the most we can ever do is make an observation which tells us whether the centre of mass of the weight lies within some finite interval on the x axis; and similarly for momentum. The interval can be made as small as we like, but it can never be shrunk to a single point.)

We now come to the second, key feature of quantum mechanics that distinguishes it so sharply from classical physics. *Not all observables are simultaneously measurable.* Suppose one measures two quantum-mechanical observables, one immediately after the other. Quantum mechanics may make quite different predictions for the probabilities of getting certain specific values of these observables, from what it predicts for a measurement of the observables in the reverse order. If so, the two observables are said not to be *compatible*. Two observables are compatible if and only if the corresponding observable operators *commute*. A and B are said to commute just in case, for any vector ψ, $AB\psi = BA\psi$. Now if one makes a nonperturbing measurement of an observable, and immediately afterwards measures that observable again, one will invariably get the same result, if no significant time has elapsed and one's instruments are reliable. But if A and B fail to commute, and one measures A, B and A again, with no significant lapse of time, then in general the two measurements of A will yield different eigenvalues.

This brings us to the famous Heisenberg *uncertainty principle*. The principle is usually applied to position and momentum, and, so applied, reflects the fact that position and momentum are not compatible observables, in the sense just defined. If one measures the position of a particle, and immediately afterwards measures its momentum, an immediately subsequent repeat measurement of the position will in general yield a different result; and similarly, if one measures momentum, position and then momentum. Moreover, the more precise one's measurement of the position – the smaller, that is, the region within which the measurement allows one to locate the particle – the larger, correspondingly, will be the region within which the momentum may be found to lie in a subsequent measurement. And, of course, conversely; that is, interchanging position and momentum. Heisenberg's principle gives a precise statement of this reciprocal indeterminacy.

The above characterization of compatible observables applies only to pairs of observables. If, as promised, I am to offer a quantized version of the Russellian conception of phenomenal qualities which was presented earlier, the notion of compatibility must be generalized, so as to apply to a set of observables with an arbitrary number of members. A set of observables may be said to be a *compatible set* if and only if the observables in the set have a common *eigenbasis*. By that is meant a set of vectors which (a) are eigenvectors with respect to all the observables in question, (b) are mutually orthogonal, and (c) constitute a basis for the corresponding Hilbert space: that is to say, any arbitrary vector may be represented as a linear combination of vectors in the set. (For the limiting case in which there are just two observables, saying that they have a common eigenbasis is equivalent to saying that the corresponding operators commute.) Repeated measurement of the same observable, drawn from a compatible set, with a negligible intervening time interval, is guaranteed to yield the same result, regardless of what other observables in the set have been measured in the interim.

This allows us to restate, in a manner appropriate to quantum mechanics, the Russellian account of phenomenal qualities that I have been defending in this and the previous chapter. An n-dimensional phenomenal quality space is now to be identified, not, as suggested previously, with an n-dimensional physical state space, but rather with *an n-dimensional space of observable attributes, each point of which is associated with some n-tuple of eigenvalues of the spectra corresponding to the shared eigenstates (eigenvectors) of a set of n compatible brain observables.* My contention is that quantum-mechanical observables are inherently perspectival. Observation is always from a point of view. But this claim, with regard to quantum mechanics, depends on a particular way of interpreting the theory, which I shall explain and attempt to vindicate in the next chapter.

The concept of a maximal or nondegenerate observable, which was introduced earlier, may also be generalized, so as to apply to sets of compatible observables, the individual members of which are in general nonmaximal. A compatible set of n observables is complete or maximal if and only if every vector in the shared eigenbasis is associated with a distinct n-tuple of eigenvalues of the n observables. To put it another way, any two distinct vectors in the shared eigenbasis must, for at least one of the observables in the set, be associated with distinct eigenvalues. In the limiting case where we have just one observable, this clearly reduces to our earlier definition of a maximal or nondegenerate observable. As with an individual maximal observable, joint measurement of all the observables in a complete set of compatible observables yields the maximum amount of information about the system, at the time of the measurement, that is simultaneously available to an observer.

It follows from the definitions given above that every maximal observable, or complete set of compatible observables, of some physical system, corresponds to a way of imposing a *coordinate system* or vector basis on the corresponding Hilbert space. These coordinate systems or bases are what are known as *representations*. And the energy representation is just the particular representation that corresponds to the Hamiltonian; that is to say, the energy observable, which for the simple harmonic oscillator is itself a maximal observable in the required sense. There is, in fact, a potential infinity of distinct ways of representing the Hilbert space for, say, our simple harmonic oscillator. Only a handful of these have, in general, much to recommend them, either conceptually or in terms of facilitating calculation. But if one is concerned with the measurement of a particular (maximal) observable, then it is often convenient to express the state vector in the corresponding basis; that is, as a linear combination of the unit vectors representing the eigenstates of that observable. For then the square moduli of the coefficients in the corresponding terms of the linear combination give the respective probabilities that the measurement will yield the associated eigenvalues. There is, as I shall be arguing in the next chapter, an intimate connection here, between the fact that a maximal observable or set of compatible observables corresponds to a choice of coordinates, and what I was saying just now about quantum-mechanical observables being inherently perspectival.

In general, physical systems change over time. And according to the conventional wisdom, quantum-mechanical systems can do so in two distinct ways, which von Neumann referred to as *processes of the first* and *second kinds*, respectively. I shall start with processes of the second kind, which are what are supposed to occur in *isolated* quantum-mechanical systems – free, that is, from external interference – on which no measurements are being carried out. Processes of the second kind are what most closely resemble the deterministic development of an isolated system in classical mechanics. One speaks, in both cases, of the *time evolution* of a physical system; and indeed, the time evolution of a quantum-mechanical system is likewise deterministic. (Contrary to popular belief, quantum mechanics cannot, therefore, be said to be *in*deterministic in the same sense in which classical mechanics is deterministic.) Now there are two ways of conceiving quantum-mechanical time evolution. The formalism of quantum mechanics makes contact with observation and experiment via the expectation values of the observables and the probabilities associated with their various eigenvalues. And these, as we have seen, are jointly determined by a state vector and the observable operators. The required change over time may thus be achieved, formally, in one of (at least) two distinct ways. We could keep the state vector constant and make the observable operators time-dependent, or we could make the state vector time-dependent and keep the observable operators constant. Heisenberg, in effect, went for the first option, and Schrödinger for the second; they are thus known, respectively, as the Heisenberg and Schrödinger *pictures*.

A simple analogy may make it clearer just what a choice between these two pictures involves. I said earlier that every vector parallel to a given vector corresponds to the same quantum state. Conventionally, one often takes the unique unit vector in this set of parallel vectors (that is, vector with a length equal to one) to represent the corresponding state. One could think of this as positioned with its tail at the origin. Now the time evolution of a quantum state corresponds mathematically to a rotation of this unit vector with respect to the coordinates; that is to say, the unit vectors that comprise one's chosen *basis*. Think now of the obvious analogy with ordinary Euclidean geometry. Given a set of coordinates, and an arrow with its tail at the origin, a relative rotation could be achieved in either of two ways. One could rotate the arrow, keeping the coordinates fixed; or one could keep the arrow fixed, and rotate the coordinates. The first option corresponds to the Schrödinger picture; the second to the Heisenberg picture. In view of the fact that a complete observable defines, by way of its eigenstates, a basis (that is, a coordinate system for Hilbert space), a decision to let the observables evolve over time, while the states remain constant, is equivalent to representing the time evolution of a physical system by way of a rotation of the coordinates. One might think that this choice of pictures is simply a matter of convenience. But I do not believe it is just that. On the contrary, I am convinced that the Heisenberg picture is, from a philosophical standpoint, the correct one. My reasons for saying that will emerge later. For the moment, in order to avoid prematurely committing myself to either picture, I shall simply speak of the *system*, rather than its state, as evolving.

What, then, of processes of the first kind? Well, these are supposed to occur when a measurement or observation is carried out on a quantum-mechanical system. Just what does happen, when one measures a quantum-mechanical observable, is a matter of intense controversy; and I shall be giving my own view in the next two chapters. But there is a standard view of the matter, due to von Neumann, which is to be found in practically every textbook, and which I must now briefly outline. This is the doctrine of *state vector reduction* or *collapse of the wave function*, encapsulated in von Neumann's *projection postulate* (so labelled by Margenau). According to this doctrine, the effect of carrying out a measurement of a maximal observable, or a simultaneous measurement of a complete set of compatible observables, is to project the state of the system being measured into the eigenstate corresponding to the resulting eigenvalue(s). Suppose that our simple harmonic oscillator is in a state that is not an energy eigenstate – not, that is, one of the states corresponding to the basis vectors of the energy representation. Then, according to the projection postulate, the result of carrying out a measurement of the energy is to precipitate an instantaneous and discontinuous change: the system immediately goes into the energy eigenstate associated with the observed energy. (The measured state can always be expressed as a linear combination or superposition of the eigenstates of the measured observable. If what is being measured is a degenerate observable – one that has more eigenstates than eigenvalues – then, according to the projection postulate, the system will go into a state corresponding to what remains of this linear combination, when we delete all terms except those which correspond to eigenstates that have as their eigenvalue the value obtained in the measurement. Carrying out a measurement may thus be thought of as analogous to passing the state through a filter, which allows through only those elements in the superposition that are associated with the measured eigenvalue.)

This, supposedly, is where indeterminism enters the picture. For according to the projection postulate, it is in general impossible to tell, from the prior state of a quantum-mechanical system, into which eigenstate of an observable the system will be projected upon measurement of that observable. Rather, the system will have certain probabilities of going into one or other of the observable's eigenstates, the probabilities in question being simply the probabilities that the measurement will yield the corresponding eigenvalues. Only if the system is already in an eigenstate of the measured observable, at the time of measurement, can one know what state it will be in immediately after the measurement: namely, the same state. (In this limiting case, the state is 'projected' into itself.)

I must emphasize that this postulated projection of the state of the system into an eigenstate of the measured observable has, on the face of it, nothing whatsoever to do with any changes that may take place in the state of the system being measured *simply in consequence of the need physically to interact with it.* (In fact it can readily be demonstrated that no physical interaction whatsoever could possibly have this effect.) The reduction or collapse, for those who believe in it, is supposed to take place equally with perturbing and nonperturbing measurements – nonperturbing measurements being ones where the time evolution prescribes no intrinsic change in the object being measured, in consequence of the measurement interaction. It is quite possible, within quantum mechanics, for a physical system – in this case the object being measured – to act without being acted upon. State vector reduction, in this respect, is a process that is supposed to transcend all ordinary physical inter-actions (such as involve only von Neumann's processes of the second kind).

This is undoubtedly, for practical purposes, quite a helpful way to think of measurement, in a quantum-mechanical context. But there are various reasons, which I shall shortly explain, for doubting whether it corresponds to what actually happens. It is no exaggeration to say that what does happen in a quantum measurement is the most fundamental question raised by modern physics (though whether it should be regarded as a physical or rather as a metaphysical question is itself a matter of dispute). We shall be exploring this issue in the next two chapters.

12

The Paradox of Schrödinger's Cat

Schrödinger's cat (*Felis paradoxicalis Schrödingeri*) made its first appearance in a paper that Schrödinger published in *Die Naturwissenschaften* (Schrödinger, 1935). Jauch gives the following literal translation of the relevant passage in his *Foundations of Quantum Mechanics* (1968, p. 185):

> A cat is placed in a steel chamber, together with the following hellish contraption [*Höllensmaschine*] (which must be protected against direct interference by the cat): In a Geiger counter there is a tiny amount of radioactive substance, so tiny that maybe within an hour one of the atoms decays, but equally probably none of them decays. If one decays then the counter triggers and via a relay activates a little hammer which breaks a container of cyanide. If one has left the entire system for an hour, then one would say that the cat is still living if no atom has decayed. The first decay would have poisoned it. The ψ-function of the entire system would express this by containing equal parts of the living and dead cat. [See figure 12.1.]
>
> The typical feature of these cases is that an indeterminacy is transferred from the atomic to the crude macroscopic level, which can then be *decided* by direct observation. This prevents us from accepting a 'blurred model' so naively as a picture of reality. By itself it [i.e. reality] is not at all unclear or contradictory. There is a difference between a blurred or poorly focussed photograph and a picture of clouds or fog patches.

Jauch adds a gloss (p. 185): 'The paradoxical aspect of the example', he says, 'is to be found in the supposed reduction of the state from a superposition of macroscopically distinct alternatives to one of the events during the act of observation.' I include this gloss, not because it sheds

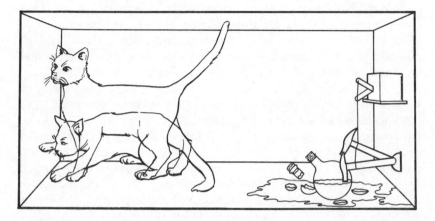

Figure 12.1 *Schrödinger's cat.* (From Paul Davies 1986: Time asymmetry and quantum mechanics. In Raymond Flood and Michael Lockwood (eds), *The Nature of Time*, Oxford: Basil Blackwell, p. 110.)

any light on what Schrödinger actually meant, but on the contrary, because it embodies a very common misreading of Schrödinger's example. A careful study of the passage shows that it is really intended as an argument for the *incompleteness* of the quantum-mechanical description, as expressed in the state vector or wave function. In fact, Schrödinger's article was one of a series he published in response to the celebrated Einstein–Podolsky–Rosen (EPR) paper (first published in 1935), in which these authors, too, argued for the incompleteness of the quantum-mechanical description, though on quite different grounds (Einstein, Podolsky and Rosen, 1970).

Schrödinger's point I take to be this. There has been a persistent tendency to regard the wave function of a subatomic particle, say, in which distinct eigenstates of the energy, for example, are superposed, as a complete description of a state of affairs in which the particle has no exact energy. It is this interpretation of the wave function that Schrödinger compares to 'a picture of clouds or fog patches'. However, the argument continues, no one would be prepared to accept as objective, in this sense, a description in which distinct values of a macro-observable, such as cat-alive and cat-dead, were thus superposed. Here we should be bound to regard any indeterminacy as a feature of the description, rather than of the state of affairs described.

We may call Schrödinger's position the *ignorance interpretation* (by analogy with the so-called ignorance interpretation of quantum-mechanical *mixtures*, which has quite a different status): the cat is determinately alive or dead, but in a given state of knowledge, the best we may be able to do is to give a description which assigns to various determinate states different probabilities of actually obtaining. But it is perfectly possible to arrange interactions between microsystems and macrosystems, in which the states of the one come to be correlated with states of the other, so that if the microsystem exists in a certain superposition of microstates, then, after the interaction, the macrosystem exists in a corresponding superposition of macrostates. Since, in Schrödinger's view, the latter superposition can, on pain of absurdity, *only* be understood along the lines of the ignorance interpretation, it follows that the superposition of microstates, from which it derives, should be similarly understood. Not, that is to say, as a picture of something intrinsically fuzzy, such as a cloud or a fog-patch; but rather as a blurred or out-of-focus picture of something with perfectly sharp outlines. What Schrödinger describes is just such an interaction. The time evolution of the system as a whole, quantum-mechanically regarded, does not only lead to a superposition of distinct states of the radioactive substance, corresponding to at least one atom's having decayed and to none having done so. Given the interaction, via the Geiger counter, between the radioactive substance and the cat, it leads to superpositions of distinct states of the whole system, corresponding to at least one atom's having decayed and the cat's being dead, and to none having done so and the cat's being alive.

Notice that, in this reconstruction of Schrödinger's line of thought, I have said nothing about acts of measurement or observations: Jauch's paradox is not Schrödinger's. What Schrödinger finds paradoxical is quite simply the idea of the system's *being*, objectively, in a state that amounts neither to the cat's being dead nor to its being alive, but to a linear combination of the two. Now it is no doubt also paradoxical that, by the projection postulate, the very act of opening the chamber and peering inside should then reduce the superposition, 'collapse' the wave function, thereby making it a reality that the cat is, as the case may be, alive or dead. If it's dead, are we to conclude, as some wag has it, that curiosity killed the cat?

This, as I say, is a paradox right enough, but it is not the one that Schrödinger had in mind. However, if Schrödinger were right in supposing that superpositions can be understood along the lines of the ignorance interpretation, then this second paradox would be automatically resolved also. For we should then be entitled to think of the collapse of the wave function, not as any kind of physical event, but simply as the collapse of ignorance into knowledge – a matter merely of discovering what had been true, albeit unknown, even while the chamber remained sealed and its contents isolated from outside interference.

How come, then, that the problem, over half a century later, remains with us? Why is it that, alive or dead, Schrödinger's cat refuses to lie down. Well, quite simply because the ignorance interpretation of superpositions is generally accounted untenable. Some time in the early 1970s, I heard a talk (at Columbia University) by Hilary Putnam, in which he used a fairy story to illustrate the key objection to the ignorance interpretation. To the best of my recollection, the story ran as follows.

Once upon a time there was a king who had a beautiful daughter, so beautiful, indeed, that she was surrounded by suitors. These suitors, as far as the king was concerned, were beginning to make a thorough nuisance of themselves. So in order to stem the flow somewhat, he instructed the court magician to set the suitors a test, involving a puzzle which was very difficult to solve. Anyone who succeeded in solving it could have his daughter's hand in marriage; but anyone who failed to do so would be instantly beheaded.

The puzzle that the magician had devised was deceptively simple. There was a box with three chambers, and the suitors were told that three balls were distributed amongst the chambers, one in each, and that two of them were white and one black. What the suitor had to do was select two chambers. If both contained white balls, he could marry the princess. If, on the other hand, either chamber contained a black ball, he would die. Several brave suitors decided to risk their lives. But on every occasion, no matter what chambers they chose, if the first contained a white ball, the second was bound to contain the black.

From that one might have been inclined to conclude that the magician had cheated, and placed black balls in two of the chambers before each test. Had that been so, however, the two chambers chosen would sometimes have been found both to contain black balls. And this never happened. Moreover, the magician steadfastly denied that he ever interfered with the boxes while the test was taking place.

After a great many suitors had lost their lives, there came a brave knight to whom the princess lost her heart immediately she set eyes on him. Desperately afraid that he too would fall victim to the magician's fiendish puzzle, she pleaded with him not to go through with the test. But the knight told her that he had studied the puzzle and had fathomed its secret. He believed that he had a chance of succeeding where the other suitors had failed.

The time came for the test. When the magician asked the knight which chambers he wished to choose, he pointed to one and said: 'Open that chamber first'. It was duly opened and revealed a white ball. The knight visibly relaxed. 'Right', he said, 'Open either of the remaining two chambers, I don't care which. The chamber *I* choose is the other one.' At this point the magician frowned and began to protest that this was against the rules. But the king could see no reason to disallow the knight's rather strange way of making his choice, and ordered one of the other chambers to be opened. It contained the black ball. 'It appears, sir,' said the king, 'that you have won my daughter's hand. But, just as a matter of interest, I would now like to see the contents of the third chamber.' At this, a look of panic came into the magician's face. A pair of courtiers tugged at the lid of the third chamber, but try as they might, it wouldn't open.

Feeling that he had not been playing fair with the suitors, the king ordered the hapless magician to be beheaded. The knight and the princess, meanwhile, married and lived happily ever after.

The operations of opening the chambers and looking inside here correspond to quantum-mechanical observables. And the fact that only two chambers can be opened at a time corresponds to the fact that these observables commute only in pairs. The three operations, taken together, correspond to what is not a set of compatible observables. Incompatibility, in the quantum-mechanical sense, does not by itself represent an obstacle to the ignorance interpretation. But the point of Putnam's fairy story is that there is no consistent hypothesis one could adopt, regarding the distribution of balls with respect to the chambers of the box, which could possibly account for the fact that, whatever pair of chambers one chooses to open, one of them will be found to contain a black ball and the other a white.

This situation arises in real life. There is a curious property, possessed by subatomic particles, known as spin angular momentum, which is measured in units of Planck's constant divided by twice pi, symbolized as $\hbar$ (and pronounced 'h-bar'). Angular momentum (angular velocity times mass) is a vector quantity: its complete specification, classically speaking, requires knowledge of the components of angular momentum with respect to three distinct axes. Spin-1 particles have the property (which makes no sense at all from a classical standpoint) that, along whatever axis one measures the spin, the component of spin angular momentum in that direction will turn out to be $+\hbar$, $-\hbar$ or zero. Now the observables, S_x, S_y and S_z, corresponding to measurement of the components of spin angular momentum of a spin-1 particle along three mutually orthogonal spatial axes x, y and z, are not simultaneously measurable. But the observables S_x^2, S_y^2, S_z^2, representing the squares of the corresponding components, are simultaneously measurable. Moreover, they will always be found to be, two of them, equal to one, with a third equal to zero. This is so no matter what triple of mutually orthogonal directions one chooses.

The reader is now invited to think of spatial directions as analogous to the chambers in Putnam's fairy story, and the infinite totality comprising all directions in space as analogous to the box as a whole, to all three chambers. The fact that one can measure the square of the spin angular momentum in at most three directions at once corresponds to the fact, in Putnam's story, that one can only examine the contents of at most two chambers at a time. The obstacle to making rational sense of Putnam's story is that we cannot conceive of a distribution of balls with respect to chambers that will result in any given pair of chambers always comprising one that contains a black ball and one that contains a white. The corresponding problem for the ignorance interpretation of the wave functions of spin-1 particles is that of conceiving a distribution of squared spin values, with respect to directions in space, that will result in every triple of mutually orthogonal directions comprising one direction that is associated with the value zero and two that are associated with the value one.

We could represent a direction in space by a unit vector positioned with its tail at the origin of our coordinate system. The set of all directions would then be a dense cluster of such vectors, all sticking out at different angles. And the tips of these vectors would form the surface of a sphere. The association of a value of one (for the squared spin value) with a given direction could then be represented by an infinitesimal spot of red on the point of the sphere's surface defined by the tip of the corresponding vector. And likewise, the association of the number zero (for the squared spin value) could be represented by an infinitesimal spot of blue on the corresponding point on the surface of the sphere (see figure 12.2). The problem of distributing squared spin values to directions in space, in the required way, may thus be graphically reformulated as one of colouring the surface of a sphere, using only two colours – red and blue, say – subject to the constraint that any three points on the sphere's surface that correspond to the tips of three mutually orthogonal vectors, with their tails at the centre of the sphere, must comprise two red points and one blue. This is known as the *two-colour problem*; and it can be rigorously shown that no such colouring exists. It is a logical impossibility to colour the surface of a sphere red and blue, subject to the stated constraint. (The issue is not *quite* as clear-cut as I may have made it sound, in view of a theoretical loophole discovered by Pitowsky (1985); but the general opinion seems to be that Pitowsky's result is one of which no hidden variable theory could, realistically, take advantage.)

Interpretations of quantum mechanics according to which the quantum-mechanical description, as embodied in the state vector or wave function, is incomplete are known as *hidden variable* theories. The idea is that, corresponding to a single quantum-mechanical description, there is in fact a whole range of distinct states; the postulated hidden variables are simply the parameters with respect to which these states differ from one another. And the values, at time t, of a system's hidden variables, taken together with the system's quantum-mechanical state description at t, are

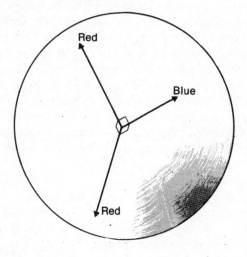

Figure 12.2 *The two-colour problem.*
The diagram shows three mutually orthogonal vectors radiating from the centre of a sphere, with their tips just piercing the surface. Two of the corresponding points on the sphere's surface are associated with red, and one with blue. The task, which can be demonstrated to be impossible, is to colour the surface of the sphere in such a way that, for all such triples of vectors, two will emerge in a red area and the remaining one in a blue area.

held jointly to determine what the result would be of measuring any of the system's observables at t.

These hidden variables needn't necessarily be anything exotic. To suppose, as did Einstein and Schrödinger, that an electron invariably *has* some exact position and momentum, even though no exact position or momentum values are assigned to it by the system's state vector, is to give *classical* position and momentum the status of quantum-mechanical hidden variables. Likewise, squared spin values are hidden variables, if we suppose that a spin-1 particle has a comprehensive set of such values, corresponding to every direction in space. The obstacle to assuming this, which we have just explained, is a special instance of a celebrated 'no-go' theorem proved by Kochen and Specker (1967), which establishes the impossibility of interpreting quantum mechanics by way of *non-contextual* hidden variables. Non-contextual hidden variables are ones that serve, in conjunction with the state vector, to determine the results of measuring observables, in a way that is independent of what other observables one chooses to measure at the same time. A contextual hidden variable theory, as applied to the magician's box in Putnam's fairy story, would make what was found when opening one chamber dependent on whether another chamber was being inspected at the same time, and perhaps also on which chamber. Likewise, in the spin case, a contextual theory would say that the value one got for the squared spin in a given direction would, in general, depend on the other squared spin measurements in the context of which this particular measurement was being carried out. Such a theory would assign a determinate triple of numbers, comprising a zero and two ones, to every triple of spatial directions, and likewise a determinate pair of numbers to every pair of directions, and a single number to every single direction. But a given direction, as it figured in a triple, would not necessarily be assigned the same number which it received as a member of a pair or when taken individually.

The postulation of contextual hidden variables might seem quite an attractive option, were it not for another, even more celebrated, no-go theorem, due to John Bell (1964). Bell's theorem states that hidden variables are required also to be *non-local*, if they are faithfully to reproduce the predictions of quantum mechanics. In quantum mechanics there are *correlated* states, in which the values of certain observables, as measured on one system, are systematically correlated with the values of the same or different observables, as measured on the other. For example, one can produce a pair of particles with anticorrelated spins, which then fly apart. If two observers measure the components of spin angular momentum of these two particles, then the smaller the angle between the two directions of measurement, the greater is the likelihood that they will get opposite results: if they are spin-½ particles, say, then if one observer gets the value $+\hbar/2$, the other gets the value $-\hbar/2$. If the directions of measurement are the same, the observers are certain to get opposite results; if they measure the spin in opposite directions, then they are bound to get identical results. But the directions of measurement can be freely chosen by these two observers, independently of each other, and when the two correlated particles are an arbitrary distance apart. Given that fact, Bell was able to show that one could account for these correlations by means of hidden variables, only on the assumption that there was some kind of communication between the two particles, or the associated measuring devices, whereby a change in the values of the hidden variables of the one system produced a corresponding change in the values of the hidden variables of the other. Moreover, in order successfully to reproduce the predictions of quantum mechanics, such communication would sometimes be required to take place at a speed faster than light. More to the point, perhaps, it would, in general, require 'action at a distance' – that is to say, action without any dynamical contact or spatio-temporally intervening process.

Now of course it could be that quantum mechanics is in error, in so far as it predicts a degree of correlation in excess of that which any non-local hidden variable theory could account for. But that has now been tested, most notably by Alain Aspect et al. (1982) in the crucial case where the influence would have to propagate faster than light. And the predictions of quantum mechanics have been triumphantly confirmed.

Incidentally, the famous EPR paper, which prompted Schrödinger's cat example, itself concerned a case of two correlated particles; though the correlated observables, here, were position and momentum, rather than spin. In their imagined example, a measurement of position on particle 1 after the particles have ceased to interact, enables one to predict with certainty the result of a measurement of position on particle 2. Likewise a measurement of momentum on particle 1 enables one to predict with certainty the result of a measurement of momentum on particle 2. (And in each case, vice versa.) If, without disturbing a physical system, it is possible to predict with certainty the result of a certain measurement, then it follows, so these authors argued, that the result of such a measurement is an 'element of reality'; the system must actually possess the corresponding attribute, regardless of whether the measurement is actually carried out. Consequently, the two particles must simultaneously possess, as elements of reality, the positions and momenta corresponding to these hypothetical measurements. But, as we have seen, the quantum-mechanical description embodied in the wave function does not tell us, with certainty, what the results of such measurements would be. Hence the quantum-mechanical description is incomplete: the conclusion that Einstein and the other authors intend us to draw from their thought-experiment is clearly that some sort of hidden variable theory must be true. It would be interesting, therefore, to know what Einstein's response would have been to Bell's theorem and the subsequent Aspect experiment. For, ironically, what these results seem to show, in regard to correlated systems, is that the only sort of hidden variable theory that would do the job Einstein, Podolsky and Rosen had in mind is one the adoption of which would involve rejecting one of the premises on which their argument is based: namely that the correlated systems have indeed ceased to interact.

These results (Kochen and Specker, Bell, Aspect) seem to me effectively to dish the ignorance interpretation. It is not so much that it is impossible to give a hidden variable interpretation of quantum mechanics (as von Neumann, for example, mistakenly believed). It is rather that the price of adopting such a theory has been shown to be too high. The assumptions one is required to make in order to run a hidden variable theory – namely, contextuality and non-locality – are, in sum, so extravagant as to rob the enterprise of its rationale. If the adoption of a hidden variable theory is a proliferation of implausibilities, rather than their elimination, then one is surely better off taking quantum mechanics as it comes, instead of adding gratuitous epicycles.

As I said earlier, Jauch's paradox, concerning the quantum-mechanical interpretation of what happens when an observer looks inside Schrödinger's feline gas chamber, is not Schrödinger's. Nevertheless, it is a perfectly good problem in its own right, and forces us to re-examine the standard account of what is involved in carrying out an observation. The starting point is von Neumann's theory of measurement (von Neumann, 1955). According to von Neumann, a measurement comprises two elements. The first is a process that can be broken down, more or less arbitrarily, into a sequence of *measurement interactions*. To start with, there is a measurement interaction between a quantum *object* and a *measurement apparatus*, whereby states of the measurement apparatus become correlated with states of the object. The object will, in general, be in a superposition of eigenstates of the observable being measured. What happens in this measurement interaction is that the combined system, consisting of object plus apparatus, goes into a superposition of states, each of which consists of an eigenstate of the observable in conjunction with a distinct state of the measurement apparatus, corresponding, say, to a particular pointer reading. What, one may ask, then happens when a human observer looks at the pointer on the dial, to see what it is reading? According to von Neumann, another measurement interaction then takes place, in which states of the retina, say, become correlated with states of the combined system, consisting of object plus apparatus. And so on, and so on, until we finally arrive at a correlation that incorporates states of the observer's consciousness.

This is known as *von Neumann's chain*. Thus far described, the whole process is a deterministic, quantum-mechanical time evolution which, if one adopts the Schrödinger picture, is described by the Schrödinger equation. At no point will the application of this equation, by itself, result in a reduction of the superposition to a single eigenstate of the measured observable. If we allow the process to proceed uninterrupted until conscious states of the observer become correlated with eigenstates of the observable being measured, then, according to Schrödinger's equation, the observer's consciousness will itself go into a superposition of states, each containing a perception of a different disposition of the pointer.

From the fact, presumably, that the pointer will invariably appear to the observer to be pointing in just a single direction, von Neumann concludes that the process does not proceed uninterrupted right into the observer's consciousness. This goes back to what we were saying at the end of chapter 11. Somewhere along the line, smooth deterministic evolution, by way of the Schrödinger equation – a process of the second kind – gives way to a process of the first kind: a discontinuous collapse into an eigenstate of the measured observable (with a probability proportional to the square modulus of the corresponding coefficient, when the state vector is expressed as a linear combination of the observable's eigenvectors).

Now there is nothing in von Neumann's theory to say where, along the chain, a process of the first kind occurs, precipitating a reduction of the state vector, save that *it must occur no later than the point at which the result of the measurement registers in the observer's consciousness.* That it does so occur is what is asserted by von Neumann's projection postulate. Von Neumann claimed to have proved that, provided it occurred somewhere between the object and the conscious observation, it made no difference to the statistical predictions of quantum theory just where this reduction was supposed to happen. For computational purposes, one is free, subject to the stated constraint, to invoke the projection postulate at any point in the process: a von Neumann *cut*, as it is sometimes called, has, for any *one* observer (an important qualification this, as we shall see later), the same operational effect wherever it is applied. In the verificationist climate that prevailed at the time von Neumann was writing, many philosophers and physicists doubtless concluded, in view of this result, that it was meaningless to ask where it actually did occur, or where Nature imposed the cut.

But today that answer has ceased to satisfy, now that philosophers and physicists have largely awoken from their positivistic slumbers; and the whole issue of quantum measurement has, in recent years, generated a vast and ramifying literature. From a realist perspective – that is to say, a perspective according to which truth and meaning are not bounded by our powers of verification or falsification – von Neumann's account of the measurement process implies that quantum mechanics *is*, as it stands, incomplete, albeit in a quite different sense from that envisaged by hidden variable enthusiasts. It needs to be supplemented by a substantive theory of the laws or mechanism that govern the collapse, a comprehensive theory of the temporal evolution of physical systems that tells us when processes of the second kind give way to processes of the first kind.

No such theory really exists, although a number of suggestions have been offered. Some people, notably Wigner (1962), have suggested that it is consciousness itself that collapses the wave function. This has pretty strange consequences, however. It would seem to imply, for example, that whether Schrödinger's cat was, say, unambiguously dead *before* any conscious observer looked inside, or whether it only *became* unambiguously dead when the chamber was opened, would depend on whether or not it had been dreamlessly asleep during the operative period. Nicholas

Maxwell (a philosopher who has argued strenuously for the incompleteness of the standard theory) has suggested that collapse occurs with the occurrence of *inelastic collisions* between particles (excluding photons presumably), ones in which there is a change in the total energies of the particles concerned (Maxwell, 1988). Yet another suggestion, made independently by Paul Davies (1981, pp. 201–3) and Roger Penrose (1985, 1986), is that the collapse might be precipitated by the presence of an appreciable gravitational field – gravity being a phenomenon that has proved curiously resistant to quantum-mechanical treatment. On the Davies–Penrose view, I suppose one might say that the von Neumann chain collapses under its own weight!

Penrose's approach has considerable theoretical depth; and – who knows? – something may come of it. But it seems to me that, rather than trying to come up with a physical mechanism for the collapse, one should be asking oneself whether there is any good reason for believing in it. Not only do I think that there is no good reason for believing in it; I think there are very good reasons for not believing in it. The first is the fact, noted by von Neumann, that there doesn't appear to be anything in quantum mechanics itself to say where, in the measurement chain, the collapse should occur. Some extra *deus ex machina* is called for; and considerations of theoretical economy suggest that we should avoid introducing such new elements unless we are forced to do so.

The second argument has to do with correlated systems, such as we were discussing earlier. Given two spin-½ particles, a measurement of spin angular momentum on either one of them would, on the collapse view, instantly project both particles into an eigenstate of the corresponding spin observable. But what does 'instantly' mean here? We know from relativity that simultaneity is relative to frames of reference. Which frame of reference is to determine the simultaneity plane along which the collapse takes place? Again, there doesn't seem to be anything in quantum mechanics itself that is capable of providing an answer.

That remark should perhaps be qualified, slightly, in view of some remarkable recent work by the American philosophers Gerrit Smith and Robert Weingard (1987). What Smith and Weingard have done is to give a proper relativistic treatment of the original EPR case. Interestingly, they have discovered that the correlations between the measured values of position and momentum obtain only on a unique set of space-time surfaces. The surfaces in question are the simultaneity planes defined by the frame of reference in which the centre of mass of the entire combined system is at rest. And from this one might conclude that it is on such a surface that collapse, consequent upon measurement, occurs.

But the fact remains: there is nothing *in general*, within quantum mechanics, to determine on what plane the collapse occurs. Smith and

Weingard's argument has, as far as I can see, no application to pairs of particles with anticorrelated spins. Unlike position and momentum, spin is an example of what is known as a *constant of the motion*, this being an observable that commutes with the Hamiltonian. The probability of getting any particular eigenvalue, upon measuring a constant of the motion, is unaffected by, or, as physicists say, invariant with respect to, the time evolution of the system. So the respective probabilities of getting the results $+\hbar/2$ and $-\hbar/2$, when measuring the component of spin angular momentum in a particular direction on a spin-$\frac{1}{2}$ particle, will be the same, regardless of when the measurement is made.

Suppose now that two observers, Tweedledum and Tweedledee, measure the spin of a pair of anticorrelated spin-$\frac{1}{2}$ particles, but in different directions. Particle 1 has its spin measured by Tweedledum in the $+x$ direction, yielding the result $+\hbar/2$, while particle 2 has its spin measured by Tweedledee in the $+y$ direction, yielding the result $-\hbar/2$. Suppose further that, relative to Tweedledum's frame of reference, the x measurement comes before the y measurement; but in Tweedledee's frame of reference, the y measurement comes before the x measurement. Tweedledum will think that the x measurement caused both particles to collapse into a joint eigenstate of the S_x observable for the combined system, corresponding to the pair of values $+\hbar/2$ for particle 1 and $-\hbar/2$ for particle 2. And then, he will think, Tweedledee's measurement of spin in the $+y$ direction, yielding $-\hbar/2$, say, precipitated a collapse of the state of particle 2 into the corresponding eigenstate of $S_y(2)$, the spin observable corresponding to the y component of spin angular momentum for particle 2, with particle 1 remaining in an eigenstate of $S_x(1)$. Tweedledee, on the other hand, will think that his y measurement caused both particles to collapse into a joint eigenstate of the S_y observable for the combined system, corresponding to the pair of values $-\hbar/2$ for particle 1 and $+\hbar/2$ for particle 2. And then, he will think, Tweedledum's measurement of spin in the $+x$ direction, yielding $+\hbar/2$, precipitated a collapse of the state of particle 1 into the corresponding eigenstate of $S_x(1)$, the spin observable corresponding to the x component of spin angular momentum for particle 1, with particle 2 remaining in an eigenstate of $S_y(2)$.

Their two stories have the same beginning and the same end, but the sequence of intervening events is different. To take the collapse of the wave function seriously, as a physical event, would be to think that there was an answer to the question which of these stories, Tweedledum's or Tweedledee's, was the correct one. But the two stories (as a simple back-of-an-envelope calculation will attest) manifestly have identical predictive consequences. That is to say, were Tweedledum and Tweedledee to repeat their observations, in identical time sequence relative to their respective frames, and for an indefinitely large number of such particle pairs, there could be nothing in the results obtained that would provide any basis for preferring one story to the other. Operationally speaking, the two accounts are equivalent. Are we to say, in spite of this, that one of the accounts corresponds to the 'true' sequence of events, albeit that the operational symmetry of the situation makes it impossible in principle for anyone to divine where the truth lies? I would prefer to believe that both accounts, literally regarded, are equally false, and that talk of 'collapse' here should be regarded as a mere *façon de parler*.

There is a final consideration that, to my mind, is the weightiest of all. Up to, but not including, the point at which the concept of collapse is dragged into the picture, quantum mechanics is a *time-symmetric* theory. Let's suppose that S is some physical system, and A and B are two observables on S. A has m eigenstates, $\alpha_1, \ldots, \alpha_m$, with the corresponding eigenvalues $a_1, \ldots, a_m$; B has n eigenstates, $\beta_1, \ldots, \beta_n$, with the corresponding eigenvalues $b_1, \ldots, b_n$. If one performs a sequence of nonperturbing measurements on S, then, given that a measurement of A, at twelve o'clock, say, yields the result a_i, one can compute the probability that a measurement of B, at ten past twelve, will yield the result b_j (where i is some integer between 1 and m, and j some integer between 1 and n). Suppose now that one has already performed a measurement of B at ten to twelve, but has forgotten what the result was. The result is stored, let us suppose, in a computer. The probability that one got the value b_j, and will find the corresponding value in the computer's memory, will be precisely the same as the probability that one will get the value b_j if one measures B at ten past twelve. Prediction and retrodiction obey the same rules.

From this point of view, the projection postulate imports into quantum mechanics an entirely gratuitous temporal asymmetry: gratuitous because it is not mirrored in any corresponding asymmetry in the observational consequences of quantum mechanics. We are invited to suppose that, at the point of carrying out a measurement, the system is discontinuously projected into the eigenstate corresponding to the observed value, whence it evolves smoothly and deterministically until the next measurement precipitates a similar jump. (Specifically, if A is measured on S and yields the result a_i, then S jumps into the state α_i. S then evolves smoothly and deterministically until B is measured, yielding, say, the result b_j, at which point it jumps into the state β_j.) This means that the process of the second kind that takes place between observations stands in a special relationship to the immediately preceding observation, the result of which sets the initial boundary conditions of the time evolution.

As far as the mathematics goes, this is completely arbitrary (as is pointed out by Penrose (1979, pp. 583–5)). One could equally well suppose that it is the immediately succeeding observation that determines the time evolution between observations, by setting the final boundary conditions. According to this time-reversed analogue of the usual picture, what happens is that the system evolves smoothly and deterministically *into* the eigenstate corresponding to the observed eigenvalue, whereupon it jumps discontinuously into another state from which it evolves smoothly into the eigenstate corresponding to the eigenvalue yielded by the next measurement, and so on. (That would mean that S was in the state α_i immediately *before* the measurement of A, at which point it jumped into another state, from which it evolved smoothly and deterministically, arriving at the state β_j immediately before the subsequent measurement of B occurred, yielding the result b_j.)

Such an account is pretty difficult to swallow, since the observables that we measure can (so we like to think) be freely chosen. The time-reversed analogue of the usual collapse picture would, in general, make the particle's state at any given time dependent on things that have not yet happened and, as one would ordinarily think, which are not yet decided: what measurements are going to be made, and what the results of them will be. But the fact that such a picture is logically available, and has observational consequences which are identical to those of the usual view, is nevertheless, it seems to me, a grave indictment of the standard account of the measurement process, serving to highlight its essential arbitrariness. It is surely a condition of adequacy of an interpretation of a physical theory that it preserve all such symmetries in the theory as are borne out by observation. The collapse theory does violence to quantum mechanics, effectively obliterating one of its most beautiful features.

For all these reasons, I shall assume in the sequel that the projection postulate is false. Two things follow at once. First, the concept of measurement ceases, as such, to play any role in the theory. (This, in fact, was cited as a desideratum of any objective quantum theory by Nicholas Maxwell (1972) in a well-known article on the measurement problem.) If by 'measurement' is meant a collapse of the state vector or wave function, in response to observation, then quite simply, there is no such thing on the present view. If, on the other hand, one means by 'measurement' a particular type of interaction, in which macrostates of some instrument become correlated with the quantum states of some object of scientific investigation, then this does occur. But the fact that one of the interacting systems is the object of scientific investigation, while the other is a system designed to function as an instrument, should be regarded as an irrelevance. When physicists speak of a *measurement interaction*, what they have in mind is merely a particular category of physical process; that a specific such process is regarded by us, in virtue of our interests and intentions in setting it up, as the *measuring* of something, is neither here nor there.

The second point is that, under some interpretation, we must now count it true that Schrödinger's sealed feline gas chamber is, after the elapse of an hour, in a superposition of states, half of which correspond to cat-alive and half to cat-dead. And, what is more, this must remain true, *even when we open the chamber and peer in*, of any larger system that includes both the chamber, with its contents, and us the curious observers. That may seem even more grossly paradoxical than either Schrödinger's original paradox or Jauch's variant. For does it not stand in direct contradiction to the evidence of our senses – that the cat, say, is manifestly an *ex*-cat?

Well does it? Wittgenstein's remark, which we quoted in chapter 2, again seems apt. Schrödinger's cat may not *look* as though it existed in a fuzzy superposition of live and dead states. But then how would it look, if it *looked* as though it were in such a state? Fuzzy?

What we need here, I suggest, is a theory that, without invoking a primitive and, within the theory, unexplained notion of measurement or observable, suitably relates the quantum-mechanical state description of a system to the *appearance* or *aspect* it should offer to an observer. This is in fact a prerequisite of any physical theory. Classical physics was able to shirk the task of giving an explicit account of the matter, only in so far as common-sense conceptions largely sufficed for its needs.

Special relativity, by contrast, cannot afford to be quite so cavalier. Nowadays, mathematicians and physicists generally favour a formulation of the theory of relativity that is couched in a *coordinate free* language and in terms of *four-vectors*. Classically, for example, one associates with a particle a certain total energy, which is a *scalar* quantity – one, that is to say, that can be represented by a single number – and a *momentum*, which is a *three-vector* quantity; a complete specification of a particle's momentum requires a specification of its speed times mass in each of three spatial directions. Relativistically, energy and three-vector momentum are united in the *energy-momentum four-vector* or *four-momentum*. This is a vector that belongs not to space but to space-time. The idea, then, is that different observers divide up the space-time continuum, relative to their state of motion, into a time component and a space component. In so doing, they will, as scientists, decompose the energy-momentum four-vector, relative to their frame of reference, into a scalar component, which is the energy, and a three-vector component corresponding to momentum. Likewise, as we have seen, a person is viewed as laid out in space-time along a spatio-temporal path known as his *world-line*. Experienced temporal passage is then to be seen as corresponding to the mathematical integral of the space-time distance, or *interval*, along the person's world-line. Special relativity, in its modern formulation, would be impossible to relate to our experience, were it not for such auxiliary notions as these. But no one would dream of supposing, for example, that this decomposition of four-vectors into a scalar and a three-vector component, relative to the observer's state of motion, was a *physical process* affecting the four-vector, in the way that projection of a Hilbert space vector on to an eigenvector of a measured observable is supposed to be.

How is it, then, with those vectors in Hilbert space? How do they project on to what Margenau (1950) has termed the *P-plane* of the observer ('P' standing for perception)? What follows is both highly speculative and extremely sketchy, but it may provide some indication of the kind of theory that seems to me to be needed.

Intuitively, we think of the universe as a whole as a physical system, and conceive of it as containing a vast number of components that are physical systems in their own right, and which in general may, in their turn, be thought of as containing physical systems as subsystems. This intuitive notion is reflected in what is known as the *product structure* of a Hilbert space. Suppose we have a physical system, P, that consists of two subsystems Q and R; and let H be the Hilbert space for P. Then if H_1 and H_2 are the corresponding Hilbert spaces for Q and R, H may be represented as the so-called *direct* or *tensor product* of H_1 and H_2, $H = H_1 \otimes H_2$. Corresponding to the direct product of a pair of Hilbert spaces, there is the direct product, $\psi = \psi_1 \otimes \psi_2$, of a pair of Hilbert space vectors, belonging to the different Hilbert spaces, H_1 and H_2. Given a set of basis vectors for H_1 and a set of basis vectors for H_2, then the set of vectors, comprising every direct product of an H_1 basis vector and an H_2 basis vector, constitutes a set of basis vectors for H. It must be emphasized that the state of a composite system cannot in general be represented by a state vector that is the direct product of state vectors belonging to the Hilbert spaces of the subsystems, but only by a superposition of such products. And this means that one cannot, in general, regard a subsystem as being in any definite quantum state. (Or at least, any definite *pure* state – one that is capable of being represented by a Hilbert space vector; I shall here ignore, as irrelevant to our purposes, the possibility of invoking in this context the concept of a so-called *mixed* state.)

The pair of spin-½ particles with anticorrelated spins that we talked about earlier constitutes a composite system in which the state of the system as a whole cannot be represented as the direct product of the vectors representing the spin states of the individual particles. Rather, the whole system is to be represented, with respect to any arbitrarily chosen spatial direction, as a superposition of two states. In one of these, with respect to that direction, particle 1 has its spin *up*, corresponding to a measured value of $+\hbar/2$, while particle 2 has its spin *down*, corresponding to a measured value of $-\hbar/2$; and in the other, particle 1 has spin down, while particle 2 has spin up. It makes no sense to ask what state particle 1, say, is in when the pair of particles exists in such a superposition. Neither particle, considered individually, can be said to be spin up, spin down, or even in a superposition of spin up and spin down states.

Given a composite system, $S + T$, and a state of that composite system, it is, however, possible to associate with any state of S a corresponding unique *relative state* of T. The concept of a relative state is due to Everett (1957, 1973). Suppose that we take a state of system S that is an eigenstate, α_i, of the S observable A, corresponding to the eigenvalue a_i. And suppose also that the relative state of the system T is represented as a linear combination of the eigenstates of the T observable B. Then the square modulus of the coefficient associated with a particular eigenstate, say β_j, with eigenvalue b_j, will be proportional to the probability of getting the value b_j when measuring B on T, given that a measurement of A on system S has yielded the value a_i. (I am assuming and will continue to assume, for simplicity's sake, that A and B are, with respect to S and T, nondegenerate observables.)

Consider, once again, our pair of particles with anticorrelated spins. *Relative to* the state, of particle 1, of being spin up in the $+z$ direction, say, particle 2 may be assigned the state of being spin down in the $+z$ direction; and vice versa. And this corresponds to the fact that, given that a measurement of spin in the $+z$ direction on particle 1 has yielded the result spin up, it is certain that a measurement of spin in the same direction on particle 2 will yield the result spin down.

Let us start, extravagantly perhaps, with a cosmic Hilbert space, the vectors of which represent states of the entire universe. This Hilbert space will be a tensor product of a vast number of other Hilbert spaces, corresponding to subsystems of the universe. And if I allow myself a certain amount of licence, I can equate one of these subsystems with that part or aspect of my brain that registers in consciousness. (The licence is called for, because I am here glossing over the fact that, quantum-mechanically regarded, the universe as a whole is in a superposition of states, in most of which I do not exist.) My fundamental assumption is that the immediate contents of awareness always correspond to the shared eigenvalues of some set of compatible observables on this subsystem. Nature, considered as a whole, may not favour any particular set of such brain observables over any other. But awareness somehow does. From the standpoint of consciousness, there is a *preferred* set of compatible brain observables. And, from the standpoint of any *particular* state of awareness, one set of eigenvalues of this preferred set of observables – and thereby the corresponding eigenstate (or, if the set is incomplete, superposition of those eigenstates that have this set of eigenvalues in common) – is selected or, as I shall express it, *designated*: '*This* is how things are with me'.

If this seems intolerably mysterious, ponder on the following parallel. A priori, there seems to be no obvious reason why time should play the central role it does in the way we experience the world. And even then, Nature does not favour *one* time over another. Nevertheless, for experience, one particular time is invariably marked out as special. Experience always designates a particular time as *now*. The designation by experience of some specific set of eigenvalues, of some preferred set of compatible observables, is in principle no different from this. Experience is operator-spectrally designative, just as it is temporally designative. That, so to speak, is part of what it is to be *in* the world, as a conscious being.

To repeat: we ourselves – our minds, brains or whatever – are really just part of a vast composite system. Moreover, many of the components of this system have interacted in the past or are now doing so. These couplings mean that all manner of correlations, of varying degrees of strength, obtain as between quantum states of our brains and quantum states of the people and things that surround us. The problem I now wish to address is that of how, given the starting point in my designative consciousness, I can proceed to construct an appearance or aspect of things that is capable of passing the usual tests of objectivity: something I can regard as my world, and yours, even if not quite *the* world.

Consider, to begin with, just two subsystems of the universe: the brain system that immediately underlies my awareness, and some other physical system (something I am observing, for example). Now from a non-relativistic standpoint (and in terms of the Schrödinger picture) there will, at any given time, be some unique vector, in the cosmic Hilbert space, which represents the current state of the entire universe. I take this state to be an objective, observer-independent, physical fact. This state, in conjunction with a given designated state of the brain system, allows one to assign to any physical subsystem a unique state – represented by a vector in its own Hilbert space – which is its state relative to the designated state. Suppose I observe, say, the golf ball to be in the hole, or Schrödinger's cat to be alive and purring. Then what that really amounts to is the following. A particular state of my brain (or, more accurately subsystem of my brain) is *designated* in the relevant act of awareness. And the perceived state of the system being observed – the nineteenth hole, or Schrödinger's cat – is its unique state, given the overall state of things as represented by the cosmic state vector, *relative* to that designated brain state.

In a measurement interaction, the states of different subsystems become correlated with each other. Suppose, then, that S_1, S_2 and S_3 are three subsystems of some composite system; and that, in consequence of measurement interactions, the states of S_1 become correlated both with those of S_2 and with those of S_3, and that the states of S_2 likewise become correlated with those of S_3. Imagine that ψ is some arbitrarily chosen state of S_1. Let ϕ then be the state of S_2 relative to the state ψ of S_1; and let χ be the state of S_3 relative to the state ψ of S_1. Then the state of S_3, relative to the state ϕ of S_2, will also be χ. That simple fact ensures that all the inferences I draw, if based on perfect correlations, will cohere. Suppose that states of the brain subsystem that registers in consciousness are correlated both with the states of some object, and also with the states of something else with which states of that object are correlated: some measuring instrument, for example, or a second conscious observer. Then I shall find myself inferring the presence of instrument readings or beliefs on the part of the other observer, regarding the observed object, that agree with my own inferences. And reliable memory, or information storage generally, will then ensure such agreement over time as well as at a time.

This last point requires elaboration. I have been speaking as though everything were happening at a single time. My awareness designates some instantaneous shared eigenstate of some favoured set of compatible brain observables. And on the strength of that I assign instantaneous relative states to other physical systems, based on the correlations between their states and those of the brain system revealed in consciousness. But that's an oversimplification. In general, states of my mind correlate with *past* states of other physical systems – sometimes, as in the case of viewing a distant star, states in the very remote past. Not only that, however. The existence of memory means that present states of my mind correlate with past states of my mind. I can construct an autobiography for myself, on the basis of relative states, using memory and other sources, including clock measurements, just as I can construct a 'public' world. By 'public', here, I mean one in which there is the appropriate intersubjective agreement: one where, as we have just seen, the relative state I assign to an object squares with the relative state that I assign to another observer of that object.

At this point, a bit of notation will come in handy. We have previously spoken of *phenomenal perspectives* or *maximal experiences*. In the present context, a phenomenal perspective may be equated with a shared eigenstate of some preferred (by consciousness) set of compatible brain observables. Let ψ_n be a phenomenal perspective that the observer has at time t_n. Associated with ψ_n, there will be a number of memories which the person could be said to have at t_n, only a small subset of which will actually figure in ψ_n. Here we shall assume, for simplicity's sake, that all and only the contents of preceding phenomenal perspectives are subsequently remembered. (In practice, of course, most of our experiences are forgotten, and moreover, we can often remember things of which we were not conscious at the time, especially by way of short-term memory; the fact that you can tell me what I just said doesn't prove that you were listening!) In order to indicate that a phenomenal perspective ψ_n is associated with a given set of memories, we shall append to 'ψ_n' a chronologically arranged list of the remembered perspectives, placed in square brackets. Finally, let us imagine (contrary to fact) that mental states form a discrete rather than a continuous sequence, so that one's conscious life consists of a first, second, third, etc. phenomenal perspective. Then the first element in the sequence may be represented $\psi_1[]$. The fact that there is nothing inside the brackets indicates that there are no memories; there cannot be, because there are no previous experiences to be remembered. The series will then continue $\psi_2[\psi_1]$, $\psi_3[\psi_1,\psi_2]$, . . . Call such a series a *biography*.

I now come to the crux of the argument. Reduction of the state vector or collapse of the wave function, *tout court*, is, so I am claiming, a myth. But collapse relative to a *biography* is a fact. It exists virtually by definition, given the way we have defined 'biography' and 'relative state'. Let's return to Schrödinger's cat, and suppose t_n to be a time at which the crucial hour has elapsed, but the chamber is still sealed and its contents isolated. The states of the observer at t_n are uncorrelated with live–dead states of the cat. Such a state, as it figures in a biography of the observer, may be represented as $\psi_n[. . .]$. Then the observer opens the chamber and peers inside. This is a measurement interaction which causes states of the observer to become correlated with states of the cat. The cosmic state vector will now be a superposition of states, in some elements of which the observer is consciously observing a live cat, while in others he is consciously observing a dead cat. (And doubtless, since this is a superposition encompassing the universe as a whole, there will be still other elements in which neither the cat nor the observer ever existed.)

But this super-superposition cannot, as such, figure in a biography of the observer; it corresponds to no phenomenal perspective. What figures in a biography, as a phenomenal perspective, must be a state of the relevant brain system; that is, a designated eigenstate of the preferred set of compatible brain observables. Suppose we take an eigenstate, at time t_{n+1}, in which the cat is alive, call it $\psi_{n+1}[. . ., \psi_n]$. Then this will be followed by a phenomenal perspective, $\psi_{n+2}[. . ., \psi_n,\psi_{n+1}]$, that is associated with a memory of this impression of a live cat. Relative to this biography, the transition from t_n to t_{n+1} is associated with a transition in the relative state of the cat from live–dead to live. That is to say, the cat, relative to the state $\psi_n[. . .]$, is in a superposition of live and dead states; but relative to the state $\psi_{n+1}[. . .,\psi_n]$, the cat is unambiguously alive.

In an absolute sense, however, there is no collapse, no cosmic state vector reduction. And this is reflected in the parallel existence of another biography, which starts with $\psi_n[. . .]$, but thereafter diverges from the one just described. The second element in the new biography may be represented as $\psi'_{n+1}[. . .,\psi_n]$, where the prime ($'$) indicates that this is a different eigenstate of the relevant set of compatible brain observables, corresponding now to a visual impression of a dead cat. This second biography continues with a phenomenal perspective associated with a memory of such an impression, $\psi'_{n+2}[. . .,\psi_n,\psi'_{n+1}]$. With respect to this biography, the transition from t_n to t_{n+1} is again associated with a reduction of the (relative) state vector of the cat. But this time, the relative state goes from a superposition of live and dead states, at t_n, to a state, at t_{n+1}, in which the cat is unambiguously dead.

This relative state formulation of quantum mechanics has much to recommend it. At the level of theory it is wonderfully economical. It can account satisfactorily for the appearance of state vector reduction, without having to postulate any physical process of collapse. Moreover, it completely removes the sting from the results, respectively theoretical and experimental, of Bell and Aspect. There is simply no need, from the present point of view, to postulate any faster-than-light propagation of influences. Suppose, as before, that there are two spin-½ particles with anticorrelated spins. I measure the spin of particle 1 in the $+z$ direction, find it to be, say, $+\hbar/2$, and in consequence know for certain that if you measure the spin of particle 2 in the $+z$ direction, you will get the value $-\hbar/2$. The problem, remember, is that if I had chosen to measure the spin in some other direction, it would have been physically possible for you, measuring the spin of particle 2 in the same, $+z$, direction, to get the result $+\hbar/2$ instead. So it looks as though my actions have contributed to an instantaneous change in another physical system that may be arbitrarily far removed spatially.

From the standpoint of the relative state formulation, however, there is no such instantaneous change, or propagation of influence. When I carry out my measurement on particle 1, my awareness selects or designates a particular eigenvalue, in this case $+\hbar/2$, and thereby the corresponding eigenstate. Relative to that designated eigenstate, particle 2 is then in that eigenstate of the observable corresponding to the z component of spin which is associated with the value $-\hbar/2$. And that's all there is to it: in selecting $+\hbar/2$ for particle 1, my awareness *a fortiori* selects $-\hbar/2$ for particle 2. But that is no more the propagation of a causal influence than the fact that, in selecting, say, 10.31 a.m., British Summer Time, 30 August 1987 as 'now', for me, sitting at a desk in Oxford, my awareness is *a fortiori* selecting that same time as 'now' for you, listening to *The Archers* on the radio in, say, Cambridge. In relativistic terms, it is simply that, in designating a particular time locally as being 'now', my experience designates by implication an entire surface in space-time, my instantaneous simultaneity plane. The situation with the two particles is entirely analogous. Suppose I am carrying out a spin measurement on one particle, and you, in some distant spot, are making a similar measurement on the other. In designating a state in the local Hilbert space associated with the relevant part or aspect of my brain, my awareness designates by implication a corresponding relative state of the larger Hilbert space that includes both particles, both sets of instruments, and your brain as well.

That is a strong point in favour of the relative state approach. But, to set against that, Schrödinger's cat remains in its live–dead limbo. The universal wave function, on the present view, does not collapse, even when the chamber is opened. Worse, the mind of the observer becomes placed in a precisely matching limbo of cat-alive cat-dead perceptual states. Thus regarded, state vector reduction is essentially an illusion engendered by our always viewing the world from the standpoint of a particular eigenstate, within our local brain subsystem, of some set of compatible brain observables. Just what we are to make of this, philosophically speaking, and what are the broader implications of the relative state approach generally, are questions we shall attempt to answer in the next chapter.

13

Quantum Mechanics and the Conscious Observer

There are, I take it, two respects in which the relative state approach which we explored in the last chapter fails to satisfy our common-sense intuitions. Somehow it simultaneously seems to give us too much and too little. It gives us too much, in so far as we are asked to take seriously, as elements of reality, all the possible outcomes of a measurement or observation, in spite of the fact that there invariably seems to us to be a unique actual outcome. At the same time, the approach appears to give us too little, inasmuch as the state of the world relative to a phenomenal perspective will only possess as much definiteness as correlations between it and the relevant states of our brain permit. To the extent that such correlations are lacking, the relative state of the world remains a superposition of such states as are countenanced by common sense – states which, from a common-sense perspective, are both mutually exclusive and jointly exhaustive. Thus the approach does not, on the face of it, give one a definite live or dead state of the cat, so long as the chamber remains sealed, even relative to one's own awareness; but for common sense, the cat simply must be *either* alive *or* dead.

A possible philosophical response to this might be to abandon what philosophers call *realism*. Very roughly, realism is the view that reality transcends experience, that propositions can be true or false, independently of our being in a position to tell which they are. One of the staunchest contemporary critics of realism, thus construed, is Michael Dummett, whose misgivings about realism derive from considerations about meaning. I do not happen to share these misgivings; and in any case this is not the place to explore the issue of realism versus antirealism. Nevertheless, it is intriguing to find, in an early article of Dummett's, an antirealist account of mathematics which would seem to fit quantum mechanics like a glove:

If we think that mathematical results are in some sense imposed on us from without, we could have . . . the picture of a mathematical reality not already in existence but as it were coming into being as we probe. Our investigations bring into existence what was not there before, but what they bring into existence is not of our own making.

(Dummett, 1978, p. 18)

Deleting 'mathematical', this is precisely what one would be obliged to say, if one equated reality with the *reduced* relative states that emerge when the relevant brain states become correlated with those of some other physical system, by way of a measurement interaction. One would then take the following view of Schrödinger's cat, when the crucial hour has elapsed, but the chamber has yet to be opened and its contents inspected. The cat is not determinately alive, nor is it determinately dead. It is not that one of the two statements 'The cat is alive' and 'The cat is dead' is true, but we don't know which. The situation is rather that neither statement is true. Reality itself contains a lacuna at that point, one which will only be filled when we open up the chamber and look inside. Then one of these statements will *become* true. Perhaps it will then become true, not merely that the cat *is* alive but also that it was alive, even before we looked. This is a strange way of speaking, but not obviously self-contradictory. What it means is that truth and falsity become relativized to times, according to a logic that would forbid the inference from '"X was F at t_1" is true at t_2' to '"X is F" was true at t_1'.

Still, this is hardly what common sense would dictate. Moreover, there is no logical guarantee that something which becomes true, on this basis, will thereafter remain true, once we relax our earlier simplifying assumption that every element in a biography leaves behind it an indelible trace that figures in every succeeding element. This relates to a rather obscure remark of Bell's (the Bell of Bell's theorem), which puzzled me when I first read it. What Bell said was that to take Everett's no-collapse, relative state view to heart was to deny the reality of the past (Bell, 1981, pp. 635–6). But it is now clear to me what he was driving at. A thought-experiment due to Wigner (1963) may serve to illustrate the point.

In Wigner's experiment, a beam of silver atoms with the spins of their valency electrons polarized in the $+x$ direction is passed through a *Stern–Gerlach* apparatus that 'measures' their spin along the z axis, by imposing a magnetic field that has the effect of splitting the original beam into an upper and a lower beam, corresponding to spin up and spin down. (The reason for the inverted commas around 'measure' will shortly become apparent.) Spatial position may then be regarded as the apparatus 'pointer' from which the spin component on the z axis may be read off. Thus far, the example is, in its essential aspects, no different from the Schrödinger's cat case. In the one, we are using presence in the upper or lower beam as a measure of spin. In the other, we are using the cat's being dead or alive to register the decay or failure to decay, within a given hour, of at least one atom of some radioactive substance. But now suppose, with Wigner, that *before any further apparatus or whatever has been allowed to interact with the atoms in the beams* (we assume that the entire set-up is screened against outside influences), they are passed through a second Stern–Gerlach apparatus that exactly reverses the operation of the first one, thereby reuniting the beams. Finally, a third Stern–Gerlach apparatus measures the spin of the particles along the x axis.

Suppose one were to regard the operation of the first Stern–Gerlach apparatus as constituting a measurement of the particles' spin. Then, taking the von Neumann view of measurement, one might be tempted to apply the projection postulate there and then. Were one to do so, one would then have to regard the atoms in the two beams as being, respectively, in two different eigenstates of the z-spin observable. If they really were, however, a measurement of spin along the x axis, carried out on the final recombined beam, would result in approximately equal proportions of spin up and spin down atoms. *And that is not what the Schrödinger equation predicts.* What it predicts is that all the atoms will be found with spin up in the +x direction, just as they were at the outset. (Some thought has been given to the question how, in practice, one might carry out Wigner's experiment. A recent analysis yielded the conclusion that for the experiment to work, the electromagnetic field would have to possess a degree of homogeneity, or uniformity, that is almost certainly beyond the reach of current technology, but which is nevertheless likely to become attainable eventually.)

We mustn't run away, incidentally, with the idea that this prediction is in any way at odds with von Neumann's consistency proof, alluded to earlier, according to which the observer is free, when carrying out a measurement, to apply the projection postulate at any point in the measurement chain. For bear in mind that no one is there to observe the two separate beams, prior to their being recombined; and without an observer, there is in a sense no genuine measurement. What von Neumann says, in effect, is that, given that the measurement eventuates in a conscious perception on the part of an observer, it is a matter of indifference, as far as that observer's subsequent predictions are concerned, where, in the measurement chain, reduction of the state vector is supposed to occur.

The moral that has generally been drawn from Wigner's imagined experiment is that it is the *de facto* irreversibility of such a correlating interaction as occurs in the Schrödinger's cat case, that allows us to think of the cat as being alive or dead before we actually look. Macroscopic objects are not, on this view, in principle different from microscopic ones; but thermodynamic (entropy-related) considerations make it possible to neglect in practice possibilities which, in the subatomic realm, we should overlook at our peril. In short, Schrödinger's chamber is, after all, in a superposition of cat-alive and cat-dead states. But in practice, no experiment we could devise would be capable of distinguishing this superposition from a situation in which the cat is determinately alive or determinately dead, each alternative having a probability of a half, but we don't know which.

Now of course, *we* have been proceeding on the assumption that the projection postulate is false anyway. Nevertheless, an analogous moral holds. Someone might wish to insist, in a realist spirit: 'The cat, before we look, must really be either determinately alive or determinately dead. In either case, we need only take seriously, as representing a description of reality, one part of the superposition making up the quantum state of the chamber. For the remainder of the superposition embodies mere unrealized *possibilities*.' This is plainly wrong. We must, at the level of theory, if not of practice, take the whole superposition seriously. For there are *in principle* possible experiments, for the correct prediction of whose outcome the entire superposition is required. But the performance of such an experiment would result in the *obliteration* of all evidence from which one could infer whether or not at least one atom had decayed in the crucial interval, and whether, in consequence, the cat had lived or died. This means that we can, in practice, regard it as a sufficient condition of a measurement's having been made that a permanent record of the result of the measurement has been created. For to describe it as 'permanent' is logically to imply that no such experiment will in fact be carried out.

In principle, however (which is what properly concerns us as philosophers), there is no record or trace that it is impossible to erase – certainly not the trace left in one's memory after something has registered in consciousness. So even when one has opened Schrödinger's chamber and observed the cat as being, let us say, dead, there is still a thinkable set of operations which some logically possible scientist could perform on the whole caboodle – observer, chamber, cat and all – which in quantum-mechanical terms would 'undo' the measurement.

A classic point of reference in quantum mechanics is the celebrated 'two-slit' experiment, in which electrons can be made to create interference fringes, similar to those that Young demonstrated in the case of light. So long as both slits are open, and there is no device present to register which slit an electron goes through, one gets an interference pattern of alternating zones of impact and non-impact, *even if the electrons are passed through one at a time, at arbitrarily large intervals.* (The corresponding phenomenon in regard to light was, in effect, experimentally demonstrated by Taylor as long ago as 1909.) So it isn't the electrons themselves that are interfering with each other. How could they be, if they are passed through, say, one every quarter of an hour (or come to that, one every twenty-five years)? Rather, the interference pattern reflects interference between the alternative trajectories of each individual electron. In other words, the path of each electron must be conceived as a superposition of the paths corresponding to passage through the different slits.

From a God's-eye view, the situation with Schrödinger's cat is very similar. Those who have seen the (1978) *Superman* film may remember the extraordinary feat at the end, where the hero puts the entire planet into reverse gear, so that a succession of catastrophic events, culminating in the death of Lois Lane, are replayed in reverse order, with their effects being correspondingly undone. In classical mechanics, this could be accomplished, in theory, by simultaneously reversing the momentum of every single particle in the system. But a similar reversibility principle applies within quantum mechanics. Just as, in Wigner's thought-experiment, the beams are recombined, so one can *imagine*, consistently with quantum mechanics, that after the crucial hour has elapsed, forces are brought into play, within the sealed chamber containing Schrödinger's cat, that induce a subsequent time evolution which is the time-reversed analogue of that undergone by the system in the first hour. Assuming that there is no collapse of the wave function, one could then open the chamber in the certainty of finding the cat alive and well, with the container of cyanide unbroken and the radioactive atoms intact.

I hardly need say that this such an experiment is not remotely feasible in practice, nor ever will be; only a God – or a Superman – could perform it. Nevertheless, it is a perfectly meaningful *thought*-experiment. Suppose, *per impossibile*, it were to be performed not just once but repeatedly, and that every time it yielded a live cat. Then that would be tantamount to a proof that the wave function had not collapsed and that at the end of the first hour the cat really was in a superposition of live and dead states. For the quantum-mechanical explanation of how the cat invariably comes to be alive, at the end of the experiment, is that the unambiguously live state is *reconstituted* by way of interference between the alternative 'trajectories' in which the cat is, respectively, killed and left unscathed. And we could go further, imagining an even more preposterous experiment, in which a human observer is allowed, at the end of the first hour, to open the chamber. Then a time evolution occurs which not only leaves the chamber resealed, but also erases the observer's memories of what happened when he opened it. Here the observer's amnesia could only be explained, quantum-mechanically, by appealing to interference between the 'trajectories' in which the cat was observed to be alive and those in which it was observed to be dead. (That would imply branching of the observer's biography, followed by reconvergence.)

Once again, there is a temptation to say: 'All the same, only one of the elements in the superposition can correspond to what *really* happened, even if it is now in principle impossible to discover where the truth lies: to discover which part of the wave function gives the true story.' That, however, one cannot say, consistently with conventional quantum mechanics. What we are now talking about, in effect, are superpositions of *histories*, rather than superpositions of instantaneous states: how the electron got from the source to the screen, what happened to Schrödinger's cat. Nevertheless, the same general point applies here as applied earlier. The supposition that there is a unique history, in the superposition, that represents what really happened, is tantamount to postulating a hidden variable theory. And that, as we have already seen, is subject to grave objections.

Most people who are acquainted with quantum mechanics would be prepared, I imagine, to accept *microscopic* states or histories, for example of an electron, that are superpositions of those that common sense would recognize as possible; but they would baulk at superpositions of *macroscopic* states or histories. This, however, is where we came in, at the beginning of chapter 12. The whole point of Schrödinger's cat example, as we saw, is to show that, given a suitable coupling, any microscopic superposition can be made to generate a corresponding macroscopic one. You cannot, if quantum mechanics is universally applicable, have one without the other. Many people, no doubt, will take that fact to show that quantum mechanics cannot, after all, be universally applicable. Well, perhaps not. But the burden of my argument has been to show that there is nothing in the character of our ordinary experience that constitutes a shred of evidence that quantum mechanics does in fact break down at the macroscopic level. What is inconsistent with the universal applicability of quantum mechanics is not our ordinary experience as such, but the common-sense way of interpreting it. And I am bound to say that, in this area, I cannot see that common sense has any particular authority, given that our intuitions have evolved within a domain in which characteristically quantum-mechanical effects are scarcely in evidence.

In the line I have so far been following, I am heavily indebted to Everett, the originator of the relative state formulation of quantum mechanics. I have, however, deliberately avoided the label most commonly applied to Everett's interpretation: the *many-worlds* theory. There are two reasons for this. First, I want to dissociate myself from a number of misconceptions which now surround the many-worlds theory, as one often finds it discussed – especially in popular accounts. Secondly, the very term 'many-worlds theory' seems to me, for reasons that will shortly become evident, a distinct misnomer for the view I am concerned to defend here (as also for what I take to be Everett's own position).

One widespread misconception – encouraged by sloppy popular exposition – is that, on the Everett view, the observer somehow splits the entire universe simply by measuring a quantum system. (This would make cosmic fission child's play compared to splitting the atom; perhaps we do it all the time, just by looking.) John Gribbin, for example, says that if someone carries out a measurement on a system that exists in a superposition of states, then according to Everett,

> the act of observation cuts the ties that bind alternative realities together, and allows them to go on their own separate ways . . . , each alternative really containing its own observer who has made the same observation but got a different quantum 'answer' . . .
>
> (Gribbin, 1984, p. 237)

What Gribbin has done here – and what exponents of Everett's theory frequently seem to do – is slip into a way of talking appropriate to a view quite different from Everett's: one that we might dub the *parallel collapse* theory. Suppose that a system is in a certain superposition of eigenstates of a particular observable. Whereas the standard von Neumann view has it that measurement of the observable precipitates collapse into just one of the eigenstates figuring in the superposition, the parallel collapse theory would postulate simultaneous collapse into all of them. On this view, the observer, so to speak, *decomposes* the superposition into its separate elements. The entire universe, observer included, accordingly divides into as many distinct copies of itself as are required to accommodate all these ostensibly incompatible outcomes. (It won't do, incidentally, to have just one world for each outcome, since that would be at odds with the fact that, in general, the different outcomes are associated with different ostensible probabilities of occurrence. What one would need is a continuous infinity of worlds, for each outcome, with a *measure*, in the mathematician's sense, that was proportional to the probability in question. Think of the worlds as like points on a line, which is divided into as many segments – sets of worlds – as there are possible outcomes to the measurement, with the length of each segment being proportional to the corresponding probability.)

This is a possible view, though I can see no good reason why anyone should wish to adopt it. Essentially, it just piles ontological extravagance on top of all the other difficulties that beset the von Neumann approach. Thus, one could ask: at what point in the von Neumann chain does the split or decomposition occur, and on what spacelike surface? The only gain is the dubious one of restoring a theoretical determinism: rather than there being only a certain *chance* of each element in the superposition's becoming actualized, the actualization of every element becomes a certainty, though measurement will still *seem* to the observer to be a probabilistic affair.

As I say, parallel collapse is not what I advocate. Nor is it what Everett advocates. (Nor, to be fair, does Gribbin really think that it is, as is clear from what he goes on to say.) According to the relative state view, there is no collapse (or decomposition) of the wave function, individual or multiple. Rather than say that, on the relative state view, the observer splits the universe by carrying out a measurement, it would be closer to the mark to say that it is the universe that splits the observer. If one starts with a quantum system, existing in a superposition of states, then what really happens according to the relative state theory is that a causal influence proceeding *from* the system *to* the observer, via the measuring apparatus, results in the observer's going into a corresponding super-position. Putting it that way, however, makes it clear that there's no real call to bring in the *universe*, as such, at all; for the transaction is a purely local one.

That brings me to a second respect in which the majority of accounts of the many-worlds theory are liable seriously to mislead. Such accounts regularly speak of the *whole universe* dividing every time a measurement takes place or, more generally, every time a quantum interaction occurs. For example, Peter Gibbins (1987, p. 112) says that 'upon each measure-ment the universe splits up into myriad new universes'. The impression is thereby conveyed that, say, any routine demonstration in the Clarendon Laboratory here in Oxford has instantaneous cataclysmic consequences, affecting the entire universe, right out to the Andromeda galaxy and beyond. This apparent implication is made absolutely explicit by de Witt (quoted by Davies (1980, pp. 136–7); Davies doesn't give the reference):

> Our universe must be viewed as constantly splitting into a stupendous number of branches ... Every quantum transition taking place on every star, in every galaxy, in every remote corner of the universe is splitting our local world into myriad copies of itself. Here is schizophrenia with a vengeance.

De Witt is a leading champion of Everett's views: Huxley to Everett's Darwin. But if this passage is anything to go by, he and I are talking about different theories. As I interpret it, the relative state view has no such implications as he alleges. It postulates no causal influences beyond what conventional physics would countenance, and certainly none that propagate faster than light. (Indeed, as I indicated at the end of the last chapter, it seems to me to be a principal virtue of the relative state approach that it can avoid the problems of *non-locality* that are raised for other interpretations by the EPR thought-experiment, Bell's theorem, the Aspect experiment and so forth.)

The key point here is that 'dividing' or 'splitting', in the relative state view, is essentially a metaphor for going into a superposition; or more specifically, for going into a *macroscopic* superposition. Consider, once again, Schrödinger's cat. Schrödinger's cat is a subsystem of the universe. So if it goes into a superposition of live and dead states, then one could doubtless say of the universe as a whole that it has gone into a superposition of Schrödinger's-cat-alive and Schrödinger's-cat-dead states. That, however, is just a matter of definition: it implies no instantaneous transmission of causal influences. Only in a Pickwickian sense could the rest of the universe be said to be instantaneously 'affected' by what befalls Schrödinger's cat: the same Pickwickian sense in which an astronaut on Mars, whose wife back on Earth sleeps with another man, may be said to be 'affected' by instantaneously (in a shorter time even than it takes for light to travel between the two planets!) becoming a cuckold.

It must already be becoming apparent why I consider the 'many-worlds' label something of a misnomer. But there is more to be said on that score. If this talk of 'many worlds' is just a graphic way of saying that the universe is in a superposition of states, and if it's a sufficient condition for the universe to be in a superposition of states that some subsystem is, then it follows that *every realist interpretation of quantum mechanics that eschews hidden variables should be regarded as a many-worlds theory.* This would apply even to the standard von Neumann construal of quantum mechanics, which acknowledges real superpositions at the microlevel. Why, then, is the many-worlds metaphor supposed to be uniquely appropriate to a theory that postulates *macroscopic* super-positions? I can only suppose that people have failed fully to wean themselves away from the classical prejudice that macroscopically distinct states simply won't mix. Being unable to make sense of the idea that macroscopically distinct states can be linearly combined within the *same* universe, they feel obliged to interpret proposed superpositions of such states as implying a kind of doubling up of reality itself. But that's just a confusion, and one that is liable to prompt all manner of irrelevant or otherwise unfounded objections to the Everett view. Consider, for example, Peter Gibbins's charge (1987, p. 112) that the many-worlds theory involves 'an extreme violation of the principle of conservation of mass-energy'. The appearance of a violation of that principle could only result from illicit multiple counting: taking a state of the universe that is a macroscopic superposition, and then treating each element in this superposition as though it referred to something that was a distinct universe in its own right. We must not lose sight of the fact that, on the relative state view, a superposition of live and dead states of Schrödinger's cat is still a unitary quantum state of a unique cat, inhabiting a single universe.

It may be helpful, at this point, if I briefly summarize the position that I am here concerned to defend. Nonrelativistically conceived, the universe is to be thought of as a seamless whole that evolves smoothly and deterministically in accordance with the Schrödinger equation. This evolving system can be decomposed, in a vast number of different ways, into subsystems. To the extent that there are correlations between the subsystems, no subsystem can be thought of as being in any determinate quantum state at any given time. If, however, one selects a particular subsystem, and chooses some possible state of that system – not, I repeat, the state that it is 'really in', for in the presence of correlations there is no such state – then one can assign to any other subsystem a determinate quantum state, relative to the chosen state of the original subsystem. For a conscious subject, at any given time at which it is conscious, it is invariably *as though* a particular state of a particular subsystem has been selected: namely, a state of whatever physical system within the subject's brain immediately underlies the subject's stream of consciousness. I say of this state that it is *designated* by consciousness. Not just any state of the relevant brain system is eligible for designation, only those states that are shared eigenstates of some favoured set of observables on the relevant brain system. A conscious subject, at any given time, is entitled to think of any other subsystem, from the whole of the rest of the universe on down, as having a determinate quantum state relative to this designated state. What one would normally think of as *the* state of anything, at a given time, should really be thought of as merely its state relative to the given designated state of oneself; and this goes for the state of the universe as a whole.

I said that only shared eigenstates of the preferred set of brain observables are eligible for designation. Let me now be a little more specific. Suppose that the state of the entire universe is represented as a superposition of states, each of which is a tensor product of the states of its subsystems, under some suitable decomposition into subsystems and some suitable choice of representation for each subsystem. I say the *entire* universe; but actually, it would suffice to consider the smallest subsystem of the universe that includes the relevant brain system as a subsystem and which is *self-contained*, in the sense that its states are not correlated, in the quantum-mechanical sense, with those of any other subsystem of the universe (with the exception of those already contained, in whole or in part, within itself). For that subsystem will have – as the relevant brain system will not – a determinate well-defined, objective quantum state. (This smallest self-contained subsystem will, however, coincide with the entire universe, unless – as seems improbable – there are parts of the universe that have never interacted with the rest.)

Suppose, further, that the brain subsystem underlying my awareness is one of the subsystems and that the representation chosen is the one defined by the favoured set of brain observables just referred to. Then, at any given time, a necessary condition for a particular shared eigenstate of the preferred set of observables to be designated is that it is included in one of the tensor products that figure in the universal superposition – or, more precisely, that it appears in an element of that superposition which is associated with a nonzero coefficient. I say that this is a necessary condition for a given state of the relevant brain system to be designated; but it is also a *sufficient* condition. All the states that satisfy this condition will be simultaneously designated, thus generating parallel phenomenal perspectives which are all equally mine. That is the literal meaning which should be attached to talk of a 'split' or divided observer, in the context of measurement.

It is, incidentally, senseless to ask – as do some commentators on Everett – 'Why do I find myself in *this* state?' For it isn't as though I find myself to be in one of the eligible states *as opposed to* any of the others. On the contrary, for each of the parallel states, I have an experience of finding myself in it – though these experiences are not, of course, co-conscious. It's very like asking 'Why is it now *now*?' Once again, the question embodies a confusion, because I don't find it to be now *now* – 12.00 noon, 1 February 1989 – as opposed to any of the myriad other times at which I have been, or will be, conscious; I have experienced, am experiencing or will experience as 'now' all the times that figure in my conscious biography. (What I have just said applies to Jammer's remark (1974, p. 518) that 'the many-worlds interpretation may be criticized for not giving a sufficient explanation of why the observer is localized in that branch of the splitting universe in which he happens to be'; the whole point, if one insists on talking this way, is that the observer is 'localized' in all the relevant branches.)

To what extent my own position, as I have just presented it, coincides with Everett's I'm not sure. In his own writings, Everett was nowhere near as explicit on certain crucial philosophical matters as I am here aiming to be – thus bearing much of the blame for the confusion evident amongst his commentators; nor, it must be said, did he show the least inclination to repudiate the more extravagant formulations of the many-worlds view promoted in his name by de Witt and others. But in any case, I am not concerned in this book with exegesis of Everett's writings. Suffice it to say that this seems to me clearly to be what Everett *ought* to have held, given the logic of the relative state approach.

There are several points about the relative state view, as I have interpreted it, that still require clarification. First, there is the question of the role of *probability* in all of this. For the conventional, collapse interpretation, probabilities arise from the indeterministic character of the collapse. When a measurement is carried out, the system state vector is projected into one of the eigenstates of the measured observable, with a probability that is proportional to the square modulus of the associated coefficient, when the measured state is represented as a linear combination of these eigenstates. The relative state formulation, however, realistically interpreted, is fully deterministic, and there is no collapse, objectively speaking. What one has to do, therefore, is somehow associate probabilities with the branching structure of the biographies. Take the case, considered in the last chapter, of a spin-1 particle. Suppose I am measuring the square of the spin, measured in units of $\hbar$, along just a single axis, say the z axis. According to quantum mechanics, I am twice as likely to get the result 1 as 0. What could this mean in our present terms?

At this point I adapt an idea due to Deutsch (1985a). That part of the formalism of quantum mechanics which is concerned solely with the representation of quantum *states* is, as it stands, a piece of mathematics. In order to constitute a physical theory, it requires interpretation. We saw earlier that biographies form a branching structure. If one makes the simplifying assumption that the elements of a biography form a discrete series, then each element may have a multiplicity of successors. Thus, in the case just considered, measurement of the square of the z component of spin, of a spin-1 particle, results in distinct continuations of my pre-measurement biography. These will involve, respectively, succeeding phenomenal perspectives in which I have the impression of having got the result 1, and in which, on the contrary, I have the impression of having got the result 0. What we now need is a new way of thinking about these biographies: a new model.

The model up to now has been that of a branching line. Now think instead in terms of a solid, elongated object, with a cross-section of uniform size; a cylinder, for example. Let the long dimension represent time, and a biography correspond to a straight line running along it parallel to the sides (see figure 13.1). A slice through the solid reveals a coloured, but in general not uniformly coloured, surface. The colour at a point corresponds to the phenomenal character of the phenomenal perspective, at the time to which the slice corresponds, in a biography that passes through that point. If we take a slice at the point immediately before the measurement, we find that the surface is a homogeneous green. That corresponds to the fact that the interaction which carries the observer's brain into a superposition of eigenstates has not yet taken place. If we take a slice at a higher point, after the measurement is completed, we shall find that the surface is divided into two regions of different colours, blue and yellow, corresponding to the results 1 and 0 of the square spin measurement. And *the blue region is twice the area of the*

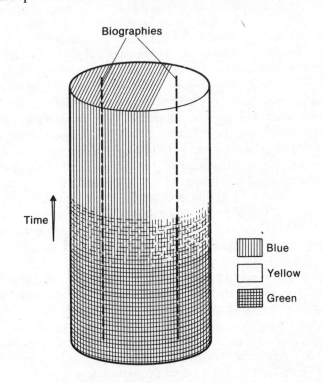

Figure 13.1 *Biographies are depicted as lines through a cylinder, parallel to the sides.*

The transition from homogeneous green to two distinct regions – a larger blue one and a yellow one, half the size – corresponds to the time evolution of the relevant brain system, when the observer makes a quantum measurement that, as we should ordinarily think of it, has two possible outcomes, one twice as likely as the other. In fact, the true outcome is a superposition – encompassing the observed system, the measuring apparatus and the observer – in which there figure brain states appropriate to both results of the measurement. The appearance of one result's being twice as probable as the other corresponds to the fact that an arbitrarily chosen line – biography, that is – which starts in the green region, is twice as likely to pass into the blue region as into the yellow.

yellow region. What this means is that if we take an arbitrary straight line, that is to say biography, running along the solid, parallel to the sides, it is twice as likely to run into the blue region as the yellow.

From one point of view, what we have done is replace a single stream of consciousness, as would be acknowledged by common sense, with a continous infinity of parallel such streams. And, rather than branching, these are now to be thought of as *differentiating* over time. But putting matters that way may serve to make it sound a more extravagant move than it really is. These biographies, as I have repeatedly stressed, are, objectively regarded, merely an abstraction from the quantum-mechanical time evolution of the universe as a whole. What I am proposing, following Deutsch, is that we interpret the mathematical formalism of quantum mechanics in such a way that the fact of a physical system's being in a superposition, with respect to some set of basis vectors, is to be understood as the system's having a *dimension* in addition to those of time and space. It is unproblematic that a system can be in different energy states, say, with respect to different points on the time dimension, like our damped harmonic oscillator, steadily running down. Similarly, I am suggesting, a harmonic oscillator's being in a superposition of energy eigenstates at a *given* time can be thought of as its having different determinate energies at different points on a new dimension running, so to speak, perpendicular to time and space. (Seeing that any state may be represented as a superposition in an infinity of different ways, we shall, strictly speaking, need an infinity of such extra dimensions; but one will suffice for present purposes.) This dimension can be thought of as of arbitrary finite size, and divided into as many regions as there are eigenstates of the corresponding observable, each with a size that is proportional to the square modulus of the coefficient associated with the corresponding eigenstate, as it figures in the superposition. These are only dimensions in a Pickwickian sense, since there will be no counterpart of spatial or temporal order. All of this, in fact, is just a vivid way of conveying the essential point – that the components in a superposition must be given a model which admits of their being assigned a measure that is proportional to the corresponding probability. (For a more rigorous exposition see Deutsch, 1985a.)

Common sense acknowledges variations, in phenomenal perspectives belonging to the same person, in only the time dimension (though in chapter 6 we questioned the assumption that even a normal brain is associated with just a single such perspective at a given time). Now I am suggesting that we should be prepared to countenance something further: variations in phenomenal perspective along an imaginary dimension, corresponding to a shift from component to component within a single instantaneous superposition. I hardly need say that this is an exceedingly radical proposal. Its appeal is likely to be confined to those for whom argument and elegance of explanation are to be accorded greater intellectual weight than is common opinion. For my own part, I would say only that this conception seems to me to be vastly superior to any other proposed *interpretation* of quantum mechanics, where interpretation is to be contrasted with modification. Consequently, it should, I contend, be regarded as the preferred view, unless and until some evidence emerges that quantum mechanics itself breaks down at the macroscopic level, in such a way as to block the creation of macroscopic superpositions.

This may be an appropriate point to reflect on what is entailed by 'macroscopic' in this context. Ordinary observation of common-or-garden objects may, as von Neumann demonstrated, be construed quite happily as measurement in the quantum-mechanical sense. Thus, it must be associated with a corresponding range of observables. When I observe the pencil on my desk, I am *inter alia* making a 'measurement' of a position observable; and likewise when I observe the woman crossing the road, I am making a 'measurement' of velocity. And if I use a ruler to measure the distance of the tip of the pencil from the right and front edges of my desk, or glance at the speedometer (and, for direction, compass) of my car, there again I am measuring macroscopic position or velocity observables. These coarse-grained macroscopic observables must not, however, be confused with their idealized quantum-mechanical counterparts. Macroscopic observables have two key characteristic features. First, every set of macroscopic observables is a compatible set; macroscopic observables invariably commute. Secondly, macroscopic observables are massively degenerate, in the quantum-mechanical sense; that is to say, every eigenvalue – that is, every possible distinct result of an ordinary observation or measurement – corresponds to a vast *eigenspace* of distinct quantum-mechanical states, between which ordinary observation or measurement is incapable of distinguishing.

It would strike most people as unremarkable that things always appear to us to have determinate macroscopic attributes. The macroscopic observables are a fundamental given that we ordinarily take for granted. But in the context of quantum mechanics there is a puzzle here. And it is frequently cited as an objection to the relative state view that it assigns a special status to one particular way of decomposing state vectors: namely, that in which the components are eigenstates of macroscopic observables. Why should we always observe things as being in eigenstates of *those* observables, as opposed to some other set of observables, with eigenstates that are superpositions of the eigenstates of the macroscopic observables? In short, what's so special, from Nature's point of view, about these observables, and that way of decomposing Hilbert space vectors? This is known as the *preferred basis* problem.

The first thing to be said here is that, contrary to what many people seem to think, this is no more of a problem for the relative state view than it is for the conventional view. Think of a measurement as having two stages. At Stage 1, there is a measurement interaction in which macroscopic states of the apparatus become systematically correlated with microscopic quantum states of the observed system. This interaction between apparatus and observed system is then followed, at Stage 2, by a second measurement interaction which results in introspectively distinguishable states of the observer's brain becoming correlated with those same macroscopic states of the apparatus. It is worth noting that Stage 1 interactions are, in a sense, freely chosen, subject to the technology being available to implement them. Stage 2 interactions, on the other hand, are a physical and biological given, depending as they do on the operations of our nervous system and the character of sound, light and so forth.

Now the conventional view, as I see it, runs into the preferred basis problem at Stage 1. For according to this view, objects can only ever exist in eigenstates of the macroscopic observables. The measurement interaction thus results in a reduced state, for the composite system, in which the apparatus exists, as it must, in an eigenstate of some macroscopic observable; and this, by virtue of the correlation, is associated with the observed system's being in the corresponding eigenstate of the observable that it is the purpose of the exercise to measure. For the conventional view, therefore, the preferred basis problem arises in the form: 'Given that macroscopic objects are constrained to exist only in eigenstates of *some* set of observables, why should it be those ones, the ones we think of as macroscopic observables? Why aren't objects constrained, instead, to exist in eigenstates of some other set of compatible observables, and hence in superpositions of the states we actually appear to find them in?'

For the relative state approach, by contrast, the problem – if it is a problem – arises at Stage 2. On this view there is no state vector reduction, and objects do, in general, exist in superpositions of eigenstates of macroscopic observables. Hence, there is nothing occurring at Stage 1 which favours any particular representation over any other. Stage 2, however, involves macroscopic states becoming correlated with brain states on which *consciousness* somehow imposes a preferred basis. It is not, as suggested by Wigner, that our awareness precipitates a state vector reduction, at this stage. Those states of our brains to which consciousness is sensitive can, on the present view, happily evolve into superpositions that mirror superpositions in the apparatus and the observed system. These superpositions are not, however, experienced as such. There is, apparently, a preferred set of compatible brain observables, such that only eigenstates of that set constitute phenomenal perspectives. A superposition of phenomenal perspectives can exist; but it is not a phenomenal perspective in its own right. Rather, its existence is associated with the simultaneous presence of all the phenomenal perspectives thus superposed.

In chapter 1, we saw how the secondary qualities, meaning and the flow of time have all been pushed into the mind by philosophers eager to preserve a suitably austere conception of physical reality. Within the context of the relative state approach to quantum mechanics, as I have been developing it in the past few chapters, one might do the same to Nature's ostensible preference for a particular basis, which threatens to mar the rotational symmetry of Hilbert space. Once again, something that is an embarrassment to physics could be construed as a mere creature of the mind, which is, in effect, projected outwards on to external reality. Alternatively, one might take a more objectivist tack, seeing the character of our experience, here, as reflecting something that is quite generally true, and in no way peculiar to mind.

What one might try to show, if one took this second line, is that a preferred basis arises quite naturally within quantum mechanics itself, in the context of measurement. This is what David Deutsch argues (1985a). According to him, the very occurrence of measurement interactions depends upon the universe having a certain structure. The fact that we can carry out the measurements that we do requires the Hilbert space for the universe as a whole to be representable as a tensor product of Hilbert spaces, between which certain specific sorts of relation hold – the latter Hilbert spaces being the state spaces for the various subsystems. And from the product structure possessed by the universe at any given time, it is possible, he argues, to derive a preferred basis – what he calls the *interpretation basis* – that evolves over time, as new measurement interactions occur. This is to express the idea in terms of the Heisenberg picture; in terms of the Schrödinger picture, a different basis will be preferred at different times. (At different places too, one would have to add, in a properly relativistic formulation.) Deutsch makes the intriguing suggestion that this evolution of the interpretation basis may be what underlies our impression of the flow of time.

Deutsch's motivation, here, is actually rather different from mine. For he is inclined to adopt a more literalist interpretation than I am of the metaphor of division into separate worlds. One problem that faces anyone who wants to regard this as something more than a mere metaphor for superposition is the fact that there is an infinity of different ways of representing the state of the universe as a superposition, corresponding to the infinity of available bases. Objective splitting, it would seem, requires that one unique basis – or at any rate, a unique basis at any given time – should be regarded as canonical: superpositions with respect to that basis, but no other, are to be taken to correspond to genuine 'fractures' or 'fault-lines' within reality itself. Deutsch, therefore, sees his interpretation basis as providing a unique recipe for universal fission – or, more accurately, differentiation – and, occasionally, fusion or convergence. (It should be emphasized, however, that relativistically conceived, Deutsch's view doesn't imply *instantaneous* global fission. A split that is initiated in one region of space is to be thought of as akin to a blister that becomes progressively more extensive over time, as the states of increasingly more far-removed physical systems become correlated by measurement interactions with the original superposition. The 'blistering' here corresponds to a local separation of space-time itself into distinct parallel sheets. A similar picture is mooted, though not endorsed, by Penrose (1979, pp. 592–5).

Deutsch's proposal raises a host of technical questions which I cannot go into here. But Sara Foster, a philosophy research student at Oxford, and her supervisor Harvey Brown have succeeded in demonstrating that the proposal does not work as it stands (Foster and Brown, 1988). The problem is that the conditions of the interpretation basis that Deutsch lays down turn out not to define a *unique* basis, as they are intended to; and Deutsch himself has failed, so far, to find any plausible way of amending the conditions so as to meet Foster's objections. So the approach, at the moment, doesn't look particularly promising. But anyway, as we have seen, my own version of the relative state view doesn't call for the kind of literal splitting of space-time that Deutsch envisages. Consequently, it has no need to postulate a preferred vector basis for the universe as a whole, independently of mind. The problem that Deutsch's theory confronts at the global level, mine faces only in microcosm: at the level of the branching or differentiating *biographies*. For there *is*, on my view, a preferred basis with respect to which biographies may be said to divide or differentiate. But even here, I am not suggesting that the brain systems whose activities are constitutive of streams of consciousness are, *qua physical systems*, associated with any preferred basis. What is preferred here is preferred only from the point of view of awareness itself: from a point of view that has phenomenal perspectives as its windows on reality.

In short, I see the preference for a particular basis as being rooted in the nature of consciousness, rather than in the nature of the physical world in general. I do not pretend to know, in general, how and why the eigenstates of a particular set of compatible brain observables correspond to, or figure within, phenomenal perspectives, while others don't (though our discussion of time, in chapter 15, will have some bearing on this question). Yet that does not seem to me to be any more of a mystery than the problem that arises, independently of quantum mechanics, of why only certain aspects of what goes on in the brain register in consciousness anyway. In both cases what we have is a certain selectivity that seems, in our present state of ignorance, arbitrary. But that some such selectivity exists is, from the point of view of any theory that stops short of panpsychism, an inescapable fact about consciousness. The grain problem is one manifestation of this selectivity: the fact that the phenomenal content of any conscious state seems insensitive to the fine structure of any plausible corresponding brain state.

But here, I would argue, we have the makings of a powerful unification of the classical and quantum-mechanical manifestations of selectivity. For both, surely, can be encompassed within the single consideration that consciousness favours a particular set of brain observables on a particular brain subsystem. Indeed, the grain problem seems to me to lose its bite, once it is appreciated that the contents of consciousness are required to correspond to the simultaneous eigenvalues of a set of quantum-mechanical *observables*. For, in quantum mechanics, no observables are a priori privileged, or to be regarded as more fundamental than any others. And it is open to us to suppose that what consciousness favours are observables that involve a degree of *averaging* over spatial or spatio-temporal regions. (Indeed, such averaging is unavoidable in quantum mechanics; in the context of *quantum field theory*, no sense can be attached to a measurement of the electromagnetic field quantities at a precisely defined point, any more than, in elementary quantum mechanics, one can attach a meaning to a precise measurement of position or momentum.) Once again, this reflects the perspectival character of what is presented in consciousness; but as I emphasized in chapter 11, that in no way detracts from its objectivity or immediacy with respect to the underlying neurophysiological reality. The proposal remains Russellian in spirit.

Anyway, given such a preferred basis at the level of consciousness, it follows inexorably that it will become reflected in the objects of sense perception themselves, *as we perceive them*. What we think of as the ordinary, classical, macroscopic observables will simply be those who eigenstates are correlated by the mechanisms of sense perception with eigenstates of the preferred set of compatible brain observables. Thus, we shall inevitably view objects as possessing determinate eigenvalues of these observables, just as we view them as possessed of secondary qualities such as colour.

We began, in chapter 11, with the idea of physical reality as in some sense a sum of perspectives. We have now seen how such an idea arises very naturally in the interpretation of quantum mechanics. A set of perspectives is generated by the combination of a physical system P, a preferred set of compatible observables on P, and the actual quantum state of the smallest self-contained subsystem of the universe that includes P – which will then determine which shared eigenstates of P are designated. For only certain physical systems, and only for certain sets of compatible observables, will the resulting perspectives be *phenomenal* perspectives. We might introduce the notion of a set of *generalized* perspectives here, to be understood in such a way that any arbitrary choice of a physical system and a set of compatible observables on that system would, taken together with the quantum state of the smallest self-contained system that has the given system as a subsystem, define a set of generalized perspectives. Then phenomenal perspectives would be those generalized perspectives that are, so to speak, illumined by consciousness.

Assuming that the quantum-mechanical description of the physical world is essentially correct, one can say of it what Russell (rightly in my opinion) insisted we should say in regard to physical descriptions generally. It represents the physical world as having a certain formal structure; but to grasp the theory is not to know how that structure is qualitatively fleshed out. Nevertheless, it must be fleshed out in some way or other. In order for the theory to be true, the structure must be concretely realized; the physical world must have an intrinsic nature which instantiates the structure in question. And I wish to argue that, in consciousness, that intrinsic nature makes itself manifest. In one of its aspects, one must add. Thus a phenomenal perspective carries with it a transparent grasp of one part or aspect of what it is that concretely realizes the formal structure of the quantum-mechanical state description.

Much remains obscure, however. For example, can one meaningfully ask (always? sometimes?) what it would be like to experience, to have as one's current state of awareness, a generalized perspective that is in fact not illumined by consciousness, and is thus not, as things stand, a *phenomenal* perspective? Are there generalized perspectives on my brain which are potentially phenomenal perspectives, such as the phenomenal perspective I would have had a moment ago, had I been attending to the perception of a tree that currently occupies the periphery of my visual field? Thus can one regard it as, to some degree, a contingent matter which generalized perspectives make it into awareness? If so, does this depend on the preferred set of brain observables not, after all, remaining constant over time, but being (within certain limits) adjustable by the brain? I think the answer to all these questions is probably yes, though I have yet to work out the consequences. I incline to the view that there is a larger preferred set of (not necessarily all mutually compatible) observables, from which the brain, at different times, selects different compatible subsets. (In dreamless sleep it would, in effect, be selecting the *null set* of observables, the set with no members.) Clearly, one would need to take some such line, in order to preserve the *disclosure* view of phenomenal qualities, which I defended in chapter 10.

Finally, we can ask (again with an eye to the argument in chapter 10): if not all generalized perspectives are even potentially phenomenal perspectives, then does this limit, in a philosophically objectionable way, the logical possibility of having a transparent grasp of the intrinsic character of reality? Or does it suffice, for the purposes of the Russellian view, that in principle the intrinsic nature of reality can always be grasped, subsystem by subsystem, under some representation or other? These, and the other questions just raised, are ones that I shall not attempt to pursue further in this book; but I commend them to anyone who is sufficiently sympathetic with the point of view that I have been developing in the last three chapters to think it worth exploring its deeper implications.

14

Could the Brain be a Quantum Computer?

Nothing I have said in the last three chapters should be taken to imply that there is anything *distinctively* quantum-mechanical about the brain, the mind or consciousness. Mind and brain doubtless are quantum-mechanical, if quantum mechanics is universally applicable. And so construing them has, as we have seen, far reaching, not to say startling, implications. But there is nothing in any of this, taken by itself, to suggest that anything beyond classical physics and chemistry is needed, if one is to provide an account of the workings of the brain that is *functionally* adequate at the level relevant to psychology. That the brain can indeed be regarded as a classical system, for the purposes of understanding the physiological basis of cognitive processes, is assumed by the vast majority of workers in the field.

Nevertheless, there are some who have argued that, on the contrary, the brain may have evolved in such a way as specifically to exploit peculiarly quantum-mechanical effects. And consciousness itself, it has been suggested, may in this sense be a quantum-mechanical phenomenon. Roger Penrose (1987) is a leading advocate of this approach.

Two questions arise here. First, is there any advantage that might accrue from the exploitation of quantum-mechanical effects? Are there things that a quantum brain could do, which a classical brain couldn't, and which might give its possessor some adaptive advantage? Second, given what we know about the physics of the brain, is it at all plausible to suppose that quantum-mechanical effects, of the kind required to give the brain these extra powers, could be occurring within it? We shall consider these questions in turn.

The answer to the first question is a qualified yes; the exploitation, by the brain, of specifically quantum-mechanical effects might indeed, in principle, enhance its computational powers. It all depends on whether the brain might be functioning, in part, as a *quantum computer*. The study of quantum computers is still in its infancy; and it is a wholly theoretical discipline at present. No one, as yet, has ever constructed a quantum computer, and it is unknown at present whether it is even possible to do so. But the theory of quantum computers has already yielded some remarkable results, mainly through the work of David Deutsch (1985b). The concept of a quantum computer is a generalization of that of a *Turing machine*.

Alan Turing conceived the notion of a Turing machine in the 1930s as a way of giving a precise meaning to the mathematical concept of an *algorithm*, a procedure that can be carried out mechanically. In 1900, the mathematician David Hilbert had listed a number of unsolved mathematical problems which he thought it might be fruitful for mathematicians to work on in the coming century. And Alan Turing, as a young research student at Cambridge, became interested in the 23rd Hilbert problem, which was that of finding a mechanical way of testing whether an arbitrarily chosen formula of *first-order predicate logic* was a theorem. An example of a formula of predicate logic, translated, more or less, into English, would be: 'For every x, if x is F, then x is G', which is a long-winded way of saying 'Everything that's F is G'. Another example is 'For every x, there is a y, such that y is R to x', which, with 'R to' interpreted as 'larger than' becomes a truth about the natural numbers, to the effect that there is no largest number. A formula of predicate logic that is also a theorem is 'If there is an x, such that x is F, then it is not the case that, for every x, x is not-F'; what makes it a theorem is that whatever you substitute for 'F', you get a truth. A mechanical test of theoremhood is known as a *decision procedure*.

Anyway, Turing conceived the notion of an ideal machine, a Turing machine, which was capable of performing any mathematical task that one would intuitively think of as being susceptible of being performed by an algorithm, or mechanical procedure. Addition and subtraction, multiplication and division are obvious examples of tasks that admit of being performed by way of simple algorithms, which most of us will have been taught at school. Turing was then able to recast Hilbert's 23rd problem in a mathematically precise form as that of whether one could design a Turing machine which, given an arbitrary formula of predicate logic, could determine whether or not it was a theorem.

A Turing machine is a mathematical abstraction rather than a piece of hardware. Nevertheless, Turing gave us a way of visualizing it. We are to imagine a device, a little like a typewriter, with an endless paper tape, only a finite portion of which is ever used at one time, divided into segments or *squares*. Just what the contents of these squares are is a matter of convention; but it is convenient to think of every square as containing either a 1 or a 0. At any given time, the machine will be scanning just a single square and will be in some specific internal *state*. The state that it is in, in conjunction with the symbol that is currently being scanned, can cause three sorts of thing to happen. First, the machine 'prints' either a 1 or a 0 on the square being scanned, where 'printing' a 1 means either leaving the square as it is, if it already contains a 1, or else deleting the 0 and replacing it with a 1. Second, it may change its internal state. Thirdly, it will either halt, or else move the tape, so that it comes to scan the adjoining square on the left or right. This is called moving left or right. The machine's operations, when it is started off scanning a particular square of a particular tape, may be exhaustively described in a *machine table* (see figure 14.1). The machine table lists, for every internal state, what the machine will do when it is in that state and is scanning a 1 or a 0. Thus the entry in the machine table for internal state 34 and 1 on the tape, might be abbreviated, '0, R, 12'. That would mean that when the machine is in internal state 34, and is scanning a 1, it erases the 1, prints a 0, moves right, and goes into state 12.

Internal state	Symbol read on tape	
	0	1
1	0,1,R	0,2,R
2	1,3,R	1,2,R
3	Halt	Halt

Figure 14.1 *Simple Turing machine table for the addition of two numbers expressed in unary notation.*

The two numbers are initially represented on the tape separated by a single 0, with 0s on all the other squares. The machine starts out in state 1, scanning one of the squares to the left of the numbers to be added. It then moves right until it encounters the first 1, deletes it, moves right until it encounters a 0, replaces it with a 1 and then halts.

With a little ingenuity, one can readily devise machine tables that will perform such operations as addition and multiplication, given some way of representing 'input' numbers on the tape. The simplest way would be to represent the numbers in *unary* notation, so that 3 and 5, say, were represented by a tape consisting entirely of 0s, save for 111 and 11111, separated by a single 0. Then a machine table for multiplication might cause the machine, if it was started off somewhere to the left of the input numbers, to move right until it came to the first 1, and then perform a series of operations which ended with the machine halting, scanning a 0, with the string 111111111111111 immediately to the left of this square, and every other square of the tape containing a 0. Using such relatively simple functions as building blocks, one can fairly easily build up more complicated ones, since it is reasonably straightforward to combine the machine tables corresponding to simpler operations, so as to yield machine tables corresponding to combinations of such operations.

Turing was able to demonstrate, using the concept of a Turing machine, that Hilbert's 23rd problem was insoluble; the algorithm envisaged by Hilbert simply didn't exist. This he did by showing that the problem of deciding whether an arbitrary formula of predicate logic was a theorem was mathematically equivalent to the *halting problem*. As anyone with the slightest experience of programming computers will know, one of the commonest signs that there is something amiss with a program is that it causes the computer to 'loop'; it starts to perform the same sequence of operations over and over again, without ever getting anywhere. (Though sometimes, of course, that is the programmer's intention.) A computer that gets into a loop never halts, so long as it continues to follow the program. Likewise, assuming that it is started off in a particular state, scanning a particular square of a tape with a particular configuration of 0s and 1s, a Turing machine may eventually halt or it may not.

Turing showed that, by adopting a suitable set of conventions, it is possible to take any machine table one likes and encode it as a string of 0s and 1s. All possible Turing machines admit of being so represented, using only this meagre 'alphabet'. Consequently, one can, in effect, put a description of a Turing machine on to a Turing machine tape. And obviously, one could combine that with a description of the contents of any finite segment of tape, together, by some suitable convention, with an indication of the starting square and the starting state. (Usually, a machine is started off somewhere to the left of the first 1, and in a standard initial state that causes it to move right until the first 1 is encountered.) The question then is whether one could devise a Turing machine which, given a tape containing all this information, could perform a series of operations the upshot of which was the following. It would be guaranteed, in due course, to halt, scanning, say, a 1 or a 0, depending on whether the corresponding Turing machine, under the specified conditions, would or would not eventually halt. Turing was able to prove that this was in principle impossible; and the insolubility of this halting problem could be shown logically to entail the impossibility of devising a mechanical decision procedure for first-order predicate logic.

But the possibility of encoding a specification for an arbitrary Turing machine, in the form of a string of 0s and 1s, has an amazing corollary. For Turing also showed that one could devise a *universal* Turing machine, with the following remarkable property. Given, on its tape, a specification of an arbitrary Turing machine, the universal Turing machine would, having read the specification, proceed to behave, with respect to the contents of the remainder of the tape, exactly like the specified machine. That means that the universal Turing machine, if supplied with an appropriate sequence of 1s and 0s on its tape, can perform absolutely any task of which any Turing machine is capable! This discovery constitutes the theoretical foundation for the modern digital computer. Any modern computer is, in essence, a universal Turing machine. Its *random access memory* corresponds to the tape; and programming the computer is tantamount to instructing it to behave like a specific Turing machine. The sole limitation of the digital computer, as compared to Turing's mathematical idealization, is that it has only a finite memory, whereas the Turing machine has an infinitely long tape. (Seeing, however, that a Turing machine doesn't really need an *infinite* amount of tape, but only an arbitrarily large finite amount, that limitation could in principle be removed by building the computer in a modular fashion that enabled extra memory units to be plugged in as required, without limit.)

At the heart of Turing's work lies a *hypothesis* that does not really admit of proof. Consider any arithmetic function, where each input value or set of input values – which mathematicians refer to as the function's *argument(s)* – is associated with a unique output, the *value* of the function for the given argument(s). Such a function is said to be *computable* if and only if there exists a mechanical procedure for calculating the value of the function for any given argument(s). The so-called *Church–Turing hypothesis* states that a function is computable in the intuitive sense if and only if it is *Turing machine computable*, that is, if there exists a Turing machine which, given a tape containing the argument(s), will eventually halt, having printed the value of the function for the argument(s) in question.

Putting things this way gives the impression that all a Turing machine is good for is computing arithmetic functions. But of course that is no more true of a Turing machine than it is of a modern computer. For a cognitive task need not be mathematical in character in order to admit of being arithmetically encoded; and, to the extent that it can be arithmetically encoded, any task that requires some unique appropriate output to be provided for any given input, may be represented as that of finding the value of some arithmetic function for given argument(s). Moreover, it seems plausible to suppose that absolutely any cognitive task that can be precisely described can also be arithmetically encoded.

Thus the range of functions that a device is capable of computing provides an indication of its computational powers in general, not just in relation to arithmetic. Nevertheless, not every task that is susceptible of being arithmetically encoded can be represented as the computation of a function. For functions have *unique* values for given inputs. Some tasks, on the other hand, involve operating on the input in such a way that the output is not wholly determined by the input; identical input may, on different occasions, result in different output. Or the task may sometimes fail, in such a way as to yield no output at all. The first possibility, that of producing unpredictable output, could be modelled on a Turing machine with a random number generator. The second, failure to produce any output at all, is effectively modelled on a Turing machine by failure ever to halt. But the crucial point is that the computational power of a device encompasses its performance on these sorts of task just as much as its performance on those tasks that can be represented as the computation of functions.

A further dimension of computational power that is neglected when one says merely *which* tasks a device is capable of performing, whether or not they admit of being equated with the computation of functions, is speed of operation. Now, of course, in one sense speed is wholly relative to technology. Nevertheless, the study of Turing machines yields a rich theory of how the time taken to perform a task increases, in the ideal case of maximally efficient programming, as a function of the increase in the numerical value(s) of the input(s), and/or the number of inputs. This is known as *complexity theory*. A good example is the *travelling salesman* problem. A salesman has to visit a number of cities, and wants to know the shortest route that will take him through every city on his itinerary. Its mathematical idealization is that of finding, for a set of points on the plane, the shortest continuous line that passes through every point at least once. The time it takes to calculate this rises sharply as the number of points increases. Every algorithm so far discovered that is guaranteed to find a shortest path has the distressing property that, as the numbers become larger, the number of basic operations the algorithm calls for eventually rises faster than any power of the number of points. That is to say, if the number of points (cities) is n, then for any number m, the number of operations required to find the shortest path, as n gets larger, will eventually start to rise faster than n^m.

Let us assume, as is generally believed, that any algorithm or Turing machine for solving the travelling salesman problem will prove to have this same property. Then one says that the travelling salesman problem is *not soluble in polynomial time*. Suppose that a problem is soluble in polynomial time. And let n be the number that measures whatever it is about the input that gets larger in such a way as to affect the scale of the task (usually the value(s) of the input number(s) or the number of inputs). Then an increase in n will, for a suitable choice of algorithm, result in an increase in the number of basic operations required to solve the problem, which, for some value of m, is less than or equal to the corresponding increase in n^m.

Broadly speaking, problems that are not soluble in polynomial time become intractable, for large values of n, *if what one is looking for is a guaranteed best solution*. In the case of the travelling salesman problem, which has considerable practical bearing on such things as circuit design, there are some highly efficient algorithms, operating in polynomial time, which will produce paths that either have a high probability of being the shortest possible, or else that have lengths that are unlikely to be much longer than the shortest possible paths.

A Turing machine is the ultimate serial computer. So one might suppose that one could evade the constraints imposed by complexity theory by using a computer with a number of processors working in parallel. Well, so one could, to a limited extent. But complexity theory is interested in what happens in the long run, as the crucial parameter n gets ever larger. And these limitations will instantly re-emerge as soon as n, in effect, exceeds the number of component serial processors.

A quantum computer, however, could in principle evade some of these limitations. Quantum computers have their own complexity theory, which differs from that of Turing machines. As yet, though, I have not explained what a quantum computer is, and must now proceed to do so. A Turing machine, as we saw, has a tape, which we took to consist of a sequence of squares, each containing a 1 or a 0, a scanning and printing head capable of moving right and left relative to the tape, and an internal structure capable of assuming a finite number of states. And the operations of the whole are governed by a machine table. A quantum computer has all these things too. But there is one crucial difference. Both internal states of the device and states of the tape can be superpositions. Thus, rather than determinately containing a 1 or a 0, a particular square of the tape may be in a linear combination of its containing a 1 and of its containing a 0; likewise with the contents of any *set* of squares. And the internal state of the machine may be a superposition of one or more conventional Turing machine states. Take a conventional Turing machine, and imagine the sequence of operations it would go through when started off in a particular state, scanning a particular square of a tape containing a particular configuration of 0s and 1s. Now take an identical machine, but with a different tape; it, in general, will go through a different set of operations. In theory, there could be a quantum computer with a time evolution that corresponded to a superposition of the sequences of operations of these two conventional Turing machines. The tape would start in a superposition of the two imagined tapes, and there would follow a sequence of operations each of which was a superposition of the operations respectively followed at that stage by the two machines considered separately. And, if it eventually halted, it would end up with a tape that was in a superposition of the final states of the two tapes considered individually.

That, however, would achieve no more than could be achieved by having the two original Turing machines running simultaneously. Actually it would achieve less, because an observation of the final state of the tape could not, in general, reveal its contents in *both* components of the superposition. To exploit the full power of a quantum computer, one has to supply it with a suitable machine table. This must associate general states of the square of tape being scanned, not just those of determinately containing a 1 or a 0, and general internal states, including superpositions of the conventional ones, with scanning shifts that may result in superpositions of its scanning different squares. It is possible, by these means, to describe a universal quantum computer which is the appropriate analogue of a universal Turing machine, in that it is capable, given a suitable tape as input, of simulating any arbitrary quantum computer.

Any function whose values could be computed by a quantum computer would also be computable in the intuitive sense. So what would have been really exciting is if it had turned out that quantum computers could compute functions that Turing machines couldn't. For then the Church–Turing hypothesis would have been shown to be false. (Although the hypothesis does not admit of being proved, it certainly admits of being disproved.) In fact, however, the set of functions computable by a quantum computer is precisely the same set of what Church called *recursive functions*, that are computable by a Turing machine. More disappointing still, Deutsch has shown that, as far as *functions* are concerned, quantum computers and Turing machines have the same complexity theory. A quantum computer is not going to be able, for example, to solve the travelling salesman problem in polynomial time if a conventional computer can't.

But not all tasks correspond to the computation of functions. And with regard to tasks that do not correspond to functions, quantum computers have a complexity theory that differs from that which applies to Turing machines (and classical computers generally). The reason for this, intuitively speaking, is that a quantum computer is capable of a kind of *quantum parallelism* which, unlike conventional parallel processing, is not restricted as regards the number of tasks that can be performed simultaneously.

Consider the following task. The input consists of two things. The first is an algorithm for computing some function, F, that runs in polynomial time; that is to say, a mechanical procedure (in the form, say, of a suitably encoded Turing machine table) which, for some number m, is guaranteed to yield the value, $F(n)$, of the function F, for any given number n, in a number of steps that is less than n^m. The second item in the input is an integer of the form $2n$: in plain language, an even number equal to twice n. Given the algorithm and the integer, the task is to find a true statement that belongs to the following pair:

(i) Not every number in the set $\{F(1), \ldots, F(2n)\}$ is even;
(ii) It is not the case that exactly half (that is, n) of the numbers in the set $\{F(1), \ldots, F(2n)\}$ are even.

Logically, at least one, and possibly both, of these statements must be true.

It is crucial to the argument that the performance of this task, taken as a whole, does not amount to the computation of a function. And the reason why it doesn't is that a function has a unique value (output) for a given set of arguments (inputs). But that is not true of the present task. For some values of F and $2n$, statements (i) and (ii) will both be true, in which case either will serve as output. Thus, there is not a unique acceptable output value for every pair of input values. No classical computer or Turing machine would be capable of solving this problem in polynomial time. But a quantum computer could; in principle it could solve it in a number of steps proportional to the logarithm of n. The increase in the time (or number of steps) taken by a Turing machine to solve the problem, as n gets larger, is *exponentially* greater than what could in principle be achieved with a quantum computer. (I am here drawing on unpublished work by Deutsch.)

This is a remarkable result. But one mustn't exaggerate the difference between quantum and classical computers here. A Turing machine with a random number generator could, for given F and $2n$, *probably* solve the problem in the order of log n steps. However, the time within which it could *guarantee* to do so would again be exponentially greater than this. The way one puts this is to say that, for a Turing machine, the problem is not soluble in polynomial time, but it is soluble in *random* polynomial time. For an idealized quantum computer, however, it is soluble in polynomial time proper; and this is still an advance on what is possible classically.

There is a different sort of task in which a quantum computer has an advantage, and which may better serve to illustrate the possible practical utility of such a device. Suppose someone had devised an algorithm for calculating an ideal investment strategy, which tells one how to play the market tomorrow, on the basis of given data, including information that becomes available only at the close of trading today. For every share, the algorithm needs a certain set of figures. These might include opening price, closing price, day's high, day's low, current price–earnings ratio, total capitalization, whether pre-dividend or ex-dividend, current year's high and low, etc. Given these vital statistics as input, the algorithm requires a certain calculation to be performed, individually for each company. The final strategy is then computed as a function of the results of all these calculations. Thus, one has first to calculate the value of a function of a large number of variables, for a large of number of different sets of input values. Then one has to calculate the value of another function G, for a set of input values which are the various values of F.

Let us suppose that the algorithm issues excellent investment advice, but is unfortunately useless, as performed on the fastest available conventional computer, since it takes sixteen hours to run. If one sets it going at the end of today's trading it will not come up with the desired strategy until well into tomorrow's trading, by which time it is inapplicable (rather like the Emperor's messages in Kafka's short story 'The Great Wall of China'; or the generals' commands in battle, which Tolstoy tells us, in *War and Peace*, were invariably irrelevant to the tactical situation as it had developed by the time these commands reached their intended destination).

What a quantum computer can do here is first, in effect, to go into a superposition of as many distinct Turing machines as there are distinct shares whose statistics go into the calculation. Let n be the number of shares, and hence of elements in the superposition. The evolution of this superposition, in accordance with the quantum computer's machine table, then corresponds to the calculation, in parallel, of all the various values of F. Next the computer goes through some further operations, the upshot of which is that, within eight hours and thus before the start of tomorrow's trading, it ends in a state with the following property. If we carry out on its memory (the equivalent of the tape) a measurement of observable A, we get either a 0 or a 1. One day out of every $1/(n^2 - 2n + 2)$, we get the value 0, which means that the program has 'failed', and we are best advised to steer clear of the market the next day. But on the other days, when we measure A, we get the value 1. That tells us that the measurement of another observable B, will produce the number that embodies the desired investment strategy. On those days we do invest and, in due course, we get rich – celebrating in champagne the advent of the quantum yuppie!

Deutsch thinks that quantum computers, were it possible to construct them, would constitute a powerful argument for his own preferred interpretation of quantum mechanics, according to which there is an infinity of parallel universes. He says of this interpretation that it 'explains well how the computer's behaviour follows from its having delegated subtasks to copies of itself in other universes' (Deutsch 1985b, p. 114). So it does. But I should prefer to say simply that the existence of quantum computers (or the proven possibility of constructing them) would be an argument for taking seriously *all* the components in a quantum-mechanical superposition. The time evolution of a quantum computer, as it works on the stock exchange problem, must, at the first stage, be seen as involving the genuine simultaneous computation of F, for all n shares, quite as much as if we had a room containing n classical Turing machines all beavering away at once. One might take the fact that a measurement of the 'tape' can, at best, yield the result of just one of these calculations, as an argument for saying otherwise. But the supposition that only one of these calculations *really* occurs is surely refuted by the fact that, one day out of $1/(n^2 - 2n + 2)$, a measurement of the tape observable B will yield a value for G that could not (at any rate in classical terms) have been arrived at other than by the computer's having had, at some stage, simultaneous access to all n values of F.

It is too early to say whether the fact of quantum computers having a different complexity theory from classical computers, as regards tasks that do not correspond to the computation of functions, would, as such, give them any *practical* edge over classical computers. But they would, in any case, undoubtedly have great practical utility, since they are inherently more flexible. The point is that the concept of a quantum computer is a *generalization* of that of a classical computer or Turing machine. Any Turing machine algorithm (or program) will run on a universal quantum computer; but not every quantum computer algorithm will run on a universal Turing machine. For any given task, therefore, it is possible that there exists a quantum computer algorithm that performs the task in a smaller number of steps than any Turing machine algorithm. And this is true even of tasks that do correspond to the computation of functions. The most efficient quantum computer algorithm won't run in polynomial time if no Turing machine algorithm does, though it may well, for *all* input values, perform the task in a smaller – perhaps much smaller – number of steps than any Turing machine algorithm could. Complexity theory, after all, is concerned only with how the number of steps *increases*, as the input gets larger; and two algorithms can have the same rate of increase, even though one is vastly more efficient than the other.

But could quantum computers exist in reality? Deutsch himself is convinced that they could and, indeed, that they will someday be built. As a matter of fact there exist already, as he points out, devices that are possible candidates for quantum computer memory elements. I am referring to so-called *superconducting quantum interference devices*, or SQUIDs. These are rings of superconducting material, pinched in at one point to form a narrow constriction or *neck*. (A material is said to be *superconducting* if its electrical resistance is zero, so that a current flowing through it will not become attenuated, as it does in an ordinary wire, in consequence of the conversion of electrical energy into heat; this phenomenon of *superconductivity* occurs in some materials when their temperature falls below a certain critical value.) SQUIDS have been around now for over a quarter of a century and have a host of practical applications, including use in body scanners. In 1980, however, Tony Leggett (then at the University of Sussex) suggested that SQUIDS might, under certain conditions, be demonstrated to exist in what are, in effect, macroscopic superpositions. (Let me emphasize, though, that 'macroscopic' here just means large-scale. We are not talking now, as we were in the last chapter, of superpositions of states corresponding to distinct eigenvalues of such 'classical', mutually commuting macroscopic observables as macroscopic position and velocity.) Leggett's ideas have prompted a spate of theoretical and experimental work which has tended to bear out his original suggestion (see Leggett, 1980; Eckern, 1986; and Spiller and Clark, 1986a, 1986b). A SQUID, so it would seem, behaves in many respects as a macroscopic analogue of the microscopic systems that are more usually thought of in connection with quantum mechanics. The flow of current around the superconducting ring creates a magnetic flux. And this flux and the electric charge at the neck behave as noncommuting quantum-mechanical observables, obeying an uncertainty relationship analogous to that of the position and momentum of a single electron. Thus, just as an electron can (indeed, strictly speaking always does) exist in a superposition of position eigenstates, so a SQUID can exist in a superposition of distinct eigenstates of the macroscopic magnetic flux observable.

That, at least, is the claim. And if it is correct, it has far-reaching consequences. First, if SQUIDs can exist in superpositions of macroscopic states, why not Schrödinger's cat? The insistence that there cannot exist superpositions of more familiar macroscopic states is coming, in the light of this work, to seem increasingly arbitrary and implausible. Secondly, the ability to form macroscopic superpositions, that can be prepared and measured at will, is precisely what is required of something that is to serve as a memory element for a quantum computer. What we want is a device that can be put into an 'on' state (1), an 'off' state (0), and any linear combination of these; and SQUIDs appear to answer to this requirement. Nevertheless, the construction of a quantum computer, using SQUIDs, would present difficulties that today's technology is probably incapable of overcoming.

Is it possible, however, that quantum computers already exist? Could Nature have got there first? Is it conceivable that the brain itself functions, in part, as a quantum computer, making use of quantum interference effects within the nervous system? Deutsch himself is inclined to think not, on the grounds that the brain is ostensibly too hot to sustain the kinds of so-called *coherent* states that systematic quantum interference calls for. Indeed, superconductivity has itself, until recently, seemed to be an essentially low-temperature phenomenon. But this argument is hardly decisive. In the first place, as anyone who reads the newspapers will be aware, superconductivity has recently been demonstrated at far higher temperatures than hitherto; hence, there is now a distinct possibility that it might exist at room temperature or even blood temperature, given suitable materials. Even so, the idea promoted by some authors (for example, Walker, 1970) of there being superconductivity in the brain still seems pretty far-fetched. More to the point, therefore, is the fact that superconductivity is just one particular instance of a more general quantum-mechanical phenomenon known as *Bose condensation*. And the existence of other sorts of Bose-condensed states in biological systems has already been proposed on independent grounds by the physicist Fröhlich. (It was Ian Marshall who first drew my attention to Fröhlich's work. Strictly speaking, as Marshall has pointed out to me, Bose condensation is defined only for so-called *perfect Bose gases*, so that such things as superconductivity, superfluidity, laser light and the phenomena postulated by Fröhlich should be regarded merely as *analogous* to Bose condensation. But, in common with several other authors, I shall continue to use the term in its broader and looser sense).

In order to grasp the concept of Bose condensation, we need first to understand what a *boson* is. Imagine, to begin with, that we have a system, similar to a Bagatelle, in which metal balls are fired towards a partition, set up in such a way that any given ball is equally likely to end up on the left side of the partition or on the right. And suppose, now, that we fire off two balls, *a* and *b*, in succession. What then is the probability that we shall find both balls on, say, the left side? Clearly, it is ¼, since this state is one of four distinct, equally likely, possibilities: ball *a* on the left, ball *b* on the right; ball *b* on the right and ball *a* on the left; both balls on the left; and both balls on the right.

This classical reasoning presupposes, however, that the two balls are distinct. If we were talking, not about macroscopic objects, but about photons, say, or electron pairs such as are involved in superconductivity, the classical reasoning would produce wrong predictions. And this is because, in quantum mechanics, we are not allowed to regard indistinguishable particles as having distinct identities. If the 'balls', in the bagatelle case, were *bosons* – photons, say, or helium atoms, or electron pairs in a superconducted current – then the probability that two of them would end up on the left would be greater than ¼. And this reflects the fact that we are not allowed to regard, as distinct states, the 'two' situations in which particle *a* ends up on the left with *b* on the right, and that in which *b* is on the left with *a* on the right. Quantum-mechanically speaking, these are just alternative descriptions of one and the same state. Thus there are only three distinct possibilities here, not four: both particles on the left, both particles on the right, and one particle on each side. Accordingly, the probability that both particles will end up on the left is ⅓, with a probability of ⅔ that they will both end up on the same side, left or right. Bosons are, by definition, those particles that obey this kind of statistics.

(Bosons may, in this respect, be compared to money. Suppose I give you two pounds, say, asking you to give 'a pound of that money' to each of your two children. It makes no sense, in general, for me then to ask which pound, of the two pounds I gave you, went to Susan and which to Christopher. What, after all, if I had given you a two pound cheque, which you had duly cashed? This feature of money is referred to by lawyers as *fungibility*; but it is not peculiar to money. I may walk into a TV showroom, see a model I like and buy one, for later delivery. But I will not necessarily have bought any *particular* one: the delivery of any television of the specified model may fulfil the implied contract. Fungibility, in law, arises with contracts or transactions which are indifferent to the identity of the items involved, being concerned only with more or less precise numbers of items of a certain specified kind: types matter, tokens do not. The great nineteenth-century jurist John Austin observes, quite reasonably (1885, p. 780): 'Things are fungible or not fungible, not in their own nature, but with reference to the terms of the given obligation.' Quantum mechanics, however, says different: bosons precisely *are* fungible in their own nature.)

What we see here is thus a statistical tendency for bosons to crowd into the same state. (The other category of particles, *fermions*, which includes electrons and protons, has the opposite tendency: it is impossible for more than one fermion to occupy any given state.) Classically, the probability that both particles will end in the same state, where there are two particles and two equally probable states, is ½; but if the particles are bosons, the probability, as we have seen, is ⅔. Suppose there are three particles and two states. Then, classically, the probability that all three particles will end in the same state, if each state is equally probable, is ¼; if the particles are bosons, however, the probability is ½. For four particles and two states, the probability that all will be found in the same state is ⅖ if they are bosons, as compared to only ⅛ if they are classical particles. And, in general, this crowding tendency becomes more marked the more particles there are, whatever the number of available states.

Bose-condensed states are states where all or practically all of a set of bosons are occupying the same state. But there are various ways in which this may come about. A key notion in modern physics is that of *thermal equilibrium*. Suppose we think of our set of bosons as immersed in a *heat bath*: some source of energy with which the bosons are in constant interaction. Suppose further that the bosons and the heat bath together constitute a closed system; no energy can get in or out. Random exchange of energy between the bosons, and between the bosons and the heat bath, will then cause the system of bosons to come into equilibrium with the heat bath, a state in which the net exchange of energy between the system of bosons and the heat bath over any interval of time is, on average, zero. When that equilibrium state has been reached, the bosons will be distributed with respect to different energy states according to a formula first postulated, in 1900, by Max Planck: the so-called *Planck distribution*. (The formula itself is the consequence of a statistical argument.)

This Planck distribution is a function of temperature. And Planck's formula implies that for any closed system consisting of a set of bosons in equilibrium with a heat bath the bosons will be concentrated in the lowest energy level, if the equilibrium temperature is sufficiently low. Hence, one way of achieving Bose condensation is through cooling. By lowering the ambient temperature – that is to say, the temperature of the heat bath – one, in effect, chases the bosons into their lowest energy state, from where they have nowhere else to go. That, essentially, is why superconductivity is easiest to achieve at low temperatures. The bosons in this case are *Cooper pairs* of electrons with anticorrelated spins and momenta, and they crowd into the lowest energy state when the ambient temperature drops sufficiently.

Cooling, however, is by no means the only mechanism whereby Bose condensation can occur. It may also, under appropriate conditions, be achieved by way of artificially maintaining one's system of bosons in a *nonequilibrium* state, a process that is known as *pumping*.

Any vibrating system has a set of what are called *normal modes* of vibration. These are states of vibration in which every element in the system is oscillating about its equilibrium position with the same frequency. Any arbitrary vibrational state of a system can be represented as a superposition of the normal modes. Moreover, each of these normal modes can be regarded as a harmonic oscillator in its own right. As such, it will have a discrete spectrum of energy levels, or amplitudes, which we can label 0, 1, 2, 3 . . . (The energy of the nth level will be equal to h times the frequency times $(n + \frac{1}{2})$.) An energy eigenstate of the entire system is exhaustively specified, when we say, for each normal mode, how many 'notches' up the energy spectrum the system is. In quantum field theory, photons are regarded as nothing but notches on the energy spectra of the normal modes of the electromagnetic field; in other words, they are the *quanta* of the electromagnetic field. If one of the normal vibrational modes of the field is at energy level n, then we may be said to have n photons of the relevant frequency and polarization. And the fact that photons travel at the speed of light reflects the fact that transverse vibrations in the electromagnetic field propagate at that speed.

This correspondence between photons and the quanta of the electromagnetic field is just a special example of something far more general. All elementary particles can be construed as the quanta of the normal modes of some corresponding field. Not only that; whenever one has a vibrational system, with a set of normal modes, the associated quanta can for many purposes be thought of as particles. And this is true, in particular, for ordinary vibrations in matter, of which the vibrations we detect as sound are just a special example. Matter vibrations are electrical. That is to say, the forces involved in these oscillations are forces of electrical attraction and repulsion between atoms. *Phonons* are the notional particles which stand to the electrical vibrations in matter as do photons to the oscillations of the electromagnetic field; and, so construed, these phonons behave like bosons. Physicists will speak of a phonon 'gas', in which the phonons can collide with and scatter each other, just like a literal gas. The physical substrate will be a set of molecules, vibrating under the influence both of mutual intermolecular, and of internal interatomic, forces of electrical attraction and repulsion. But instead of thinking of the system in terms of these physical components, we can think of it instead as a collection of interacting phonons. The components are now taken to be the quanta of the collective normal vibrational modes of the system, rather than the entities whose vibration is in question.

There are, as Fröhlich points out, a number of biological entities that make excellent electrical *dipole* oscillators – systems, that is, possessing both a positive and a negative electrical pole. Certain so-called *dielectric* protein molecules are dipole oscillators in their own right. And molecules in cell membranes are also excellent candidates. For the voltage gradients across cell membranes are often amazingly steep, especially, though by no means exclusively, in nerve cells. Yet another possibility involves nonlocalized electrons; that is to say, electrons whose position wave function is spread out over a relatively large area. Fröhlich considers the system of phonons associated with normal collective *longitudinal* frequency modes of a system of such biological oscillators, vibrating at microwave frequencies of around 10^{11} Hz. (Longitudinal waves are ones in which the direction of oscillation coincides with the direction in which the wave is travelling: pressure waves, in other words, like those of sound in air or water. These are to be contrasted with *transverse* waves, which lie perpendicular to the direction of travel, like those of light, or sound waves in an incompressible medium such as glass.)

Fröhlich argues that, for such a system, Bose condensation is in principle achievable at ordinary temperatures. What we have, in Fröhlich's model, is a system of biological dipole oscillators immersed in a heat bath which is maintained at a *constant* temperature. These oscillators vibrate under the influence of two types of force: first, the short-range electrical forces between the positive and negative poles of single oscillators; and second, long-range *Coulomb* forces between the oscillators. These long-range forces mediate the transmission of kinetic energy from one oscillator to another; the stronger these long-range forces, the greater, therefore, is the tendency for the oscillators to vibrate in unison.

The bosons of this system are, as we have seen, the quanta of the normal collective frequency modes of the oscillators. But the set of oscillators, and the heat bath in which they are immersed, are not now to be thought of as a closed system, nor is the system allowed to reach an equilibrium state. Rather, the individual oscillators are supplied with a constant source of energy from outside, by pumping; and it this that prevents them from ever settling into thermal equilibrium with the heat bath. (This pumping energy might be conveyed to dielectric molecules in cell membranes via a cell structure known as the *cytoskeleton*.) Earlier, we saw that Bose condensation can be achieved by withdrawing energy from the heat bath, and allowing the system to settle into equilibrium. In Fröhlich's model, however, condensation is achieved by keeping the temperature of the heat bath constant, while supplying energy to the individual oscillators. Much of this energy is, of course, transferred to the heat bath, and then dissipated by way of whatever processes serve to maintain the temperature at a constant level. But when the rate at which energy is supplied to the oscillators is sufficiently high, a proportion of the energy, instead of being dispersed in this fashion, is effectively *stored* in the phonon system by being channelled into the lowest collective frequency mode; new phonons are created in this mode. And the result is a coherent state: one, that is to say, which exhibits long-range spatial order. More precisely, spatio-temporally separated points in the system will be associated with *phase and amplitude correlations*. Oscillations at one point will coincide in frequency with those at other points, and will differ in phase and amplitude by a fixed amount, like properly adjusted clocks in different time zones. Very roughly, an incoherent state might be compared to the surface of a pool on a windy day: a chaotic mass of waves and ripples, with no discernible pattern. By contrast, a coherent state, such as Fröhlich envisages, would be like the same pool on a calm day; not with a flat surface, however, but containing *standing waves* that involve the surface, at every point, moving in a coordinated way.

These Bose-condensed states could have considerable biological utility.

For one thing, they could be used as biological amplifiers. A very weak signal could 'trigger' such a system, so as to produce a very powerful, because coordinated, output – which, indeed, is precisely what happens in a laser. But also, again as with laser light, such states could be used to encode, within a very small region, a vast amount of information. One possible way of doing this will be mentioned shortly.

There appears to be no question but that the mechanism Fröhlich proposes is a theoretical possibility. Writing nearly twenty years after the appearance of Fröhlich's original article (and see also Sewell, 1986), Bond and Huth (1986, p. 294) observe:

> The prediction of the existence of a phenomenon analogous to Bose–Einstein condensation, as in Fröhlich's vibrational model, has been confirmed via several other approaches, namely, via a transport theory formalism by Kaiser and a molecular Hamiltonian approach by Bhaumik *et al.*, and also by Wu and Austin; the basic concept has been shown to be on firm theoretical ground.

That is not all, however. There is also a certain amount of evidence that coherent states of this kind do actually exist in biological systems; though it must be stressed that the evidence in question is indirect and circumstantial. One piece of evidence is the fact that one can cause marked changes in the behaviour of living cells by exposing them to microwave radiation. For example, one can change, by a factor of ten per cent or so, the rate of growth of yeast cells by exposing them to microwave radiation far too weak significantly to affect the temperature of the cells. What is more, there are sharply defined 'resonance' frequencies at which the phenomenon is observed. Further evidence stems from the discovery of a *Raman effect* in living cells; this has to do with the way a system scatters laser light. It is difficult to explain either effect, other than on the assumption that there exist, in living cells, cooperative processes similar to those that Fröhlich has postulated (see Fröhlich, 1986).

The first person, as far as I know, to put forward the idea that Bose condensation, in such *pumped phonon* systems, might be the basis of *mental* states and processes is Ian Marshall (to whom, incidentally, I am indebted for the pool analogy). Marshall (a practising psychiatrist with a training in mathematics) has argued (1989) that the collective, and indeed holistic, character of these Bose-condensed states might be the physical basis of the unity of consciousness. His own calculations suggest, moreover, that a Bose-condensed state of the kind proposed by Fröhlich would easily be capable, within the space of a cubic centimetre or less, of carrying as many bits of information as are contained within what I would call a single phenomenal perspective, or maximal experience. (Since phenomenal perspectives ostensibly possess temporal 'depth', as well as spatial 'width' – a feature of phenomenal perspectives that I shall be discussing at length in chapter 15 – it may actually be more to the point to consider how much information could be contained within a given *spatio-temporal* volume.) Marshall suggests that such information might be encoded – all within the lowest collective frequency mode – by appropriately adjusting the amplitudes of, and phase relations between, the dipole oscillators. (He even suggests that amplitude and relative phase may, respectively, be the physical basis of the intensity and quality of our sensations.)

Marshall points out that his theory is fully consistent with what is known, or generally believed, concerning the action of general anaesthetics. There is, as yet, no generally accepted detailed theory as to how such anaesthetics achieve their effect, and why it is that general anaesthesia can be brought about by means of such a seemingly heterogeneous set of chemical agents. But it seems likely that they operate by binding to specific proteins or lipids on cell membranes, thereby affecting their permeability (Evers et al., 1987). This is entirely consistent with their preventing certain key neurons in the brain from firing, seeing that the action potential requires a very specific pattern of exchange of positive and negative ions across the walls of the axon. But it could equally well be, as Marshall suggests, that the obliteration of consciousness is directly connected, not so much with any effect on the action potential, but rather with an impairment of the ability of certain cells to participate in molecular dipole oscillation. General anaesthetics may work by so affecting the membranes of the cell bodies as to level, or greatly to reduce, the voltage gradient. Though that, no doubt, would also affect the action potential, it may not be the effect on the action potential as such that is directly implicated in loss of consciousness. Moreover, if Marshall is right, it may not only be neurons, but other sorts of cell as well, whose cell membranes help to sustain the collective oscillatory states that, on this view, constitute consciousness.

Marshall is not the only person to have suggested that consciousness might have, as its physical basis, a state of the brain exhibiting quantum coherence. Roger Penrose (1987, p. 274) has speculated along similar lines:

Quantum mechanics involves many highly intriguing and mysterious kinds of behaviour. Not the least of these are the *quantum correlations* . . . which can occur over widely separated distances. It seems to me to be a definite possibility that such things could be playing an operative role over large regions of the brain. Might there be any relation between a 'state of awareness' and a highly coherent quantum state in the brain? Is the 'oneness' or 'globality' that seems to be a feature of consciousness connected with this? It is somewhat tempting to believe so.

If one is inclined to succumb to this temptation, then Fröhlich's Bose-condensed oscillatory states certainly seem to fit the bill. They are indeed global, with respect to the individual oscillators. Within such a system, information would be non-localized, transcending the states of individual oscillators, in a sense even stronger than that in which information could be said to be 'distributed' within a neural network or a hologram. In phonon terminology, the coherence of these states means that the associated phonons have sharply defined momenta, and hence, by the uncertainty principle, highly indeterminate positions; the phonons, or more strictly, their position wave functions, are spread out over the area occupied by the coherent state. (As the jargon has it, the phonons are highly localized in *momentum space*, but unlocalized in *configuration space*.)

Whether or not, however, *consciousness* may somehow be grounded in Bose condensation, these Bose-condensed states are exactly the sort of thing that is needed if the brain is to operate as a quantum computer. They lend themselves to coherent superposition, with constructive and destructive interference, in just the way that is required of quantum computer memory states. They could, in principle, serve the same sort of function in biological systems that Deutsch has suggested could be served by SQUID states in an electronic quantum computer.

I hardly need say that the foregoing line of thought is highly speculative. It is still not known for certain whether mechanisms of the kind Fröhlich has proposed exist at all, let alone whether they are to be found in the brain. And even if the brain does contain such Bose-condensed states, it is a substantial further step to suppose that they are used to run quantum computer algorithms of the kind described by Deutsch. But evolution is the ultimate opportunist. If the possibility is there, we shouldn't baulk at the thought that natural systems may have taken advantage of it.

Technical note

If one wants a mental picture of Fröhlich's vibrational model, one could think of it in the following terms. First, one has a lot of tiny, powerful springs. These are the electric dipole oscillators, and the force of the spring represents the short-range electrical force between the positive and negative poles of the dipole. Then one should imagine these small powerful springs linked together by longer, weaker springs, through which energy can be transferred from one oscillator to another. These linking springs represent the long-range Coulomb forces between the individual oscillators. But the longer springs have a rather strange property: they must be thought of as getting stronger, as the amplitude of vibration of the little springs, the individual dipole oscillators, is increased. This means that the greater the amplitude of the dipole oscillators, the more energy it would take to remove one such oscillator from the system, overcoming the Coulomb forces binding it to the other oscillators.

Let μ represent the (average) amount of energy required to remove one oscillator from the system, divided by Planck's constant h; technically, μ (or rather hμ) here represents a *chemical potential*. Let ω_j be the *angular frequency* associated with the jth collective frequency mode, that is to say, the frequency of this mode multiplied by 2π; e is 2.71828 . . ., the base of the natural logarithms, and k is Boltzmann's constant. Let n_j be the *expectation value* of the *particle number* associated with the mode ω_j; that is to say, the average number of phonons one would find associated with that mode if one were to carry out repeated measurements. Finally, assume that we are dealing with a stationary state: one in which the rate at which energy is supplied to the individual dipole oscillators equals the rate at which it is lost to the heat bath. Then the following relationship holds:

$$n_j = \frac{1}{e^{h(\omega_j - \mu)/kT} - 1}$$

In terms of this formula, a Bose-condensed state is one in which n_1, the average particle number associated with the ground state, ω_1, is very large in comparison to the particle numbers associated with the other energy levels or frequency modes. Suppose we start with a situation in which μ is small in relation to ω_1. Holding μ constant, we then get Bose condensation if we reduce the temperature T. This is conventional Bose condensation by cooling. But equally, holding T constant, we get Bose condensation if we increase μ, allowing it to approach the value of ω_1. That, in a nutshell, is the mechanism proposed by Fröhlich. Increasing the rate at which energy is supplied to the individual dipole oscillators *ipso facto* increases the value of μ, which is a function of the total number of phonons. (To get a mathematical feel for Bose condensation, the reader is invited to try the experiment of substituting different figures, in the formula, for T, ω_j and μ. Since k and h are constants, the numerical values of which depend on an essentially arbitrary choice of units, they may both, for this purpose, be assigned the value 1. The reader will find that the ratio between the values of the particle numbers associated with the ground state ω_1 and any higher frequency mode ω_k approaches infinity as T approaches 0, or as μ approaches ω_1, regardless of what specific values one assigns to ω_1 and ω_k.)

15

Time and Mind

Time, as construed by modern physics, comes in two forms. There is *coordinate time*, which is time as a fourth dimension, additional to the three dimensions of space. And there is *proper time*, which is time as a measure of the space-time distance between two points on an object's world-line, as measured along the world-line itself (see figure 15.1). How far any physical process has progressed, from one time to another, within an object, is dependent on proper time; and likewise with biological processes, including, no doubt, the psychological sense of time passing. But the *passage* or flow of time, as we saw in chapter 1, is a dynamic concept which is essentially alien to relativity. Different pairs of points, on a person's world-line, are separated by proper time intervals of different lengths. There is, however, no notion here of time passing, any more than there is a notion of space passing in respect of spatial distances measured along a piece of string.

When shown a space-time diagram (such as figure 15.1), incorporating a world-line that is intended to represent the life of a human being, one has an almost irresistible urge to interpret it dynamically. One tends to think of the individual as like an ant that crawls along the line from one end to the other. (Or as climbing the world-line like a ladder – see figure 15.2.) Or perhaps one thinks of the world-line as like a tendril that grows, as time passes. But, on the face of it, no such interpretation is logically permissible. *For time is already included in the diagram.* It isn't as though the situation were to be described by a continuous succession of space-time diagrams, corresponding to successively later times, in which the 'ant' is progressively further along the world-line – or, to shift to the alternative metaphor, in which the world-line has grown progressively further in the direction of the point at which the individual ceases to exist. That, in effect, would be to make the world five-dimensional, with each cross-section corresponding to a different four-

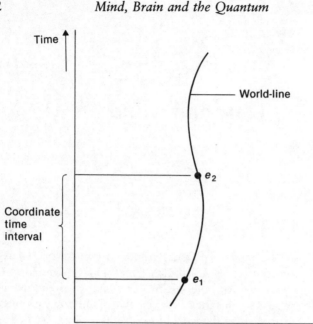

Figure 15.1 *The world-line of an individual human being; e_1 and e_2 are two
events in this individual's biography.*
The coordinate *time interval between* e_1 *and* e_2, *in the chosen frame of reference, is equal to
their separation with respect to the time coordinate. Their* proper *time separation, by
contrast, is equal to the space-time distance between them, as measured along the world-
line. It is the proper time interval that is reflected in* experienced *time, degree of ageing and
so forth. Appearances to the contrary, the proper time interval between* e_1 *and* e_2 *is actually
less than the coordinate time interval. And this accounts for the well-known* time-dilation
*effect, which would lead astronauts who had done a lot of travelling at high speeds to
return home having aged significantly less than their stay-at-home contemporaries.*

dimensional space-time diagram. And the successive positions of the
'ant', or the point to which the 'tendril' has grown, will then define a new
world-line in this five-dimensional universe (see figure 15.3). Then, no
doubt, one would be tempted to interpret this new world-line dynamically;
and so on, for ever higher dimensions.

This is essentially what J. W. Dunne does, in his *An Experiment with
Time* (1981; first published 1927). What he ends up with (pp. 160–89) is
an infinite hierarchy of 'static' temporal dimensions, which he compares
to Chinese boxes. In his model, the whole shebang is then presided over
by a dynamic 'absolute time', the time of the conscious observer, who is,
as Dunne puts it, positioned 'at infinity' – perhaps at 'Dunneromin'!
Here, surely, we have a recipe for nonsense. In philosophy, the

appearance of this sort of infinite regress is almost invariably a sign that it was a mistake to take the first step.

In what follows, I shall assume without argument that the space-time conception of time is, in its own terms, correct and adequate. Accordingly, I shall concentrate on the problem of explaining, on that basis, what it is about the way time figures in our experience that leads us to think in terms of temporal flow. A good starting point here is the so-called *specious present*, which we discussed briefly in chapter 6. It seems to be a brute fact about experience that events which are contained within a sufficiently small interval can be experienced as a group, encompassed within a single phenomenal perspective, without thereby being experienced as simultaneous. There could be no appreciation of music, for example, unless groups of notes could be grasped by the mind in the form of temporally extended Gestalts. But there is a puzzle at the outset as to how one is to describe what is going on here. Bear in mind that the events we're talking about are to be construed as events within consciousness. When I say, for example, that temporally separated notes

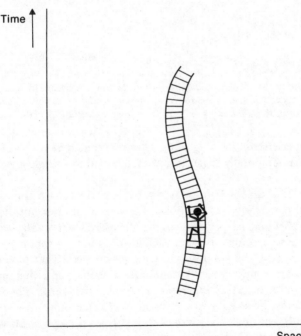

Figure 15.2 *Erroneous picture. An individual is shown 'ascending' his or her world-line, here depicted as a ladder.*

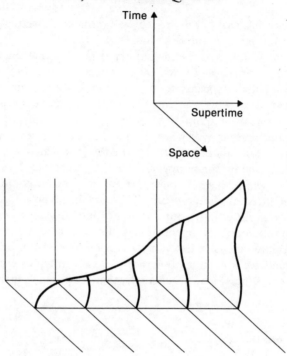

Figure 15.3 *5-D super-space-time.*

An additional supertime *dimension has been added to the four dimensions of Einsteinian space-time. Each successive cross-section, perpendicular to the supertime axis, corresponds to a distinct conventional space-time diagram (with two spatial dimensions suppressed), in which the world-line has 'grown' or progressed a little further.*

can be experienced as a group, I mean that *phenomenal* notes, experienced as temporally separated, can figure within a single phenomenal perspective.

From the fact that a pair of notes are experienced, within a single phenomenal perspective, *as* temporally separated, it does not, however, follow that phenomenal perspectives are themselves temporally extended. That they are so extended is what is claimed by many proponents of the specious present. Other philosophers, however, insist that phenomenal perspectives are tightly tied to temporal moments, and that any two things that are directly experienced within the same phenomenal perspective must be strictly simultaneous with each other. An article by Plumer (1985), entitled 'The myth of the specious present', ends with the words 'a continuously changing sensation is hardly itself a sensation of continuous change'. That, of course, is true on any account. But his contention is that 'the sensory present is an instant', that we are only ever aware of our sensations as they are at some particular moment. When we listen to music, there is, he would argue, *only* a succession of auditory experiences. For any given phenomenal perspective, there will be some specific time t – intuitively, the time at which the perspective occurs – such that whatever one is directly aware of within that perspective must be occurring at t. And that, in turn, implies that an experience of succession cannot be construed as involving a direct awareness of temporally separated events.

Anyone who takes this second line is obliged to look for *surrogates* for past conscious events, that are capable of figuring in subsequent experiences: surrogates by way of which one can have an *indirect* awareness of events experienced earlier, that is strictly simultaneous with direct awareness of later such events. Several possibilities suggest themselves. One is that experiences may, so to speak, reverberate in the mind, by a mechanism analogous to that whereby a pianist can prolong a note by depressing a pedal. This notion may be dismissed at once, as an attempt to explain how the mind can form a single Gestalt out of a succession of temporally separated auditory experiences. For, to the extent that such neural prolongation was at work, they wouldn't be perceived *as* temporally separated but, if they are musical notes, as a chord (or perhaps, rather, as a sort of squashed arpeggio). And, again as a matter of brute fact, the component notes in a musical Gestalt can appear to us to be sharply temporally delimited, and not in the least 'smeared out' over time. (This point is made by Chisholm, 1981.)

Another, and more obvious, candidate is memory – specifically what one might call short-term experiential memory. Experiential memory here is to be distinguished from factual memory. Recalling an experience is not the same as remembering a fact, not even the fact that one had the experience in question. One may remember *that one had* a given experience, without being able to call the experience to mind. Suppose that someone hears the notes a, b and c, in rapid succession. Then, appealing to memory, one might credit the hearer with the following sequence of experiences. First, the hearer has the experience of hearing a. Then he has the experience of hearing b, whilst having a short-term memory experience of having just heard a. So far so good; but what then?

As a first shot, one might think of the hearer as having the experience of hearing c, whilst having a short-term memory experience of having heard a followed by b. That, however, is circular. For we're talking about short-term *experiential* memory. Thus the hearer cannot have a short-term memory of having heard a followed by b unless he can also hear, within a single phenomenal perspective or maximal experience, a followed by b. But it is precisely this experience of succession that we're supposed to be analysing. Nor will it do to appeal to factual memory, saying that the hearer has an experience of c whilst simultaneously remembering that, in fact, he has recently had an experience of a, shortly followed by an experience of b. In the first place, this introduces an intellectual element into the experience of succession of a kind that clearly doesn't belong. And secondly, it would fail to explain the qualitative difference between hearing three notes within the space of a second-and-a-half, and hearing them within the space of a minute-and-a-half or an hour-and-a-half. It obviously won't do, either, simply to say that the hearer has an experience of c, whilst simultaneously remembering having heard a and remembering having heard b. For that fails to capture the fact that a was heard before b, or, more precisely, that b was heard *as* occurring after a.

What a defender of this approach might say here is that the hearer has the experience of hearing c whilst having a short term memory of having heard a, and a short-term memory of having heard b whilst having a short-term memory of having heard a. But the very complexity of this formulation is surely a decisive objection to it. It's bad enough with three notes; make it five, and we're dealing with memories of memories of memories of memories. Beyond the first couple of terms, such nesting of short-term memories within short-term memories like Russian dolls is a psychological absurdity.

Attempting, in this fashion, to appeal to short-term experiential memory, in order to account for a musical Gestalt, encounters another problem having to do with the intervals between the notes, and indeed the lengths of the notes themselves. Of course, one could add, to one's favoured formulation, short-term experiential memories of gaps. But bear in mind that the notes and the gaps *are themselves temporally extended*. Those who wish to defend the point of view we are in process of exploring are thus faced with an impossible dilemma. Either they admit that someone can be directly aware of a temporally extended note or gap, as a whole; or else they deny that this is possible. If they admit it, then how can they consistently deny the possibility of being directly aware, within a single phenomenal perspective, of two or three notes separated by gaps? If the fact of temporal extension counts against this, surely it must also count against hearing a single note, seeing that it will inevitably be temporally extended to some degree? If, on the other hand, they deny the possibility of being directly aware of the whole of a note, within a single phenomenal perspective, and insist on appealing to memory even here, they will need as many distinct short-term memories as there are phenomenally distinguishable times. This approach therefore seems to me to be hopeless.

What strikes me as a more promising account of our experience of succession is one proposed by the German philosopher (and lapsed Catholic priest) Franz Brentano (1838–1917), who pioneered the so-called *phenomenological* method in philosophy. (Phenomenology is, in essence, the logical analysis of experience. The whole of this discussion of the specious present is thus an example of phenomenological analysis, as understood by Brentano.) In the last of several attempts to give a satisfactory account of the experience of succession, Brentano began, in 1911, to apply to our experience of time the concept of a *mode of presentation*. (Professional philosophers will be familiar with this concept in the rather different context of Frege's philosophy of language. In its Fregean guise, the notion was invoked briefly in chapter 8, in our discussion of physicalism. Perhaps, indeed, Brentano borrowed the concept from Frege, or possibly vice versa.) The idea is that one and the same object may be presented to the mind in different ways. And this, Brentano in effect argues (1973, p. 279), can be so even in regard to what we are directly aware of. One and the same phenomenal item, a sound for example, may present itself either as present, or else as past, with as many distinct possible degrees of 'pastness' as there are phenomenally distinguishable times within the specious present. Thus, when the notes *a*, *b* and *c* occur in rapid succession, there will be a continuous sequence of overlapping phenomenal perspectives that include the following: (i) an experience of *a* under the mode of presentation *present*; (ii) an experience of *b* under the mode of presentation *present*, together with an experience of *b* under the mode of presentation *just past*; (iii) an experience of *c* under the mode of presentation *present*, together with an experience of *b* under the mode of presentation *just past* and an experience of *a* under the mode of presentation *further past*. Here *just past* and *further past* represent two specimen positions on a phenomenally continuous spectrum of temporal modes.

This appears to be correct, as far as it goes. But there are, it seems to me, grounds here for doubting the adequacy of the temporal mode of presentation approach, notwithstanding that it is plainly a great advance on the other views we have considered. For the immediate contents of awareness are presented to us as *temporally ordered*. Moreover, this is, from a phenomenological point of view, a primitive fact about experience. We do not, as it were, first observe that the note *c* is presented to us under the mode of presentation *present*, *b* under the mode of presentation *just past*, and *c* under the mode of presentation *more than just past*, and then *infer* that their temporal order is *a*, *b*, *c*. That they are so ordered is immediately apparent to us, without analysis. And it is a phenomenal feature which is invariant with respect to the position, within a phenomenal perspective, of the group as a whole. When *c* itself is presented under the mode of presentation *just past*, provided *a* is still sufficiently recent to lie within the same specious present, the ordering is phenomenologically no different from when *c* is presented under the mode of presentation *present*. It is arguable, indeed, that this perceived temporal ordering is phenomenologically prior to Brentano's temporal modes of presentation. To be aware of a note as present, just past, more than just past, and so forth is, perhaps, precisely to be aware of it as thus-and-so temporally related under this primitive ordering to some shifting reference point: the phenomenal now, or the forward temporal boundary of the specious present.

One great advantage of this way of viewing the matter is that it allows for the following fact, briefly alluded to in chapter 4. Where *a* and *b* are objects of immediate experience, it is not invariably true that we are aware of *a* either as occurring before *b*, or as occurring after *b*, or as occurring simultaneously with *b*. A pair of sounds are usually presented to us as occurring either simultaneously, or in a definite order, and likewise with a pair of visual presentations. But a flash of light cannot, in general, be unambiguously ordered with respect to a tone, if the physical stimuli are close together in time.

Let me emphasize that I am not talking here about our ability temporally to order the external physical events that our senses are registering. Present people with two flashes of light sufficiently close together in time, in slightly different positions in the visual field, and they will indeed be unable to tell which flash came first. That, in general, will be because the corresponding phenomenal items will seem to be simultaneous. In the case of a flash and a sound, however, the situation may be different. They may seem to the subject to be neither simultaneous nor temporally ordered in an unambiguous way; they merely seem close to each other in time. Here is a breakdown of *phenomenal* ordering itself, not just of the ability to *infer* the temporal order of a pair of physical stimuli from the phenomenal relationship between the corresponding objects of immediate awareness. The present view can accommodate that fact simply by allowing that the *phenomenal* temporal ordering of items within awareness is only a *partial ordering*, in the logician's sense. Phenomenal items are presented as temporally ordered, in the sense that there are phenomenal temporal relations holding between items within experience. But not every two items, within a given phenomenal perspective, will stand to each other in one of the phenomenal relations *earlier than*, *later than* or *simultaneous with*.

I have presented Brentano's theory and my subsequent elaboration of it as though it were an alternative to accounts of our experience of time that relied on short-term memory. But it need not be so regarded. For someone might argue as follows: 'When Brentano speaks of "*b* under the mode of presentation *just past*" what he is describing is, in reality, only a *memory* of *b*, through which we are acquainted with *b* only indirectly. Wherever an experience figures, in its own right, within a phenomenal perspective, it invariably does so under the mode of presentation *present*.' Now admittedly, no criterion has yet been offered for distinguishing a vivid short-term memory of a note, say, from a direct awareness of that note under a mode of presentation that labels it as past. So it might be thought that anyone was free to describe this as a memory. And, if one so describes it, there is nothing then to prevent one from invoking the notion of temporal modes of presentation in relation to such memories themselves. Bertrand Russell (1915) speaks, confusingly, of 'immediate memory' in this context, whilst simultaneously insisting that we are, in his technical sense of direct awareness, *acquainted* with past sounds, shapes and so forth that lie within the specious present. He explicitly contrasts this with other cases, involving phenomenal items further removed from the present, where what we are actually acquainted with is only a 'memory image' of the experience, and not the experience itself.

One might begin to suspect that the question whether what we are directly aware of is the past (phenomenal) sound itself, or merely a memory of it, is simply a verbal issue. It seems to me, however, that there is after all a factual issue here, if the arguments of chapter 5, for assigning a spatio-temporal location to experiences, are accepted. For one can then ask: what sort of spatio-temporal region is occupied by a phenomenal perspective or maximal experience? One possibility, it would seem, is that every phenomenal perspective corresponds to a three-dimensional spacelike *surface* – a slice through the world-tube of the relevant brain system. One might think of this as a *psychological* simultaneity plane. Even if this surface were flat, it would still be true that, with respect to most frames of reference, phenomenal perspectives were temporally extended. And if it weren't flat – being more akin in shape to a popadum, say, than to a playing-card – then it would be temporally extended relative to every set of rectilinear space-time coordinates. Nevertheless, it would have zero *depth* or *thickness* in the temporal direction. That is one possibility. The other is that each phenomenal perspective corresponds, rather, to a four-dimensional *chunk* of space-time, more analogous to a slice of Swiss roll than to an infinitely thin sheet of paper.

On the face of it, these two possibilities are equally consistent with the phenomenological account just given. The first possibility would correspond to the *teleprompter model*, mooted in chapter 6. If phenomenal perspectives lack temporal depth, then something other than temporal separatedness must be used to *encode* perceived temporal relations between items that are comprehended within a single specious present. Think of the way that a teleprompter screen contains, all at once, a sequence of words that, as spoken, take a *period* of time to enunciate; on the screen, the words are presented in a *spatial* order that *represents* a temporal order. Analogously, so the suggestion would run, if one is listening to music, each instantaneous state of awareness contains, all at once – that is to say, all within the same psychological simultaneity plane – a sequence of phenomenal notes whose external counterparts take a period of time to play.

According to this teleprompter model of temporal perception, one is not directly acquainted with the temporal ordering, or degrees of 'pastness' of the notes, even *qua* phenomenal items. When one is aware of two notes following in rapid succession, what one is directly acquainted with are phenomenal items that are physically located on the same spacelike surface (namely, that containing the contents of the phenomenal perspective of which these items form a part), standing in a phenomenal relation that merely *represents* the temporal order of the corresponding external events. And likewise, when one apprehends a pair of notes under the respective modes of presentation *present* and *just past*, what one is directly acquainted with are phenomenal items, again physically located on the same (relevant) spacelike surface, but possessed of distinct phenomenal attributes which *represent* presentness and just-pastness. *Phenomenal* before and after, and past and present, must, on this view, be distinguished from *physical* before and after, past and present, even in relation to the immediate contents of awareness.

Figure 15.4 gives a schematic representation of what, on the teleprompter model, would be involved in hearing the diatonic scale, Do, Re, Mi, Fa, So, La, Ti, Do, played at such a speed that three successive notes could be embraced within a single phenomenal perspective. The boxes represent successive time-slices of the hearer's stream of consciousness, corresponding to cross-sections of the world-tube of the hearer's brain, each encompassing the entire contents of a single phenomenal perspective or maximal experience. (One must think of there being an infinity of further such boxes between the ones shown.) If one ignores the subtleties introduced by relativity, one can think of the phenomenal items contained in each box as simultaneous events, albeit caused by temporally separated external events. These items are, however, phenomenally ordered in a manner that systematically reflects the objective temporal ordering of the external events that give rise to them.

Brentano observes that, when a note is becoming 'more and more past . . . it appears as one and the same unitary note, which is only such that it is apprehended by us successively with a different temporal mode' (Brentano, 1978, p. 247, as quoted, in his own translation, by Chisholm, 1981, p. 16). This, clearly, is a feature that any theory of our perception of time must somehow accommodate. On the teleprompter model, Do,

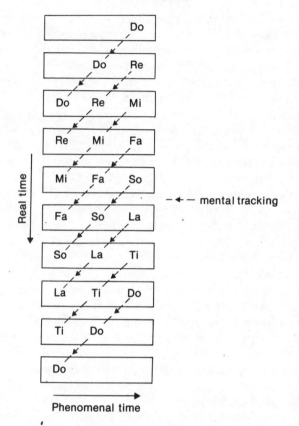

‑Figure 15.4 *Teleprompter model of the specious present.*

as it appears in the first box, cannot literally be regarded as the same phenomenal item as Do, as it appears in the second box – shifted to the right, and hence phenomenally shifted into the past. Nevertheless, as Brentano quite rightly says, they appear to consciousness 'as one and the same unitary note'. What we must invoke here is the notion of *mental tracking*. Where the phenomenal landscape changes, over time, in a more or less continuous fashion, the mind has the capacity to 'lock on' to phenomenal items or features. This it does, with respect to any such item, in such a way that its 'descendants' in succeeding phenomenal perspectives are mentally identified with the original, and automatically come to occupy the same cognitive niche established by the initial locking-on. This mental tracking is represented in figure 15.3 by broken lines.

It might be argued that the teleprompter model is covertly invoking (short-term) memory – albeit in a manner significantly different from that suggested earlier and found to be inadequate. 'Strictly speaking', someone might insist, 'Do, as it figures in the second and third boxes in the diagram, is only a vivid *memory* of the original perception of the note, represented in the first box.' Now, of course, it *could* be so described; this is what Russell meant by 'immediate memory'. But then so could anything to the left of the rightmost boundary of each box, corresponding to the present (as opposed to past) boundary of the corresponding phenomenal perspective. A certain time elapses, even between the beginning and end of a single note. So one could argue that, by the end of the note, the beginning of the note is only a memory. Indeed, the phenomenal present could, by this logic, be shrunk to an extensionless point, so that, in effect, everything contained within a phenomenal perspective is, strictly speaking, a memory. However we describe matters, the key point is that there is phenomenal *continuity* here. 'Immediate memory', in Russell's sense, is at least phenomenally continuous with perception (continuous in a way that, as I shall argue presently, short-term memory, properly so regarded, is not); so that saying where one ends and the other begins would involve an essentially arbitrary decision. But any vagueness which may attach to the question whether a given note is or is not encompassed by a particular phenomenal perspective hinges not on *that* arbitrariness, for everything that Russell would count as immediate memory is to be included. Rather, it hinges on the question where, in a process of gradual fading from consciousness, one should regard the note as no longer forming a part of the phenomenal landscape.

The alternative to the teleprompter model is what I shall call the *temporal overlap* model. On this latter model, phenomenal perspectives possess genuine temporal depth; and phenomenal items, such as musical notes, typically figure in a continuous sequence of overlapping phenomenal perspectives, under different temporal modes. This model is represented in figure 15.5, where braces serve to indicate the respective scope of successive phenomenal perspectives. As in figure 15.4, the perspectives shown in the diagram must be thought of as merely discrete samples of what would, in reality, be a continuous series.

The question that now arises is whether this view is philosophically coherent. I argued in chapter 6 that there is nothing, as such, philosophically objectionable about the idea of overlapping phenomenal perspectives. This, indeed, is simply the consequence of allowing the relation of co-consciousness, as between experiences, to be nontransitive. But more than that is involved in the temporal overlap model of temporal perception. For it is not simply that Do figures in a succession of distinct phenomenal perspectives. The point is rather that *it is experienced differently in each*; under the mode of presentation *present* in the first,

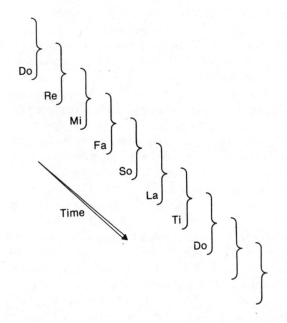

Figure 15.5 *Temporal overlap model of the specious present.*

just past in the second, and *further past* in the third. In other words, these are *different* experiences. And if they are different experiences, what can be meant by saying that the phenomenal perspectives genuinely overlap. Does the overlap model really make sense?

It seems to me that it does make sense, provided that we do not say that the self-same *experience* can be encompassed, *as a whole*, by several distinct, temporally overlapping phenomenal perspectives. We can, to be sure, think of the temporally extended experience of the note Do as persisting through a sequence of phenomenal perspectives, represented by the first three braces in the diagram. But then, this temporally extended experience is not fully encompassed by any of these perspectives, taken by itself. On the other hand, we could focus, more narrowly, on the experience of Do under the mode of presentation *present*. This experience (if we ignore the fact that the note is itself temporally extended) is confined to the phenomenal perspective represented by the first of the braces in figure 15.5, but is only part of the larger, temporally more drawn out, experience just considered. What is envisaged by the temporal overlap model is that some single phenomenal item, in this case the note Do, not itself temporally drawn out, is the object of a continuous sequence of distinct experiences, as it is apprehended under different temporal modes of presentation.

It may be easier to see what is meant if one thinks in terms of brain events. Corresponding to the playing of the note Do, there is a certain brain event to which consciousness is sensitive (doubtless itself temporally extended, but ignore that). This is the physiological correlate of the phenomenal item, Do. But to this single brain event (or phenomenal item), there corresponds a *sequence* of distinct experiences of hearing the note; the correspondence between brain events and nonmaximal experiences (ones that form only a part or aspect of a complete phenomenal perspective) is thus a one–many relation. The selfsame brain event can be constitutively involved in a succession of distinct phenomenal perspectives, in which it (or the corresponding phenomenal item) figures under different temporal modes. The mind is, so to speak, apprehending the same brain event from successively different temporal perspectives.

At first sight, it may seem that this picture is implicitly invoking a most unsatisfactory form of dualism, with the mind or self somehow standing outside the brain, or rather the corresponding world-tube, viewing it from different angles. In fact, no such dualism is involved here. If any dualism is involved, it is merely the innocuous dualism of states and observables. I argued in chapters 12 and 13 that there must, from the point of view of consciousness, be some preferred set of compatible brain observables. Now in elementary quantum mechanics, which largely ignores relativity, one tends to think of observables as being applied to states which correspond to time-slices of the physical system in question. But in a relativistic context, it is more natural to think of the observables as being applied to *space-time regions*. These regions *can* be spacelike surfaces, devoid of temporal depth, though they need not be. As far as I can see, it is simply a contingent question whether the preferred set of brain observables is defined on spacelike cross-sections of the world-tube of the relevant part(s) of the brain, as implied by the teleprompter model, or on something more like world-tube *segments*, possessed of temporal depth. And the latter supposition automatically gives rise to the temporal overlap model, and has no particular dualistic implications. That the view is at least coherent, on the assumption that phenomenal perspectives are indeed embedded in reality in the way that my interpretation of quantum mechanics implies, thus seems to me beyond serious question.

Whichever of these alternative views is correct, phenomenal perspectives may be thought of as being possessed of *phenomenal* temporal extension; in this sense, the specious present is an inescapable feature of the phenomenology of our experience, regardless of whether it is grounded in an objective temporal extendedness on the part of phenomenal perspectives (as is implied by the temporal overlap view, but denied by the teleprompter model). But it is questionable, it seems to me, whether this phenomenal temporal extension casts much light on our experience of the flow of time. Indeed, it may perhaps seem to make it more, rather than less, difficult to make sense of the temporally dynamic character of our experience. For it serves to make the temporal aspect of our experience very similar, in its phenomenological structure, to its spatial aspect, as manifested, say, within the visual field. There too, items are presented as ordered, this time spatially. And the way in which, on the view I have been defending, one's phenomenal perspective presents itself as temporally extended, with a fuzzy temporal boundary, might seem closely analogous to the way in which the visual field presents itself as spatially extended, with a fuzzy spatial boundary. Yet we do not experience, by way of vision, a flow of space.

Some philosophers would have us equate the experience of temporal passage with the experience of change. And it might be thought that the concept of the specious present, regardless of whether it is interpreted along the lines of the teleprompter or the temporal overlap model, allows for a single phenomenal perspective to encompass processes of change – to encompass them in their own right, if the temporal overlap model is correct. That, however, is less of an advance than it may seem. For there is nothing inherently 'dynamic' about change, if all that is meant by change is that different times are associated with different (phenomenal) attributes. After all, it is equally true that within one's visual field different places are associated with different attributes: for example, blue to the left, green to the right. Why, then, should the fact that the phenomenal time dimension is associated with phenomenal variation serve to render time dynamic in a way that phenomenal space is not?

What is needed here, one might argue, is some kind of concept of second order change. On the one hand, there is temporal change *within* a phenomenal perspective: the change in tone, within the compass of a single specious present, of the sound made by the engine of a jet fighter streaking overhead. This I shall refer to as *first order* change; it is analogous to variations in colour within one's visual field, say when looking at the sky. By *second order* change, I mean variations in the way that a single phenomenal item is presented from one phenomenal perspective to another. This seems to me to have no spatio-visual analogue. And it is here, perhaps, that vivid short-term experiential memory comes into its own. To the extent that memory of this kind is being exercised, a phenomenal perspective recapitulates, within itself, a portion of the stream of consciousness of which it is the immediate issue. A phenomenal perspective always presents itself as the latest element in a continuous, overlapping, temporally ordered series. There is thus a phenomenal ordering, not just within any given perspective, but of the perspectives themselves. Within any phenomenal perspective, there are presented vivid memories of previous perspectives, which are given to us as temporally ordered, both amongst themselves and with respect to the present, directly experienced perspective. Not only, then, do we have phenomenal variation associated with temporal shifts within a *single* perspective; we are also given, by way of memory, phenomenal variation associated with temporal shifts within the *series* of perspectives. And, in particular, we are conscious of variation in the way in which (what presents itself as) the same object of direct awareness is apprehended, with respect to successive phenomenal perspectives, when the object in question lies within the area of phenomenal temporal overlap.

Two things need to be added to this. First, in vividly recollecting an earlier perspective we remember it *as present*, whilst simultaneously placing it in the relation *earlier than* to the present perspective in which this memory figures. Vividly to remember an earlier phenomenal perspective is to remember what it was like to experience it; and, as experienced at the time, it was itself the latest in the series. Could our experience of the flow of time perhaps be grounded in part in this simultaneous *dating* of a recollected perspective as *past*, whilst *recollecting* it as *present*? And grounded likewise, as just suggested, in our being aware of some phenomenal item – a musical note, for example – as, say, *just past*, whilst vividly remembering that same item as given in the mode *present*. I say 'in part' because one also needs to appeal to expectation. The recollection of phenomenal perspectives, present as experienced but now become past, yields, by immediate induction, an expectation that the currently given phenomenal perspective will, in its turn, become past and give way to new perspectives. Moreover, phenomenal items presented as *present*, within a given perspective, are associated with the expectation that they are shortly to be presented as *just past*. Present experiences, it is tempting to suggest, are coloured by such instinctive expectations; and their contents thereby come phenomenally to strike us as shifting and ephemeral (see figure 15.6).

Here it may be instructive to reflect on the *dis*analogy between a phenomenal perspective in relation to time and our visual field in relation to space. It is essential to the account just offered that we are enabled, by way of memory, to conceive of time itself as extending beyond the boundaries of the current phenomenal perspective. Likewise, of course, the fact that we can shift our gaze and move around enables us to conceive of physical space as extending beyond the boundaries of our visual field. But there the similarity ends. For we do not conceive of what lies beyond the boundaries of our current visual field as in general an object of actual visual experience, or not, at least, of *our own* visual experience. By contrast, it is not just *physical* time that we think of as extending beyond the boundaries of our current phenomenal perspective; it is time *as experienced by ourselves*. We think of our own conscious

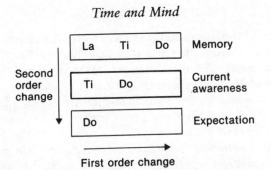

Figure 15.6 *First and second order phenomenal change.*
The middle box represents one's current phenomenal perspective; the transition within this box, from Ti to Do to silence exemplifies first order change. Second order change is exemplified by the change from one perspective (box) to another. The top box is intended to represent a phenomenal perspective which precedes that corresponding to the middle box, but which still lingers in vivid, short-term experiential memory; the bottom box represents a succeeding phenomenal perspective which is the subject of lively anticipation.

lives as being thus extended. The combination of experiential memory and current perception renders us simultaneously conscious of the temporal limits of current awareness, and the existence of other temporally distinct awarenesses (that is, phenomenal perspectives) which are equally our own.

That by itself, however, does not amount to a conception of time as flowing or passing. For one could think of these multiple awarenesses simply as existing in parallel, distributed as a continuous, perhaps overlapping, series along one's world-line. What one needs, in addition, is a conception of oneself – more than that, a *sense* of oneself – as progressing through the series. And that is something that this conception of a continuous series of phenomenal perspectives (punctuated by periods of unconsciousness), laid out along one's world-line, fails to capture. Indeed, it fails to capture one's sense of *personal* temporal progression for essentially the same reasons that the space-time conception, taken as a whole, fails to capture an objective, *universal* 'flow' of time.

When matters are viewed in this light, the appeal to memory and expectation turns out to be less helpful than it appears. In memory and expectation, one may picture to oneself phenomenal perspectives extending beyond the temporal boundaries of current awareness. And within certain such perspectives, neighbouring on the present, one may picture phenomenal items of which one is currently aware being presented under different temporal modes. Merely to do that, however, is not yet to see oneself as progressing *from* the perspectives revealed in memory, *through* current awareness, *towards* those which are the subject of imaginative expectation. Nor is it to see the objects of one's awareness as *emerging* from the future and then *receding* into the past. To be sure, memory and expectation carry just such connotations. But the very fact that they do so means that there is an inevitable element of circularity in appealing to memory and expectation by way of *explanation* of our sense of temporal progression. Even so, that does not render the foregoing account vacuous. To say that our sense of temporal progression depends, in this way, on memory and expectation is to make a substantive claim that may prove susceptible to being tested empirically. It is in the nature of a psychological hypothesis. (If correct, it might, for example, be appealed to in order to explain the sense of 'timelessness' reported by many mystics. On the present view, this might be achieved precisely through the suppression of memory and expectation.)

To believe that the foregoing account, or something along similar lines, was the correct account of our sense of temporal flow, or progression, would *ipso facto* be to regard it as an illusion. It does for temporal progression something similar to what Hume's theory of causation did for the concept of causal connection. Hume argued that there was, in reality, nothing more to causation than a constant conjunction of similar pairs of events. It is just that when we have, on a number of occasions, experienced an event of type *A*, closely followed by an event of type *B*, without ever experiencing an *A* without a *B*, we come to expect a *B* whenever we are presented with an *A*. And this expectation is then illicitly *projected* on to the reality, read into the objects of our experience, in such a way that we come to think of *A* and *B* as being objectively connected with one another by some relation of necessitation. The tendency of the mind to pass from an impression of an *A* to an idea of *B*, is, to use a Freudian term, externalized as a propensity in the world for *A* to make *B* happen. The theory just proposed, regarding our experience of time, is very much in this Humean tradition. For it too invokes the notion of projection. The objects of immediate awareness are regarded by us as fleeing into the past, because we project upon them our expectation of phenomenal perspectives in which they are either presented as more past, or no longer presented at all.

But in neither case does the Humean account carry complete conviction. There is something in most of us that wants to retort: 'Yes, there may be a large element of truth in this, considered as a piece of psychology. But, for all that, surely the *fundamental* reason why we tend to view things this way is because they *are* that way. There are causal connections in the world. And *in some sense* we do progress through time.' For that reason, and in a spirit of open-mindedness, I would like to offer the reader another line of thought. It is very sketchy and speculative; and even if it is on the right track, it need not, as I see it, be regarded as wholly invalidating the suggestions already made. The accounts are, to a degree, complementary to one another, with what I have just been saying belonging to philosophical psychology (or phenomenology), and what I am about to say belonging to metaphysics. I want to start with the traditional philosophical problem of our identity through time, on which I have briefly touched in previous chapters.

In a suitably relativistic representation, that part of the brain that is directly implicated in consciousness may, as remarked above, be pictured as a spatio-temporal world-tube. And, as a first approximation (ignoring quantum mechanics), a phenomenal perspective can be thought of as occupying a slice or segment of this tube. Most philosophers who have grappled either with the problem of the perceived flow of time or with that of personal identity, if we transpose their discussions into this space-time framework, start, in effect, with these perspectives, and then try to *construct out of them* a persisting sentient being or a temporal progression. In either case, they find themselves faced with an uphill struggle. It has, however, always struck me as curious that these philosophers should be so confident about what is the appropriate starting-point of their enquiries. The exercise of logical construction can only be expected to work when it proceeds from the genuinely more fundamental, or *primitive*, as philosophers say, towards something that is less fundamental, or, in philosophers' jargon, *derived*.

For my own part, I am far from convinced that phenomenal perspectives do possess the requisite primitiveness. What we need, it seems to me, is the right conception of how consciousness maps on to the world, so to speak. Implicit in a view that takes the concept of a phenomenal perspective as primitive with respect to that, say, of a persisting sentient being, is the thought that *slices or segments of world-tubes* are the immediate target of the relevant mapping. A very quick way with the problem of personal identity – far *too* quick – would be to claim that, on the contrary, consciousness maps all in one go, as it were, on to the discontinuous four-dimensional object that embraces all of the world-tube of a living brain that is associated with stretches of waking life. (This is a four-dimensional analogue of what a philosopher would call a *scattered particular*.) That, however, would then leave it as a complete mystery why one's entire conscious life is not comprehended within a single phenomenal perspective – why we do not experience the whole of our lives at once.

But what, in any case, entitles one to assume, as do both of these proposals, that what consciousness maps on to has to be something static? This may strike the reader as a curious question. For isn't the space-time conception of the universe inherently static, with time spatialized? Well, in a sense, no doubt, it is. There remains, though, a perfectly good mathematical distinction between things that are and things that are not a function of space-time location; one still, in relativity, has equations of motion. Thus, the acceleration of a particle is an obvious example of an attribute that takes on different values for different space-time locations along its world-line. The acceleration at any given point on that line is given by the degree of curvature at that point – how rapidly it is changing direction. It would be somewhat dogmatic, I should have thought, to insist that the concept of acceleration *as a function of* (space-time) position on an object's world-line was less fundamental than the concept of acceleration *at* a specific location.

In a similar fashion, why should one not think of consciousness itself as mapping on to some aspect of one's brain that, in general, takes on different values with respect to different locations along the world-line, or world-tube, of the relevant part of one's brain? Instead of taking as primitive the concept of a spatio-temporally extended *series* of phenomenal perspectives, why not think, rather, in terms of a *single* phenomenal perspective which is a function of location on the world-tube? The image of a collection of distinct perspectives, which require somehow to be conceptually synthesized into a single conscious life, will then give way to a different image. We are to think, rather, in terms of a phenomenal *frame*, something like an empty picture frame, which can be moved over a huge landscape; what lies within the frame will, in general, depend on where the frame is positioned; the contents are a function of position – dependent, that is, on where the frame happens to be. I would argue that this concept of a phenomenal frame does far better justice to our intuitive conception of our own awareness, in relation to time, than does the more conventional philosophical model of a temporal series. Intuitively, the conscious mind is a persisting but ever-changing *plenum*: a vessel with a perpetual turnover of contents, rather than a mere parade of states or occurrences.

A phenomenal frame, as I envisage it, is defined by that preferred set of compatible brain observables to which I have been alluding in previous chapters. But the implication of thinking of a phenomenal frame as a function of location on the relevant world-tube is that it is has to be a set of observables conceived along the lines of the Heisenberg rather than the Schrödinger picture, as I explained these notions at the end of chapter 11. That is to say, what we really have here is a constant state, which is simply the overall state of the relevant brain system, conceived as a four-dimensional object laid out in space-time. This, clearly, is something which it makes no sense to speak of as changing or evolving. That is why the Heisenberg picture is so compelling, from a relativistic perspective. In the Heisenberg picture, as we saw in chapter 11, it is the observables which, so far from being constant with respect to time as in the Schrödinger picture, have different forms at different points along the world-tube of the physical system to which they apply. And accordingly, it is these to which the equations of motion come to apply. But, whereas in nonrelativistic quantum mechanics we think of Heisenberg observables as a function merely of time, we must now think of them rather as a function of *space*-time location. Thus, each observable in our preferred set (the set which defines a phenomenal frame), is to be thought of as a *variable*; for different space-time locations, the observable will correspond, in general, to distinct determinate Hermitian operators. (As was remarked earlier, the preferred set of observables will itself be defined on finite *regions* of space-time; hence, by 'location' here I mean the location of a region, rather than of a space-time point.)

This notion of a phenomenal frame does not, as it stands, accommodate temporal progression. But could we, perhaps, go further? There is a perfectly well-defined *mathematical* operation that corresponds to transporting the frame along the world-tube (see figure 15.7). (Central to the mathematical theory of so-called *Riemannian manifolds*, a class of spaces which includes both ordinary three-dimensional space and the four-dimensional space-times of relativity, is a somewhat similar concept of *parallel transport* of vectors within the manifold.) Such an operation is well-defined, moreover, just in case we know the path along which the transport occurs, and its direction, or *sense*. No meaning, here, could be attached to the notion of the transport occurring at any particular *rate* or

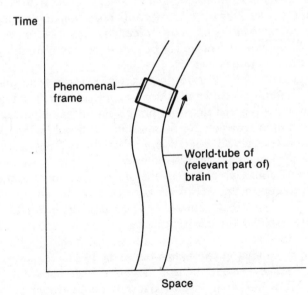

Figure 15.7 *Transport of phenomenal frame.*

speed. For it is not a *physical process* at all. Is it possible that consciousness maps on to the four-dimensional geometry of space-time in such a way that a *conscious life* corresponds to the *mathematical* operation of transporting a phenomenal frame along a world-tube?

So to suppose would not, it seems to me, commit one to holding that there there is any *physical* progress of, or progression through, time, either in respect of the universe as a whole, or on the part of conscious beings. Nor would it commit one to supposing that there is any more structure to the world than is capable of being accommodated within the space-time picture; certainly it does not imply an evolution of conventional space-time structures within some overarching time, as Dunne would have us believe. No; if the present suggestion were correct, the flow of time should be regarded, rather, as a reflection of the manner in which consciousness is embedded within the four-dimensional reality. That one sees oneself as progressing through time would be just another instance of the general truth that, though there is no gap between immediate awareness and the brain processes that are constitutive of our conscious lives, still one cannot but perceive reality, even one's own reality, from a distinctive point of view. There would be no overall, perspective-independent, temporal progression, any more than on the view defended in chapters 12 and 13 there is any perspective-independent collapse of the wave function. Yet *from our own point of view*, there would be temporal progression, just as *from our point of view* the wave function collapses. Just as the wave function may be said to collapse *relative to a biography*, so, *relative to the (abstractly conceived) operation of transporting a phenomenal frame along the world tube corresponding to the relevant part of a living brain*, events might be said to be transported backwards from the future into the past.

One thing that does seem to me to emerge clearly from this line of thought is that it is not, after all, a decisive objection to the intuitive idea that we progress through time that one cannot meaningfully speak of a *rate* or speed of progression; for the appropriate model, as I say, could be that of a mathematical operation, rather than a physical process. (Compare the way that, in a geometrical context, it makes sense to distinguish rotations according to the angle of rotation, and whether they're clockwise or anticlockwise, but not according to the speed of rotation.) But, for all that, I am inclined to doubt whether, in the end, the proposal is viable. Although we may be able legitimately to block the question 'How fast are we progressing through time?', there is unfortunately another question, first put to me by Harvey Brown, which is perhaps equally embarrassing and which I do not know how to answer. This is the question how our experience would or could be different, if the direction, or sense, of the phenomenal frame transport were to be *reversed*. In the absence of a satisfactory answer to this question, the goal of erecting some semblance of temporal progression within the framework of relativistic space-time would seem, yet again, to have eluded us. I want, therefore, to turn now to a rather different issue, where I feel myself to be on somewhat firmer ground; albeit that what I have to say may well strike the reader as even more wildly speculative.

Thus far, quantum mechanics has played only a minor role in the discussion of this chapter. Yet it offers, it seems to me, a radically new way of thinking about time in relation to consciousness. For present purposes, it will be convenient to return to our original space-time picture, in which phenomenal perspectives are conceived as distributed along the world-line of a conscious subject – or at least, those parts of it that correspond to continuous stretches of sustained awareness. In chapter 12, I suggested that there was a close analogy between the way experience designates a specific set of eigenvalues of the preferred set of brain observables, and the way experience designates a specific time as now. Just as other times, within the scope of one's conscious life, are designated as now, with respect to other (past or future) phenomenal perspectives which are equally one's own, so, I suggested, alternative eigenvalues are similarly designated as actual within parallel phenomenal perspectives that also belong to oneself. Now, however, I want to suggest that this may be far more than an analogy.

Suppose it were possible to construe time itself as an observable in the quantum-mechanical sense. As such, it would have a spectrum of eigenvalues that corresponded to a range of possible times. And each of these different times would appear as *the* time – as now, that is – from the standpoint of a corresponding phenomenal perspective. Thus the fact that one is presented, in the course of one's conscious life, with a range of phenomenal perspectives, each associated with a different time, wouldn't just be *analogous* to what, on my version of the relative state theory, is true of phenomenal perspectives in relation to eigenvalues of the preferred set of brain observables. Rather, it would be a specific *instance* of the more general principle. Time, here, would differ from other observables in the preferred set only in so far as one has, by way of memory, access to eigenvalues (which is to say times) alternative to that which is associated with any given phenomenal perspective.

That, then, is the suggestion: time itself is an element – no doubt a key one – in the preferred set of brain observables to which I referred in earlier chapters. Kant tells us that time is the form of the inner sense. One could, perhaps, recast Kant's remark in the language of quantum mechanics: a necessary condition for any brain observable to figure in the preferred set is that it commute with time, understood as a brain observable in its own right. But some further observations are in order here. First, there cannot, strictly speaking, be any such observable as one that has *precise* times as its eigenvalues; this must be so, for reasons parallel to those that apply to the conventional position operator. There could be no such thing as a perfectly precise measurement of time. So the time observable with which all of the other preferred brain observables are required to commute must be an observable the measurement of which (from outside) would suffice only to locate the time within a certain small finite interval.

I referred earlier to the familiar philosophical problem of personal identity, understood as the problem of defining the relation in which successive person time slices have to stand, in order to be counted as belonging to one and the same individual. A surprising and intriguing implication of taking time itself as an element in the preferred set of brain observables is that the relation which holds between successive time slices of the same individual turns out to be one of superposition! Persisting sentient beings can, on this view, be construed as linear combinations of time eigenstates of the relevant brain system. Just what relevance, if any, this observation might have to the traditional problem of our identity through time is a question that would merit further consideration.

All of this, however, may be thought to founder on one very familiar fact: within quantum mechanics, as conventionally formulated, it is impossible to treat time as an observable at all! (Even, that is to say, in the extended sense in which position and momentum can be treated as observables.) To explain just why this is so is beyond the scope of this discussion. Suffice it to say that I do not regard this fact as a decisive objection to what I have been suggesting. For there have been discovered a number of ways in which, subject to limitations parallel to those which apply to the position operator, one *can*, after all, treat time as an observable. What is indeed not possible is to construct a Hermitian operator on *Hilbert space* which has the properties required of a time observable. This was rigorously demonstrated by Pauli many years ago (Pauli, 1933, p. 143), though his proof has not prevented other theoreticians from attempting to square this particular circle. But there are independent reasons for doubting whether Hilbert space is fully adequate, as a quantum-mechanical state space. And people have found other ways of formulating quantum mechanics which do allow for the construction of a time operator with more or less the required properties. (I have in mind particularly the 'super Hilbert space' approach of Rosenbaum (1969).)

What, then, are the 'required properties' of a quantum-mechanical time operator? Well, what people have mostly been looking for is an operator that stands to the energy observable, the Hamiltonian, in a relation of reciprocal indeterminacy, analogous to that in which position stands to momentum. (Technically, such pairs of observables are known as *canonical conjugates*.) One way of seeing why this is a natural requirement is to reflect that, from the standpoint of special relativity, momentum and energy are merely the projections, on to space and time respectively, of a unitary so-called *four-momentum*, a four-component vector in space-time. Thus, energy is to time as momentum is to (spatial) position. This will make sense to the reader who thinks back to our discussion of the simple harmonic oscillator. Almost any system that evolves in a predictable way could, in principle, be used as a clock, though, in practice, we tend to choose systems with periodicities that match our conventionally chosen temporal units. A simple, classical harmonic oscillator functions as a clock, in the sense that a joint measurement of the position and momentum of the bob would suffice to tell one what the time was, within, or as mathematicians say, *modulo*, its period of oscillation. (Every position is visited twice in every orbit, but associated with opposite momenta.)

But now think about the simple harmonic oscillator in the light of quantum mechanics; and imagine that it is in an energy eigenstate. We know that for the system to be in an energy eigenstate is for it to be in a *stationary* state. And that means that the expectation values of all observables whatsoever remain constant over time. So, without even being told what form the time observable is going to take, we know that when the energy is fully determinate, the time must be wholly indeterminate. Whatever a measurement of time is supposed to consist in, quantum-mechanically, it must have the following feature. When the system on which the time observation is being made is in an energy eigenstate, the likelihood of finding the time to lie within any given finite interval must be exactly the same as that of finding it to lie within any other interval of equal size: all times are equally probable.

Now there are, in fact, close analogies between the universe, as regarded in modern cosmology, and the simple harmonic oscillator. General relativity yields a whole class of cosmological models, including a subclass, particularly beloved of cosmologists, known as the *Friedmann models*. In some of the latter the universe expands for ever; in others it expands for a while, starting with the *big bang*, and then contracts, finally collapsing in the *big crunch*. The key parameter, in the Friedmann models, is R, the *radius of curvature*. The standard way of visualizing the expanding universe, in its spatial aspect, is as the three-dimensional analogue of the two-dimensional surface of a balloon which is being blown up. Dots drawn on the surface of such a balloon will all recede from each other, as the balloon expands, at a rate that is proportional to their spatial separation, just like the galaxies. Each dot can regard itself as the centre of the expansion, inasmuch as all the other dots will be moving away from it; but the truth is that there is, on the surface, no centre of expansion, no unique place at which the big bang may be said to have occurred.

On this model, R corresponds to the radius of the balloon. The balloon model, however, is appropriate only to the case where the rate of expansion, in relation to the density of matter within the universe, is such that the expansion will eventually cease and give way to a subsequent contraction. Here, R is positive. If, on the other hand, the universe is expanding at more than cosmic escape velocity, at a rate sufficient, that is to say, to overcome the gravitational forces tending to pull the galaxies back together, we have a different geometry which is less easy to visualize. R is now negative (or zero if the rate of expansion is at the precise minimum required to prevent recollapse); the universe is spatially infinite; and it has, in every region, a geometry that is the three-dimensional analogue of the surface of a saddle (or, if R is zero, of a flat Euclidean surface).

Anyway, R plays a role in the Friedmann models that is closely analogous to that played by the position coordinate in regard to the simple harmonic oscillator. One can even associate with R a canonically conjugate *generalized momentum*, P, that stands to R as ordinary momentum stands to position. And the total energy of the universe as a whole (or at least the kinetic energy associated with the expansion plus the gravitational potential energy associated with the gravitational forces between the galaxies) may be represented by a Hamiltonian that is a function of R and P.

Quantum cosmology, as the name suggests, is the attempt to study such systems from the standpoint of quantum mechanics. Ideally, one would want do this in a way that was fully relativistic, combining quantum field theory and general relativity. Unfortunately, though, this is something that physicists don't yet understand how to do. Indeed, Penrose (1985) takes the view that the superposition of different space-time curvatures, or *metrics*, is in principle impossible; and this is one reason why he believes that the coupling of a system to a gravitational field, of a certain minimal strength, will cause its wave function to collapse: Nature, as he sees it, is forced to choose between alternative metrics that cannot meaningfully be combined. Most people who have tackled the task of quantizing gravity have avoided – or perhaps one should say evaded – this problem by treating gravity (if only as a first approximation) as a quantum field in *flat* space-time, in which the quanta of the field, the *gravitons*, are particles of spin 2. For many years, this approach failed to produce meaingful results, the problem being that it generated infinities of a kind that did not admit of being swept under the carpet – as do the infinities arising in other quantum field theories – by the device of *renormalization*. Penrose has been inclined to find support, in this fact, for his own belief that what is needed here is a radically new theory, synthesizing general relativity and quantum mechanics, and incorporating a mechanism for physical collapse of the wave function.

In the mid-1980s, however, there occurred something of a breakthrough for the more orthodox approach. Michael Green, of Queen Mary College, London, and John Schwartz, of Caltech, have apparently succeeded in getting rid of these embarrassing infinities which arise within conventional quantum field theory, by treating elementary particles as one-dimensional entities or 'strings' – loops of string, in the currently favoured version of the theory – rather than extensionless point-particles (see Green, 1985, 1986). In this theory, which is known as *superstring theory* and which automatically incorporates gravity, it is also necessary to suppose that space-time is really ten-dimensional rather than four-dimensional, with six of the spatial dimensions being curved back on themselves in such a minute radius that they are, for ordinary purposes, undetectable. There is some reason to hope that, within this theory, Penrose's problem of how to superpose metrics may ultimately be solved by treating as fundamental, here, not space-time, but rather the *configuration space* of the strings (the dimensions of which correspond to the *degrees of freedom* of the strings: the independent ways in which the strings can change state or store energy). Space-time itself, on this view, should be thought of as being grounded in a string-like microstructure.

Whatever may be the truth here, it is, in any case, possible to get quite a long way in quantum cosmology (and effect a kind of ersatz superposition of metrics), by adopting a semi-classical approach – what Padmanabhan (1987) refers to as 'a poor man's quantum cosmology'. If one follows this line, one is obliged to contemplate states of the universe in which different values of R (or of P) are superposed. (Indeed, strictly speaking there can be no state in which either R or P is fully determinate.) And, in particular, one can consider the energy eigenstates of the universe. Just as with the harmonic oscillator, these will be stationary states, in which the expectation values of all observables, including R, remain constant over time.

Now what those who work in the field of quantum cosmology normally end up supposing is that the universe, at any given time, is in a so-called *coherent state*. These coherent states can be represented as superpositions of the energy eigenstates. The supposed virtue of these coherent states is that their time evolution resembles that of the state of the universe in the Friedmann models; specifically, the *expectation value* of R, considered as an observable, evolves in a manner analogous to that of the radius of curvature in the classical theory, thus allowing for an expanding universe and so on. (The expectation value of R never goes to zero, however, as does the radius of curvature in the classical theory, if we suppose expansion of the universe to be eventually followed by recontraction into the 'big crunch'. And this may allow for subsequent re-expansion: in short, an oscillating universe.)

Page and Wootters (1983) have, however, challenged the assumption that the expectation value of R is required to change over time in order to square with astronomical observation. Their argument turns on some highly technical considerations which I cannot go into here. But the upshot is that, according to them, *there is nothing to prevent our supposing that the universe as a whole is in a stationary state*. Objectively speaking, the universe may not be evolving at all! One might think that this supposition was contradicted by the fact that things seem to us to change, and, in particular, by the fact that the galaxies are observed by astronomers to be receding from one another (assuming this to be the correct interpretation of the galactic red shift). In fact, though, all observations carried out from *within* the universe are consistent with the supposition. From a relative state point of view, the fact that the universe seems to us to be expanding is fully explained by the following consideration. If we divide the universe into subsystems, one of which is a properly adjusted clock (strictly, clock-cum-calendar), and the other of which comprises the rest of the universe, then the states of these two subsystems will be correlated with each other. More precisely, they will be correlated in such a way that relative to the state of the clock in which it registers, say, 21 November 2987, the remainder of the universe will be in a state associated with a larger expectation value for R; but relative to the state of the clock in which it registers 21 November 1987, the remainder of the universe will be in a state that is associated with a smaller expectation value for R. If we then modify the example slightly, partitioning the universe into three subsystems, the third being an astronomer with a set of instruments, it follows that he will find, if he lives long enough or his instruments are sufficiently sensitive, that observations of higher (later) clock readings are associated with the measurement of higher values for R. All of this is entirely consistent with the universe as a whole, objectively regarded, remaining in a stationary state throughout. Only a measurement performed by an observer who, *per impossibile*, was situated outside the universe altogether could prove the supposition to be false. But it will presumably still be true that *relative* to the designated state of the observer, the remainder of the universe may be regarded as being in something like a coherent state, in the quantum-cosmological sense.

This point can now be generalized. According to the version of the relative state theory defended in chapters 12 and 13, what one would normally take to be the objective state of the world is, properly regarded, the state it is in relative to a certain state of a certain subsystem of the universe: namely, that physical system in one's brain whose activities are constitutive of awareness. Ultimately, then, the fact that the world seems to us to change is a consequence of the fact that this preferred subsystem of the brain is itself capable of functioning as a clock, albeit an imperfect one; the world seems to us to change, inasmuch as the states of things are referred to 'clock states' of our own brains. Of course, we also make use of external clocks; but they would not seem to us to change state, save for correlations between their states and states of ourselves. A given phenomenal perspective, so I have been arguing, corresponds to a set of eigenvalues of some preferred set of compatible brain observables. It is only in so far as eigenvalues of what amount to *time* observables on the relevant brain subsystem are themselves included in the sets associated with phenomenal perspectives, that these perspectives come collectively to generate *streams* of consciousness or biographies.

Earlier in this chapter, I suggested that one's sense of the flow of time, or of our own progression through time, was, if not simply an illusion, then at any rate no more than a perspective-relative phenomenon: something that could be said to occur only from the point of view of the conscious subject itself. Now, however, I am suggesting something far more radical. It must at the very least, one would think, be an objective, observer-independent fact that the state of the world changes over time, that different times are associated with different constellations of features. But that assumption too is one that the discussion of the last few paragraphs calls into question. The whole logic of the relative state approach tends to the conclusion that a system can be regarded as changing, only to the extent that distinct states of the system are correlated with distinct time eigenstates of some other system designated as a clock. We ourselves perceive the world as changing, only because we refer the states of things to certain preferred states of ourselves. And these preferred states both contain, and are ordered on the basis of, 'clock readings' of our own brains.

All this may seem to constitute a surprising vindication of Henry Ford's remark that 'History is bunk'. But of course, history is not bunk. I am not claiming that nothing ever really happens. Rather the reverse: on a relative state view, absolutely everything that (physically) can happen does happen, in the sense that it is to be found somewhere in the cosmic wave function. What I think of as *the* history of the world is really its history relative to a particular biography, and only one of my many biographies at that. In that sense, history as one ordinarily thinks of it is something *abstracted* from an underlying matrix that contains countless alternative histories. And the assumption that this entire system is, in its own right, changing or evolving (or that it is not) is at best gratuitous;

and at worst meaningless. Archimedes is alleged to have said, apropos of his theory of leverage: 'Give me a place to stand, and I can move the whole universe.' There is no such place, however; nor is there an Archimedean point from which, even in principle, one could make the observation that alone would establish whether or not the universe as a whole is in a stationary state. Only in our most abstract theorizing can we disengage ourselves totally from the world, and, in Nagel's phrase (1986), contemplate the view from nowhere.

Postscript on the unity of consciousness

A question that was left hanging at the end of chapter 6 is whether it makes sense to suppose that co-consciousness could be a matter of degree. If it is not an all-or-nothing matter, so the argument ran, then we are not, *pace* Descartes, required to think of the unity of consciousness as an absolute unity. But, on the other hand, the introduction of intermediate degrees of co-consciousness seemed to lead to absurd consequences. Consider the following simple schematic example. We have three states or events, *A*, *B* and *C*. (*B* could be a headache, *C* a velvety tactile sensation induced by an item of clothing one was in the process of putting away in a drawer, and *A* the passing thought that the constant conjunction of stinging nettles and soothing dock leaves might be evidence of divine providence.) *A*, we imagine, is co-conscious both with *B* and with *C*; but *B* is only *quasi*-co-conscious with *C*. That is to say, it stands to *B* in a relation that is somehow intermediate between not being co-conscious with *C* at all, and full co-consciousness with *C*. The result, presumably, is a phenomenal perspective unambiguously comprising *A* and *B*, with *C* sitting ambiguously on the periphery; and symmetrically, a phenomenal perspective unambiguously comprising *A* and *C*, with *B* sitting ambiguously on the periphery (see figure 15.8). If we imagine the degree of co-consciousness between *B* and *C* being gradually strengthened, then the result will be a gradual fusion of these perspectives. The point is, however, that the question when this occurs will not, on this model, admit of any precise answer.

Why, then, does this appear to lead to absurdity? Well simply because we have what purport to be the same experiences, *B* and *C*, figuring ambiguously in one perspective and unambiguously in the other. And that must mean that their phenomenal character is different with respect to the two perspectives. But if the phenomenal character is different, then they cannot, after all, be the *same* experiences.

This objection seems, on the face of it, unanswerable. Consider, though, the parallel objection that could be raised to the temporal

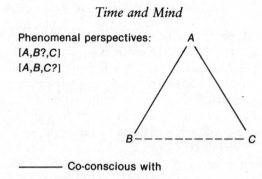

Phenomenal perspectives:
[A,B?,C]
[A,B,C?]

——————— Co-conscious with

– – – – – Quasi-co-conscious with

Figure 15.8 *Three experiences,* A, B *and* C.
A is unambiguously co-conscious both with B *and with* C. B, *however, stands to* C *in a relation intermediate between full, unambiguous co-consciousness and non-co-consciousness: a relation of* quasi-co-consciousness. *Correspondingly, we have a phenomenal perspective such that it is ambiguous whether or not it contains* B, *and a phenomenal perspective such that it is ambiguous whether or not it contains* C.

overlap model of our experience of time, discussed earlier in the chapter. What this model envisages, after all, is that the very same phenomenal item – the note Do, for example – should, in its own right (and not merely through the proxy of short-term memory), figure in distinct phenomenal perspectives under different temporal modes of presentation. This seems clearly to be a coherent view, whether or not it is true to the facts of our experience of time, since it surely must be a contingent question whether the spatio-temporal regions to which phenomenal perspectives correspond do or do not possess temporal depth. Yet it makes no sense to say that the very same experience of hearing the note Do figures, under different modes of presentation, in distinct perspectives.

The key point now is that the strategy employed earlier on to save the temporal overlap model from incoherence may be straightforwardly carried over to our simple model involving quasi-co-consciousness. According to the temporal overlap model, the sense in which the note Do, as it figures in successive phenomenal perspectives is the *same* (phenomenal) note, albeit clearly not the same experience, is quite simply that it corresponds to the same brain event. What led us into contradiction was the idea of degrees of co-consciousness between *experiences*. No such contradiction arises, however, if we think instead in terms of a relation of co-consciousness *defined upon brain states and events*, and allow this relation to be a matter of degree. Two brain states or events are co-conscious, we shall now say, if and only if they figure constitutively within the same phenomenal perspective. (Thus construed, co-consciousness ceases to be a reflexive relation; a brain state or event will be co-conscious with itself only if it figures constitutively in at least one phenomenal perspective, which not all brain states or events do.) The advantages of this move should be immediately apparent. No contradiction is generated by the supposition that one and the same brain state figures constitutively in each of two phenomenal perspectives, wherein it is experienced somewhat differently: centrally and unambiguously in one, peripherally or ambiguously in the other; or under the mode of presentation *present* in one, under the mode *just past* in the other.

Still, isn't this inconsistent with maintaining an identity theory of the relation between mental states and events and brain states and events? For identity is a one-to-one relation, whereas the present proposal involves saying that a single brain event may correspond to several distinct mental events or experiences – a one–many relation. Well, it is certainly inconsistent with a version of the identity theory that would have us identify maximal *and nonmaximal* experiences with brain states or events, that is to say, experiences that are not and experiences that are parts of larger experiences. But all that shows, I now want to argue, is that this is not the form that an identity theory should take. An identity theorist should be content, it seems to me, to identify *maximal* experiences – which is to say, entire phenomenal perspectives – one-to-one with corresponding constellations of brain processes. For then our mental lives will themselves have been equated, without remainder, with sets of physical goings-on. It is simply not necessary to insist that nonmaximal experiences be susceptible of one-to-one identification with brain states or events, in their own right. Nor does the impossibility of such one-to-one identification have any dualistic implications. All that it implies is that the phenomenal character of nonmaximal experiences is a partly *contextual* matter.

Suppose we have a pair of distinct, overlapping phenomenal perspectives. These may be temporally overlapping, or else overlapping in the way in which, in chapter 6, I speculated that concurrent phenomenal perspectives might overlap in commissurotomy patients. Then it will be possible to pick out some brain event which lies within the overlap zone and hence figures constitutively in each of the perspectives. How that brain event manifests itself, phenomenally speaking, in each of the two perspectives will, I am suggesting, depend partly on what other brain events figure constitutively within that same perspective, and the relations in which the chosen brain event stands to those other brain events. (This kind of contextuality is what we were appealing to earlier, when we suggested that the temporal mode of presentation of a musical note, say, within the context of a given phenomenal perspective, could, from the standpoint of the temporal overlap model, be seen as being grounded in the (spatio-) temporal relation of the corresponding brain event to (the events at) the forward boundary of the perspective. Relative to a given phenomenal perspective, the further a brain event is from the forward boundary of that perspective, which is to say the phenomenal present, the further back in time the corresponding feature of our experience will appear to be.) There is, surely, nothing here that is in the least inconsistent with a thoroughgoing materialism, or which would give any comfort to a mind–body dualist.

Tentatively, therefore, I am inclined to conclude that the nature of our experience does not, after all, logically oblige us to believe in an all-or-nothing unity of consciousness, such as would constitute an obstacle to a materialist programme. But co-consciousness itself is still, of course, a complete enigma, in materialist terms; as, indeed, is consciousness *simpliciter*. We are no closer now than we were in the first chapter to knowing how or why certain brain events should conspire to form integrated perspectives, illumined by awareness. And mere empirical investigation seems to me as powerless to shed light on this question as is the conceptual clarification that used to be thought the proper province of philosophy. That is not to say that more neurophysiological data, and more neuropsychological data – information about how the neuro-physiology correlates with psychological phenomena – is simply irrelevant to these questions. The point is rather that such data cannot by themselves enable us to make any headway with the deep questions, unless and until they inspire a radically new way of interpreting, indeed conceptualizing, the psychological facts in relation to the physical ones. What is needed here, as I suggested in the Preface, is a shift in our thinking at least as profound as that which allowed us to see space and time as merely facets of an underlying unitary spatio-temporal manifold.

16

Descartes's Legacy: Mind and Meaning, Science and Scepticism

In chapter 1, we identified four philosophically problematic features of mind or consciousness. Three of these, namely phenomenal qualities or 'qualia', the unity of consciousness, and the 'flow' of experienced time, have now been extensively discussed, with an attempt being made, in each case, to reconcile them with a conception of mental states and events as identical with states and events in the brain. Little, however, has so far been said about the problem of meaning or intentionality; and that is one of the things I wish to talk about in this chapter. But I intend to lead into it via a discussion of external world *scepticism*, since vulnerability to such scepticism is widely believed to be a decisive objection to the kind of view of perception that I defended in chapter 9.

Our tentative rejection of the notion of an absolute unity of consciousness, if it can be sustained, represents an important break with Descartes; and of course we have had no truck whatever in this book with Descartes's conception of the mind as a self-sufficient substance, set apart from the material world though causally interacting with it. Nowadays, however, there is a widespread tendency to apply the term 'Cartesian' to a broad range of philosophical positions which have in common only the fact that they share Descartes's view of our epistemological predicament. In this broader sense, the whole approach adopted in this book is likely to be perceived as exceedingly Cartesian – and to that extent, some will think, hopelessly wrong-headed.

The term 'Cartesian', thus understood, is usually employed as a term of disparagement. It tends to be associated with a widely held view of the history of modern philosophy according to which Descartes somehow set the subject on the wrong track. Many contemporary writers – some of whom, the avant-garde, describe themselves as 'postmodern' or 'post-analytic' philosophers – would have us regard the bulk of modern philosophy as the product of a seductive, but radically misguided, conception of the relationship of mind to 'external' reality, which has been passed down from Descartes, and which exercises a malign influence even on philosophers who would totally reject Descartes's metaphysical dualism. We are invited to see Cartesianism, in this sense, as a kind of incubus from which philosophy must liberate itself if it is ultimately to make any progress. (Indeed the very notion of the material world, in general, as 'external' to the mind might be seen as part of this Cartesian inheritance; so I should stress that my own references, in this chapter, to the 'external world' are in no way intended to beg the question in favour of the Cartesian viewpoint.)

I need hardly say that I do not share this fashionable view of the Cartesian legacy. Nevertheless, there is one respect in which I do have some sympathy with the contemporary reaction against Cartesianism. It is important, it seems to me, to distinguish two main elements in Cartesianism, as the term is used by these contemporary writers. The first element involves a package of views, one of which is a conception of the mind as standing at one remove from the external world, being directly acquainted only with what appears on an internal stage. Compare Hume (*Treatise*, bk I, pt III, sec. XIV):

> The mind is a kind of theatre, where several perceptions successively make their appearance; pass, repass, glide away, and mingle in an infinite variety of postures and situations.

This 'inner stage' conception of the mind is combined with *realism* – the view that there is an objective reality logically independent of the knowing or conceiving subject – and the *correspondence theory of truth*, according to which the truth of a belief, theory or assertion consists in an appropriate match or fit between the content of the belief or whatever, and the way things actually are. Precisely which elements in this package should be rejected is a matter on which critics of Cartesianism differ amongst themselves.

Unfashionable though it is, this entire Cartesian picture seems to me essentially correct. Actually, it would be a grave historical error to suppose that this view was, in any sense, invented by Descartes. A clear statement of it is to be found in the writings of Augustine, whom Descartes is very likely to have read. (See, for example, Augustine's *De Trinitate* X, XI and *De Genesi ad Litteram* XII.) And Augustine, Descartes and Locke were plainly all influenced by Stoic and Academic thought (as conveyed, for example, in Cicero's *Academica*), in which there are striking anticipations of Cartesian and Lockean epistemology (see Arnold, 1911, pp. 130–44; Cicero, 1867; Long and Sedley, 1987, 236–53). Where Descartes differs from Augustine is that he thinks, as

Augustine does not, that such a conception of the mind, in relation to external reality, gives rise to an epistemological crisis. Having, so to speak, cut the mind off from external reality, Descartes then became preoccupied with the question how he was to re-establish contact, how he was to avoid scepticism – a preoccupation which subsequent philosophers have inherited.

This second element in Descartes's thinking has indeed, it seems to me, proved an unfortunate legacy. The whole enterprise of trying to prove the existence of an external world, or of other minds, or that the future will resemble the past, or whatever – or else of trying to show that scepticism, in these matters, is somehow logically incoherent – has, in my view, been an exercise in futility, comparable to trying to square the circle. Moreover, the obsession with scepticism has, far too often in modern philosophy, resulted in the epistemological tail being allowed to wag the metaphysical dog. This can be said of views as diverse as Berkeley's idealism on the one hand, and behaviouristic or Wittgenstein-inspired quasi-behaviouristic theories of mind on the other. And it can be said, *par excellence*, of the current resurgence of common-sense realism regarding perception, discussed at length in chapter 9.

Here I think Descartes may indeed have been guilty of a fundamental mistake; at any rate, the mistake is undoubtedly one which his writings have helped to propagate. The mistake, as I see it, is that of thinking that the adoption of a view of the mind as being directly acquainted only with its own 'private' contents has any tendency at all to *create* a sceptical problem about the existence of the external world. Don't misunderstand me; I'm not denying that there *is* a sceptical problem. I am denying, rather, that this problem is a product of any particular, idiosyncratic conception of the relation between mind and reality. I would hold that, on the contrary, it is totally *irrelevant* here whether one adopts the Cartesian (Augustinian/Lockean/Humean/Russellian) 'inner stage' view of the mind, or, instead, some version of common-sense realism according to which we are directly or immediately acquainted in perception with a part or aspect of the external world. What gives the sceptics their opening is not some particular philosophical or scientific way of conceiving perception, but, rather a certain prosaic and uncontroversial fact. This is that the conditions which have to be satisfied, in order for one genuinely to perceive a material object answering to a certain description – a patch of green paint, say – *are not self-intimating*. To judge that these conditions are satisfied is to impose a certain *interpretation* upon one's experience. And this interpretation is never *necessitated*, or forced upon one. That is to say, it is invariably true that one could – logically could – have been in a state that was subjectively indistinguishable from one's actual state, consistently with this preferred interpretation's being false: there may be no patch of green paint, only a green after-image.

When one appreciates that this is the real crux, one sees that the Cartesian and the common-sense, direct realist are in precisely the same boat. To be sure, they give different accounts of what it is to perceive something. For the Cartesian this is a matter of being directly acquainted with some appropriate purely mental item, which is caused, in the right sort of way, by some external material object. For the common-sense or direct realist, on the other hand, it is a matter of being directly acquainted with, or conscious of, the material object itself. But whichever is the correct *analysis* of perception, the subjective character of one's experience can never be such as logically to guarantee that what is actually going on, on any particular occasion, answers to this analysis. Knowing or believing that genuine perception is a matter of being directly acquainted with a material object, doesn't tell you whether what is going on now really is an instance of being directly acquainted with a material object, as opposed to being subject to some sort of perceptual illusion (caused, say, by direct stimulation of the visual cortex). Indeed, one cannot, on either view, logically rule out the possibility that what actually goes on *never* meets the conditions of genuine perception. The analysis of perception proffered by the common-sense realist provides, by itself, no bulwark even against wholescale scepticism regarding the external world.

Here I am largely repeating points already made in chapter 9, though with a rather different emphasis. For what I am now suggesting is that many contemporary critics of Cartesianism are choosing the wrong point of attack. These critics would have us suppose that Descartes engineered a spurious epistemological problem, by foisting upon us a false conception of our relation to reality. But people who take this line show that they themselves are still labouring under what I believe to be the key Cartesian misconception: namely that there is some *connection* between adopting a Cartesian picture of the mind and vulnerability to scepticism.

If I am right about this, then it means that I am under no particular obligation, given my own views, to show how scepticism regarding the external world can be countered or kept at bay: it is no more of a problem for me than it is for any other realist. I have, in any case, nothing here to add to what others have already said. I regard a belief in an objective, external material world, of things that occupy space and persist through time, as having the status, essentially, of a *theory* – a theory whose justification lies in its power to make sense of the motley of sense experience. We are justified in believing in it, on the basis of our sense experience, for the same sorts of reasons that a scientist is justified in believing in electrons, on the basis of experimental data and the observed functioning of electronic equipment and so forth. Suppose one has a theory which imposes a rational order upon a range of diverse phenomena. Suppose, further, that predictions based on this theory are constantly confirmed, and no other genuinely distinct theory that anyone has been able to dream up is remotely comparable to it either in explanatory or predictive power. Under these conditions, it is, it seems to me, rational to believe that the theory is at least partially or approximately correct – that there is a substantial degree of correspondence between the theory and the nature of the reality to which it is applied. And these conditions are met, *par excellence*, in the case of our belief in the material world, and the perceptual judgements which routinely invoke this theory. Our entire lives could be thought of as consisting of repeated experiments which go to confirm the theory. We are constantly basing predictions on this conception of an external reality, which are just as constantly being borne out by subsequent experience.

(One thing that puzzles me, incidentally, about common-sense realism, intended as an answer to external world scepticism, is how it is supposed to cope with such things as electrons. Either common-sense realists think that we are justified in believing in electrons, or they don't. If they think that we are not justified in believing in electrons, on the grounds that electrons do not admit of being directly observed, then they are still lumbered with a most implausible form of scepticism. If, on the other hand, they think that this belief *is* justified, then surely they must accept that a Cartesian can, for exactly the sorts of reasons that a scientist is justified in believing in electrons, be justified in believing in external material objects; and this in spite of the fact that, according to the Cartesian, such objects cannot be directly observed. And in that case their own insistence on our being able directly to perceive material objects loses its principal rationale.)

What I have just given is, of course, only the merest sketch of an answer to the question what justifies us in believing in the external world. Properly to do justice to this issue would involve a major excursus into the theory of scientific method. Just what constitutes a good theory, and under what conditions a theory may be thought of as highly confirmed, are themselves difficult and complex questions on which philosophers of science are divided. Nevertheless, I am convinced that it is in the theory of scientific method that a justification of our belief in the material world must be sought. Of course, nothing we shall find there will serve to refute the very determined sceptic. We cannot hope to *prove* that there is an external world, or even to *prove* that there probably is. And this isn't the *Cartesian* predicament, it is simply the human predicament. For our justifications must themselves, on pain of an infinite regress, rest ultimately upon certain premises which we are unable to justify. Certain things must be assumed, without argument, which it is perfectly possible to deny without contradiction. In the end, there is nothing one can do with determined sceptics other than acknowledge the logical consistency of their position and then get on with the job regardless.

Thus far, I have been talking about knowledge. But, as we saw in chapter 9, there are those who see Cartesianism as placing the material world beyond our ken altogether: as something which cannot even be an object of coherent thought, let alone of knowledge. This brings us naturally to the problem of intentionality. If I am directly acquainted only with the private world of my own consciousness, how can my thoughts *mean* or refer to something external? We have this image of the mind somehow reaching out into the world and grasping this or that object, in order to make it a subject of thought. Compare Wittgenstein (*Zettel*, sec. 13):

> In some spiritualistic procedures, it is essential to *think* of a particular person. And here we have the impression that 'thinking of him' is as it were nailing him with one's thought.
>
> (Wittgenstein, 1967, p. 4e)

Such images, one might think, simply make no sense from a Cartesian perspective. For the Cartesian mind is ostensibly unable to roam beyond the confines of the private stage.

It is worth pointing out here how closely parallel are the common-sense view of perception and the common-sense view of thought. Just as it is natural to think of *con*ceiving an object as a kind of cognitive grasping, so it is natural to think of *per*ceiving as a kind of sensory grasping. Geoffrey Warnock (1978, pp. 2–3) put this very nicely, in a discussion of the causal theory of perception:

> [S]o far as the *concept* goes, . . . one might want to represent seeing Socrates rather as something that I do to him, than as something that he does to me – as more like netting a fish, than being hit by a cricket-ball.

If one thinks of thought and perception in these terms, then it is natural to conclude that the two are intimately related. It is tempting to think that it is only because we are able to get a *per*ceptual purchase on the material world, of the kind that our common-sense notion of perception implies, that we are able to get a *con*ceptual purchase on it. And this, in turn, may seem to be a *reductio ad absurdum* of the Cartesian view of the mind. Were we really in the predicament that this Cartesian view implies, the external world would be not merely unknowable but unthinkable.

The idea that a Cartesian view of the mind threatens 'loss of the world' was also discussed at some length in chapter 9. It seems to me, however, that there is a very simple way of showing that this concern *must* be misplaced. And this is by that favourite device of philosophers, the resort to science fiction. Were the Cartesian right, so the argument runs, and one was directly acquainted only with the private contents of one's own mind, then there would be no way of establishing contact, even in thought, with an external reality. But this line of reasoning has, it seems to me, a wholly implausible consequence that McDowell and others who take this line appear to have overlooked.

Suppose, for the sake of argument, that the common-sense realist is right, and we *are* directly acquainted, in perception, with external objects. Still, we can perfectly well *imagine* someone who wasn't, or at least wasn't in direct perceptual contact with the objects of normal perception: the common-or-garden furniture of the world. Such a person might be suffering from some extreme form of immune deficiency which would make any direct contact with the outside atmosphere fatal. So she's been kitted out, from birth, with a protective suit, rather like a space suit. There are no windows in the suit: it is both lightproof and soundproof. Everything is done by remote sensing. What the person actually sees, sees directly, is a television image, relayed from a pair of video cameras mounted outside the suit, and viewed through stereoscopic lenses. What she actually hears comes from a pair of loudspeakers, wired up to external microphones. And her tactile sensations, rather than being the consequence of forces transmitted directly through the suit, are immediately caused by pressure plates mounted on her skin, and activated by external sensors. Since this is science fiction, we could imagine all of this being done so cunningly that it was several years before the person herself became aware that she was in any way abnormal: for example, the outside of the suit might be cleverly contrived to look exactly like normal skin (and be able to expand to match the growth of the body it enclosed).

From the standpoint of common-sense realism, such a person would be, *vis-à-vis* the world in the neighbourhood of the suit, in a position that is, in relevant respects, just like that which, according to Descartes, we are all of us in *vis-à-vis* the material world in the neighbourhood of our own bodies. Just as, in Descartes's view, we are directly acquainted only with our own percepts, so the person envisaged is directly acquainted only with material objects lying within the protective suit. (These objects are, of course, only *de facto* private, since someone else could in principle open the suit and peer in; whereas I cannot peer in at your percepts. But that hardly seems a relevant disanalogy.) Yet, for all that, no one, surely, would suppose that a person thus situated would have the least difficulty in forming a concept of the external world – a concept of the world no different, in essence, from our own. (Mackie (1976, pp. 44–7) argues along similar lines.)

By reflecting on this example, one comes to see that any adequate account of how reference to material objects is possible at all would have to be of such a kind that Cartesians could, *mutatis mutandis*, avail themselves of it as readily as common-sense realists. For, on pain of absurdity, such an account would have to be capable of accommodating the object-directed thoughts of people who *de facto* were never, from the point of view of common-sense realism, in direct perceptual contact with any of the objects that figured in their thoughts. (I have in mind someone like the girl in our example before she becomes aware of her situation.) Whatever problems, therefore, there may be in giving a philosophically satisfactory account of intentionality, these cannot be any greater for the Cartesian than they are for the common-sense realist. It cannot, after all, be true that Cartesianism threatens 'loss of the world' in this sense, any more than it is true that Cartesianism creates any special sceptical problems regarding knowledge.

What we must do, clearly, is free ourselves from the grip of two opposing but equally misleading images. On the one hand is the image of the mind reaching out into the world. And on the other hand, there is this image (intended as a *reductio ad absurdum*) of the Cartesian mind as imprisoned within a windowless cell, unable so much as to contemplate a world beyond. Both, in their different ways, are travesties of the truth. The second picture fails to do justice to the fact that the contents of the mind embody *information* about the external world, and that the senses are, *inter alia*, information channels. Still, one must be careful here. There is a technical sense of *information*, according to which the mind could be said to embody information about the external world simply in virtue of its states being nonaccidentally correlated with states of the world. And one way of looking at perception is as a process whereby external states and events causally bring about states of, and events within, the mind, so as to promote a systematic such correlation. What must be emphasized is that information, in this technical sense, does not as it stands amount to information in the ordinary sense. A message in Morse code may, in the technical sense, embody the same information as a page of typescript. But the message will convey nothing to me unless I understand Morse code. What may encourage the idea that a Cartesian mind would be irretrievably cut off from external reality is the thought that it would have no way, so to speak, of *decoding* the messages it receives from the senses. To do that, people think, it would have to achieve a vantage point whereby it could survey both ends of the information channel, seeing just how states of the external physical world correlate with the sensory states to which they give rise. (This, of course, is the point of McDowell's distinction, alluded to in chapter 9, between an 'end-on' and a 'horizontal' picture of perception. McDowell, in effect, invites us to see a causal theory of perception, in the Cartesian mould, as pragmatically self-refuting, inasmuch as it credits the mind only with an 'end-on' perspective, from which the theory itself is literally unthinkable; the theory, he thinks, denies to the mind just that 'horizontal' perspective on which the intelligibility of the theory depends.)

Here again, it seems to me, we must beware of allowing a picture to hold us captive, as Wittgenstein puts it. What is really going on, in perception, according to a causal theory? Well, there are surely two aspects to the process. On the one hand, the external world acts upon us in such a way as to produce internal states that, in the austere technical sense, embody information as to what is happening externally. And on the other hand, these states are taken by us *as* perceptions of this, that or the other external objects and happenings. It is in the second of these two aspects that the intentionality of perception lies. It is perceiving or conceiving *as* that serves to render internal states, that would otherwise count as information only in the technical sense, information in the literal sense. An appropriate, and appropriately caused, isomorphism between an internal and an external state has no power, in and of itself, to prevent these states from remaining semantically inert. What is called for, in addition, is that these states receive the appropriate *construal*.

Thus, perceiving or conceiving *as* is what, crucially, requires explanation here. And once again, we see that the task facing the Cartesian is essentially no different, let alone any more difficult, than that facing the common-sense realist. Suppose the mind, in perception, *were*, as the common-sense realist alleges, in direct contact with some part of the external material world, so that a certain building (or the visible portions of its surface), say, were immediately present to the mind. Still, it is one thing to see a building, and another to see it *as* a building, and yet another to see it as some particular building, say Buckingham Palace. How does the common-sense realist think that this is accomplished?

Viewing matters in this light, one sees how misleading is the notion that our being able, *per impossibile*, to survey both ends of the causal transaction involved in perception – being able, as McDowell puts it, to adopt the horizontal perspective – would make any essential difference. For here too the right kind of construal would be called for, if such a God's-eye vision were to generate any kind of enlightenment: the objects at one end of the causal chain would have to be perceived *as* material objects, and so forth. Yet the question how one could possess the conceptual resources so to construe them is no less problematic, philosophically, than that of how one could possess the conceptual resources to construe, straight off, one's perceptions as perceptions of external objects. And by now it should be evident that it is a sheer confusion to imagine that this latter problem is rendered any more tractable by abandoning the Cartesian approach.

If the question is asked 'How, then, *are* we able to construe our perceptions as perceptions of this, that or the other external object?', a natural answer might be that we have something like a *mental map* of reality, to which these perceptions are referred. What allows us to conceive ourselves as part of a larger reality, with which we are causally interacting, is our possession of a mental model of the world, in which *we ourselves*, or our minds, symbolically figure as embedded within a larger structure. This is very much in the spirit of the sort of theorizing that contemporary cognitive scientists engage in. (And incidentally, most of them appear, in the sense we have been using the term, to be unregenerate Cartesians.) Much of the talk, these days, is of 'mental representations' or 'mental models'. The latter term is used by Johnson-Laird (1983, 1988), who has speculated interestingly about the role active manipulation of mental models may play in thought about the world. (It may be worth mentioning, in this context, that real-time imaging of the visual cortex of monkeys required to recognize shapes in an unfamiliar orientation, has recently revealed patterns of neural activity apparently corresponding to the rotation of mental images.) Of course, the intentionality of perception does not require that material objects and events be construed as *external*, presupposing as this does a prior distinction between self and non-self. Babies and lower animals presumably have a more primitive mental map of reality, which would not distinguish, in this respect, between, say, pain and rain – both being classified as unpleasant things that happen from time to time.

But however plausible one may find these speculations, there's a clear sense, it seems to me, in which they fail even to address the central *philosophical* problem of intentionality. And this is because they go no way towards answering the question what *makes* a mental structure – even one to which consciousness has access – into a mental model, map, representation, or whatever. Once again, one wants to insist, it is only by being taken or conceived *as* a model of reality, or of this or that aspect of reality, that a mental structure comes to count as such a model.

These remarks have a direct bearing on John Searle's celebrated *Chinese room argument* (Searle, 1980), designed to undermine some of the more extravagant claims made on behalf of artificial intelligence. (Searle is Professor of Philosophy at Berkeley.) Much recent work in the field of artificial intelligence has been concerned with language. And there are some very impressive programs that allow one to conduct a dialogue with the computer, in which the computer behaves, in many respects, like a native speaker of the language. Imagine now that such programs become increasingly sophisticated. More specifically, the linguistic behaviour generated by the program gets closer and closer to that of a native speaker, and this behaviour is the product of rules that are closer and closer to the principles that govern actual human linguistic behaviour. Then there are those who argue that, at a certain point, the computer, in following the program, will not merely be behaving *as though* it understood what was being said to it, and what it said in response; *it would really and literally understand what was being said*, in precisely the same sense that a native speaker would. Searle dubs this thesis *strong AI*.

By way of attempting to refute this thesis, Searle asks us to imagine that the program for which this remarkable claim is being made is one for command of Chinese. Now instead of this program's being run on a computer, Searle supposes that *he*, Searle, is running it instead. He is placed in a large room, furnished with rows of baskets, containing Chinese characters, and a book, perhaps several books, of rules. This room has two slots, an input slot and an output slot. Strips of paper, containing sequences of Chinese characters, enter the room through the input slot. Searle then refers to the book of rules, which tells him, according to what is on the input strip, to select certain characters from the baskets and paste them in a certain order on to another strip of paper, which he then 'posts' through the output slot. From the standpoint of an external observer, it may seem that what is taking place is an intelligent conversation: the input strips may be questions, to which the output strips contain appropriate and informative answers. Searle's point, however, is that he could, in principle, perform this task impeccably *without understanding a word of Chinese*. And if Searle can perform this task, without understanding any Chinese, surely there can be no grounds for supposing that, when the task is performed by a computer, *it* understands Chinese either.

This argument of Searle's has generated a host of responses and counterarguments by other authors (several of which accompany Searle's 1980 article). The commonest response goes like this. Searle, in the Chinese room example, is really playing the role that in a computer implementation of an artificial intelligence program is played by the computer's central processing unit (CPU). But it's a misunderstanding of strong AI to suppose that it is committed to holding that the *CPU* understands Chinese, when the computer is running a suitable program for the comprehension and generation of Chinese sentences. Rather, it is *the system as a whole* that could be said to understand Chinese. Thus, what, if anything, would understand Chinese, in Searle's example, would be the contents of the room taken *en bloc*, including the baskets of characters and the book(s) of rules. Hence, the fact that *Searle*, considered in isolation, does not understand Chinese is neither here nor there.

But to this counterargument Searle has a convincing answer. There is surely no reason, in principle, why Searle should not *memorize* the rules and the characters, perhaps in their spoken, rather than their written form, so that he had no need of the baskets of characters, strips of paper or rule book. Yet the ability to run the program, doing all the requisite computations in his head, would still imply no understanding of Chinese.

One thing that must be made clear is that Searle is not claiming that it would be impossible to build a machine that genuinely understood language. He is not even claiming that it would be impossible to build a *computer* that was capable of understanding language. His point is the more modest one that no device could be said to understand language merely in virtue of following some program, no matter how sophisticated that program was. That is to say, the explanation of how a given device was able to understand, say, Chinese, would have to appeal to some feature of the device over and above the fact that it was running this, that or the other program.

This claim seems to me clearly correct (regardless of whether Searle's Chinese room argument succeeds in establishing it). And it may help one to see why if one considers an interesting response to Searle's argument which is due to Stuart Sutherland (Professor of Experimental Psychology at the University of Sussex). Suppose, he says, the questions that were being put to the Chinese room were questions about Chinese geography. Then intuitively, one would be more inclined to credit the individual in the room with an understanding of the questions if he or she made essential use of a map of China, or better still a relief map of China, in the process of answering them. (This might be likened to an artificial intelligence program running on an analogue, rather than a digital, computer.)

Now there seems to me to be something right about this response. No one, plainly, could have mastery of a language unless he or she had mastery of a whole lot of other things as well. Of course, any artificial intelligence program that was capable of sustaining a reasonable conversation would be bound to embody a vast database of general nonlinguistic information about the world. But the point is that the form in which this information is embodied seems, intuitively, crucial to understanding. In many artificial intelligence programs, this information itself takes the form of sets of sentences, written in a special symbolic language, such that inferences may be drawn from them, according to a well-defined set of logical rules. (This is true, in particular, of programs written in PROLOG, which stands for programming in logic; here the symbolic language is a version of the *predicate calculus*, briefly alluded to in chapter 14.) Thus, there is a level of description of the computer's behaviour, when running the program, at which it can be said that all it is really doing is carrying out syntactic transformations upon strings of symbols. Searle would cite this as yet another reason for denying that the computer should be said to understand the symbols that it is manipulating: as he puts it (1984, p. 31), 'a computer program is only syntactical, and minds are more than syntactical'. Other philosophers, however, have seized upon this computational paradigm with enthusiasm, regarding it as a plausible and illuminating model for what we ourselves do when engaged in sequential thought. The mind, according to the American philosopher Jerry Fodor, may be conceived as a vast 'syntactic engine', operating upon a so-called *language of thought*.

This is not as silly as may sound. Contemporary philosophers who have addressed questions about thought and meaning have tended totally to neglect the dynamics of thinking: how it is that one thought can lead to another, in such a way as provide solutions to problems, and so forth. Logical inference is clearly one aspect of the dynamics of thought, the tendency to pass from thoughts to other thoughts which logically follow from them. And any attempt to give a systematic account of inference, to formulate rules of inference, for example, is bound to end up characterizing it (in part at least) in terms of propositional structure. Take, for example, the inference 'If it rains, the match will be cancelled; it will rain; therefore the match will be cancelled'. The validity of this argument depends essentially on the fact the conclusion is identical with the second clause of the first premiss, and that the second premiss is a syntactic variant of the first clause of the first premiss. How, it can reasonably be asked, is inference at the level of thought possible – even the primitive kind that it is plausible to ascribe to some lower animals – unless thoughts themselves have something analogous to a syntactic structure, with parts in common and so forth? That, in a nutshell, is the sort of consideration that underlies the thinking of Fodor and like-minded philosophers.

But it seems to me, first, that logical inference of this kind is a very poor model on which to base a theory of sequential thought in general. And secondly, the purely syntactic manipulation of symbolic strings (though doubtless a fruitful mathematical idealization) is, in any case, very implausible as a model of what is involved in actual, real-life logical inference. For, in real life, syntactic and semantic considerations ostensibly play an equal role in such inferences. Thus, it is, on the face of it, no more difficult to infer from 'If it rains the match will be cancelled', and 'The weather forecast is bad', to 'The match will probably be cancelled', than it is to make the same inference when 'The weather forecast is bad' is replaced by 'It will probably rain'. The syntactic approach would be obliged to postulate – implausibly in my view – a subsidiary (doubtless subconscious) inference, in the first case, from 'The weather forecast is bad' to 'It will probably rain', using the auxiliary premisses, say, that 'If the weather forecast is bad, and it is not winter, then it will probably rain' and 'It is not winter' (given that in winter the 'badness' of the weather forecast might imply snow, rather than rain). But I don't believe that there is any such subsidiary inference. The real point, surely, is simply that *understanding* 'the weather forecast is bad', given one's seasonally and contextually adjusted psychological set, automatically carries with it an expectation of rain (with a degree of confidence that depends on the faith one is disposed to place in such forecasts). (Fodor (1987, pp. 139–40) would deny understanding any such causal efficacy. For he explicitly rejects the idea that, in mental causation '[semantic] contents per se determine causal roles' (p. 139). According to him, it is the structure of mental states, rather than their content that does the work here, albeit that content is correlated with structure. By analogy – Fodor's own analogy – being tall doesn't really cause one to have tall children. It is rather that being tall correlates with, and indeed is caused by, the possession of certain genes; and it is these genes, or copies thereof, that cause one's offspring to be tall.)

In any case – though this is hardly germane to the issues Searle raises – far more attractive models of sequential thought, in general, and logical inference, in particular, are now emerging within the context of the connectionist approach, where the concept of a *constraint network* is proving very fruitful. It is no longer necessary to think of inference as a linear progression from premisses to conclusion. Rather, we can think of those items of knowledge or belief that inform one's reasoning – what the logician would represent as premisses, axioms, and rules of inference – as features of a neural network, ultimately embodied as a set of synaptic weights, which *constrain* the evolution of the network. One can visualize sequential thought as analogous to a ball rolling on a landscape, the *energy surface* of the network. The position of the ball on the landscape represents one's instantaneous state of mind. In this landscape there are dips and bumps, hills and valleys, and it is these features of the landscape that represent constraints on one's thinking; beliefs and desires alike are probably best conceived as constraints of this kind, helping to guide or channel one's thought in certain directions. Periodically, the ball will settle into a dip on the landscape, before it jostles its way out again. It is helpful to think of the ball as having a certain intrinsic vibratory motion that enables it to escape from these *local minima* on the energy surface; indeed it helps to think of this vibratory motion as something that the brain is capable of adjusting at will, so that it is higher when one is thinking hard than when one is engaged merely in desultory daydreaming. A train of thought, as registered in consciousness, might then correspond to a succession of dips, in which the ball temporarily comes to rest (see Rumelhart et al. 1986b).

Irrespective, it seems to me, of the merits of this particular approach, the foregoing considerations cast considerable doubt on the concept of a language of thought, as conceived by Fodor. Of course, there is a trivial sense in which all language users have a language of thought (mine is English, mainly British but with a trace of New York American): all language users think their respective languages as well as speaking them. But the crucial point is that even when we are, in some sense, thinking in words, the words draw semantic sustenance from the overall patterns of mental activity in which they are embedded. Thinking *with* words cannot – in principle cannot – be reduced to thinking purely *in* words. In much the same way that Wittgenstein insisted that a language game is ultimately inseparable from a form of life, so even the most verbal forms of thought are logically inseparable, *qua* thought, from the life of the mind in general. What Sutherland has put his finger on, it seems to me, is the need for an appropriate extralinguistic mental *context*, if the manipulation of symbols is to carry with it any sort of understanding – if, indeed, the symbols are to *symbolize*, from the standpoint of the conscious subject.

What is right about Fodor's claims, and perhaps all that is right about them, is that sequential thought requires that mental states possess structure, sub-elements of which are common to different states, and that the productivity of thought essentially depends on this fact. What then is wrong with it, beyond what I have already said? Well, first, there is no good reason to suppose that, in general, this structure has anything distinctively in common with the syntactic structure of sentences, or that the way in which this structure facilitates sequential thought has any very intimate resemblance to the way in which the syntactic structure of a formula in symbolic logic facilitates the manoeuvres involved in giving a formal proof or derivation. Secondly, there is no good reason to suppose that it is only structural features of mental states (whatever precisely that means) that contribute to their productivity; a priori, any properties whatsoever that the brain is capable of discerning may be relevant here. And finally, though it is of course true that we often do think with words, language, here, is only one system of mental representation amongst others, and – as I have already stressed – almost certainly not a semantically self-sufficient one. There is a host of nonlinguistic systems of representation, or types of mental model, which are deployed or manipulated in sequential thought; and it is unlikely that language could, at the level of thought, be a vehicle for understanding were it not that its deployment automatically brought some of these other systems into play at the same time. (And incidentally, there is some very interesting work by Johnson-Laird (1988), showing how our intuitions about the logical relations between concepts and propositions may be grounded in the 'mechanics' of these mental models – so that real-life inference is constrained by the state spaces of the models, rather than by abstract logical laws. The way he puts it – though taken at face value this would be objectionably psychologistic, seeing that logic itself cannot depend on psychology – is that logical relations are *emergent* features of mental models.)

Having said all of that, however, the obvious answer to Sutherland, from Searle's point of view, is that a map of China will do nothing to further understanding unless the individual in the Chinese room construes the map *as* a map; indeed, he will not fully understand the questions, or the answers, unless he can construe it as a map of *China*. And the point can be generalized. It is one thing to run a program for the interpretation of Chinese sentences, and another to see what one is thereby doing *as* the interpreting of Chinese sentences. Conceiving or perceiving as seems to me ubiquitous, in the study of intentionality or understanding, linguistic or otherwise. So much so that one is reminded of what J. L. Austin (1961, p. 179) said of the word 'can': it is something 'that we seem so often to uncover, just when we had thought some problem settled, grinning residually up at us like the frog at the bottom of the beer mug.'

This is not to deny there might *in some sense* be a viable account of meaning that did not, either explicitly or implicitly, invoke this notion. I am thinking especially of certain sorts of causal–functional theories of meaning, which are all the rage in certain circles (see, for instance, Millikan, 1984, 1986). The sort of theories I have in mind might enable one to say, for example, that a given dance by a given bee *meant* that there was food in such-and-such quantities in such-and-such a direction at such-and-such a distance from the hive. This would be rendered true roughly because (a) there was some approximate causal law linking such dances, occasion by occasion, with dispositions of food sensorily encountered by the bees who perform the dances; and relatedly, because (b) such dances can be regarded as having a biologically grounded, information-embodying and transmitting *function*, in the same sense that the heart has a biologically grounded pumping function.

Such theories scarcely touch our present concern, however, which is with the question what it is for a sentient being to *find something meaningful*. An account, along the lines just indicated, may allow us to regard as genuinely meaningful the dance of a bee. But it doesn't even address the question what would make the dance *mean something to the bee*. For all we know, after all, bees may not possess even the most rudimentary mentality; they may, in effect, be insensate automata. And even if they do possess some sort of inner life, their situation, *vis-à-vis* the dances, might still resemble that of Searle, in the Chinese room, *vis-à-vis* sequences of Chinese symbols; their behaviour may, in this respect, be semantically opaque both to each other and to themselves.

Now there is another respect in which these reflections about thought and understanding may be thought to be vitiated by Cartesian prejudices: for am I not assuming that meanings and thoughts are 'in the head'? And hasn't this view been effectively exploded, if not by Wittgenstein, then certainly by contemporary causal theories of meaning? It seems to me that thoughts and understanding are in the head (given my views, of course, this is no metaphor), in approximately the same sense in which husbands can be in Spain, while their wives are in England. The point is that a husband may be in Spain, but what makes it true that a given man *is* a husband may depend on his relations to something else that is not in Spain. Likewise, a thought or a state or act of understanding can be quite genuinely in the head, even though that in virtue of which a given mental state or event answers to that description – what makes it the thought that it is, or even what makes it, in some sense, a thought at all – may be its relation to things outside the head. Thus, I defended, in chapter 9, Evans's view that there are 'Russellian thoughts', thoughts that depend for their existence on the existence of suitable referents for their subjects. There can be no such thought as the thought 'That bird is a chaffinch' if there is no bird there, and I have been deceived by a trick of light and shade, playing on the leaves. This makes perfectly good sense, if by a thought one means the entertaining of a certain determinate proposition; for if there is no bird, then there is no subject, and hence no proposition. Nevertheless, something is going on in my mind, intrinsically similar to what would be going on in my mind if I were having a thought about a particular bird to the effect that it was a chaffinch (something that it would be quite natural to call a 'thought', using that term in a way that did not imply propositional content). There is still a certain man in Spain, intrinsically similar to a husband, even if there is no husband, seeing that the putative marriage was, unbeknownst to the man, invalid for some reason.

Likewise with understanding, and with perceiving or conceiving as, which I take to be at the heart of all understanding, linguistic or otherwise. There are Russellian 'taking as's.' The reality of Buckingham Palace (its existence now or in the past) is a necessary condition, not merely of one's seeing it, but also of one's taking a visual impression *as* a perception of Buckingham Palace. It is necessary that one's cognitive capacity so to construe one's visual impression be causally related to

Buckingham Palace in the right sort of way. And that requires both the past reality of Buckingham Palace, and that Buckingham Palace itself enters essentially into any sufficiently complete explanation of one's current cognitive responses. Understanding *is* 'in the head', it seems to me, but it is certainly answerable to what takes place beyond the head. In a fascinating discussion in his *Zettel*, Wittgenstein (1967, secs 7–35 *passim*, pp. 2–8e) considers such questions as what determines whom one is writing to, if one happens to have two friends with the same name, both of whom fit the content of the letter. Gareth Evans (1973, p. 191) considers a similar example. Suppose you are musing on a girl you have met and fallen in love with, who happens to be one of a pair of identical twins. Elaborating a little, let's suppose that you met the girl at a party, where both twins were present (perhaps wearing identical dresses), and that you don't know the name of either of them. As Evans remarks (echoing Wittgenstein, 1967, sec. 36, p. 8e), 'Even if God had looked into your mind, he would not have seen there with whom you were in love, and of whom you were thinking.' The point, in regard to Evans's example, is that there might be nothing in the phenomenal character of your thoughts that would, by itself, reveal which twin you were thinking about: the descriptive content of these thoughts might match either twin. Which twin your thoughts referred to would depend on the causal provenance of the thoughts: how your present musings causally relate to what happened at the party. (And what goes for object-directed thoughts also, as Hilary Putnam has shown (1975), goes for general thoughts. To be thinking of water, for someone ignorant of its chemical composition, it is essential that one's concept be grounded in causal transactions with the right kind of stuff, as opposed to a chemically wholly distinct but subjectively indistinguishable liquid.)

However, it is the intrinsic character of what does, by any reckoning, go on 'in the head' that constitutes a problem for a materialist theory of mind. The causal aspects of meaning are thus, once again, largely irrelevant to our present concerns. To repeat, *taking as* is the crux, the frog at the bottom of the beer mug. But is there anything that can usefully be said, by way of illuminating this notion further? Well, in one sense, no. It is possible to say illuminating things about what it is to have this, that or the other *specific* concept, and what it is, therefore, to bring it to bear on a given occasion, which is what taking as amounts to. But as for the question what *in general* it is to have a concept, what in general it is to perceive or conceive *as*, that – at least in the present state of the art – seems to me to defy philosophical and scientific analysis alike.

Nevertheless, I have one or two observations to offer. In the first place, it seems to me that the problem of taking or construing as is not really a distinct problem from that of consciousness itself. More specifically, I would claim that there is no consciousness, no sentience, without taking as. Some philosophers appear to think that the possession of concepts, as opposed merely to behavioural discrimination, is something that goes way beyond mere sentience, and is perhaps restricted to higher mammals. To me, however, it seems, on the contrary, that it is simply incoherent to suppose that there could be a creature that was aware of certain phenomenal qualities or qualia, without being aware of them *as* anything at all. One source of resistance to the idea that even the most primitive sentience must carry with it some minimal conceptualization, is the fact that any concept we humans possess, or at any rate for which we have a word, is likely to be far too sophisticated plausibly to be attributable to the most lowly possessors of consciousness. But of course this problem arises even at the level of dogs; one can say that the dog is wagging his tail because he construes the ring of the door bell as betokening the arrival of his master. Presumably, however, the dog does not possess *our* concept of 'master' or 'doorbell', and probably not 'arrival' either. Even so, dogs surely have beliefs, and beliefs call for some concepts or other.

If I am right in this claim – that taking as is a precondition of sentience – then, at least at the most primitive level, various sorts of taking as could perhaps be regarded simply as different modes of consciousness: different ways of being aware of the phenomenal character of what is immediately present to the mind. At this level, where all one has, I take it, is bare classification, construing as may simply be a matter of the warp and weft of awareness itself: the grain of consciousness.

Things get more complicated, of course, with concepts that import a measure of theory; and for the reasons just discussed, one cannot, in any case, regard as merely a mode of consciousness any form of taking as that counts as such partly in virtue of its causal antecedents. And then there is the fact that one is inclined, intuitively, to ascribe understanding even in the absence of conscious attention. We have made several references, in this book, to the stock example of the philosopher so engrossed in conversation that he has no conscious awareness of his driving or the road ahead. Perhaps, though, it would be possible for a very experienced philosopher, in the presence of a novice pupil asking familiar and predictable questions, to carry on the conversation on automatic, whilst being conscious only of his driving. Set against that, however, is the fact that one would intuitively be very reluctant to ascribe even unconscious understanding to anything other than a conscious subject. That suggests that all genuine understanding is somehow grounded in consciousness; and that it is *conscious* taking as which is central to the meaningfulness of thought. But of course, the mental structures that make meaningful thought possible will in general outrun awareness. And those same structures that underpin conscious taking as may also, on other occasions, be at work subconsciously: so that it might be natural to think of these subconscious processes as involving understanding of a sort, albeit only in an extended and derivative sense. Conscious taking as would still be the key.

This linkage of consciousness with conceptualization is itself very Cartesian in spirit. (Indeed, it was, in effect, Descartes's scepticism about the conceptual capacities of lower animals that led him to the wildly implausible conclusion that they lacked sentience altogether.)

Let me end this rather discursive chapter (and with it, the book), with a final plug for Descartes's *conception of philosophy*, and its relation to science. Throughout much of the twentieth century, philosophy in the Anglo-Saxon world has been viewed as sharply demarcated from science, and in some sense aloof from it. Unlike science, philosophy, it is frequently supposed, is not concerned with empirical facts, or with theorizing about the fundamental nature of reality. Rather, it is concerned with conceptual and methodological issues. It is concerned with analysing the language and concepts employed in science and elsewhere – the 'logical geography', as Ryle put it, of various areas of thought. The philosopher's slogan, as someone neatly expressed it, is, in effect, 'Anything you can do I can do meta!' Philosophy is metascience, metaethics, metalinguistics, and so forth. But that wasn't how Descartes saw it; and it certainly isn't how I see it. I would enter a plea for a far more traditional conception of philosophy as essentially continuous with science and other disciplines. There is no reason on earth, that I can see, why philosophers should eschew high-level theorizing that goes far beyond mere conceptual analysis. There is no reason why they should abandon their traditional role of trying to answer the big metaphysical questions; of trying to place what we know from science within a larger context; of exploring the relation of the findings of science to our prior conceptions of ourselves and reality; of trying to forge, where necessary, new frameworks, in order to make better sense of the world, as revealed both by science and daily living.

There are several reasons why academic philosophers in the Anglo-Saxon world have tended to relinquish this traditional role. And they are uniformly bad reasons. One is a hangover from logical positivism, which claimed that the traditional metaphysical questions were ultimately meaningless questions, and that the kind of high-level theorizing to which I have been alluding, precisely because it goes beyond science, is itself meaningless: meaningless because devoid of empirical content. But if the activities of the logical positivists established anything it is that there is no way of demarcating science from metaphysics. There is no criterion of empirical meaningfulness that will put metaphysical theorizing on the 'meaningless' side of the divide, whilst placing scientific theorizing on the 'meaningful' side. The celebrated 'verification principle' – according to which a statement is meaningful only to the extent that it admits of empirical verification or falsification – fails, in any of its forms, to do the job.

A second bad reason stems from the thought, inspired by the later writings of Wittgenstein, that the traditional philosophical problems – the mind–body problem, the problem of free will, and so on – are really 'pseudoproblems' that arise from a failure properly to understand and abide by ordinary linguistic usage; they arise 'when language goes on holiday'. But forty years of linguistic and conceptual analysis have done nothing to 'dissolve' these traditional problems; at best they have served to clarify the issues involved. Linguistic or conceptual analysis simply hasn't delivered the goods. And that, pretty clearly, is because these aren't, after all, merely conceptual problems; they are substantive problems, calling for a substantive solution.

Finally, there is the fear that, in attempting to tackle substantive issues, a philosopher is going beyond his or her brief or domain of professional expertise, thereby trespassing on the scientist's terrain. To that there are two answers. The first is that the distinctively philosophical questions, perhaps by definition, are precisely ones that science as currently constituted is unable effectively to address. Thus, it is in the nature of the mind–body problem that it could not be solved simply by more and better neuroscience, cognitive science, or whatever. The second answer is that there's a sense in which philosophy, thus conceived, must indeed trespass to an extent on the scientist's domain; and this in two ways. First, it must take appropriate account of scientific discoveries and theorizing. Philosophy, as I conceive it, cannot remain aloof from science. Moreover, scientific and philosophical (or metaphysical) theorizing are bound to overlap. So a knowledge of science, and a preparedness, on occasion, to confront the scientist within the scientist's own domain, is certainly called for. But the moral then is that if the philosopher lacks the relevant expertise, he or she should make efforts to acquire it. Here I would heartily endorse the following remarks of Bertrand Russell (1959, p. 254):

> One very general conclusion to which I have been led . . . is that philosophy cannot be fruitful if divorced from empirical science. And by this I do not mean only that the philosopher should 'get up' some science as a holiday task. I mean something much more intimate: that his imagination should be impregnated with the scientific outlook and that he should feel that science has presented us with a new world, new concepts and new methods, not known in earlier times, but proved to be fruitful where the older concepts and methods proved barren.

Philosophers, especially British philosophers, tend, in my experience, to combine a rather complacent ignorance of science with an excessive respect for it. And of course these things are not unrelated. The aura of mystique that surrounds fundamental physics, in particular, in many philosophers' minds, is rooted in ignorance. To become aware of what fundamental science is really about, is, as Russell says, to be transported into a wonderful new world of possibilities; those who come properly to understand relativity and quantum mechanics, so as to put classical and common-sense prejudices behind them, will never see the world in quite the same way again. But it is also to understand that even fundamental physics is a human activity, like any other, with its own limitations; it is to appreciate how philosophically shallow, and indeed, in some respects, philosophically confused are the conceptual foundations of science. (This, as we have seen, is true *par excellence* of cognitive science and quantum mechanics.)

Russell (1959, p. 230) says of philosophy that it needs the nourishment of empirical science, if it is not to 'wither and cease to grow'. That is true. But it is no less true that fundamental science, if it is to flourish, needs the nourishment of philosophy: of philosophy that is comprehending of science, without being unduly awed by it. It is, I believe, no accident that most great scientists of the past have, to some extent, been philosophers too,. and that most great philosophers have been conversant with the science of their day. If nothing else, I hope that this book – addressed as it is to philosophers and scientists alike – may help give new impetus to the symbiotic relationship in which science and philosophy have traditionally stood. Academic philosophy, if it is to play a major role in the universities, cannot afford to become too inward-looking, or too narrowly preoccupied with arcane puzzles of its own devising. It must be seen to be addressing issues whose importance is capable of being appreciated, at least by scholars in other fields, and ideally by the man or woman in the street. It needs to be perceived as having a vital contribution to make to other disciplines, and to human understanding generally. Otherwise, it will become not only increasingly marginal within our culture, but deservedly so. In that sense, if in no other, the Cartesian spirit is in urgent need of revival.

Bibliography

Aharonov, Yakir, Bergmann, Peter G. and Lebowitz, Joel L. 1964: Time symmetry in the quantum process of measurement. *Physical Review*, 134B, 1410–16.

Anscombe, G. E. M. 1959: *An Introduction to Wittgenstein's Tractatus*. London: Hutchinson.

Anscombe, G. E. M. 1963: *Intention* (1st edn 1957), 2nd edn. Oxford: Basil Blackwell.

Armstrong, David 1968: *A Materialist Theory of the Mind*. London: Routledge & Kegan Paul.

Arnold, E. Vernon 1911: *Roman Stoicism*. Cambridge: Cambridge University Press.

Aspect, Alain, Dalibard, Jean and Roger, Gerard 1982: Experimental test of Bell's inequalities using time-varying analyzers. *Physical Review Letters*, 49, 1804–7.

Austin, J. 1885: *Lectures on Jurisprudence* (1st edn 1861–3), 5th edn, rev. and ed. Robert Campbell, vol. II. London: J. Murray.

Austin, J. L. 1961: Ifs and cans (first published 1956 in *Proceedings of the British Academy*). In J. L. Austin, *Philosophical Papers*, ed. J. O. Urmson and G. J. Warnock, Oxford: Clarendon Press, 153–80.

Ayer, A. J. 1954: The terminology of sense-data (first published 1945 in *Mind*, 54). In A. J. Ayer, *Philosophical Essays*, London: Macmillan, 66–104.

Ayer, A. J. 1963: The concept of a person. In A. J. Ayer, *The Concept of a Person and Other Essays*, London: Macmillan, 82–128.

Bell, J. S. 1964: On the Einstein Podolsky Rosen paradox. *Physics*, 1, 195–200.

Bell, J. S. 1981: Quantum mechanics for cosmologists. In C. J. Isham (ed.), *Quantum Gravity 2: A Second Oxford Symposium*, Oxford: Clarendon Press, 611–37.

Block, Ned 1978: Troubles with functionalism. In C. W. Savage (ed.), *Minnesota Studies in the Philosophy of Science*, vol. IX, Minneapolis: University of Minnesota Press, 1978, 261–325.

Bond, James D. and Huth, Gerald C. 1986: Electrostatic modulation of electromagnetically induced nonthermal responses in biological mechanisms.

In F. Gutmann and H. Keyzer (eds), *Modern Bioelectrochemistry*, New York: Plenum, 289–313.

Boswell, James 1979: *The Life of Johnson* (1st edn 1791), ed. Christopher Hibbert. Harmondsworth: Penguin Books.

Brentano, Franz 1973: *Psychology from an Empirical Standpoint* (first published 1911, as *Psychologie von Empirischen Standpunkt*), ed. Linda L. McAlister, tr. E. H. Schneewind. London: Routledge & Kegan Paul.

Brentano, Franz 1978: *Die Abkehr vom Nichtrealen*. Hamburg: Felix Meiner.

Broad, C. D. 1969: *Scientific Thought* (1st edn 1923). New York: Humanities Press.

Broad, C. D. 1969: Symposium: Is there 'knowledge by acquaintance'? IV. *Proceedings of the Aristotelian Society*, supp. vol. 2, 206–20.

Brown, Harvey R. and Redhead, Michael L. G. 1981: A critique of the disturbance theory of indeterminacy in quantum mechanics. *Foundations of Physics*, 11, 1–19.

Carney, Thom, Shadlen, Michael and Switkes, Eugene 1987: Parallel processing of motion and colour information. *Nature*, 328, 647–9.

Chisholm, Roderick M. 1981: Brentano's analysis of the consciousness of time. In Peter A. French, Theodore E. Uehling, Jr. and Howard K. Wettstein (eds), *Midwest Studies in Philosophy, vol. VI: The Foundations of Analytic Philosophy*, Minneapolis: University of Minnesota Press, 3–16.

Churchland, Paul M. 1984: *Matter and Consciousness*. Cambridge, MA: MIT Press.

Churchland, Paul M. 1985: Reduction, qualia, and the direct introspection of brain states. *Journal of Philosophy*, 82, 8–28.

Churchland, Paul M. 1986: Some reductive strategies in cognitive neurobiology. *Mind*, 95, 279–309.

Cicero, M. T. 1867: *The Academic Questions (Academica)*, Book 2. In *The Academic Questions, Treatise de Finibus and Tusculan Disputations*, tr. C. D. Yonge, London: Bell and Daldy, 21–93.

Clifford, W. K. 1964: On the nature of things-in-themselves (first published 1878 in *Mind*, O.S., 5). Reprinted (in part) in G. N. A. Vesey (ed.), *Body and Mind*, London: George Allen & Unwin, 165–71.

Crick, F. and Asanuma, C. 1986: Certain aspects of the anatomy and physiology of the cerebral cortex. In J. L. McClelland, D. E. Rumelhart and PDP Research Group, *Parallel Distributed Processing*, vol. 2, Cambridge, MA: Bradford Books/MIT Press, 337.

Davidson, Donald 1980: Mental events (first published 1970 in Lawrence Foster and J. W. Swanson (eds), *Experience and Theory*, London: Duckworth). In Donald Davidson, *Actions and Events*, Oxford: Clarendon Press, 207–27.

Davies, P. C. W. 1980: *Other Worlds*. London: Dent.

Davies, P. C. W. 1981: Is thermodynamic gravity a route to quantum gravity? In C. J. Isham, R. Penrose and D. W. Sciama (eds), *Quantum Gravity 2: A Second Oxford Symposium*, Oxford: Clarendon Press, 183–209.

Davies, P. C. W. 1984: *God and The New Physics* (1st edn 1982). Harmondsworth: Penguin Books.

Dennett, Daniel 1981: *Brainstorms* (1st edn 1978). Brighton: Harvester Press.

Descartes, René 1964: *Meditations on First Philosophy* (1st edn 1642). In Elizabeth Anscombe and Peter Geach (tr./eds), *Descartes: Philosophical Writings*, London: Nelson, 59–124.

Descartes, René 1927: Selections from the *Treatise on Man* (first published 1664). In Ralph M. Eaton (ed.), *Descartes: Selections*, New York: Scribner's, 350–4.

Deutsch, David 1985a: Quantum theory as a universal physical theory. *International Journal of Theoretical Physics*, 24, 1–41.

Deutsch, David 1985b: Quantum theory, the Church–Turing principle and the universal quantum computer. *Proceedings of the Royal Society of London*, A 400, 97–117.

Devlin, Keith 1988: Doing it the brain's way. *The Guardian*, 21 January, 16.

Diels, H. and Kranz, W. 1952: *Die Fragmente der Vorsokratiker*, 10th edn. Berlin: Weidmann.

Dummett, Michael 1972: Truth (first published 1959). In Michael Dummett, *Truth and Other Enigmas*, London: Duckworth, 1978, 1–24.

Dunne, J. W. 1981: *An Experiment with Time* (1st edn 1927, 3rd edn 1934). London: Papermac.

Eckern, Ulrich 1986: Quantum mechanics: is the theory applicable to macroscopic objects? *Nature*, 319, 726.

Eddington, Sir Arthur 1935: *The Nature of the Physical World* (1st edn 1928), Everyman's Library. London: Dent.

Ehrenfest, P. 1967: Adiabatic invariants and the theory of quanta (first published 1917). In B. L. van der Waerden (ed.), *Sources of Quantum Mechanics*, Amsterdam: North-Holland, 79–93.

Einstein, A, Podolsky, B. and Rosen, N. 1970: Can quantum-mechanical description of physical reality be considered complete? (first published 1935 in *Physical Review*, 47). In S. Toulmin (ed.), *Physical Reality*, Evanstone/London: Harper & Row, 122–42.

Evans, Gareth 1973: The Causal Theory of Names, I. *Proceedings of the Aristotelian Society*, supp. vol. 47, 187–208.

Evans, Gareth 1982: *The Varieties of Reference*, ed. John McDowell. Oxford: Clarendon Press.

Everett, H. 1957: 'Relative state' formulation of quantum mechanics. *Reviews of Modern Physics*, 29, 454–62.

Everett, H. 1973: The theory of the universal wave function, Ph.D. thesis, Princeton University. In B. DeWitt and N. Graham (eds), *The Many-Worlds Interpretation of Quantum Mechanics*, Princeton: Princeton University Press, 1–140.

Evers, Alex S., Berkowitz, Bruce A. and d'Avignon, D. Andre 1987: Correlation between the anaesthetic effect of halothane and saturable binding in brain. *Nature*, 328, 157–60.

Feigl, Herbert 1967: The 'Mental' and the 'Physical' (first published 1958 in *Minnesota Studies in the Philosophy of Science*, vol. 2, Minneapolis: University of Minnesota Press). In Herbert Feigl, *The 'Mental' and the 'Physical'*, Minneapolis: University of Minnesota Press, 3–131.

Flew, Antony 1961: *Hume's Philosophy of Belief*. London: Routledge & Kegan Paul.

Fodor, Jerry A. 1987: *Psychosemantics: The Problem of Meaning in the Philosophy of Mind*. Cambridge, MA: Bradford Books/MIT Press.

Foster, John 1982: *The Case for Idealism*. London: Routledge & Kegan Paul.

Foster, Sara and Brown, Harvey R. 1988: On a recent attempt to define the interpretation basis in the many worlds interpretation of quantum mechanics. *International Journal of Theoretical Physics*, 27, 1507–31.

Frege, Gottlob, 1966: On sense and reference (first published in German 1892), tr. Max Black. In Peter Geach and Max Black (eds), *Translations from the Writings of Gottlob Frege*, Oxford: Basil Blackwell, 56–78.

Fröhlich, H. 1968: Long-range coherence in biological systems. *International Journal of Quantum Chemistry*, 2, 641–9.

Fröhlich, H. 1986: Coherent excitation in active biological systems. In F. Gutman and H. Keyzer (eds), *Modern Bioelectrochemistry*, New York: Plenum, 241–61.

Gazzaniga, M. S. 1967: The split brain in man. *Scientific American*, 217 (August), 24–9.

Geschwind, Norman and Miller, Jonathan 1983: Dialogue with Norman Geschwind. In Jonathan Miller, *States of Mind*, New York: Pantheon Books, 116–34.

Geschwind, Norman and Galaburda, Albert M. 1987: *Cerebral Lateralization: Biological Mechanisms, Associations and Pathology*. Cambridge, MA: MIT Press.

Gibbins, P. F. 1985: Are mental events in space-time? *Analysis*, 45, 145–7.

Gibbins, P. F. 1987: *Particles and Paradoxes*. Cambridge: Cambridge University Press.

Gierer, Alfred 1988: Physics, life and mind: scope and limitation of science. Unpublished paper, delivered at the Second European Conference in Science and Religion, The University of Twente, Enschede, the Netherlands, 10–13 March, 1988, 7.

Gillespie, Daniel T. 1973: *A Quantum Mechanics Primer*. London: International Textbook Company.

Green, Michael B. 1985: Unification of forces and particles in superstring theories. *Nature*, 314, 409–14.

Green, Michael B. 1986: Superstrings. *Scientific American*, 255 (September), 44–56.

Gribbin, John 1984: *In Search of Schrödinger's Cat*. London: Wildwood House.

Hardin, C. L. 1984: A new look at color. *American Philosophical Quarterly*, 21, 125–33.

Hebb, D. O. 1949: *The Organization of Behaviour*. New York: Wiley.

Held, R. and Shattuck, S. R. 1971: Color- and edge-sensitive channels in the human visual system: tuning for orientation. *Science* 174, 314–16.

Hilgard, Ernest R. 1986: *Divided Consciousness: Multiple Controls in Human Thought and Action*. New York: Wiley.

Hirsch, Eli 1986: Metaphysical necessity and conceptual truth. In Peter A. French, Theodore E. Uehling, Jr and Howard K. Wettstein (eds), *Midwest Studies in Philosophy, vol. XI: Studies in Essentialism*, Minneapolis: University of Minnesota Press, 243–56.

Hopcroft, John E. 1984: Turing machines. *Scientific American*, 250 (May), 70–80.

Hopfield, J. J. 1982: Neural networks and physical systems with emergent collective computational abilities. *Proceedings of the National Academy of Sciences (USA)*, 70, 2554–8.

Hubel, David H. and Wiesel, Torsten N. 1979: Brain mechanisms of vision. *Scientific American*, 241 (September), 130–44.

Hubel, David H. and Livingstone, Margaret S. 1985: Complex-unoriented cells in a subregion of primate area 18. *Nature*, 315, 325–7.

Innocenti, Giorgio 1987: Conversation with Colin Blakemore, recorded at IBRO Second World Congress of Neuroscience in Budapest. *Science Now*, BBC Radio 4, 14 November.

Jackson, Frank 1982: Epiphenomenal qualia. *Philosophical Quarterly*, 32, 127–36.

Jammer, Max 1974: *The Philosophy of Quantum Mechanics: The Interpretations of Quantum Mechanics in Historical Perspective*. New York: Wiley.

Janik, Allan and Toulmin, Stephen 1973: *Wittgenstein's Vienna*. London: Weidenfeld & Nicolson.

Jauch, J. M. 1968: *Foundations of Quantum Mechanics*. Reading, MA: Addison-Wesley.

Jeans, Sir James, 1934: *The New Background of Science*, 2nd edn. Cambridge: Cambridge University Press.

Johnson-Laird, P. N. 1983: *Mental Models*. Cambridge: Cambridge University Press.

Johnson-Laird, P. N. 1987: Connections and controversy. *Nature*, 330, 12–13.

Johnson-Laird, P. N. 1988: How is meaning mentally represented? *International Social Science Journal*, 115, 45–59.

Kochen, S. and Specker, E. P. 1967: The problem of hidden variables in quantum mechanics. *Journal of Mathematics and Mechanics*, 17, 59–87.

Kripke, Saul 1980: *Naming and Necessity* (first published 1972 in D. Davidson and G. Harman (eds), *Semantics of Natural Language*, Dordrecht: Reidel). Oxford: Basil Blackwell.

Land, E. 1977: The retinex theory of color vision. *Scientific American*, 237 (December), 108–28.

Leggett, A. J. 1980: Macroscopic quantum systems and the quantum theory of measurement. *Progress of Theoretical Physics* (Suppl.), 69, 80–100.

Leibniz, G. W. F. 1898: *Monadology* (written 1714). In Robert Latta (tr./ed.), *Leibniz: Monadology and Other Philosophical Writings*, Oxford: Clarendon Press.

Levinson, E. and Sekuler, R. 1980: A two-dimensional analysis of direction-specific adaptation. *Vision Research*, 20, 103–8.

Lewis, Clarence Irving 1956: *Mind and the World Order* (1st edn 1929). New York: Dover Publications.

Loar, Brian 1982: *Mind and Meaning*. Cambridge: Cambridge University Press.

Lockwood, Michael 1981: What *was* Russell's neutral monism? In Peter A. French, Theodore E. Uehling, Jr and Howard K. Wettstein (eds), *Midwest*

Studies in Philosophy, vol. VI: The Foundations of Analytic Philosophy, Minneapolis: University of Minnesota Press, 143–58.

Lockwood, Michael 1984a: Einstein and the identity theory. *Analysis*, 44.1, 22–5.

Lockwood, Michael 1984b: Reply to Gordon. *Analysis*, 44.2, 127–8.

Lockwood, Michael 1985: Einstein, Gibbins and the unity of time. *Analysis*, 45.3, 148–50.

Long, A. A. and Sedley, D. N. 1987: *The Hellenistic Philosophers*, vol. 1. Cambridge: Cambridge University Press.

Luria, A. R. 1973: *The Working Brain*. Harmondsworth: Penguin Books.

McDowell, John 1986: Experience. A pair of lectures delivered to the Philosophy Department at Harvard University in April 1986.

MacKay, D. M. and MacKay Valerie 1982: Explicit dialogue between left and right half-systems of split brains. Nature, 295, 690–91.

Mackie, J. L. 1980: *Hume's Moral Theory*. London: Routledge & Kegan Paul.

Margenau, Herbert 1950: *The Nature of Physical Reality*. New York: McGraw-Hill.

Marshall, I. N. 1989: Consciousness and Bose–Einstein condensates. *New Ideas in Psychology*, 7, 73–83.

Maxwell, Grover 1978: Rigid designators and mind–brain identity. In *Minnesota Studies in the Philosophy of Science*, vol. IX, Minneapolis: University of Minnesota Press, 365–403.

Maxwell, Nicholas 1972: A new look at the quantum mechanical problem of measurement. *American Journal of Physics*, 40, 1431–5.

Maxwell, Nicholas 1988: Quantum propension theory: a testable resolution of the wave/particle dilemma. *British Journal of the Philosophy of Science*, 39 (1988), 1–50. See also Unsigned, 1987.

Millikan, Ruth Garrett 1984: *Language, Thought, and Other Biological Categories: New Foundations for Realism*. Cambridge, MA: Bradford Books/ MIT Press.

Millikan, Ruth Garrett 1986: Thoughts without laws; cognitive science with content. *Philosophical Review*, 95, 47–80.

Minsky, M. 1975: A framework for representing knowledge. In P. H. Winston (ed.), *The Psychology of Computer Vision*, New York: McGraw-Hill, 211–77.

Mishkin, Mortimer, and Appenzeller, Tim 1987: The anatomy of memory. *Scientific American*, 256 (June), 62–71.

Moore, G. E. 1942: A reply to my critics. In Paul Arthur Schilpp (ed.), *The Philosophy of G. E. Moore*, Library of Living Philosophers, La Salle, IL: Open Court, 629–31.

Moore, G. E. 1953: *Some Main Problems of Philosophy*. London: George Allen & Unwin.

Murdoch, Iris 1959: *The Bell* (1st edn 1958). London: Chatto & Windus.

Nagel, Thomas 1979a: Brain bisection and the unity of consciousness (first published 1971 in *Synthese*, 20). In Thomas Nagel, *Mortal Questions*, Cambridge: Cambridge University Press, 147–64.

Nagel, Thomas 1979b: What is it like to be a bat? (First published 1974 in *Philosophical Review*, 83.) In Thomas Nagel, *Mortal Questions*, Cambridge: Cambridge University Press, 165–80.

Nagel, Thomas 1986: *The View From Nowhere*. New York/Oxford: Oxford University Press.

Ogden, C. K. and Richards, I. A. 1949: *The Meaning of Meaning*, 10th edn (1st edn 1923). London: Routledge & Kegan Paul.

Padmanabhan, Thanu 1987: Quantum cosmology – science of Genesis? *New Scientist*, 115 (24 September), 60–3.

Page, Don N. and Wootters, William K. 1983: Evolution without evolution: dynamics described by stationary observables. *Physical Review* D, 27, 2885–92.

Parfit, Derek 1984: *Reasons and Persons*. Oxford: Clarendon Press.

Pauli, W. 1933: Die allgemeinen Prinzipien der Wellenmechanik. In H. Geiger and K. Scheel (eds), *Handbuch der Physik*, 2nd edn, vol. 24, Berlin: Springer, 1–278.

Peacocke, Christopher 1979: *Holistic Explanation*. Oxford: Clarendon Press.

Pellionisz, A. and Llinas, R. 1985: Tensor network theory of the metaorganization of functional geometries in the central nervous system. *Neuroscience*, 16, 245–73.

Penrose, R. 1979: Singularities and time-asymmetry. In S. W. Hawking and W. Israel (eds), *General relativity: An Einstein centenary survey*, Cambridge: Cambridge University Press, 581–638.

Penrose, R. 1985: Quantum gravity and state vector reduction. In R. Penrose and C. J. Isham (eds), *Quantum Concepts in Space and Time*, Oxford: Oxford University Press, 129–46.

Penrose, R. 1986: Big bangs, black holes and 'time's arrow'. In Raymond Flood and Michael Lockwood (eds), *The Nature of Time*, Oxford: Basil Blackwell, 36–62.

Penrose, R. 1987: *Minds, Machines and Mathematics*. In Colin Blakemore and Susan Greenfield (eds), *Mindwaves*, Oxford: Basil Blackwell, 259–76.

Petersen, S. E., Fox, P. T., Posner, M. I., Mintun, M. and Raichle, M. E. 1988: Positron emission tomographic studies of the cortical anatomy of single-word processing. *Nature*, 331, 585–9.

Pinker, S. and Prince, A. 1987: On language and connectionism: analysis of a parallel distributed processing model of language acquisition. Center for Cognitive Science, MIT.

Pitowsky, I., 1985: Discussion: quantum mechanics and value definiteness. *Philosophy of Science*, 52, 154–6.

Plumer, Gilbert 1985: The myth of the specious present. *Mind*, 94, 19–35.

Pohl, W. 1973: Dissociation of spatial discrimination deficits following frontal and parietal lesions in monkeys. *Journal of Comparative and Physiological Psychology*, 82, 227–39.

Popper, K. R. and Eccles, J. C. 1977: *The Self and Its Brain*. Berlin: Springer.

Pribram, K. H. 1971: *Languages of the Brain*. Englewood Cliffs, NJ: Prentice-Hall.

Proust, Marcel 1973: *Remembrance of Things Past, vol. 1, Swann's Way, part. I* (1st edn 1913), tr. R. Scott Moncrieff. London: Chatto & Windus.

Puccetti, R. 1973: Brain bisection and personal identity. *British Journal for the Philosophy of Science*, 24, 339–55.

Putnam, Hilary 1971: The nature of mental states. In David Rosenthal (ed.), *Materialism and the Mind–Body Problem*, Englewood Cliffs, NJ: Prentice-Hall.

Putnam, Hilary 1975: The meaning of 'meaning'. In Hilary Putnam, *Mind, Language and Reality: Philosophical Papers, vol. 2*, Cambridge: Cambridge University Press, 215–71.

Putnam, Hilary 1979: Time and physical geometry (first published 1967 in *Journal of Philosophy*, 64). In Hilary Putnam, *Mathematics, Matter and Method: Philosophical Papers, vol. 1*, Cambridge: Cambridge University Press, 198–205.

Ramachandran, V. S. and Gregory, R. L. 1978: Does colour provide an input to human motion perception? *Nature*, 275, 55–6.

Ramachandran, V. S. 1987: Interaction between colour and motion in human vision. *Nature*, 328, 645–7.

Robinson, Howard 1982: *Matter and Sense*. Cambridge: Cambridge University Press, 4.

Rorty, Richard 1971: In defense of eliminative materialism (first published 1970 in *Review of Metaphysics*, 24). In D. M. Rosenthal (ed.), *Materialism and the Mind–Body Problem*, Englewood Cliffs, NJ: Prentice-Hall.

Rosenbaum, D. M. 1969: Super Hilbert space and the quantum-mechanical time operator. *Journal of Mathematical Physics*, 10, 1127–44.

Rumelhart, D. E. 1975. Notes on a schema for stories. In D. G. Bobrow and A. Collins (eds), *Representation and Understanding*, New York: Academic Press, 211–36.

Rumelhart, D. E., Hinton, G. E. and Williams, R. J. 1986a: Learning representations by back-propagating errors. *Nature*, 323, 533–6.

Rumelhart, D. E., Smolensky, P., McClelland, J. L. and Hinton, G. E. 1986b: Schemata and sequential thought processes in PDP models. In D. E. Rumelhart, J. L. McClelland and PDP Research Group, *Parallel Distributed Processing: Explorations in the Microstructure of Cognition, vol. 2 Psychological and Biological Models*, Cambridge, MA: Bradford Books/MIT Press, 7–57.

Rumelhart, D. E. and McClelland, J. L. 1986: On learning the past tenses of English verbs. In D. E. Rumelhart, J. L. McClelland and PDP Research Group, *Parallel Distributed Processing: Explorations in the Microstructure of Cognition, vol. 2 Psychological and Biological Models*, Cambridge, MA: Bradford Books/MIT Press, 216–71.

Russell, Bertrand 1915: On the experience of time. *Monist*, 25, 212–33.

Russell, Bertrand 1927: *The Analysis of Matter*. London: Kegan Paul.

Russell, Bertrand 1949: *The Analysis of Mind* (1st edn. 1921). London: George Allen & Unwin.

Russell, Bertrand 1959: *My Philosophical Development*, London: George Allen & Unwin.

Russell, Bertrand 1962: *An Inquiry into Meaning and Truth* (1st edn 1940). Harmondsworth: Penguin Books.

Russell, Bertrand 1963: Knowledge by acquaintance and knowledge by description (first published in *Proceedings of the Aristotelian Society* for 1910–11). In Bertrand Russell, *Mysticism and Logic*, London: Unwin Books, 152–67.

Ryle, Gilbert 1954: *Dilemmas: The Tarner Lectures 1953*. Cambridge: Cambridge University Press.

Sagan, Carl, 1985: *Contact: A Novel.* New York: Simon & Schuster.

Schopenhauer, Arthur 1969: *The World as Will and Representation* (1st edn 1819, 2nd edn 1844, 3rd edn 1859), 2 vols, tr. E. F. J. Payne. New York: Dover Publications.

Schrödinger, Erwin 1935: Die gegenwartige Situation in der Quantenmechanik. *Die Wissenschaften*, 23, 807–12, 824–8, 844–9.

Schrödinger, Erwin, 1967: *Mind and Matter: The Tarner Lectures 1956* (first published 1958). In *What is Life?* and *Mind and Matter*, Cambridge: Cambridge University Press, 97–178.

Searle, John R. 1980: Minds, brains and programs, with open peer commentaries. *Behavioral and Brain Sciences*, 3, 417–57.

Searle, John R. 1984: *Minds, Brains and Science* (1984 Reith Lectures, first published in *The Listener*). London: British Broadcasting Corporation.

Sewell, G. L. 1986: *Quantum Theory of Collective Phenomena*. Oxford: Oxford University Press.

Shipp, S. and Zeki, S. 1985: Segregation of pathways leading from area V2 to areas V4 and V5 of macaque monkey visual cortex. *Nature*, 315, 322–4.

Shoemaker, Sidney 1975: Functionalism and qualia. *Philosophical Studies*, 27, 271–315.

Shoemaker, Sidney 1982: The inverted spectrum. *Journal of Philosophy*, 79, 357–81.

Smart, J. J. C. 1959: Sensations and brain processes. *Philosophical Review*, 68, 141–56.

Smart, J. J. C. 1963: *Philosophy and Scientific Realism*. London: Routledge & Kegan Paul.

Smith, Gerrit J. and Weingard, Robert 1987: A relativistic formulation of the Einstein–Podolski–Rosen paradox. *Foundations of Physics*, 17, 149–71.

Smith, Peter and Jones, O. R. 1986: *Philosophy of Mind: An Introduction*. Cambridge: Cambridge University Press.

Sperry, R. W. 1966: Brain bisections and mechanisms of conflict. In J. Eccles (ed.), *Brain and Conscious Experience*, Berlin: Springer, 298–313.

Sperry, R. W. 1968a: Hemisphere deconnection and unity in conscious awareness. *American Psychologist*, 23, 723–33.

Sperry, R. W. 1968b: Mental unity following surgical disconnection of the cerebral hemispheres. In *The Harvey Lecture Series*, 62, New York: Academic, 293–323.

Spiller, Timothy P., and Clark, T. D. 1986a: Quantum behaviour of super-conducting rings. *Nature*, 321, 476.

Spiller, Timothy P., and Clark, T. D. 1986b: SQUIDs: macroscopic quantum objects. *New Scientist*, 4 December, 36–40.

Sprigge, Timothy L. S. 1971: Final causes, I. *Proceedings of the Aristotelian Society*, supp. vol. 45, 149–70.

Stich, Stephen C. 1983: *From Folk Psychology to Cognitive Science: The Case*

Against Belief. Cambridge, MA: Bradford Books/MIT Press.

Stoppard, Tom 1972: *Jumpers*. London: Faber & Faber.

Swinburne, Richard 1987: The structure of the soul. Inaugural Lecture as Nolloth Professor of the Christian Religion in the University of Oxford, delivered 18 October 1985. In Arthur Peaçocke and Grant Gillett (eds), *Persons and Personality*, Oxford: Basil Blackwell, 33–47.

Turing, Alan, 1936: On computable numbers, with an application to the *Entscheidungsproblem*. *Proceedings of the London Mathematical Society*, Second Series, 42, 230–65.

Tye, Michael 1986: The subjective qualities of experience. *Mind*, 95, 1–17.

Unsigned 1987: Particles decide the fate of Schrödinger's cat. *New Scientist*, 115 (2 July), 34.

Von Neumann, J. 1955: *Mathematical Foundations of Quantum Mechanics* (1st German edn 1932). Princeton, NJ: Princeton University Press.

Walker, E. H. 1970: The nature of consciousness. *Mathematical Biosciences*, 7, 131–78.

Warnock, G. J. 1978: The causal theory of perception: a reply to Rice. Talk given to the Philosophical Society in Oxford.

Weingard, Robert 1977: Relativity and the spatiality of mental events. *Philosophical Studies*, 31, 279–84.

Weiskrantz, L., Warrington, E. K., Sanders, M. D. and Marshall, J. 1974: Visual capacity in the hemianopic field following a restricted occipital ablation. *Brain*, 97, 709–28.

Weiskrantz, L. 1986: *Blindsight: A Case Study and Implications*, Oxford Psychology Series. Oxford: Oxford University Press.

Wigner, E. P. 1962: Remarks on the mind–body question. In I. J. Good (ed.), *The Scientist Speculates: An Anthology of Partly-Baked Ideas*, London: Heinemann, 284–302.

Wigner, E. P. 1963: The problem of measurement. *American Journal of Physics*, 31, 6–15.

Wilkes, Kathleen V. 1978: Consciousness and commissurotomy, *Philosophy*, 53, 185–99.

Windsor, Colin 1988: Recalling memories. *Physics Bulletin*, 39, 16–18.

Wittgenstein, Ludwig 1958: *Philosophical Investigations* (1st edn 1953), 2nd edn, tr. G. E. M. Anscombe. Oxford: Basil Blackwell.

Wittgenstein, Ludwig, 1963: *Tractatus Logico-Philosophicus* (first German edition in *Annalen der Naturphilosophie*, 1921), tr. D. F. Pears and B. F. McGuinness. London: Routledge & Kegan Paul.

Wittgenstein, Ludwig, 1969: *The Blue and Brown Books* (1st edn 1958), 2nd edn. Oxford: Basil Blackwell, 1969.

Wittgenstein, Ludwig, 1967: *Zettel*, ed. G. E. M. Anscombe and G. H. von Wright, tr. G. E. M. Anscombe. Oxford: Basil Blackwell.

Young, J. Z. 1978: *Programs of the Brain*. Oxford: Oxford University Press.

Zeki, S. 1974: The mosaic organization of the visual cortex in the monkey. In R. Bellairs and E. S. Gray (eds), *Essays on the Nervous System: a Festschrift for Professor J. Z. Young*, Oxford: Oxford University Press.

Zeki, S. 1983: Colour coding in the cerebral cortex: the reaction of cells in monkey visual cortex to wavelengths and colours. *Neuroscience* 9, 741–65.

Glossary

Any term that appears in **bold type** in a glossary entry has an entry of its own. Other technical terms are *italicized*.

action potential (nerve impulse, spike) A wave of electrical polarization which passes along the **axon** when a **neuron** fires. Specifically, the action potential takes the form of a local and transitory reversal of the voltage gradient across the wall of the axon (which, in the cell's resting state is positive on the outside and negative on the inside), in consequence of an exchange of potassium and sodium ions. The action potential can be triggered or inhibited by the absorption of **transmitter substances** by the cell's **dendrites**.

algorithm A mechanical procedure for solving some problem, such as could be embodied in a computer program.

antirealism The view that the meaning of a **proposition** is to be given in terms of its *assertibility-conditions*, the conditions under which one would be justified in asserting it, rather than the conditions under which it would be true or false. The antirealist rejects the idea of *verification-transcendent* **truth-conditions**, conditions which could be satisfied, even though there was, in principle, no way of establishing that they were. See **logical positivism, realism**.

awareness See **consciousness**.

axon Long fibre projecting from the **central body** of a **neuron**, along which there passes a wave of electrical polarization whenever the cell fires: the nerve impulse or **action potential**. The axon emits **transmitter substances** that are absorbed by the **dendrites** of neighbouring cells, at junctions known as **synapses**. See **action potential**.

base firing rate Frequency with which a **neuron** fires spontaneously, that is, when it is not subject to **excitatory** or **inhibitory** influences from neighbouring neurons.

basis, vector A set of vectors, such that any arbitrary vector can be represented as a **linear combination** of those in the set. See **eigenbasis**.

behaviourism In psychology, *methodological* behaviourism is the view that the task of the psychologist is merely to establish laws relating sensory input (stimuli) to behavioural output (responses), and that the psychologist should eschew the study of mental states, as such. In philosophy, *logical* behaviourism is a form of **reductionism**, according to which the meaning of mental state ascriptions consists entirely in what they imply as regards actual or possible behaviour; so that such ascriptions could, in principle, be translated into sentences making reference only to behaviour and physical circumstances.

blind-sight The ability to discriminate or identify visual stimuli presented to parts of the retina from which, owing to brain damage, the subject receives no conscious visual impressions.

boson A particle that obeys *Bose–Einstein* statistics. Given two identical bosons, *A* and *B*, and two states 1 and 2, there are three, rather than four, distinct possible configurations: both particles in state 1, both particles in state 2, and one particle in state 1 and the other in state 2. No distinction can be made between the configuration in which *A* is in state 1, while *B* is in state 2, and the configuration in which *B* is in state 1, while *A* is in state 2.

Cartesian Pertaining to the views of Descartes. In this book, 'Cartesian' mainly refers to Descartes's conception of the mind as directly acquainted only with its own private contents, with its apparently problematic implications for our knowledge of the external world.

causal realism The theory that, in perception, we are directly acquainted only with certain private mental items (variously known as *ideas, impressions, percepts, sense data*) which are caused by external objects and from which the presence of these objects is, in effect, inferred. Also known, especially in the version espoused by John Locke, as *representative realism*, on the basis that our sense impressions are to be thought of as *representing* the material objects that give rise to them.

central body That part of a **neuron** that contains the cell nucleus and from which the **axon** and **dendrites** project.

cerebral cortex The grey matter on the outer layer of the **cerebral hemispheres**, where the **central bodies** of the **neurons** of the *cerebrum* are mostly located. This is where, in human beings, most high-level processing of information takes place.

cerebral hemispheres Two halves of the *cerebrum*, linked by the **corpus callosum**.

classical In this book 'classical' usually means pre-quantum-mechanical, as in *classical physics*. Occasionally, it is used to mean 'pre-relativity'.

collapse of the wave function. See **state vector reduction.**

commissurotomy Operation of cutting the **corpus callosum** (q.v.).

common-sense realism The view that we are directly acquainted, in perception, with external material objects. See **causal realism, naive realism.**

commuting observables (observable operators) See **compatible observables**.

compatible observables The members of a set of compatible observables are all *simultaneously measureable*: repeated measurement of the same observable, with a negligible intervening time interval, yields the same result regardless of what other observables in the set are measured in the interim. Two observables are compatible if and only if the corresponding observable operators *commute*; i.e. the effect of applying each operator in turn is the same, regardless of the order of application.

complex cell Hubel and Weisel refer to a cell in the visual cortex as complex, if it responds to a stimulus of the appropriate type – if it is an **orientation cell**, a bar or edge, in the appropriate orientation – wherever, over a wide area of its **receptive field**, it is presented. See **simple cell**.

complex conjugate Given a complex number of the form a + bi, its complex conjugate is the corresponding number of the form a − bi.

complex number A number of the form a + bi, where a and b are **real numbers** and i is the square root of minus one.

conceptual analysis A philosophical methodology which concentrates on exploring the logical structure of, and logical relations between, key concepts, looking for philosophically illuminating definitions or *analyses*. See **linguistic analysis**.

connectionism That approach to understanding the workings of the brain which is based on **parallel distributed processing** or **neural networks**.

consciousness (sentience, awareness) Something is conscious (at a particular time) if there's an answer to the question what it is like to be that thing (at the time in question). Human beings are conscious when they're awake, or asleep and dreaming, but not when they're dreamlessly asleep or in a coma. Whether a crayfish, say, is conscious depends on such things as whether it ever feels anything, not on its behavioural responses, which could be variously interpreted.

corpus callosum Bundle of nerve fibres linking the two **cerebral hemispheres**.

correlated systems The states of two quantum-mechanical systems are said to be correlated, if measuring an **observable** on one system is tantamount to measuring some corresponding observable on the other. This kind of correlation was the basis of the famous *Einstein–Podolsky–Rosen* (EPR) thought experiment, in which a measurement of the position or momentum of one particle enables one to predict with certainty the result of carrying out a measurement of position or momentum on the other. Strictly speaking, when one has two correlated systems, only the combined system can be said to be in a definite quantum state; what one has here is a kind of *quantum holism*.

dendrites Branching fibres projecting from the **central body** of a **neuron**, that respond to **transmitter substances** emitted by the **axons** of other cells. Thus, the dendrites are the input fibres of a neuron, just as the axon is the output fibre. See **axon**.

deterministic Said of a process, theory or law. A process is deterministic, if later stages of the process are wholly determined by earlier stages and the laws by which the process is governed. **Classical** mechanics is said to be a deterministic theory. This is because, according to classical mechanics, the state of any *closed* system, at any one time, and the forces operating, jointly determine the state of the system at any other time during which it remains closed (i.e. free from outside influence). A law is said to be deterministic if, as applied to a closed system, it makes later states a function of earlier states; deterministic laws are thus to be contrasted with *probabilistic* or *statistical* laws, which say only that, if a system is in such-and-such a state at one time, then there is a certain probability of its being in such-and-such another state at a specified later time.

eigenbasis The set of **basis** vectors, consisting of all the **eigenvectors** of an **observable**, is known as the eigenbasis of the observable. See **basis**.

eigenvalue/vector Corresponding to everything one might measure or observe on a quantum-mechanical system (that is to say, every **observable**) there is a set of possible results or outcomes of the measurement. These are known as eigenvalues. On the conventional view, an observation or **measurement** precipitates a **reduction of the state vector** (collapse of the **wave function**) to a state corresponding to the particular result obtained. This is known as an *eigenstate* of the measured observable. When a quantum-mechanical system is in an eigenstate of a particular observable, measurement of that observable is certain to yield the corresponding eigenvalue. See **state vector reduction, observable**.

eliminative materialism The view that our common-sense ascriptions, to ourselves and others, of mental states and processes are, strictly speaking, *false*, because they embody a mistaken theory. According to the eliminative materialist, our common-sense psychological vocabulary should, if we wish to speak truly, be discarded in favour of the language of neuroscience, or whatever.

epistemology The philosophical theory of knowledge, of what we can know and how we can know it. Hence *epistemological* or *epistemic*: having to do with knowledge or the theory of knowledge.

equivalence relation An equivalence relation is one that is **transitive, symmetric** and **reflexive** (q.v.). In the domain of numbers, 'equals' is an equivalence relation.

excitatory A **neuron** is said to have an **excitatory** influence on another if, when it fires, it increases the tendency of the other cell to fire. See **inhibitory**.

expectation value The expectation value of an **observable**, with respect to a particular quantum state, is the average of the values one would obtain, if one repeatedly measured the observable on systems prepared in that same state. If one imagines a cumulative total being kept of the values obtained, then the expectation value is the *limit* to which the ratio of this total to the number of trials would tend, as the number of trials approached infinity.

exponential time If n is the parameter on which the difficulty of a mathematical task depends – the size of the number serving as input, the number of inputs, or whatever – then the task is said to run in exponential time if, for some number m, and a suitable choice of **Turing machine** program or **algorithm**, the number of steps required to complete the task is always less than or equal to m^n. Tasks that run only in exponential time or more are generally considered *intractable*, for large values of n. See **polynomial time**.

firing A **neuron** is said to fire, when an **action potential** (*spike, nerve impulse*) passes along its **axon**. See **action potential, axon**.

functionalism The theory that what makes a state of a system a *mental* state of a particular type, with the introspective features that it has, is the part it plays in the overall functioning of the system in question. The idea is that it is its causal–functional *relations* to other states of the system, and ultimately to its inputs and outputs, that make a state a mental state at all, and the type of mental state that it is. Hence, according to the functionalist, it suffices for a system to possess mental states that it have the right kind of causal–functional structure, regardless of how that structure is concretely realized (e.g., in silicon or in protoplasm).

Heisenberg uncertainty principle See **uncertainty principle**.

Hermitian operator See **observable**.

hidden variable theories Hidden variable theories attempt to interpret or modify quantum mechanics in such a way as to make the outcome of a **measurement** on a quantum-mechanical system stand in a **deterministic** relationship to the state of the system and the state of the measuring apparatus at the time of the measurement. This contrasts with the orthodox interpretation, according to which, in general, one can only make probabilistic predictions about the outcome of a measurement, given knowledge of the current state of the system. According to such theories the description of a quantum-mechanical state in terms of the **state vector** or **wave function** is essentially incomplete; the hidden variables are intended to embody the further specification that is needed to make it into a complete description.

Hilbert space An infinite dimensional *complex vector space*, used as the state space for quantum-mechanical systems. (A complex vector space is one where the **inner product** (q.v.) of two vectors is in general a **complex number**.) Hilbert space was originally conceived, prior to the advent of quantum mechanics, as an abstract space whose 'vectors' were *complex functions of a real variable* – functions which take real numbers as input and issue complex numbers as output. And it is the fact that quantum-mechanical **wave functions** (q.v.) are themselves complex functions of real variables that led to the adoption of Hilbert space as a state space for quantum mechanics. It is, however, very common nowadays to think simply in terms of state vectors, rather than wave functions *per se*, which would imply a particular way of mathematically representing these vectors.

hue The variety of colour: red, blue, orange, etc. Each colour of the spectrum is of a distinct hue. Light and dark blue, however, and likewise yellow and brown, are of the same hue, differing in **luminance**. See **luminance, saturation**.

idealism The theory, associated especially with George Berkeley, according to which material objects have no reality beyond the *ideas* (sense impressions) that occur in perception. Berkeley asserts that material objects just are 'congeries [clusters] of ideas' (including God's – Berkeley invokes an all-perceiving deity, in order to avoid the consequence that objects constantly go in and out of existence depending on whether anyone is perceiving them).

identity theory A form of **materialism**, according to which mental states and events *are* – are the very same things as – certain states and events in the brain.

imaginary number A number that is a multiple of i, the square root of minus one. See **complex number**.

inhibitory A neuron is said to have an inhibitory influence on another if, when it fires, it decreases the tendency of the other cell to fire. See **excitatory**.

inner product In Euclidean space, the inner product of two vectors is equal to the length of the one times the **projected length** of the other. The inner product of two vectors in **Hilbert space** may be thought of by analogy with this, save for the facts (i) that the inner product of two Hilbert space vectors is in general a **complex number**, and (ii) that in Hilbert space, reversing the order of the vectors in the inner product, rather than making no difference to the value as it does in Euclidean space, has the effect of replacing the original value by its **complex conjugate**.

intentionality A key feature of mental states (according to some, their defining feature) is that they are object-directed: John is afraid of the forthcoming exam; he is in love with Susan; he believes in God; and so on. This object-directedness is what is meant by intentionality (from *intendere*, in Latin, which means to aim a bow); and the objects of our mental states (which need not exist in reality) are known as *intentional objects*.

light cone The surface defined by the space-time paths of all possible light rays through a given space-time point, P. The light cone divides the space-time continuum, relative to P, into three regions: the region outside the light cone, sometimes known as the *absolute elsewhere*, the *forward light cone* or *absolute future* and the *backward light cone* or *absolute past*. According to the orthodox view of the matter, events occurring at P can be causally affected only by events in the absolute past, and can affect only events in the absolute future. The existence of *tachyons*, however (hypothetical faster-than-light particles), would conflict with this conventional wisdom; and it is arguable that an instantaneous, physical *collapse of the wave function* or **state vector reduction** would do so too.

linear combination Given a set of vectors $v_1, \ldots, v_n$, one can multiply them, respectively, by any arbitrarily chosen numbers, or *coefficients*, $c_1, \ldots, c_n$, and add the resultant vectors to yield the new vector $c_1v_1 + c_2v_2 + \ldots + c_nv_n$. This new vector is then said to be a linear combination of the original vectors, $v_1, \ldots, v_n$. A quantum-mechanical **superposition** of states is represented by a corresponding linear combination of the **Hilbert space** vectors representing the states that figure in the superposition. Of particular interest is the representation of a **state vector** as a linear combination of the **eigenvectors** of some observable. For then the **square moduli** of the coefficients are proportional to the probabilities of getting the corresponding **eigenvalues**, when the observable is measured on a system whose state is represented by the state vector. (The square moduli are *equal* to these probabilities, if the state vector is *normalized*, i.e. has a **norm** of one.) See **superposition**.

linguistic analysis A philosophical methodology which concentrates on the logical analysis of philosophically problematic words and sentences, and the way we use them. It seeks illumination on the mind–body problem, for example, by examining the way we use psychological and physical vocabulary; and on the problem of free will, by examining our use of such terms as 'can', 'free', 'responsible' and so on. See **conceptual analysis**, which comes to much the same thing.

logical positivism A philosophical school (prominent in the 1930s and 1940s), whose most characteristic tenet was that a sentence is meaningful only to the extent that it admits of being verified or falsified: the *verification principle*. Some positivists held that the meaning of a sentence *consists* in its method of verification/falsification; they would take the content of a theory to consist in its observational consequences: what observational predictions it made, for given observational input. Hence *positivist*. See **antirealism**.

luminance Lightness–darkness of a colour. See hue, saturation.

materialism The view that, as regards mind and body, there exist only the body and bodily states. Mental states do not exist over and above brain (or other bodily) states; the mind does not exist *in addition to* the body. See **physicalism**.

maximal experience See **phenomenal perspective**.

measurement, quantum-mechanical On the conventional view, a quantum-mechanical measurement involves (i) a **measurement interaction** between the observer or some instrument and the *object system* (the quantum-mechanical system under investigation), and (ii) collapse of the **state vector** or **wave function** of the object system into an *eigenstate* of the observable being measured. See **eigenvalue/vector, measurement interaction, observable**.

measurement interaction Quantum-mechanical interaction in which states of the two systems become **correlated**, in the quantum-mechanical sense. In a quantum-mechanical **measurement**, one of the systems will be a macroscopic measuring device, whose states, pointer readings for example, become correlated with the quantum states of the system being measured. See **correlated systems, measurement**.

mode of presentation See **sense**.

naive realism An extreme form of **common-sense realism** according to which objects are, independently of perception, just as they appear when perceived: perception serves merely to disclose, in part, the intrinsic nature of the objects perceived.

nerve impulse See **action potential.**

neural network Either (i) an actual array of interconnected **neurons,** or (ii) an array of actual or hypothetical artificial units, exemplifying **parallel distributed processing** (q.v.), and presumed to resemble, in its functioning, an array of neurons.

neuron Nerve cell (including those in the brain). Such cells have a **central body,** which includes the cell nucleus, a long output fibre, known as an **axon,** and input fibres known as **dendrites.** See **action potential, axon, dendrites.**

norm The norm of a vector, which is invariably a **real number,** is the **inner product** of the vector with itself. A *normalized vector* has a norm of one.

observable Any quantity that can be observed or measured on a quantum-mechanical system. Just as quantum-mechanical states are represented mathematically by **Hilbert space** vectors, so quantum-mechanical observables are represented by Hilbert space *operators,* specifically *Hermitian* operators. An operator is a function that takes Hilbert space vectors as input and yields, in general, different vectors as output. Those vectors whose direction is left unchanged by the application of the operator are known as **eigenvectors,** and the factor by which the length of an eigenvector is altered by application of the operator is known as the corresponding **eigenvalue.** In the case of Hermitian operators, the eigenvalues are invariably **real numbers** and the eigenvalues of an observable operator represent the various different possible outcomes of measuring the corresponding observable. See **eigenvalue/vector.**

ontological Having to do with existence or being.

opponent cells All **neurons** have a **base firing rate:** the rate at which they fire spontaneously, in the absence of external stimulation. In opponent cells, firing at above and below the base rate is used to encode different information. For example, some cells in the visual cortex fire at above base rate when the centre of their **receptive field** is illuminated, while the periphery is dark, and at below base rate when the periphery is illuminated, while the centre is dark. Other cells fire at above their base rate in the presence of red light and at below their base rate in the presence of green light, which has been proposed as an explanation of why red strikes us as a 'warm' colour, and green, by contrast, as a 'cool' colour.

orientation cell Cell in the visual cortex that responds preferentially to a bar or edge with a certain orientation, projected on to the retina in a suitable position (and also, sometimes, moving in the appropriate direction). See **simple cell, complex cell.**

other minds, problem of Philosophical problem of how we can know (if indeed we can know) what, if anything, is going on in the mind of another, given that all we have to go on are behaviour and physical circumstance. Am I justified in assuming that what another feels, thinks, or whatever, under given circumstances, is what I would feel or think, were I similarly situated and behaving in a similar fashion?

parallel distributed processing (PDP) Form of information processing involving a large number of relatively simple linked units, operating in parallel, whose level of activation is determined (in whole or in part) by the **excitatory** and **inhibitory** signals they receive from other units. PDP is proposed as a model of how the brain actually functions. For that reason, a set of such units is sometimes referred to as a **neural network**. Information is stored in such a network in the form of the *weights* of the various connections (which determine the strengths of the excitatory or inhibitory influences that each unit, when activated, has on those with which it is connected). By arranging for the weights to be constantly readjusted, in a self-correcting fashion, it is possible to 'train' neural networks to perform a variety of highly complex tasks. See **neural network**.

phase space Phase space is an abstract space, different points of which correspond to different possible states of some given physical system. Thus the instantaneous state of a single point-particle constrained to move in a straight line could be represented as a point in a two-dimensional phase space in which one dimension corresponded to the particle's momentum and the other to its position on the line. The development of the system over time would then define a path or *orbit* through the phase space.

phenomenal perspective (**maximal experience**) A total state of awareness. Given something, X, that one is *directly* or *immediately* aware of, the corresponding phenomenal perspective includes X itself and, in addition, everything that one is aware of together with X.

phenomenal qualities The qualities immediately present to consciousness in perception and sensation. Thus, red is a phenomenal quality, when considered as a feature of one's inner perceptual state, as opposed to an attribute of the external object, if any, which gives rise to it. See **secondary qualities**.

physicalism The view that, as regards mind and brain, an account of what is going on that is couched solely in the language of physics, chemistry and physiology leaves nothing out. According to the physicalist, there are no additional mental or psychological facts, that are incapable of being reduced to physical facts. See **materialism, reductionism**.

polynomial time If n is the parameter on which the difficulty of a mathematical task depends – the size of the number serving as input, the number of inputs, or whatever – then the task is said to run in polynomial time if, for some number m, and a suitable choice of **Turing machine** program or **algorithm**, the number of steps required to complete the task is always less than or equal to n^m. Whether a task runs in polynomial time is often taken as the criterion of whether it is to be considered *tractable*, for indefinitely large values of n. See **exponential time**.

positivism See **logical positivism**.

possible world Corresponding to every way things *might have been* – that is to say, everything past, present and future – there is said to be a possible world. Thus if I could have have been wearing a red tie today, rather than the grey tie I am actually wearing, then there is a possible world, distinct from the actual world, in which I am now wearing a red tie. The notion was originally proposed in the eighteenth century by Leibniz, who pictured God, at the creation, as having to decide which of the infinity of possible worlds (any one of which He *could* render actual) He was to confer reality upon. A proposition is said to be *necessary* if it is true in all possible worlds, and *contingent* if it is true in some worlds and false in others.

predicate calculus A mathematical language (invented independently by Gottlob Frege and Charles Sanders Peirce in the late nineteenth century), in which it is possible to represent the *logical form* of sentences of ordinary language. This allows one to state precise criteria for the validity of inferences, the truth of sentences of various different forms, and the logical consistency of sets of sentences.

primary qualities Such things as shape, size, motion and rest – considered by John Locke and others to be intrinsic attributes of objects, such as would figure in the fundamental laws governing their behaviour. See **secondary qualities**.

projected length Place two vectors, v_1 and v_2, tail to tail, draw a straight line coincident with v_1, and drop a perpendicular from v_2 on to this line. The projected length of v_2 on v_1 will then be the distance from the point of intersection to the tail of v_1, positive or negative according as the point of intersection is or is not on the same side of the tail as the tip of v_1. See **inner product**.

proper time In the theory of relativity, proper time, for a given object, is time as it would be measured by an *ideal clock* that moves with the object in question. The elapsed proper time between two points on an object's **world-line** is, in fact, a measure of the length, in space-time, of the corresponding segment of the world-line. (Clocks, in other words, are in the business of calibrating their own world-lines.) *Coordinate time*, by contrast, is time as measured by an ideal clock which, relative to one's choice of a *coordinate frame*, is at rest at the origin.

proposition The content of a belief, utterance or whatever, often expressed, in English, by a 'that' clause; what it is, for example, that is asserted or denied, believed or disbelieved, envisaged or entertained.

qualia The more standard term for what, in this book, are referred to as **phenomenal qualities** (q.v.).

real number Ordinary number such as 47, 13¾ or π. Contrasted with **imaginary** or **complex numbers** (q.v.).

realism The view that a **proposition** can be determinately true, false (or whatever other *truth-values* may be allowed) independently of one's capacity to establish which it is, or even, perhaps, to know what would count as establishing that. See **antirealism, logical positivism**.

receptive field The receptive field of, for example, a **neuron** in the visual system is that region of the retina appropriate stimulation of which can trigger or inhibit firing of the neuron.

reductionism A label applied to any philosophical theory which alleges that there are no facts about X over and above facts about Y, that, as regards X and Y, the Y facts are really all the facts there are. Such a theory aspires to *reduce* facts about X to facts about Y. **Behaviourism** (q.v.) and **physicalism** (q.v.) are reductionist theories which attempt to reduce psychological facts to behavioural and physiological facts, respectively.

reference The reference of a term is the object, if any, for which it stands. Thus the Albert Hall is the reference of 'the Albert Hall'; whereas it is doubtful whether 'Planet X', the supposed tenth planet (postulated to account for anomalies in the orbits of Neptune and Pluto), has a reference at all, though it certainly has a **sense** (q.v.).

reflexive A relation, R, is said to be reflexive if everything in the *domain* of the relation bears R to itself. 'No taller than' is an example of a reflexive relation.

saturation Saturation is a measure of the amount of colour. Thus the saturation of a blue patch is the amount of blue that is present. See **hue, luminance**.

scepticism The denial of the possibility of knowledge, in some realm or other. Thus, **other minds** scepticism is the view that it is impossible to know the mental states of others; external world scepticism is the view that one cannot have knowledge of reality external to one's own mind; and so on.

Schrödinger's cat, paradox of See **superposition**.

secondary qualities Such things as colour, taste, smell, sound, texture, considered by John Locke and others to consist merely of dispositions in objects (in virtue, perhaps, of the **primary qualities** of their microscopic parts) to induce, in suitably placed observers, certain sorts of sensation.

semantic Having to do with the *meaning* or *content* of linguistic or mental entities. See **syntactic**.

sense Roughly, the meaning of a term. More specifically, according to Frege's distinction between sense and reference, the sense of a term is the **mode of presentation** of its **reference**, what it stands for. Thus 'The Scarlet Pimpernel' and 'Sir Percy Blakeney', in Baroness Orczy's novel, have the same reference, since they stand for the same individual, but have different senses, since they present the reference in different ways: in one case as a gallant, intrepid rescuer of victims of the Terror, in the other as a frivolous, foppish English aristocrat. The manner in which a term presents its reference, its descriptive force or whatever, Frege calls the mode of presentation. Thus the sense of a term is to be equated with the associated mode of presentation.

sense datum See **causal realism**.

sentience See **consciousness**.

simple cell Hubel and Wiesel refer to a cell in the visual cortex as simple, if it responds to a stimulus of the appropriate type – if it is an **orientation cell**, a bar or edge of light of the appropriate orientation – only when it is presented at a specific location within its **receptive field**. See **complex cell**.

spacelike In the theory of relativity, a spacelike line is a path in space-time every two points on which are, relative to any frame of reference one cares to choose, separated by a spatial distance which *dominates* the temporal interval between them, in the sense that if they are, say, spatially separated by one light year, then they will be temporally separated by less than a year. A spacelike surface is a three-dimensional *hypersurface*, every line on which is spacelike. See **timelike**.

specious present The finite time interval ostensibly encompassed by a single total state of awareness (**phenomenal perspective** or *maximal experience*).

spike See **action potential**.

spiking frequency Frequency with which a **neuron fires**. See **action potential, base firing rate**.

square modulus The square modulus of a **complex number** is the product of that number and its **complex conjugate**. If the original number is of the form $a + bi$, then its square modulus is $a^2 + b^2$.

state vector A **Hilbert space** vector used to represent the state of a quantum-mechanical system. See **Hilbert space, wave function**.

state vector reduction (also known as *collapse of the wave function*) According to the standard interpretation of quantum mechanics, the effect of carrying out a **measurement** or observation on a quantum-mechanical system is to project the **state vector**, which in general will take the form of a **superposition** of states corresponding to the various possible results of the measurement, into just one of the states making up the superposition, i.e. that corresponding to the result of the measurement. This conception is, in a number of ways, deeply unsatisfactory, not least because quantum theory itself appears to provide no criterion as to exactly when, in the course of the measurement process, **state vector reduction** or *collapse of the wave function* takes place. See **eigenvalue/vector, observable, measurement**.

striate cortex So called because of its stripy or striated appearance. The striate cortex is the *primary visual cortex*: the *projection* area, in the *occipital lobe* of the cerebral cortex, to which visual information is projected first, before being passed to the *pre-striate* areas (V2–V5) for further processing.

strong AI (artificial intelligence) An extreme form of **functionalism** (q.v.), according to which a system can be said to possess any arbitrarily chosen mental attribute, provided only that it is running (and hence is capable of running) the right kind of program.

superposition Given a set of physical states in quantum mechanics, it is possible to multiply each state, or rather the corresponding **state vector**, by any number one likes, add the various products together, and get a new physical state, which is then known as a superposition of the state one started with. This is very odd, because the sum of an electron's being, for example, in place *a* and its being in place *b* has no obvious common-sense meaning. But from such a superposition one can read off the respective probabilities that, if one measures its position, one will find it in one place or the other. The *paradox of Schrödinger's cat* purports to show that if microscopic objects (like electrons) can be in superpositions of states, then so can *macroscopic* objects (like cats). The formalism of quantum mechanics seems to imply that if the fate of a cat in a closed chamber is made to depend, for example, on whether at least one atom of a radioactive substance decays within a given time interval, then the cat itself will go into a superposition of alive and dead states!

symmetric A relation R is symmetric if, whenever a is R to b, b is R to a. 'Married to' is an example of a symmetric relation.

synapse Junction between **axon** and **dendrite**, across which pass **transmitter substances**. See **axon, dendrite, transmitter substances**.

syntactic Having to do with the *form* or *structure* of linguistic or mental entities, as opposed to their meaning or content. See **semantic**.

timelike A timelike line is a path in space-time every two points on which are separated by a temporal interval which *dominates* the spatial distance. See **spacelike**.

topic-neutral A topic-neutral conception or specification of something, X, is one that fails to convey what X is like in itself, introducing X only as whatever it is that stands in a such-and-such a relation to certain other things. See **transparent**.

transitive A relation R is transitive if, whenever a is R to b, and b is R to c, then a *is R to c*. 'Taller than' is an example of a transitive relation.

transmitter substances Chemicals released at the end of an **axon**, whenever the cell **fires**, and which can have an **excitatory** or **inhibitory** effect on neighbouring cells, via their **dendrites**.

transparent One has a transparent conception of something, X, when one has a conception of what X is like in itself, of its intrinsic nature. Opposite of **topic-neutral** (q.v.). (Not to be confused with Quine's concept of *referential transparency*.)

truth-conditions Of a **proposition**, the conditions that must be satisfied in order for the proposition to be true.

Turing machine An idealized calculating device or computer, consisting of (i) an infinite tape divided into squares; (ii) a read/write/erase head capable of reading symbols from a finite set, written on the tape, erasing them, and writing new symbols from the set; (ii) a device for moving the tape right or left, one square at a time; (ii) a finite set of internal states, such that what the machine does at any stage – e.g., print a '1', move one square to the right and go into state B – is wholly dependent on its internal state and the symbol currently being read.

two-slit experiment When light is passed through a screen with two slits close together, and allowed to fall on a second, image screen, one gets *interference fringes*. This was cited by Thomas Young, who devised this experiment, as evidence of the wave nature of light. It is now known, however, that one can obtain interference fringes with electrons (or indeed, in principle, with any particles). A curious feature of the experiment (a feature predicted by quantum mechanics) is that the fringes disappear, giving way to two discrete lines of light, or regions of impact, if one has a detector capable of registering which slit a photon or electron goes through: the photons or electrons then behave like particles rather than like waves – just as they do when only one slit is open. Moreover, in the absence of such a detector, one still gets interference fringes, even if the photons or electrons are sent though one at a time, no matter at how great an interval. So what appear to be 'interfering' with each other are not the particles themselves, but rather their two possible trajectories.

uncertainty principle The principle, first put forward by Werner Heisenberg, according to which the more tightly the position of a particle is constrained, the less certain it is what value will be yielded by a **measurement** of its momentum, and vice versa. Note that the uncertainty here is not uncertainty as to where the particle really *is*; for according to quantum mechanics, particles do not possess precise positions or momenta. Rather it is an uncertainty about what outcome would result from a measurement or observation of its position or momentum. The uncertainty here stems from the fact that position and momentum are not **compatible observables** (q.v.).

verification principle. See **logical positivism, antirealism.**

wave function A mathematical function that is used to represent the state of a quantum-mechanical system. The *position* wave function, for a particle constrained to move along a single line (the position axis), is a function that takes positions on the line as input, and for each such position yields, as output, a **complex number**, the **square modulus** of which is proportional to the likelihood of finding the particle in the immediate neighbourhood of the position in question. (In terms of calculus, *integrating* the square modulus of the wave function, over an interval on the position axis, yields the probability of finding the particle within that interval.) See **state vector.**

world-line At any given time, an object will (waiving quantum-mechanical considerations) be in a particular place. From the standpoint of the theory of relativity, this (if we ignore the fact that it is spatially extended) amounts to its occupying a particular space-time point. The world-line of an object is then the line comprised of all the space-time points that an object occupies in the course of its existence. Ordinary objects, as distinct from *tachyons* (hypothetical faster-than-light particles) have **timelike** world-lines.

world-tube Similar to world-line, except that one is acknowledging the fact that an object, considered four-dimensionally, is spatially as well as temporally extended. That is to say, one is recognizing that its world-'line' has spatial thickness. Normally, we think of objects as three-dimensional, because we don't think of time as an extra dimension. An object, as it is at a particular time, corresponds to a three-dimensional cross-section of its world-tube.

Plan of the Book

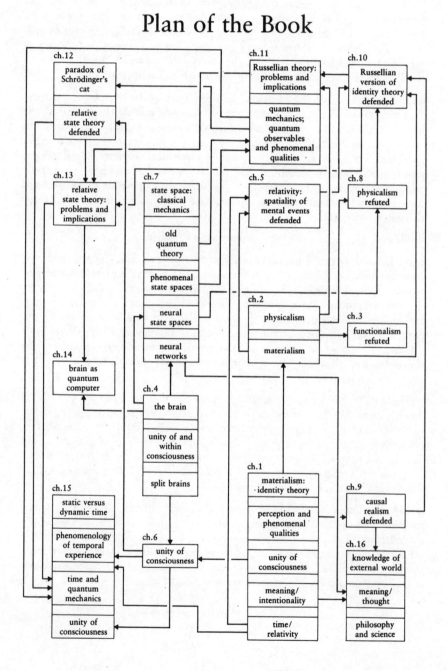

Index

(References to figures are italicized.)